Mordechai (Motti) Friedman
Theodor Herzl's Zionist Journey – Exodus and Return

Figure: Theodor Herzl, 1904; Courtesy of the Central Zionist Archives, Jerusalem.

Mordechai (Motti) Friedman

Theodor Herzl's Zionist Journey – Exodus and Return

—

ISBN 978-3-11-112182-6
e-ISBN (PDF) 978-3-11-072928-3
e-ISBN (EPUB) 978-3-11-072937-5

Library of Congress Control Number:2021932117

Bibliographic information published by the Deutsche Nationalbibliothek
The Deutsche Nationalbibliothek lists this publication in the Deutsche Nationalbibliografie;
detailed bibliographic data are available on the Internet at http://dnb.dnb.de.

© Copyright 2022 Walter de Gruyter GmbH, Berlin/Boston
This volume is text- and page-identical with the hardback published in 2021.
Cover Image: Moses and Herzl. A cover of a book honoring Herzl, given to him by the
Zionists movement of Argentina in the Fifth Zionist Congress, 1901; Courtesy of the Central
Zionist Archives, Jerusalem.
Printing and binding: CPI books GmbH, Leck

www.degruyter.com

The book was translated with the help of the
World Zionist Orgaization

A special thanks to David Matlow

Translated from Hebrew by Gila Brand

The relationship between legends and historical realities can be examined by carefully studying the lives of two of the most prominent personalities in the history of Israel in recent generations, whose influence was of the highest magnitude: the Baal Shem Tov – whose legend is the historical reality we know about him, and Binyamin Ze'ev Herzl – whose historical reality became a legend.

Ben Zion Dinur

Preface

My first encounter with Herzl occurred sometime during the 1950s. It was in the morning hours of a Jerusalem Shabbat. I walked with my grandfather from the Kerem Avraham neighborhood to Ohel Sara synagogue in the Mea Shearim neighborhood for the Shabbat prayers. On the way my eyes caught a glimpse of a big *pashkevil* (poster) on the wall. On it, printed in large bold letters, was the headline "Herzl yimakh shemo" ("May his name be erased").

The text in the pashkevil accused Herzl of attempting to push the Jewish people to convert from their faith. Since then, my curiosity regarding Herzl and my desire to understand his most inner motivations and the reasons of his success as a leader of the Jewish people has not waned.

I read and studied Herzl's writings and the writings of others. In all of these I found no answer to the question: What was Herzl's secret? How did he succeed in less than nine years, against all odds, in changing the history of the Jewish People? How did he succeed in instigating the process that led to the Balfour Declaration, the UN vote in 1947, and the declaration of the state of Israel in 1948? How did he succeed in transferring to future generations the vision of the Jewish, Zionist and democratic state – all in such a short time?

I could not decipher Herzl's secret, but the book deals extensively with some of his personality traits that undoubtedly formed part of the secret components:

Herzl's physical beauty: In my research of Herzl, I noticed that those who described him, both during his lifetime and after his death, noted his physical appearance with great admiration, from the pragmatic and rigid Ussishkin to Rabbi Shlomo Cohen, the ultra-Orthodox rabbi of Vilna. The book extensively discusses Herzl's iconography and its contribution to the success of the Zionist campaign.

The Mysteries of his Charisma: In addition to the beauty of the "Assyrian prince" many observers described the power of Herzl's charisma by which he was blessed. Thus, so many good and prominent people received his authority with love. The book discusses in detail the effect of Herzl's charismatic power on both his immediate and distant surroundings.

Unity of Opposites: Surprisingly, I found that those who described Herzl's beauty and charismatic power, also described him as a humble man. In this book I try to explain the harmony inherent in the unification of opposites.

Although blessed with these and other qualities such as total devotion and uncompromising honesty – Herzl was forced to fight forces of opposition, emanating both from home and from the outside. The chapters of this book will lead the reader along the path of Herzl's Zionist activities, from writing "The Jewish

State" through the administration of the first six Zionist Congresses until his death.

The book will deal extensively with three issues: the issue of kultura, the Altneuland affair and the Uganda affair. In all three, I argue that Herzl was right in terms of substance but erred in terms of management. For this he paid a heavy price.

To what extent can it be assumed that Herzl drew his power from his perceived resemblance to Moshe Rabbenu (the Prophet Moses) A special chapter addresses this issue in detail.

The last chapter of the book discusses two questions: Was Herzl already a legend in his lifetime, or did the legend of Herzl form after his death? Was his untimely death a blessing because he had reached his climax from which he could only have declined, as Ahad Ha'am believed, or was his early death a huge loss, as Rabbi Binyamin believed?

I am most grateful to those who read all or part of the text for their helpful comments, and to those who assisted and advised me during the translating and editing process:

Yaakov Adler, Shlomo Avineri, Moralle Bar-On, Haim Beer, Itamar Ben Ami, Anat Benin, Avraham Duvdevani, Emanuel Etkes, Ian Fisher, Shlomo Goldberg, Chaya Harel, Miriam Kaczensky, Avi Katzman, Yechiel Kimhi, Gideon Kotz, the late Yossi Lang, , Mordechai Naor, Derek Pensler, Raizy Perelman, Yosef Salmon, Shaul Shapiro, Amiel Sheffer, Avigdor Shenan, Lesley Terris and Yitzhak Weiss.

Contents

Introduction —— 1

Part 1: **His Personality**

Chapter 1
"Thine Eyes Shall See the King in His Beauty" (Isaiah 33:17) —— 21
    Herzl in the Eyes of Religious Jews —— 27

Chapter 2
Charisma —— 36
    Herzl's Looks as a Charisma Booster —— 38
    Political Genius —— 39
    Joy of Opposites —— 40
    From Diplomacy to National Pride —— 41
    The Politician and the Man —— 42
    Assertiveness and Sincerity Combined —— 46
    Long-Distance Charisma: Image and Influence —— 48
    Widening Constellation —— 50
    Letters —— 53
    Diplomatic Forays —— 55
    Iconography —— 58
    Orators and Preachers —— 61

Chapter 3
Herzl and the Press —— 69
    Herzl as Media Whiz —— 70
    Die Welt —— 77
    Die Welt in Yiddish —— 80
    Die Welt as a Unifier —— 80
    Attitude of the Hebrew Press to Herzl and Zionism —— 82
    Hamelitz —— 83
    Hatzfira —— 86
    Hamagid —— 91
    Hashiloah —— 93
    Other Jewish Newspapers —— 98
    Great Britain —— 98

United States —— 98
Palestine —— 99
Non-Jewish Newspapers —— 99
Great Britain —— 99
United States —— 100
The Non-Jewish Press in Jewish Eyes —— 101
Jewish Newspaper Circulation —— 102
Local Newspapers —— 103

Chapter 4
The First Zionist Congress —— 105
On the Eve of the First Congress —— 105
Early Initiatives —— 107
Birth of the Congress —— 110
First Zionist Congress: Unity and Adulation —— 114
Herzl's Status in Subsequent Congresses —— 121

Chapter 5
Herzl in Palestine —— 127
Background and Objectives —— 127
Journey to Palestine —— 136
Secrecy of the Mission —— 140
Herzl's Charisma in Palestine —— 141
Herzlian Charisma and its Long-Range Impact —— 145
Response of the Local Inhabitants —— 147
The Turkish Authorities —— 147
The Arabs of Palestine —— 149
The Jews of Palestine —— 150
The Old Yishuv —— 150
Rothschild's Administrators and the Colonists —— 152
Back to Europe —— 153

Part 2: Zionist Journey

Chapter 6
Opposition to Herzl —— 157
Opposition to Herzl: A Timeline —— 160
Opposition in Western Europe —— 168
Opposition in Eastern Europe —— 169

United States —— 173
The Zionist Movement in the Eyes of the Masses —— 174

Chapter 7
Opposition to Herzl in the Zionist Movement —— 178
On the Eve of the First Congress —— 178
First Category: Friendly Opposition —— 179
From Opposition to Support —— 179
Respectful Opposition —— 180
Opposition Spurred by Personal Rivalry —— 182
Second Category: Radical Opposition —— 182
"Two kings cannot serve with one crown" —— 182
Nathan Birnbaum —— 183
Ahad Ha'am —— 184
Davis Trietsch —— 185
Alfred Nossig —— 186
Homegrown Opposition —— 187

Chapter 8
The '*Kultura*' Debate —— 189
The Onset of the 'Kultura' Debate —— 190
Kultura at the Second Congress —— 193
Mounting Opposition on the Eve of the Third Congress —— 200
Third Zionist Congress: Kultura Woes —— 201
Resurgence of the Kultura Debate: Fourth Zionist Congress —— 204
Haredi Achievements —— 204
On the Eve of the Fifth Zionist Congress —— 206
Rise and Fall of the Democratic Fraction —— 206
Fifth Zionist Congress —— 209
The Democratic Fraction Gains Strength —— 209
Minsk Conference and the Compromise of Ahad Ha'am —— 217

Chapter 9
Altneuland —— 224
The Affront to East European Jewry —— 229
Freedom of Expression —— 230
The Democratic Fraction and Altneuland —— 230
From *Altneuland* to Kishinev and Uganda —— 234

Chapter 10
Uganda and the Sixth Congress —— 236
        On the Eve of the Congress —— 246
        The Congress Opens —— 250
        The walk-Out of the "Neinsagers" —— 255
        Herzl and the Dissidents in the Small Hall —— 257
        Aftermath of the Sixth Congress —— 259
        Herzl and Ussishkin —— 260
        Kharkov Conference —— 263
        Original Uganda Proposal Rescinded —— 267
        Views on Uganda —— 272
        The End of the Democratic Fraction —— 273
        The Mizrahi Movement —— 279

Part 3: **Legend and Reality**

Chapter 11
The Moses and Messiah Syndrome —— 287
        Herzl as Moses: Self-Image —— 290
        Moses Analogy Heard from Others —— 294
        Moses Analogy as an Explanation for Success —— 295
        Herzl as Moses in Jewish Sermons —— 298
        Age —— 298
        Education and Identity —— 298
        Humility —— 299
        Motivation —— 300
        Physical Appearance —— 301
        The Plan —— 301
        The People's Response – Rebellion and Skepticism —— 301
        The Plight of the Jews —— 303
        Unrelenting Pressure —— 303
        Family Life —— 304
        Personal Integrity —— 305
        Beauty —— 305
        Fate —— 306
        The Herzl-Messiah Analogy —— 306
        Herzl as a Biblical Figure: An Iconographic Comparison —— 311
        Conclusion —— 312

Chapter 12
"Akhrei Mot Kedoshim Emor" ("Speak Well of the Dead") —— 314
    Was Herzl a Legend in His Lifetime? —— 314
    Approach A: —— 320
    Approach B —— 322
    Approach C: —— 323
    1970s – 1990s —— 335
    1990s Onwards —— 336
    Conclusions —— 338
    The Kultura Controversy —— 339
    The Altneuland Affair —— 339
    The Uganda crisis —— 342

Bibliography —— 346
    Books (Hebrew) —— 346
    Books (English) —— 349
    Books (German and Yiddish) —— 350
    Articles —— 350

Index —— 353

Introduction

In late August 1897, Nahum Sokolow strode briskly towards Hotel Les Trois Rois in Basel, Switzerland. He had arrived in the city on a mission. As the editor of the Hebrew newspaper *Hatzfira*, published in Warsaw, he was in town to cover the First Zionist Congress, which was about to open at the municipal concert hall. Sokolow was a no-nonsense type, blue-eyed and fair-haired with a fleshy nose and an impish goatee, the image of the upper-class European gentleman. For the last year, his paper had been following the exploits of this personage, Dr. Herzl, a man with clearly perilous pretentions. Now Herzl had decided to hold a convention bringing together Jewish delegates from around the globe. Apparently, their intention was to ask the Great Powers to give them Palestine. This was a dangerous delusion in Sokolow's eyes. The plight of the Jews of Europe was steadily worsening. Fledgling attempts had begun to establish farm colonies in Palestine and drawing diplomatic attention to them would only sabotage these efforts. What was needed was action, not fantasies about negotiating with czars, emperors and sultans.

Back in October 1896, Sokolow had published an unusually fierce warning on the front page of *Hatzfira:*

> ...It may be unpleasant to say this, but duty is not always pleasant. Most of our readership would be overjoyed if we told them that Dr. Herzl, an assimilated Jew who has repented and become an advocate of the national idea, has successfully met with kings and is now gathering stones to rebuild the fallen tabernacle of David. Dr. Herzl, a celebrated writer in Vienna who has never before set foot in the Jewish community, is now waving the banner of Jewish renaissance on high. Here is a man untainted by greed, committed to this grand idea with all his heart, who travels from country to country preaching his message to the masses and convening with the world's high and mighty. How charming! How lovely! Such fine and noble talk! But these words are flying bullets...and nearby sits a certain enterprise, a certain threshing floor: the Jewish colonies in the Land of Israel. A spark from these bullets, a spark that flies out from beneath the hammer, and all these colonies are ashes...One has already touched the granary: All of a sudden concessions and privileges we were hoping would soon materialize have come to a standstill following Dr. Herzl's quixotic quest. It would be a crime to remain mute in the face of this interference. So we shall do our duty and say it loud and clear: Dr. Herzl's quest is merely a game. In London he achieved nothing, in Paris Baron Edmund Rothschild refused to receive him, and in cities that welcomed him, he was treated as a spectacle. We too want to honor Dr. Herzl. We too want to enjoy the spectacle. But there are loftier matters at stake, and hence we advise Dr. Herzl to desist from his prophesizing. If not, we will not hesitate to carry out our duty and let it be known that the dream pursued by this fine dreamer is his own – not that of the people. (*Hatzfira*, no. 218, October 20, 1896)

Here in Basel, Sokolow was meeting Herzl for the first time, after a year of denunciation. He observed him with interest. Theodor Herzl sat in the far corner of the hotel lobby, elegantly dressed in the latest Viennese fashion, quiet, reserved and thoughtful. He had a jet black beard, a proud hawkish nose and a melancholy air about him – so different from Sokolow, the bold reporter. Sokolow was taken aback. In his imagination, he had seen a false messiah of the Shabbetai Zvi variety, a snake oil salesman hungry for honor. He decided to give Herzl a second chance. Meanwhile, he watched with amazement as delegates from all over Europe filed in, some of them highly respected personalities. Could something of consequence be happening here after all?

The next day, Herzl and Sokolow met privately. Reflecting on the mood in the Jewish world, Herzl asked whether he thought the Jews possessed the inner strength to forge a national consciousness and an independent state. Sokolow made no reply. More than he was touched by the question itself, he was taken by the way it was phrased. A leader unfolded before his eyes. In Herzl he saw simplicity, naiveté and pure idealism but also shrewdness in the face of reality. Traditionalism and novelty combined. Sokolow felt as if he were looking at a tragic hero, the lilt of Psalms playing between his lips. He was struck dumb. He could not say whether the Jewish people was capable of following the path carved out by Herzl, but he was convinced that the Jews had a leader now like never before. From that moment on, Sokolow became a passionate follower of Herzl. The report he filed on the Congress was an ode to Herzl and his leadership. The Congress itself and the World Zionist Organization established in its wake enjoyed dramatic success, launching a process that led over time to the founding of the State of Israel. Sokolow himself went on to serve as president of the World Zionist Organization, bringing the cycle full circle. The adversary became the advocate. Years later, Sokolow's remains were brought to Jerusalem and reinterred on Mount Herzl.

Sokolow's change of heart was the perfect example of the effect Herzl had on many people. One of the most astute writers of his time, there is no way one could call him naïve. In his opposition to Herzl he was completely sober-eyed, yet one meeting was enough to transform him from a skeptic bystander into a passionate devotee and activist. What was it about Herzl that precipitated this change? What was Herzl's secret? How did a lone individual set in motion a historic process that profoundly revolutionized the existential condition of the Jewish people?

The world has not lacked for men of genius. Quite a few have left a mark on the human race. The genius of figures like Galileo, Einstein, Leonardo de Vinci and Beethoven lay in a specific God-given talent, a convergence of nature and nurture. To express their artistry or deliver their creations to the world geniuses of this ilk do not need much: Pen and ink, paper and a good head are usually enough. A much smaller number have changed the course of history, transformed political and social thought or impacted on people's daily lives and thinking. Even fewer have posthumously shaped a historical era. Geniuses in this category require a different set of skills: They need a dream, the power to make it come true, exceptional organizational ability and personal charisma.

In less than nine years, Theodor Herzl, or Binyamin Ze'ev, as his parents named him at birth, succeeded in rewriting Jewish history, and he did so against all the odds. Most of the Jewish world rejected his ideas. In our day, the idea of Zionism seems self-evident, but if one asked Jews at the end of the nineteenth century about their aspirations, few were likely to say "a sovereign state in the Land of Israel." Jews across the spectrum were united in their opposition to an independent state. The Jews who joined the socialist revolution regarded nationalism as harmful and counter-revolutionary. Reform and ultra-Orthodox Jews also rejected Herzl's vision. Even the Hovevei Zion (Lovers of Zion) movement that began to take shape towards the end of the nineteenth century did not openly espouse national goals. Hovevei Zion were "lovers of Zionism" but not necessarily Zionists. Loving something did not mean one had to be part of it. "A non-Zionist can be a lover of Zion, but a Zionist lover of Zion – out of the question," Sokolow declared.[1]

Hovevei Zion, like other Jewish aid societies, looked on confused and helpless at the misfortune of the Jews of Europe. In the lingo of the times, which today would be considered politically incorrect, it was known as the "Jewish problem." In Eastern Europe, the Jews suffered from hunger and persecution. In Western Europe, assimilation and conversion posed a threat. Nobody had the desire or audacity to talk about a Jewish state. Most Jews saw themselves as belonging to their local communities and loyal to the countries in which they lived. They did not identify as a nation with the right to self-definition. Even during the Spring of Nations, when many peoples began to clamor for national independence, the Jews opted for integration in the society around them.[2] The leaders of the Great Powers did not see them as a separate entity either: At most the Jews were treated as a confederation of communities entitled to partial or full rights as citizens of their home countries.

This changed dramatically in Herzl's day. Up until 1896, Herzl, a mediocre playwright in the eyes of the critics but acknowledged by those same critics as

---

[1] Nahum Sokolow, in: Leib Jaffe, *Sefer hacongress: 50th Anniversary of the First Zionist Congress*, Jewish Agency, Jerusalem 1950, pp. 176–177 (henceforth: *Sefer hacongress*, (1950).
[2] Benzion Netanyahu, *Khameshet avot hatzionut*, Yedioth Ahronoth, Tel Aviv 2003, pp. 15–17 (henceforth: Netanyahu, *Khameshet avot*).

a brilliant journalist, was a complete unknown to those working for the betterment of the Jews. Yet within a few short years – eight and a half years in total, he was able to turn the Zionist movement into an institutionalized political movement that led to the establishment of the State of Israel mere decades after his death. Herzl's Zionist career, officially launched on February 14, 1896, following the publication of *Der Judenstaat* ("The Jewish State"), was cut short by his premature death on July 3, 1904. He was only 44. During this brief span, Herzl managed to change the thinking of Jews and non-Jews alike, and to create consensus on three fundamental issues: The Jews were a nation, their homeland was the Land of Israel and a political solution for the nation could only be found there.

It was Herzl himself who was behind it all. The Jewish national movement cannot be understood without him. His role was unquestionably greater than any of the individual processes which would have moved ahead without him. One can conceive of Herzl without the Zionist movement – but not Zionism without Herzl. Herzl the journalist, whose ideas were opposed by forces far more powerful than he, who was deemed mad even by his closest friends, nevertheless brought about one of the greatest revolutions of modern times.

How did Herzl accomplish this, in such a short time and under fire from all sides? What was the source of strength of this man who never held a diplomatic post in his life but was able to reshape the political and international map in ways that remain valid to this day? Why did a respected journalist with a senior position at one of the leading liberal newspapers in Europe feel the need to rush to the aid of the downtrodden and assume the role of the great statesmen of the Jewish people?

It is hard to say that Herzl chose a politically auspicious moment for furthering the cause of the Jews. On the contrary, he had missed the window of opportunity created by the Spring of Nations,[3] which was open from the Congress of Vienna (1815) until the Congress of Berlin (1878). If the Jewish national movement had emerged earlier, it might have enjoyed the same support and solidarity enjoyed by other national liberation movements, says Israeli historian Benzion Netanyahu.[4] After the Congress of Vienna, however, Europe turned imperialistic. Colonialism spread to trade routes far and wide and nationalist aspirations were ruthlessly suppressed. At the same time, the industrial revolution expanded,

---

[3] In the 1840s, Europe experienced a wave of revolutions and uprisings with a common denominator: wresting free of the Great Powers and winning political independence. The liberation process, advanced by nurturing national sentiment through the mass media, became known as the Spring of Nations.

[4] Netanyahu, *Khameshet avot*, p. 15.

leading to the emergence of socialist and social-democratic movements that preferred cosmopolitanism as a solution to poverty and distress over nationalism, which was perceived as a reactionary ideology that did not contribute to the welfare of the masses.[5] The rise of nationalism actually posed an obstacle for the handful who clamored for Jewish self-determination. The surge of anti-Semitism that followed served as an important wake-up call for the Jews regarding their prospects for integration, and dashed any hopes for self-determination. It was clear that declaring Jewish national aspirations would only fan the flames of anti-Semitism. Thus Herzl did not win the international backing he might have garnered a few decades earlier. Ideologically, he was operating in utterly hostile surroundings.

Herzl's personal life does not provide a definitive answer either. An outside observer would never guess from his upbringing, schooling or occupation that he would one day become the founding father of the Jewish national movement. This is Herzl's biographical sketch of himself, published in London's *Jewish Chronicle*:

> "I was born in 1860 in Budapest, in a house next to the synagogue, where lately the Rabbi denounced me from the pulpit in very strong terms, because, forsooth, I am trying to obtain for the Jews more honor and greater freedom than they enjoy at present...
>
> First of all I was sent to a Jewish preparatory school, where I enjoyed a certain authority because my father was a wealthy merchant. My earliest recollection of that school consists of a caning which I received from the master, because I did not know the details of the Exodus of the Jews from Egypt. At the present time a great many schoolmasters want to give me a caning, because I recollect too much of that Exodus from Egypt.
>
> At the age of ten I went to the *Realschule* (a grammar school, where the modern side is more looked after than classics, in contradistinction to the Gymnasium, a grammar school where the study of Latin and Greek is more cultivated than Euclid and natural science). Lesseps was then the hero of the hour, and I had conceived the idea of piercing the other isthmus, that of Panama. But I soon lost all my former love for logarithms and trigonometry, because at that time a very pronounced anti-Jewish tendency prevailed at *Realschule*. One of our masters explained to our class the meaning of the word 'heathen,' by saying 'To that class belong the idolaters, Mohamedans and Jews.' After this peculiar definition, I had quite enough of the *Realschule*, and wanted to become a classical scholar. My good father never constrained me into a narrow groove for my studies, and I became a pupil of the Gymnasium. But for all that I had not yet quite done with Panama. Many years later, as the Paris correspondent of the *Neue Freie Presse*, it became my duty to write about the notorious incidents of that scandalous episode in the history of France. At the Gymnasium, the Jewish boys formed the majority, and therefore we had not to complain of any *Judenhetze*. In the upper seventh wrote my first newspaper article – of course, anonymously, otherwise I would have been 'kept in' by the headmaster. While in the highest

---

5 *Ibid.*

class in the Gymnasium, my only sister died, a girl of eighteen; my good mother became so melancholy with grief that we removed to Vienna in the year 1878.

During the Shivah week Rabbi Kohn called on us and asked me what were my plans for the future. I told him that I intended to become an author (*ein Schriftsteller*), whereupon the Rabbi shook his head just as dissatisfied as he disapproved of Zionism only the other day. A literary career is no real proper profession, concluded the discontented Rabbi.

In Vienna I studied law, took part in all the stupid students' farces, including the wearing of a coloured cap of a *Verbindung*, until this Association one fine morning passed a resolution that no Jews should henceforth be received as members. Those who were members already they kindly permitted to remain in the *Verbindung*. I said good-bye to these noble youths, and commenced to devote myself seriously to work. In 1884 I took my degree as Dr. Juris, and entered the Geirchts Praxis (an unsalaried appointment in the Law Courts as a judicial clerk under the supervision of a Judge).

I held this appointment in the Law Courts of Vienna as well as in Salzburg. In Salzburg the work seemed to be much more attractive, the scenery in and around the town being most beautiful. My office was in an old castellated tower just under the belfry, the chimes sound sweetly pretty to me three times every day.

Of course, I wrote much more for the theater, than for the law courts. In Salzburg I spent some of the happiest hours of my life; I would have liked to have stayed in this beautiful town, but, as a Jew, I could never have advanced to the position of a Judge. I, therefore, bade good bye to Salzburg and to the law business at the same time. Again I caused a great deal of worry to the Rabbi in Budapest; for instead of going in for a real profession or for an 'art,' I commenced to travel and to write for newspapers and for the theatre. A great many of my plays were performed at different theatres, some with great applause, other fell flat. Until this minute I cannot understand why some of my plays met with success, while others were hissed off the stage. However, this difference of the reception of my plays taught me to disregard altogether whether the public applauded or hissed my work. One's own conscience must be satisfied with one's work (*min muss es sich selbst recht machen*), all the rest is immaterial...In 1889 I married, I have three children, a boy and two girls. In my opinion my children are neither ugly nor stupid. But of course I may be mistaken.

While travelling in Spain in the year 1891, the *Neue Freie Presse* made me the offer to become its correspondent in Paris. I accepted this position, though I detested and despised politics up to that time. In Paris I had occasion to learn what the word politics means, and I expressed my views in a little book, 'The Palais Bourbon.' In 1895 I had quite enough of Paris and returned to Vienna.

During the last two months of my residence in Paris I wrote the book 'The Jewish State,' to which I owe the honour of having been asked by you of some biographical data of my humble person. I do not recollect ever having written anything in such an elevated frame of mind as that book. Heine says that he heard the wings of an eagle beat over his head while writing certain verses. I do believe that 'something also beat' about my head while I wrote that book. I worked at it every day until I was completely exhausted; my only relaxation in the evening consisted in listening to Wagner's music, more especially to 'Tannhauser,' which opera I went to hear as often as it was performed. Only on those evenings, when there was no performance at the Opera, I felt doubts about the correctness of my thoughts.

At first I had conceived the idea to write my pamphlet concerning the solution of the Jewish question, only for private circulation among my friends. The publication of these views did not enter into my plans until later; I had not intended to commence a personal agitation for the Jewish cause. Most people will be surprised at present when they hear of this former resolution. I considered the whole matter as only fit to be acted on, and not to be talked about. Public agitation should only become my *ultima ratio* if my private advice was not listened to or not obeyed.

When I had finished my book I asked one of my oldest and best friends to read the manuscript. While reading it he suddenly commenced to cry. I found this emotion quite natural, as he was a Jew, and I had also cried several times while writing the book. But to my dismay I found that he gave quite a different reason for his tears. He thought that I had gone mad, and, being my friend, my misfortune made him very sad...I then passed through a very serious crisis; I can only compare it to the throwing of a red-hot body into cold water. Of course if that body happens to be iron, it becomes steel by the process.

...On that day my troubles with the *Judenstaat* commenced. During the two years and more since that time I experienced many, many sad days, and I am afraid many more sad days will still follow.

In 1895 I commenced to keep a diary; four stout volumes have been filled already. Should I ever publish them, the world will be surprised to learn what I had to put up with; who were the enemies of my plan, and on the other hand who stood by me.

But one thing I consider as certain, as beyond a doubt, the movement will last. I do not know when I shall die; but Zionism will never die. Since the days at Basle the Jewish people has again a popular representation; consequently, the *Judenstaat* will arise in its own country. I am now at work to start the bank and I expect it will prove to be as great a success as the 'Congress.'"(*The Jewish Chronicle*, 'An Autobiography,' Theodor Herzl, January 14, 1898).

Herzl paints a picture for the Jews of England that emphasizes his Jewish upbringing in Budapest, in contrast to his life as a student, journalist and playwright in Vienna and Paris from which Judaism was largely absent. His interest in the Jewish question returns as the divine spirit hovers above him while writing *Der Judenstaat*. Finally, he proclaims the immortality of Zionism and voices the certainty that a Jewish state will be born. For a chronicle of his life from 1898 until his death in 1904, we have Herzl's Zionist diaries. In these volumes, we see how he devoted all his energy and fortune to furthering the programs that led over time to the establishment of a Jewish state in the Land of Israel.

When *Der Judenstaat* was published, it actually came as a surprise to many that Herzl was a Jew. His emergence as a public figure took some unusual turns, and his early schemes to resolve the Jewish question were bizarre, to say the least. In 1893, for example, he proposed that the Jews convert en masse to Christianity in the presence of the Pope in front of St. Stephen's Cathedral in Vienna, a theatrical ploy with little connection to reality. One comment from the editor of his newspaper and he shelved it. If it had not been recorded in his diary, nobody would have been the wiser.

Conventional historiography links Herzl's debut and anti-Semitism. The claim is that Herzl hoisted the banner of political Zionism in response to anti-Semitic incidents in the 1890s. While Herzl was born in Budapest, he spent his finest years in Vienna, a city emblematic of the spirit of the times. Vienna was the hub of the crumbling Austro-Hungarian Empire and a symbol of the old, antiquated European order. It gave birth to anti-Semitism and cosmopolitanism (with quite a few anti-Semites claiming to be cosmopolitan); to the psychoanalysis of Herzl's neighbor Freud, which became known as "Jewish science"; to the expressionist movement in art; to the sense of dissolution that preoccupied writer and dramatist Arthur Schnitzler; to the modern romantic music of the Jewish composer who converted to Christianity, Gustav Mahler; to Stefan Zweig and his lament for the lost world in *The World of Yesterday.* Vienna created both the cure and the disease, Herzl and Hitler. The streets of Vienna were swarming in those days with would-be reformers, idealists, dreamers and inventors peddling their solutions for Europe's political ills.

Herzl was a serious man, a respectable Viennese gentleman. Nearly everyone who knew him tried to make him understand this. He was endangering his family's livelihood and risked being branded a quack and a charlatan, they told him. But Herzl did not relent. From his seat in Vienna he had sized up pre-World War Europe and realized it was no longer a place for Jews. He watched as Karl Lueger, the head of the anti-Semitic Christian Social party won the mayorship three times in a row, although the election results were sanctioned by the emperor, Franz Josef, only after his third victory (1897). Herzl's cultural world, shaped in Vienna, was dashed in Paris of the Belle Epoque, where he served as a political correspondent for *Neue Freie Presse*. There, exposed to the anti-Semitism of Edouard Drumont[6] and the Dreyfus affair,[7] he sensed that hatred of the Jews was seeping like poison into the heart of Europe.[8] In time, anti-Semitism actually worked in Herzl's favor: As universities in Russia barred their doors to Jewish students, they were forced to leave for European universities. These students became his first and most important band of followers. In

---

6 Edouard Drumont, a French journalist. In his book *La France juive,* published in 1886, he claimed that the Jews were an inferior race with a despicable religion. He was the editor of an anti-Semitic newspaper.
7 The Dreyfus affair made headlines at the end of 1894 when Alfred Dreyfus (1859–1935), a French Jewish army captain was falsely accused by anti-Semitic officers of passing military secrets to Germany. Herzl, who was present at the degradation ceremony at which Dreyfus' stripes were ripped off and his sword broken, witnessed the crowd chanting "Death to the Jews." The affair ended in 1906 with Dreyfus' complete exoneration.
8 Netanyahu, *Khameshet avot*, p. 15.

the short run, anti-Semitism acted as a catalyst and wake-up call for Herzl, but anti-Semitism on its own does not reveal his secret. Even if anti-Semitism was critical in opening his eyes to the status of European Jewry, it does not explain why he chose to act as he did, let alone why the Jews embraced him. It provides no clue to Herzl's meteoric success, to his transformation into a man of both vision and action, the star of a drama he could never write for the stage. Ahad Ha'am once made a witty comment that "anti-Semitism gave birth to Herzl, Herzl gave birth to the Jewish state, the Jewish state gave birth to Zionism, and Zionism gave birth to the Congress."[9] While this statement may be historically true, it leaves out the causes. Like other great leaders of the Jewish people, Herzl's genius cannot be explained by anti-Semitism alone. Suffice it to say that Herzl succeeded in doing what no one before him thought possible: playing statesman without a state.

Herzl was preceded by a long line of people who sought a solution for the Jewish problem. First came the "Dorshei Zion" ("seekers of Zion"), among them Moshe Hess, Rabbi Yehuda Hai Alkalai, Rabbi Yosef Natonek and Rabbi Zvi Hirsch Kalischer. Their contribution was small and primarily ideological, but constituted a first step toward putting Zion on the agenda. Next were the "Hovevei Zion" ("lovers of Zion"), who also failed to come up with a genuine solution for alleviating Jewish distress or furthering the Zionist cause. While they began to encourage settlement in Palestine and financially support it, their ambitions and initiatives were modest. They did not dare to think big. To do so, they needed a visionary like Herzl. If they had managed to raise greater sums and convince Jews to settle in Palestine on a large scale, they could have been an agent of change and aspirations for a national homeland might have eventually sprung from that.

However, Palestine at this time was in a very different place. The Jews subsisted mainly on charity collected from overseas which was distributed to Torah scholars in the Holy Land awaiting messianic redemption. The agricultural colonies relied heavily on donations from Baron Rothschild and would not have survived without his aid. Although the colonists dreamed of independence, they did not dare to wave the nationalist banner: The colonies were controlled by Rothschild's officials, and Rothschild was an opponent of Herzl's initiatives. The colonists also feared the Ottoman regime, which looked askance at nationalist endeavors perceived as a threat to the empire.[10] Furthermore, the Hovevei

---

9 Ahad Ha'am, Asher Zvi Ginsburg (1856–1927), one of Herzl's fiercest critics. We will discuss Ahad Ha'am and his relations with Herzl in the course of this book.
10 For more on the colonists' fear of the Ottoman authorities, see below.

Zion movement in Russia was struggling. It was organizationally weak, its leadership was anemic, and its arms were tied by the prohibition on Zionist activity. It had not succeeded in introducing any real change. So when Herzl began to create waves, Hovevei Zion benefitted, too. In the same way that Dorshei Zion created the psychological infrastructure for Hovevei Zion, Hovevei Zion created the organizational and human infrastructure that formed an important part of the political Zionist administration established by Herzl. Later, when Herzl organized the First Zionist Congress and founded the political Zionist movement, the Hovevei group became political Zionists.

One can therefore say without exaggerating that Herzl was directly responsible for the consolidation of the Jewish national movement. It is hard to imagine how it would have developed without him, if at all. The most dramatic turnabout in the history of the Jews in the Diaspora, which made it possible for them to leave and realize the dream of returning en masse to Zion, was entirely the doing of Benjamin Ze'ev Herzl – and he did it in a hostile environment whose part in setting the stage for Jewish self-determination was acknowledged only later. Herzl stood alone, dreaming and battling, even when his closest friends began to wonder whether he was hallucinating.

Der Judenstaat, whose publication on February 14, 1896 launched Herzl's Zionist journey, was not the first book on Jewish nationalism. On the face of it, there was no logical reason for this book to ignite the Zionist revolution. A whole series of like-minded publications had preceded it, most of them unknown to Herzl. *Rome and Jerusalem* by Moses Hess had come out in 1862, but Herzl read it for the first time while visiting Palestine, when he was already deeply involved in the Zionist cause.[11] He read *Auto-Emancipation*, a Zionist pamphlet published in 1882 by Hovevei Zion leader Yehuda Leib Pinsker, only on the eve of the First Zionist Congress:

> "Read today the pamphlet entitled Auto-Emancipation which [Joseph Samuel] Bloch gave me. An astounding correspondence in the critical part, a great similarity in the constructive one. A pity that I did not read this work before my own pamphlet was printed. On the other hand, it is a good thing that I didn't know it – or perhaps I would have abandoned my own undertaking."[12]

He knew nothing of *Aruchas bas ammi* by Isaac Rulf of Memmel, rabbi and teacher of David Wolffsohn, who succeeded Herzl as chairman of the World Zion-

---

[11] *The Complete Diaries of Theodor Herzl*, edited by Raphael Patai, Herzl Press and Thomas Yoseloff, vol. 3, p. 1090 (henceforth: *Complete Diaries*).
[12] *Complete Diaries*, vol. 1, p. 299.

ist Organization, which was published in 1883 in response to Pinsker's book.[13] Neither had he read Max Bodenheimer's *Whither the Russian Jews?* (published in 1891),[14] or Nathan Birnbaum's pamphlet "*The national revival of the Jewish people in its land as a solution to the Jewish question*" (published in Vienna in 1893).[15] Some of these authors took issue with Herzl, whom they saw as an interloper. They accused him of stealing ideas that they had developed long before him. But Herzl had no knowledge of their work, which is astonishing in itself and evidence of his intellectual powers. The Zionist movement was certainly the richer for it. Never had a revolutionary movement gained more from its leader's ignorance of what had gone before. At the same time, Herzl conceded that the idea behind *Der Judenstaat* was not new: "The idea which I have developed in this pamphlet is a very old one: it is the restoration of the Jewish State... I wish it to be clearly understood from the outset that no portion of my argument is based on a new discovery."[16]

Nevertheless, he offered a combination of vision and action that was not found in the books of his predecessors. Herzl's Zionist activism was not a product of his acquaintance with Zionist materials or propaganda. It emanated from a deep spiritual need and perhaps even a sense of historic urgency. His Zionist journey began with the composition of a 68-page letter to the Rothschild family, which went on to become the basis for *Der Judenstaat*. Herzl's ideas, fleshed out by deeds, chalked up phenomenal success. Two years after the publication of his book, the Zionist Organization was born.

In retrospect, the fact that Herzl arrived at his Zionist ideology without familiarity with the "Zionist street" was a disadvantage that became an advantage. As Menachem Ussishkin put it:

> "He will be a great boon to the Zionist movement. There is no question that with his charming demeanor he will captivate all the Jews of Russia and perhaps also the Jews of the West. While he has a very serious defect, looking at the situation as it is now, this defect may actually work to his benefit: He does not know the Jews and is therefore certain that the only obstacle to Zionism comes from outside, not inside. Better that he should not be told the truth, lest it diminish his faith in the project."[17]

---

13 Shmuel Leib Citron, *Lexicon Tzioni*, S. Shreberk, Vilna 1924, p. 654
14 *Ibid.*, p. 145.
15 Nathan Birnbaum, Die Nationale Wiedergburt des jüdischen Vokes in seinem Lande, als Mittel zur Losung der Judenfrage, Ein Appell an die Guten und Edlen aller Nationen, 1893.
16 Theodor Herzl, *The Jewish State*, American Zionist Emergency Council , New York, 1946 (henceforth: *The Jewish State*).
17 Ernest Laharanne, French author and secretary of Napoleon III, published a treatise in 1860 called *La Nouvelle Question d'Orient: Empires d'Egypte et d'Arabie: reconstitution de la nationa-*

Such comments only add to the Herzl mystique. How did Herzl end up on the stage of one the most spectacular dramas of Jewish history? None of the publications that predated *Der Judenstaat* were influential to such a degree, and certainly, none gave rise to a mass political movement. Herzl's modest book, started out as a letter, could barely find a publisher, and truth be told, was far from being a literary masterpiece. Yet it influenced history in a way that few other books can claim. So what was the secret of its success? The secret was undoubtedly Herzl himself. *Der Judenstaat* won adulation more because of its author than for its own sake. As Herzl attested, he poured into it all his hopes and dreams, writing it non-stop over a few weeks in Paris, sometimes in a state of reverie, sometimes in tears. But apart from this personal component, we believe there are other factors that contributed to this reception of Herzl and his ideas.

First, the target audience of *Der Judenstaat* was not only Jewish: It was a book written for the world. Herzl saw anti-Semitism – the "misery of the Jews," as he called it, as a global problem. With his keen understanding of how anti-Semitism worked, it was clear to him that despite the process of emancipation in Europe, full integration of the Jews was not going to happen. From his perspective, the Jewish problem was a universal one that needed to be addressed by a universal audience. The world would remain troubled until a solution was found. Towards this end, Herzl worked tirelessly to convince kings and heads of state to join him. It was not enough for him to appeal to the Jews. He invested tremendous energy in diplomacy, meeting with the German emperor, the Russian minister of the interior, the king of Italy, Ferdinand prince of Bulgaria, the British secretary of state for the colonies, the Pope, and many other dignitaries to mobilize support for a Jewish state in Palestine. He was prepared to form alliances with anti-Semites who wanted to rid their countries of Jews, in the hope of sweetening the bitter pill. He harnessed the whole political arena to his cause, with political acumen matched by no other Zionist leader.

Another important factor was Herzl's sober assessment of the emancipation. He wisely discerned the futility of attempts to better the lot of European Jews through artificially granting them rights. This ran counter to the conventional wisdom among Jewish activists of the time, who perceived the hardship of the

---

lité juive in which he proposed settling Jews in Palestine. Sir Lawrence Oliphant, a British diplomat and journalist, expressed similar ideas in *Land of Gilead*, published in 1879. John Henry Dunant (1828–1910), the Swiss founder of the Red Cross, also worked toward this end. See Pinhas Blumenthal, *Ein zu agada*, Am Oved, Tel Aviv 1964, pp. 152–153 (henceforth: *Ein zu agada*). Alfred Nossig, a member of Hovevei Zion and later a Zionist movement leader, proposed the establishment of a Jewish state in Palestine an article that appeared in 1887. See Yigal Elam, *Elef yehudim ba'et hakhadasha: Lexicon*, Zmora-Bitan, Tel Aviv 1985, p. 223.

Jews as temporary. East European Jewry, bowed by physical suffering, hunger and government edicts, believed that emancipation was around the corner and life would improve, in the same way that it had for the Jews of Western Europe. Jews and non-Jews alike saw the emancipation as a promise, and even if it had not yet been realized in full, they were certain the process would gradually bring about equality for all. Herzl disagreed. In his view, emancipation was a failure and the only answer was the creation of a Jewish state. His arguments led to a profound shift in Jewish and world opinion. But in addition to altering the public mindset, Herzl published a book that offered a detailed road map for solving the problem.

What was special about *Der Judenstaat* is that it was not just a prophetic treatise but a brilliant operational plan worked out in extraordinary detail, with a clarity that far exceeded the visions of other prophets and dreamers. The publication of *Der Judenstaat* was part of a process: As a man of action, Herzl sought to translate his grand ideas into political achievements. Fusing ideology and organizational skills, he called conferences, launched public relations campaigns and initiated diplomatic forays. The pinnacle of his activity was the Zionist Congress and the establishment of the World Zionist Organization in 1897. He chose this channel after realizing that diplomacy and talks with the world's high and mighty were not enough. To solve the problem, he needed to recruit the masses. Spearheading a national movement was no simple matter. Such a movement could easily deteriorate into populism and anarchy. For Herzl, the Viennese aristocrat, the transition from his desk to the organizational and diplomatic world was a formidable challenge. He was suddenly called upon to exercise a different talent: public leadership. Through his cultivation of the Zionist organization as an all-inclusive Jewish body, it was perceived within a short time as a worldwide representative of the Jewish people, in the eyes of the Jews themselves as well as the outside world. No such organization had existed since the destruction of the Second Temple, and Herzl was its progenitor.

Publishing *Der Judenstaat* was one successful stop on Herzl's Zionist journey. However, the reasons cited above for the tremendous influence of his book do not yet explain the success of Herzl the man. They do not tell us what it was about the finely nuanced persona of this gentleman – ultimately one journalist and dramatist in a crowd, however gifted – that enabled him to reprogram the worldview of his generation in such a way that the aspirations of the Jews for a state, which was not even defined as a goal by the Jewish masses before he appeared, became acceptable to both Jews and the world at large. Fully unraveling Herzl's secret is a daunting task. However, probing certain less studied aspects of his life and work may shine some light on the Herzl enigma. There were several factors underlying his diplomatic, organizational and ideological triumphs that may have helped him dramatically alter the course of history. These factors, outlined below, will be explored in depth in the course of this book.

One of the key factors was Herzl's lofty social standing. He was a highly acclaimed journalist. What he failed to achieve in the theater, he achieved in the newsroom. Herzl was appointed literary editor of *Neue Freie Press* (*NFP*), one of the leading liberal newspapers of the time, after four years as its correspondent in Paris. He was known far and wide as an outstanding feuilletonist and a spirited travel writer. On numerous occasions, his journalistic fame helped to open doors that were closed to ordinary folk. Herzl put this advantage to good use to establish connections with world leaders. However, he was careful not to mix journalism with his Zionist activities, as his bosses were unforgiving on that score.

Herzl's family fortune was another factor whose importance cannot be underestimated. From the earliest stages of his Zionist campaign, Herzl paid out of his own pocket. He never took a penny from the public coffers until his dying day. In his mind, financial independence was essential for integrity and intellectual independence. It was not so much fear of being the butt of criticism as a desire to pursue the Zionist dream on his own terms without being beholden to others. He was handsomely paid by the NFP and his plays brought in a nice income, but there were also times when money was tight. The family's household expenses were high, and Herzl's outlay on Zionist schemes was substantial. Whenever funds were low, Jacob, Herzl's wealthy father stepped in willingly to cover the deficit. He contributed generously and spurred Herzl on at important junctures that involved a major financial investment such as the establishment of the newspaper *Die Welt* and the Jewish Colonial Trust. The dowry of his wife Juliette (nee Naschauer) was also a great help. According to Austrian law, Herzl was the beneficiary of this money, and indeed, a large portion of it was channeled into the Zionist cause. There is no question that without these economic resources, the Zionist movement would not have achieved the same degree of influence and the enterprise as a whole might have floundered.

Herzl's physical appearance, upon which we will elaborate in the following chapters, was also a key component. Many who met Herzl testified to his striking looks and the powerful impression he made on them. They describe his appearance in almost photographic detail: his deep-set eyes, perceived as beautiful or sad; his long, full beard; his raven-black hair; his statuesque height; his finely shaped head, his slender build; his captivating laugh; his clear voice; his large, strong hands; his regal bearing and elegant body language; and above all, the exquisite harmony of all these features in combination. In addition, people extolled his intellectual abilities and human qualities as a man and a leader, as well as his great personal warmth and passion. It was this amalgam of character and physical beauty that endeared him to the public and contributed to the aura of leadership and trust he inspired in those around him. Such accounts are particularly surprising when they come from people who disagreed with him or how he was assessed by others. Nearly every depiction of Herzl, even by bitter opponents, cites his dashing appearance. People spoke of his looks and personality in the same breath, as if his physical appeal were an integral part of his persona as a Jewish leader and visionary.[18]

Herzl's sweeping charisma was yet another factor in his success. Many people who met him were struck by his ability to charm his interlocutors and change their minds. His effect on Nahum Sokolow, mentioned above, is a case in point, and he was hardly the only one. A combination of brilliance, good looks and integrity produced a dynamic and charismatic leader who was hard to resist. Herzl was a man of many opposites: action and vision, imagination and pragmatism, authoritarian and humble. He was a loner who did not get the respect from his family that he did from the Jews. While he may have had difficulty relating to his friends as equals, there was no one more attuned to the feelings of the masses. Many have pointed out the contradictions and conflicting elements in his personality. In other people, such contradictions would be their undoing; in Herzl, all the strands harmonized perfectly. That Herzl was able to push through a monumental historic change in such a short span of time was a tribute to his charisma. On the following pages, we will analyze the nature of Herzl's charisma and how it affected those around him – both those in his close circle and those who never met him. In particular, we will discuss how Herzl's charisma went beyond borders, as borne out in his visit to Palestine.

The seminal event that made Herzl a towering figure in the Jewish world and beyond, constituted a vital component of his success and marked a key juncture in his Zionist odyssey, was the First Zionist Congress. Herzl did not rely only on his own abilities or diplomatic contacts attained as a result of his social standing and personal magnetism. When he failed to advance the Zionist revolution from the top down with the aid of Baron Hirsch and Rothschild, he made up his mind

---

18 History professor Robert Wistrich wrote about this special synthesis of "form and content" in the case of Theodor Herzl. He claims that the Herzlian ethos, fusing political idealism and sublime beauty, worked its charms on the Jews of Eastern Europe and impressed them deeply. Persecuted under the Czarist regime, they sought a way out, and Herzl was their messiah. See *Mitos vezikaron: Gilguleha shel hatoda'a hayisraelit*, eds. Robert S. Wistrich and David Ohana, Hakibbutz Hameuhad and Van Leer, Jerusalem 2005, p. 130 (henceforth: *Mitos vezikaron*). Wistrich dwells on Herzl's impact in East Europe, but as we shall see, many Jews in Western Europe also fell under his spell.

to mobilize the people. Many geniuses work alone, at the easel, in the laboratory or in the study. Few succeed in rallying the masses. The Zionist Congress was the first national convention that purported to represent the Jewish people in its entirety and shape its aspirations as an independent nation.[19] Herzl was the playwright, stage director and star of this phenomenal show. He succeeded in transforming the Congress into a watershed event, utilizing it to mold the spirit of the nation and gain international recognition for Jewish self-determination. The Congress and the institutions created under its auspices continued to serve as the central instruments for the advancement of Zionist goals long after Herzl was gone. The Congress was both an affirmation of Herzl's success and a contributing factor. Herzl's public persona was shaped at the Congress, and he remained the figurehead in the six congresses he chaired before his death. It was not easy work – not at the first and second congresses, and not at those that followed. Opposition to Herzl mounted from one congress to the next, slowly sapping his strength. Yet he stood his ground and was able to push through unanimous resolutions in spite of the raucous debates that took place along the way. At the congresses, Herzl's charisma unfolded in all its glory. Even the stiffest opposition could not erode his status. Although some delegates challenged him, he managed to preserve the special atmosphere year after year, for five congresses in a row. The sixth congress, which revolved around the Uganda debate, posed some particularly trying moments for Herzl that we will analyze in detail.

The parallel between Herzl and great Jewish leaders of the past was another point that worked in his favor – in the Jewish world, but sometimes among non-Jews as well. Herzl was often compared to Moses. That Herzl had emerged from a secular environment impressed the Jews deeply. In that respect, he reminded them of Moses, who grew up in Pharaoh's court. Herzl's book on the Zionist project took both Jews and non-Jews by surprise. It had never even occurred to many of them that this "Dr. Herzl" was a Jew. Zionism was thus thrust into the limelight and enjoyed unprecedented exposure. If such aspirations had been articulated by some other Jew, people would have pronounced him delusional, but coming from Herzl, they were taken seriously.

The similarities between Herzl and Moses are quite striking. Moses went out to the Israelites from the royal court where he lived as a free man, an Egyptian

---

19 While the vast majority of Jews lived in Europe, it was important to Herzl that the Zionist Congress represent Jews from all over the globe. Towards this end, he sent emissaries and letters to communities throughout the world. The first congress already included delegates from the United States and Algeria. There were only a quarter of a million Jews in North Africa, but the General Zionist Council sought to recruit them to the Zionist Movement and sent out an appeal to communities in the region in 1900.

prince, untainted by slave mentality. Herzl descended from the heights of journalism, from his post as the literary editor of one of Europe's most prestigious newspapers. He was not affiliated with the Jewish community. The suffering of the Jews did not touch his life or affect his standing in any way. If he had not witnessed anti-Semitism in Europe with his own eyes, chances are he would never have taken an interest. But Herzl did not allow his lofty social status to blind him. Convinced that the Jews had no future in Europe, he went down to the people, like Moses in his day, out of a sense of historic calling. He acted to save the Jews, to lead them to freedom and a better future. Like Moses, who looked like an Egyptian, Herzl was the quintessential European. Both Jews and gentiles saw him in this light. He was "Dr. Herzl" – Theodor, not Benjamin Ze'ev. The Jews stood in awe of him. That Herzl identified with the character of Moses himself helped to boost his spirit in the face of the obstacles that came his way at home and abroad. On the following pages, we will look at other points of convergence between the two and discuss their significance.

Although he wielded extraordinary influence, Herzl's path was not strewn with roses: Alongside his triumphs, he grappled with one trial after another. Ideological opponents and people with vested interests were never in short supply. The publication of *Der Judenstaat* was greeted with derision and scorn, and until his dying day, he faced opposition at home and farther afield. Some rejected Herzl's leadership altogether, dismissing him as a lunatic and a dreamer. Even those who acknowledged the Jewish problem and believed in the importance of intervention were openly confrontational. Within the ranks of the Zionist movement, he was challenged by members whose agenda differed radically from his own. Sometimes their disagreement was a cover for personal resentment. Outside the Zionist movement Herzl faced a motley crew of opponents that included rabbis from the Reform and ultra-Orthodox movements. Herzl coined a term for them: the *"Protest Rabbiner"* (protest rabbis). Opposition also came from Hovevei Zion, which supported settlement and eventual immigration to Palestine but viewed Herzl's diplomatic overtures as superfluous and risky. His activism was seen as endangering the colonies. To some he was an unfair competitor, appearing out of nowhere and usurping a project that was theirs. There were those who were jealous and attacked him personally, claiming he was not worthy of leading the Zionist movement. In the end, some of these individuals joined the movement and became part of the opposition that stubbornly fought him from within. They made Herzl's job harder, but the Zionist movement gained momentum nonetheless.

Herzl's influential status was sometimes exploited and his words twisted. He complains about this on more occasions than one. The phenomenon itself is not surprising. Historic personalities are talked about, and it is not uncommon for both admirers and foes to draw upon them for justification of their own views. "I am already so accustomed to [being] misunderstood, that I am altogether confused when for once... my words are not distorted," Herzl wrote to the editor of the *Jewish Chronicle*.[20]

The distortion has become even more widespread since Herzl's death. His celebrity status seems to attract slanted and biased portrayals. Herzl scholar Georges Yitshak Weisz argues that Herzl has become "the butt of a campaign of distortion and misrepresentation aimed at justifying a priori ideological positions, political or religious."[21] But such distortion, based on cherry-picked readings and abridged citations from his writings, did not start today. In 1934, Berl Katznelson was already protesting the falsification of Herzl's legacy in the Zionist world "by malice or by ignorance."[22] To unravel the secret of Herzl means contending with such falsehoods. We will look at the misreading of Herzl over the course of his career, examine the motives of those behind it, and weigh the impact on Herzlian charisma. The paeans of praise heaped upon Herzl, some written while he was alive and some posthumously, are another important subject, which will be explored in the final chapter of the book.

Our intention is not to observe Herzl from afar but to closely scrutinize the arenas in which he worked and the strategies that helped him bring his ideas to a wider public. Employing in-depth scholarship, we hope to deepen our understanding of Herzl, the Viennese gentleman who dreamed a dream, strove to make it a reality and successfully launched a historic revolution. This book is about his journey.

---

20 See Alex Bein, "Some early Herzl letters," *Herzl Year Book* (henceforth: *HYB*) vol. 1 (1958), p. 316, in: Georges Yitshak Weisz, *Theodor Herzl: A New Reading*, Gefen, Jerusalem 2013, p. 25, note 89.
21 *Ibid.*, p. 22.
22 Berl Katznelson (1877–1944), one of the leaders of the Labor Movement and Zionist socialism, and a founding member of the Zionist Organization. See Berl Katznelson, *Bekhavlei adam: Al morim vehaverim*, Am Oved, Tel Aviv 1945, p. 68 (henceforth: *Bekhavlei adam*).

Part 1: **His Personality**

Chapter 1
"Thine Eyes Shall See the King in His Beauty" (Isaiah 33:17)

The focal point of this book is Herzl's personal profile: his personality, his persuasive abilities and also his physical appearance, which so deeply impressed those who saw him. Some, as we shall see below, committed their thoughts to paper.

For the title of an essay about Herzl, the German Jewish artist Hermann Struck, one of several artists who sketched, painted, photographed and sculpted Herzl in his lifetime, chose a verse from the Book of Isaiah: "Thine eyes shall see the king in his beauty." An ardent Zionist and lifelong admirer of Herzl, Struck wrote:

> "What I wish to say about Herzl, our leader whose memory shall remain forever with us, I have already tried to express in some of my etchings, which attempt to portray his extraordinary appearance. I know very well that these efforts are far from perfect, as Herzl was a man endowed with divine beauty. And I must confess that it was this divine beauty – a gift from the heavens – that left the most enduring impression on me. His tall, slim figure, the marvelous harmony of every feature, his graceful movements – all came together to form an ideal paradigm of beauty. The monarchs he met presumably felt the same way. 'Their eyes saw the king in his beauty.' I believe he represented the ideal that everyone – Kaiser Wilhelm II, the king of Italy, Edward VII, Franz Josef, Alfonso of Spain – saw in their minds. Even the visions of the prophets pale in comparison. This nobility, difficult to put into words, combined with an almost princely generosity of spirit, instantly charmed his interlocutors."[1]

Struck does not discuss individual components of Herzl's beauty, but speaks in general terms about the tremendous visual impact his looks had on those around him. Struck admits that his own artistic endeavors to capture this beauty succeeded only in part: Herzl's charm and good looks were a gift of God and thus impossible to convey in a picture. But physical beauty was only one dimension. Struck goes on to talk Herzl's aristocratic bearing and compassionate nature, which left anyone who had dealings with him enchanted and added to his charisma.

---

[1] Yitzhak Mann, *Hermann Struck: Ha'adam veha'oman*, Dvir, Tel Aviv 1954, p. 174 (henceforth: *Hermann Struck*).

Ephraim Moshe Lilien was another artist who incorporated images of Herzl in his work. Like most of his colleagues in the Democratic Fraction,[2] he was a great admirer of Herzl even though the Fraction as a group battled Herzl fiercely on "kultura"[3] and other matters. The famous photograph of Herzl leaning on the railing on the balcony of Hotel Les *Trois Rois* in Basel was taken by Lilien, and many of the biblical leaders that appear in his artwork, among them Moses, Aaron and Joshua, sport Herzl's features. The stained-glass windows Lilien designed for the B'nei B'rith club in Hamburg, Germany depict Herzl as Moses.[4]

Herzl was the perfect foil for the stereotypical nineteenth-century East European Jew. Mordecai Ehrenpreis writes about Lilien's use of Herzl's imposing features to represent the "authentic" Jew, the Jew of the olden days. In Herzl's visage Lilien saw nobility, vitality, strength and charisma – all the traits ascribed to the Jews of antiquity in the Romantic novels of George Eliot and Benjamin Disraeli's *Tancred*. On Herzl's wondrous melding of the physical and spiritual, Ehrenpreis says:

> "He was majestic not because of his scheme to found a state but because majesty was an intrinsic part of him ... He was a king from head to toe, regal in body and mind."[5]

There were differences of opinion, however, on what exactly Struck and Lilien's portraits of Herzl conveyed. Comparing Lilien's balcony photograph and Struck's famous etching,[6] Ehrenpreis agreed that Struck's etching was important as a work of art, but he was disturbed by its "exilic" connotations: "This is the face of a deeply passionate man tortured and tormented by the labors of the mind ... But it is a Galut-suffused grandeur existing more in the imagination of the masses than in reality."[7] Struck wished to transmit grandeur in his por-

---

2 The Democratic Fraction was a separatist group that debuted at the Fifth Zionist Congress. It was at the forefront of the battle for secular national culture. For more on the Fraction, see the chapter on the kultura debate.
3 The Fraction demanded that the Congress focus on "kultura," not politics (in the spirit of Ahad Ha'am). In the opposing camp sat the rabbis, who fiercely objected to any programming that was not under their supervision. Herzl, fearing a split in the Zionist movement, tried to put off the discussion of culture until after the establishment of a Jewish state. For more on the Fifth Congress and the issues raised there, see Chapter 4.
4 For more on the comparison between Herzl and Moses in literature and art, see Chapter 11.
5 *Sefer hacongress* (1950), p. 235.
6 In May 1903, Struck drew a number of sketches of Herzl at his home that became the basis for this etching.
7 *Sefer hacongress* (1923), pp. 189–190.

trait, but what he depicted was exilic grandeur, which was alien to Herzl. He felt that Lilien's rendering of Herzl was different:

> "Here we have a calm face, soft and gentle, suffused with all the sorrow of the human race. Not bitterness or irritability ... but the quiet melancholy of a lyrical soul. This Herzl has a harmonious face, the face of a man who knows how to dream, the face of a whole and healthy man free of worldly inhibitions, a symbol of Jewish refinement and breeding, neither enslaved nor submissive. His greatness lies in being the essence of an entire chapter of history, a composite of all the precious values of the national soul, a cross between a king and a dreamer. That is why the people followed him."[8]

Karl Schwarz, an art critic and friend of Struck, disagreed with Ehrenpreis. In Struck's etchings he sees greatness free of exilic association, and describes the symbolic importance of his work in mythic terms:

> "The artist sought to portray Herzl as a paragon and prophet of Israel, and in this he succeeded. Struck has drawn the Theodor Herzl who lives in our hearts. His is the ultimate portrait of Herzl, a visionary deep in thought, his eyes gazing out into the future."[9]

Despite these differing interpretations, the portraits of Struck and Lilien do share something: charisma. Both artists portray a man who exerts an involuntary influence on those around him, whose looks are irresistibly appealing and whose presence radiates brilliance, majesty and prophetic vision.

Other descriptions of Herzl hone in on specific physical traits, the harmony of his features and his majestic bearing. This is how the Austrian-Jewish novelist Stephan Zweig recalled his first meeting with Herzl at the offices of the *Neue Freie Press* (NFP):

> "Theodor Herzl rose to greet me, and instinctively I felt there was a grain of truth in the ill-intentioned joke about the King of Zion – he really did look regal with his high forehead, his clear-cut features, his long and almost blue-black beard and his deep-blue, melancholy eyes. His sweeping, rather theatrical gestures did not seem affected, because they arose from a natural dignity and it would not have taken this particular occasion to make him look imposing to me. Even standing in front of the shabby desk heaped high with papers in that miserably cramped editorial office with its single windows, he was like a Bedouin desert sheikh; a billowing white burnoose would have looked as natural on him as his black morning coat, well-cut in an obviously Parisian style."[10]

---

[8] *Sefer hacongress* (1950), p. 234.
[9] Hermann Struck, pp. 30–31.
[10] Stefan Zweig, *The World of Yesterday: An Autobiography*, University of Nebraska Press, 1964, p. 105.

Moving from Vienna to London, the famous Anglo-Jewish author Israel Zangwill, who claims to have been the second person Herzl recruited to the Zionist cause after Max Nordau, describes Herzl as "a majestic Oriental figure , [who] draws himself up and stands dominating the assembly with eyes that brood and glow – you would say one of the Assyrian Kings, whose sculptured heads adorn our museums, the very profile of Tiglath Pileser. In sooth, the beautiful somber face of a kingly dreamer ..."[11]

In explaining what made Herzl the "greatest of them all," the celebrated author and thinker Max Nordau (1849–1923), the first to join Herzl on his Zionist adventure,[12] also lingered on Herzl's physical appearance.

> "Herzl was a gifted writer and an outstanding orator with a wonderful, fertile imagination, but at the same time, quick and practical of mind ... Herzl was less of a poet than Heine, less of a speaker than Disraeli and less of an organizer than Baron Hirsch ... but he was the greatest of them all because he had everything: 'He is all-powerful and contains them all.'[13] And let us not forget: He was endowed with those external features, seemingly a matter of chance, that are invaluable in human relationships. He was tall, handsome and well-built, with a noble brow, imposing black eyes, a hearty laugh and a clear voice that carried far but also radiated sincere emotional warmth."[14]

Many of those who initially opposed Herzl for a variety of reasons were later won over by his charms and became loyal followers. One of the leading Jewish journalists and writers of the time, Nahum Sokolow, was skeptical when *Der Judenstaat* was published, mainly because he feared that political Zionism and its goal of a Jewish state endangered the Hovevei Zion movement which was in the process of establishing farm colonies in Eretz Yisrael. As related above, Sokolow changed his mind after meeting Herzl at the First Zionist Congress. Like many others, he breaks down his impression of Herzl into three stages: First he was

---

11 Israel Zangwill, *Dreamers of the Ghetto*, Harper & Brothers, New York and London, 1898, p. 306; Sefer hacongress (1950), p. 143.
12 Nordau and Herzl had much in common: Both were born in Budapest and became writers and journalists, and both were witnesses to anti-Semitism. Some compared the duo to Moses and Aaron, see: Netanyahu, *Khameshet avot*, p. 134. Both were famous but not known as Jews. Ussishkin relates that when he met Herzl in 1896, Herzl asked to send regards to Nordau in Paris. Ussishkin asked: Which Nordau? The famous author? What, he is a Jew? And Herzl replied: "Not just a Jew but a good Zionist." See *Sefer Ussishkin*, p. 353. Nordau was the first to encourage Herzl to embark on his Zionist journey, and opened doors for him in England by introducing him to Israel Zangwill. See *Haderech la'atzmaut (The Road to Independence)*, p. 1.
13 A reference to God in "Vekhol ma'ameenim," a piyyut recited in the Rosh Hashanah prayer service.
14 Joseph Heftman, *Herzl bikhazon hador*, Uma Umoledet Ltd., Tel Aviv 1946, pp. 23–24.

struck by Herzl's height: "Standing before me I saw a tall man." Then he goes into greater detail: "My first impression was of a handsome man, serious and important-looking, whose expression was constantly changing ... He tended to look directly into the face of his interlocutor, his gaze penetrating as an eagle, his eyes mesmerizing in their beauty and captivating power." When the meeting is over, Sokolow observes Herzl from a distance:

> "From the first moment I knew I was in the presence of an unconventional personage. There was something brooding in his appearance. His head was large and slightly elongated but marvelously symmetrical – a blend of strength and charm. He reminded me of the marvelous carved heads of the kings of Assyria in ancient reliefs, a resemblance enhanced all the more by his magnificent black beard. Under his moustache, a little smile of amusement flitted across his lips. Conflicting somewhat with all this princely Oriental glory and splendor were his large, powerful hands, as if testifying that their owner was a man of strength and action."[15]

Sokolow attributes Herzl's sorrowfulness to the sorrow of the Jews and their yearning for a homeland, which under Herzl's devoted leadership could now be channeled into energy and action.

As a close friend, however, Sokolow began to notice changes over time that signified a process of premature aging:

> "I had been observing him for many years. The head, held high over all others in Herzl's younger days, the beautiful high brow, the hair black as tar, this grand head, so finely chiseled, which seemed to glow with radiance in later days, became draped in sorrow, Jewish sorrow. The impression he left on the serious-minded viewer was deep and profound...In his youthful days, the beauty of this head was conveyed in lively movement. Over time, a new beauty joined the flash of intellect in his eyes, the beauty of deepening wisdom ... Gone was the man of the salon, replaced by an ancient sage, one of the sages of Israel, endowed with the spirit of a prophet. But one thing remained unchanged: With that same imposing head and enormous, piercing eyes, the essence of his character continued to reveal itself – the indomitable will."[16]

Sokolow's chronicle of Herzl's life thus provides us with a record of his physical change: The freshness of youth gives way to old age, but the impressiveness of his looks remains undiminished. Not all of them said so, but it was clear that people meeting Herzl for the first time could not ignore his appearance. When Menachem Ussishkin, who was not enamored with *Der Judenstaat*, was asked to assist in its distribution, he replied: "I read the pamphlet carefully but see

---

15 Nahum Sokolow, *Hatzofeh leveit yisrael*, Hasifria Hatzionit, Jerusalem, 1961, p. 470.
16 *Ibid.*, pp. 466–481.

no reason to distribute it because there is nothing that the Russian Jew will find new after reading the pamphlets of Pinsker and Lilienblum." He was equally unimpressed by what he had heard about Herzl. When he arrived in Vienna, two Zionist activists, Nathan Birnbaum[17] and Johann Kremenezky[18] suggested that he go see Herzl, but he refused on the grounds that he saw no benefit in such a visit. The next day, Birnbaum handed him a visiting card he had received from Herzl with the following message: "I heard that you are one of the noted activists in the field of Zionism which interests me now. Please do not deprive me of the honor of hosting you at my home today, at 5 o'clock." At that point, Ussishkin gave in and accepted the invitation. With all his suspicion and misgivings, not to mention his own dogmatism, he could not help but comment on Herzl's appearance: "When we came in, Dr. Herzl rose from his chair and walked over to greet me. He surprised me at once with his beauty, freshness and youth." After the visit, he wrote: "He will be a great boon to the Zionist movement. There is no question that his charming demeanor will win over the Jews of Russia and perhaps Western Jewry too."[19] Avraham Ludwipol, who reported on the First Zionist Congress for the Hebrew newspaper *Hashiloah*, wrote at length about Herzl's looks:

> "... Even in his outward appearance he is destined for the top. Herzl is handsome in every sense of the word. His features overflow with Eastern beauty and the ancient peoples of the East. Not without cause, Zangwill compared his countenance to the Chaldean kings. Imagining what Bar-Kokhba looked like, Herzl's face has come to mind more than once: tall, broad-shouldered but not excessively so, sparkling black eyes, broad forehead, but again not overdone, long straight nose, direct, penetrating glance, full black beard almost down to his chest, cheeks not too full but also not too thin, dark complexion and a mouth conjuring up inner conviction...What a delight to gaze upon this face. There is no

---

[17] Dr. Nathan Birnbaum was the head of Kadimah, a Zionist students association. See *ibid.*, pp. 199–200.
[18] Johann Kremenezky, an Odessa-born engineer who introduced electric lighting to Vienna, was a member of Kadimah and a founding director of the Jewish National Fund. He was a close friend of Herzl and one of the executors of his will. Another Kadimah member, Isidor Schalit, writes: "Our movement was not taken very seriously in Vienna. We were mocked and ridiculed...and altogether treated like fools...In the end, those Jewish students from Kadimah will grow older and wiser, and forget this nonsense. If not, they should be sent to the madhouse. But not Herzl, the poet who spoke of his visions...He was a handsome man, the people's favorite..." *Sefer hacongress* (1923), p. 67.
[19] *Sefer Ussishkin*, pp. 352–354. Dr. Nathan Birnbaum was the head of the Zionist students association Kadimah. See *ibid.*, pp. 199–200.

doubt about it. The look of this man sets off the imagination and fires up our emotions. One has to like him."[20]

Finally, we have the testimony of Dov Haviv Lubman, one of the leaders of the agricultural colony of Rishon Lezion, who remembers Herzl's visit in 1898 and the community's unusual response to his looks:

> "He captivated all who saw him. Pregnant women picked their way through the crowd to get nearer and gaze upon his comeliness for good luck, in the hope of bearing children like him. Indeed, little Herzls and Herzliyas were born that year and named for him, some of them darling and beautiful, if not exactly in his image ..."[21]

Herzl in the Eyes of Religious Jews

Herzl's looks attracted attention across the social spectrum. Amid the plethora of commentary on his appearance, the remarks of the religious community are worthy of special note. Among religious Jews, after all, a leader was judged by his inner qualities, not by his façade. Beauty and grace were perceived as skin deep – sheer vanity and deceit, to quote the Book of Proverbs.[22] In his study of Herzl and religious Zionism, Dov Schwartz discerns two different approaches. Some, like Rabbi Eliezer Meir Lifshitz,[23] looked inside to explain Herzl's power of influence. Lifshitz hailed Herzl as a genius who managed to unite all the strands of Zionist ideology and practice by dint of his personality.[24] Rabbi Meir Bar-Ilan says something similar:

> "Very often one finds true greatness – personal greatness – in individuals who are upheld as legends in their lifetimes. When they walk among men, their virtues and flaws are visible, as they are for everyone else, and yet they are perceived as extraordinary. They are not treated as ordinary mortals but as a chapter of history. Herzl was such a one."[25]

---

20 Avraham Ludwipol, "Impressions and reminiscences of the First Congress," in: *Luah Ahiasaf*, 1903, p. 56.
21 Aharon Vardi, *Malki betzion*, Hapoel Hatza'ir, Tel Aviv, 1931, p. 75.
22 *Proverbs* 31:30
23 Rabbi Eliezer Meir Lifschitz (1879, Galicia – 1946, Jerusalem), a Jewish educator and scholar, one of the founders of Hamizrachi.
24 See *Herzl az vehayom: Medinat hayehudim bemedinat hayehudim*, eds. Avi Saguy and Yedidya Stern, Bar Ilan University and Hartman Institute, Ramat Gan-Jerusalem, 2008, p. 313 (henceforth: *Herzl az vehayom*).
25 See Dov Schwartz, "Hatzionut hadatit veherzl: Dgamim shel tadmit," in: *Herzl az vehayom*, pp. 312–313.

Others, however, directly referenced Herzl's appearance. Hermann Struck, an artist but also a religious Jew, was one of those who embraced the aesthetic approach. While Rabbi Lifshitz and his colleagues looked for a rational explanation for Herzl's success, Struck rejected the power of words and saw Herzl's elegance and body language as the key."[26] Avraham Zvi Glicksman of Lodz was another religious Jew who adopted this approach.[27] Failing to understand why the rabbis were not backing Herzl, whose ultimate goal he said was to "rescue the Jews from a life of sorrow, hunger and persecution," Glicksman went to the offices of the newspaper *Die Welt* to set up a meeting with him.[28] The fact that a pious Jew was so taken with Herzl's physical beauty that he wrote about it in his memoirs underscores how powerfully Herzl's looks impacted on those who laid eyes on him:

> "When I saw Herzl in the flesh I was astonished and moved beyond words. Never in my life had I seen anyone so magnificent, head and shoulders above ordinary mortals. His beard was long, his hair black as a raven's and his posture erect. Wisdom shone from his face, which overflowed with an abundance of kindheartedness and goodness. He could not have been more than forty. *Ben porat alei ayin* ["Joseph is a fruitful vine, a fruitful vine by a fountain," Genesis 49:22], I said to myself. Happy is the nation that has sons like him."[29]

Yet another religious figure who was impressed by Herzl's regal bearing was Rabbi Shlomo Hacohen, a leading Vilna rabbi. In 1903, Herzl passed through Vilna on his return from St. Petersburg after meeting with top Russian government officials in the wake of the Kishinev pogrom.[30] Rabbi Hacohen wore his rabbinic garb to greet the guest and welcomed him with the Priestly Blessing. Yehuda Leib Maimon, one the founders of Hamizrahi, recounted the story of this meeting after Herzl died:

> "When I had the honor of hosting Rabbi Shlomo a year before his death, I asked him in the course of conversation about his impressions of Herzl. The dear rabbi placed his wizened hands on my shoulder and in a voice laden with grief told me: All those who were with me

---

26 *Ibid.*, pp. 291–322.
27 A Kotzker hasid and one of the great industrialists of Lodz.
28 While the exact date is unknown, the meeting was reported in *Hamelitz* in 1900, so it presumably took place sometime before that.
29 Avraham Zvi Glicksman, *Tiferet adam: Biographical sketches and letters*, Kultura, Lodz, 1923, p. 63 (henceforth: *Tiferet adam*).
30 See p. 246.

on that occasion were convinced that our eyes beheld the King of Israel in his splendor. Woe to beauty buried in the earth!"³¹

Finally, David Shub, one of the pioneers of Rosh Pina, shared his memory of Herzl in Vienna during the winter of 1897: "From the very first moment, he captured my heart with his beautiful face and exceptionally fine features …"³²

Up to this point, no distinction has been made between the testimony of Jews from Eastern and Western Europe. But Robert Wistrich argues that Herzl's appearance was of special importance to the East Europeans. The Herzlian ethos, with its combination of political idealism and physical attractiveness, spoke to them first and foremost because they were suffering from oppression and hardship. They needed a savior and Herzl was a perfect fit. In Wistrich's opinion, Herzl's beard played a starring role as a symbol of religious Jewry and messianic ideology. His elegance, the fact that he was bearded, and the message he conveyed, created a package that endeared him to this public:

> "Herzl's impressive beard was, without doubt, an important detail in the dissemination of his myth and that of Zionism itself, as a movement of genuine national unity. The thick black beard was reassuring in the sense that it also recalled *traditional* Judaism and its messianic hopes. It appeared to reinforce the link between Herzl, political Zionism and the revered image of the ancient Hebrew prophets."³³

Wistrich brings a quote from David Ben-Gurion, one of many that attest to the significance of the beard:

> "When [Herzl] appeared in Plonsk, people greeted him as the Messiah. Everyone went around saying, 'The Messiah has come,' and we children were much impressed. It was easy for a small boy to see in Herzl the Messiah. He was a tall, finely featured man whose impressive black beard flowed wide down to his chest. One glimpse of him and I was ready to follow him then and there to the land of my ancestors."³⁴

---

31 Yehuda Leib Maimon, *Sarei hame'ah: Reshumot al gedolei yisrael*, vol. 6, Mossad Harav Kook, Jerusalem 1999, p. 17.
32 Moshe David Shub, *Zikhronot levait david: Sheevim shnot avoda besadeh hat'hiya vehayishuv*, Reuben Mass, Jerusalem, 1973, pp. 20–11 (henceforth: *Zikhronot levait david*).
33 *The Shaping of Israeli Identity: Myth, Memory and Trauma*, eds. Robert Wistrich and David Ohana, p. 29 (henceforth: *The Shaping of Israeli Identity*).
34 David Ben Gurion, *Recollections*, London 1970, p. 34; *The Shaping of Israeli Identity*, p. 128, note 28.

Michael Berkowitz[35] offers a similar theory with respect to Herzl's beard and its connection to religious Judaism:

> "Herzl's physiognomy, to most Zionists, was the purest symbol of Zionism's aspirations. One might say his was the specific countenance of the movement. Herzl was presented as serious, proud, intelligent, noble, attractive, unique and at the same time – recognizably Jewish ... His manliness and handsome looks consciously rebuked the anti-semitic stereotype of Jewish effeminity and ugliness while his dark complexion and face were perceived and extolled as the perfect face in which the Zionist movement and Jews could take great pride."[36]

While Wistrich and Berkowitz draw a link between Herzl's beard and traditional Judaism, the question is whether beards at that time were indeed associated with religion. Beards were fashionable in those days in both Eastern and Western Europe. Looking broadly at the comments about Herzl's beard, it seems clear that the context was often aesthetic and not related to religious observance.[37] Even the remarks of the East European Jews were not specifically religious. For the most part, they refer to the beard as a component of his distinguished appearance that only added to his charisma, with no religious or messianic connotations.[38]

In his memoirs, Zionist activist Sammy Gronemann wrote about the iconic status of Herzl's beard:

> "A certain secretary of state told Wolffsohn, looking at Herzl with awe: 'I think that the whole reputation of Zionism rests on the beauty of your president. If he shaved his

---

[35] A professor at the University of London (not to be confused with Herzl's secretary of the same name).

[36] *The Shaping of Israeli Identity*, p. 29, 128, note 28.

[37] For the most part, the speakers are not East European or religious Jews. They are remarking on Herzl's handsome looks, with his beard singled out for special praise. Hermann Struck, born in Germany, associated it with the ideal male beauty of the biblical world. Eulogizing Herzl, the Anglo-Jewish writer Israel Zangwill, wrote "It seems only the other day that a black-bearded stranger knocked at my study door" (*Haderekh la'atzmaut*, p. 71, *Jewish Herald*, Houston, Texas, October 16, 1908). Stefan Zweig, an Austrian Jew, described Herzl's beard as blue-black and priestly (in a Christian sense) (*The World of Yesterday*, p. 105).

[38] Nahum Sokolow, an East European Jew, impressed by Herzl's amalgam of regal grace and power, notes that his handsome black beard only enhanced that impression (*Sefer hacongress*, 1950, p. 179). Glicksman mentions Herzl's beard as beautiful, not as a sign of religiosity. That Herzl donned a *kippa* in Glicksman's presence seems unlikely (*Tiferet adam*, p. 63). Recalling Herzl's visit to Palestine in 1898, an unnamed speaker in Aharon Vardi's *Malki betzion* describes him as a majestic figure with a long black beard (*Malki betzion*, p. 90).

beard – that would be the end of Zionism.' To which Wolffsohn amusedly replied: 'Perhaps, but then Zionism would instantly grow back.'"[39]

Beards were enormously popular in Herzl's day. Looking at photographs from the late nineteenth century from both Eastern and Western Europe, the number of bearded men far exceeds the number of men who were clean-shaven. In the group photograph of the First Zionist Congress, 94 of the male delegates are bearded out of a total of 151, with 43 sporting moustaches. Only one man in the picture has no facial hair.[40]

Marcus Cohn (1890–1952), son of the chief rabbi of Basel, Rabbi Asher (Arthur) Cohn, attended the Congress as a child. In his memoirs, he writes:

> "The First Congress looked very different from congresses in our day. Very few women participated or had the right to vote, and most of the men had full beards – not only leaders like Dr. Herzl ... Dr. Ehrenpreis, Dr. Nathan Birnbaum, Menahem Ussishkin and David Wolffsohn, but a great many other delegates ..."[41]

Among the heads of Hovevei Zion, there were many who were bearded without being religiously observant. These included Leon Pinsker and Moshe Leib Lilienblum who hailed from Eastern Europe. The same was true for many West European Zionist leaders, who wore beards but were not Orthodox, such as Max Bodenheimer and Birnbaum. The obvious conclusion is that Herzl's beard, however impressive, did not necessarily have religious significance.

Herzl's height is another subject of interest. While many testimonies describe him as being tall, Israeli journalist and author Amos Elon challenged this assumption:

> "He was invariably described by his admirers as ... towering over everyone. In his army medical examination papers, however, he is described as being of medium height; the French Prefecture de Police listed his height as five feet eight inches."[42]

After the publication of Elon's biography in the 1970s, Herzl's historic and public image took a turn and the focus of discourse shifted to Herzl as a private per-

---

39 Sammy Gronemann, *Zikhronot shel yekke* (translated from the German: Dov Stock), Am Oved, Tel Aviv, 1946, pp. 184–195.
40 Dan Ben Amotz, *Ma nishmah*, Ahiasaf, Jerusalem, 1965, pp. 238–239.
41 Marcus Cohn, "Erinnerungen eines Baslers an den ersten Zionistenkongress," in: *Festrschrift zom 50 Jahrigen bestehen*, Federation Suisse des Communautes Israelites, pp. 225–336.
42 Amos Elon, *Herzl*, Holt, Rinehart and Winston, 1975, p. 9.

son.⁴³ Elon's depiction of Herzl as short became entrenched in the public mind, although Georges Yitshak Weisz, among others, accuses Elon of distorting the facts:

> "The misrepresentation of Herzl ... has extended as far as his appearance. Amos Elon, one of Herzl's first Israeli biographers, thought it appropriate to comment about his physical characteristics. He was described ... as 'majestically tall' ... five feet eight inches... In the corresponding passage of the Hebrew version [of Elon's book] ... Herzl has shrunk to 1.65 meters, or approximately 5'5". [If so], all the people around him must have been scarcely more than five feet all themselves – a manifest impossibility."⁴⁴

Herzl's Austrian passport lists him as "tall," writes Weisz. He even discovered that records of the Paris police, which kept track of Herzl's movements (as it did for all foreign correspondents),⁴⁵ give his height as 1.74 meters.⁴⁶ This was definitely above the norm in the late nineteenth century.⁴⁷ The height controversy fits in with Getzel Kressel's criticism of Elon's biography.⁴⁸ Elon is a master of dramatization, he argues. Although he admits to reading the book with great pleasure, he finds countless statements that infuriate him.⁴⁹ "Elon might have produced a wonderful book if only he had devoted more time to studying his subject,"⁵⁰ Kressel concludes. Indeed, if Elon had inquired further, he would have found innumerable references to Herzl's height. The descriptions fall into two categories: those that emphasize the way Herzl carried himself and those that speak of his physical height.

The observations of Shmuel Pineles fall into the first category: "His physical appearance captured every heart ... and with his erect carriage, he was head and shoulders above the entire nation."⁵¹ Isidor Schalit also notes "his wondrously fine form and monumental height."⁵² Of course, accounts of his stately bearing are not evidence of physical height, as even short people look taller if they have good posture.

---

43 Daniel Gutwein, *Iyunim betkumat yisrael*, vol. 12, 2002, pp. 29–73.
44 Georges Yitshak Weisz, *Theodor Herzl: A New Reading*, pp. 23–24.
45 Foreign correspondents were kept under surveillance.
46 CZA, H1 2211, see p. 34.
47 *Ibid.*
48 Getzel Kressel, "Dramatizatsia lehayav upoalo shel Herzl" in: *Moznayim*, 46, Tevet 5738 (1978), p. 128.
49 *Ibid.*
50 *Ibid.*, p. 133.
51 *Sefer hacongress* (1923), p. 56.
52 *Ibid.*, p. 74.

In the second category are descriptions that leave no doubt about Herzl's actual height. Max Nordau wrote: "He was tall and handsome."[53] Itamar Ben Avi, who met Herzl when he visited Palestine, was in Berlin when Herzl's death was announced. Recalling the moment in his memoirs, he writes: "Everyone sensed that we were parting from a man who towered above the people, physically and spiritually."[54] Nahum Sokolow relates how Herzl rose to greet him and he found himself facing a "tall man."[55] The writer Mordechai Ben Hillel Hacohen also remarks on his height.[56]

In his account of the First Zionist Congress, Ehrenpreis writes: "Binyamin Zeev Herzl took the podium, tall and awe-inspiring."[57] When Herzl and Wolfsohn traveled together to Constantinople, Sokolow compared their height: Wolfsohn, who was taller than average, looked short compared to Herzl.[58] Reuben Brainin quotes the writer Hermann Bahr:

> "As if it were yesterday, I see myself strolling down the city street with a colleague … and a tall fellow with a dark complexion passes by … I was struck by the astonishing beauty of this man. I was also surprised by the sudden bashfulness of my colleague, who was usually quite bold … The name of this young man, my colleague revealed to me, was Theodor Herzl."[59]

Another interesting recollection appears in the autobiography of the Jewish conductor and composer Joseph Rumshinsky, who heard Herzl speak to an assembly of British Jews when he was in London en route to New York.[60] Taking advantage of Herzl's presence in the country during which he met secretly with members of the British parliament, the Jews organized an informal meeting to present their views on the Jewish question. The hall was packed with all kinds of Jews – bearded and clean-shaven, working class and aristocrats – and buzzed with arguments in different languages. The meeting had not opened yet. Everyone awaited the entrance of two distinguished guests – Sir Francis Montefiore and Theodor Herzl. As they entered the hall, Rumshinsky remembers how they looked:

---

[53] Heftman, *Herzl bikhazon hador*, pp. 223–224.
[54] Itamar Ben-Avi, *Eem shakhar atzma'utaynu: Zikhronot khayav shel hayeled ha'ivri harishon*, Public Committee for the Publication of the Writings of Itamar Ben-Avi, Jerusalem, 1961, p. 152.
[55] *Sefer hacongress* (1923), p. 11.
[56] Ibid., p. 103.
[57] Ehrenpreis, *Bein mizrakh lama'arav*, p. 74.
[58] Shmuel Leib Citron, *Herzl: Khayav upe'ulotav*, Shreberk, Vilna, 1921, p. 101.
[59] Reuben Brainin, *Khayei Herzl*, vol. 1, pp. 52–53.
[60] Joseph Rumshinsky, *Klangen fun mein leben*, Biederman, New York, 1944, pp. 224–239.

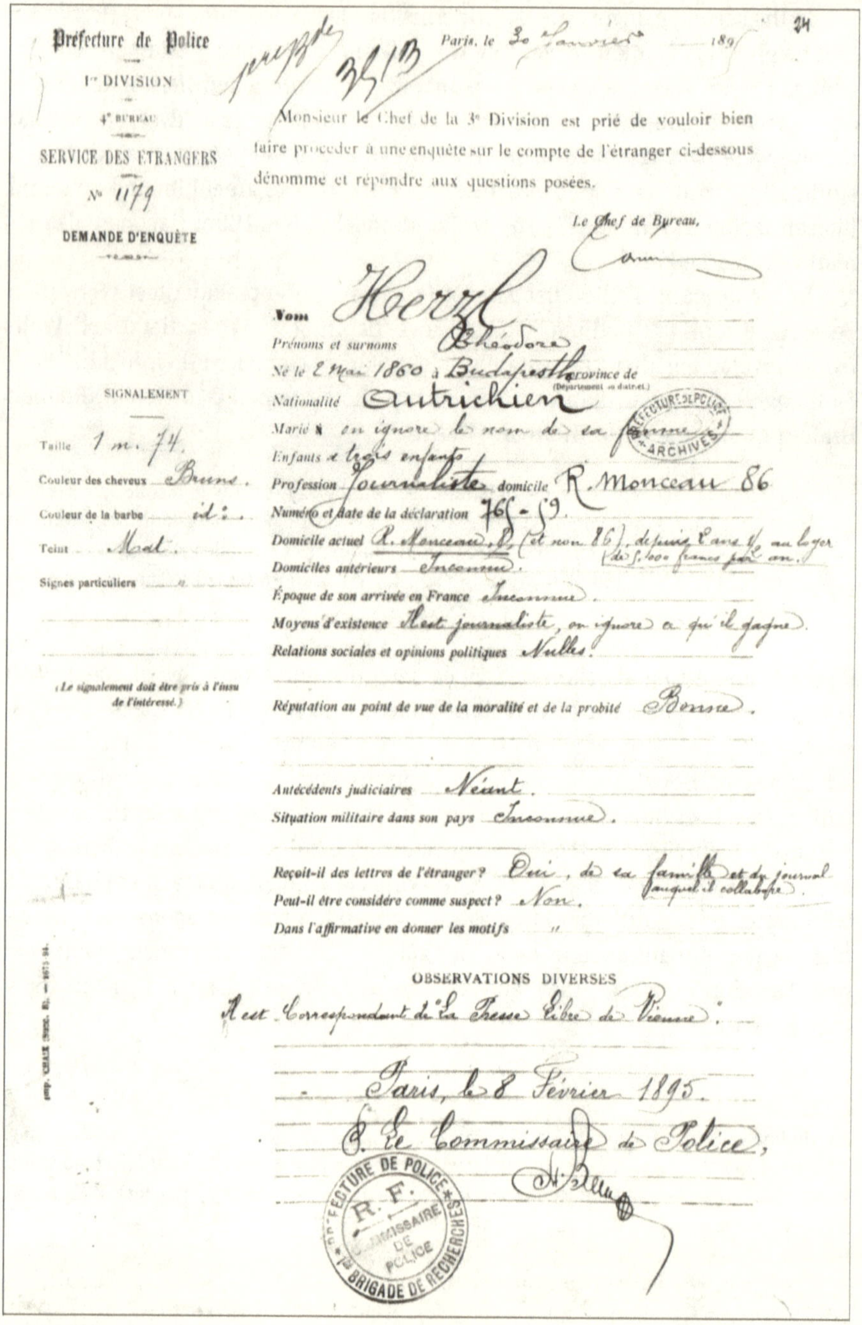

Préfecture de Police

1re DIVISION

4e BUREAU

SERVICE DES ÉTRANGERS

No 1179

DEMANDE D'ENQUÊTE

Paris, le 30 Janvier 1895

Monsieur le Chef de la 3e Division est prié de vouloir bien faire procéder à une enquête sur le compte de l'étranger ci-dessous dénommé et répondre aux questions posées.

Le Chef de Bureau,

Nom Herzl

Prénoms et surnoms Théodore

Né le 2 Mai 1860 à Budapesth province de (Département ou district)

Nationalité autrichien

Marié on ignore le nom de sa femme

Enfants a trois enfants

Profession Journaliste domicile R. Monceau 86

Numéro et date de la déclaration 765 – 59.

Domicile actuel R. Monceau, 8 (et non 86), depuis 2 ans ½ au loyer de 5.000 francs par an.

Domiciles antérieurs Inconnu.

Époque de son arrivée en France Inconnue.

Moyens d'existence Il est journaliste, on ignore ce qu'il gagne.

Relations sociales et opinions politiques Nulles.

Réputation au point de vue de la moralité et de la probité Bonne.

Antécédents judiciaires Néant.

Situation militaire dans son pays Inconnue.

Reçoit-il des lettres de l'étranger? Oui, de sa famille et du journal auquel il collabore.

Peut-il être considéré comme suspect? Non.

Dans l'affirmative en donner les motifs "

SIGNALEMENT

Taille 1 m. 74.

Couleur des cheveux Bruns.

Couleur de la barbe id.

Teint Mat.

Signes particuliers "

(Le signalement doit être pris à l'insu de l'intéressé.)

OBSERVATIONS DIVERSES

Il est Correspondant de La Presse Libre de Vienne.

Paris, le 8 Février 1895.

Le Commissaire de Police,

PRÉFECTURE DE POLICE – R.F. – COMMISSAIRE DE POLICE – 1re BRIGADE DE RECHERCHES

Figure 1: The document written by the Paris police indicating the height of Herzl, Courtesy of the Central Zionist Archives, Jerusalem, cf. footnote 46.

"Francis Montefiore was six feet tall, but Herzl's poise made him look taller. Of all the interesting characters at Kings Hall the one who stood out above all was the majestic figure of Theodor Herzl."

From this account, we see that Herzl gave the impression of being taller than Montefiore. If Herzl was 1.74 meters tall, and Montefiore was 1.80 meters (which is equivalent to six feet), Herzl might have appeared taller by the way he carried himself. But if Herzl was only 1.65 meters high, as Elon claims, such an optical illusion would have been impossible.

So from all the evidence we have compiled, it seems that Herzl was not just perceived as tall, or taller than he really was because of the way he carried himself. He was in fact taller than average for his day, and sufficiently so for many people to remark upon it and accentuate it.

In conclusion, Herzl was endowed with numerous traits that helped him on his Zionist journey, but to truly understand the secret of his success within such a brief period of time, one cannot ignore the component of physical attractiveness. From the testimony cited above, it seems clear that Herzl's handsome exterior was a key aspect of the charisma that opened doors for him, enabling him to launch political Zionism as a movement and lay the groundwork for a future Jewish state.

Chapter 2
Charisma

> *"In an atmosphere suffused with adoration and nervous excitement, his stature loomed larger than life. Before us he stood, powerful and majestic and beloved. We were as dreamers."*[1]

Charisma (Latin: χάρισμα) is a divine gift. The German sociologist Max Weber described charisma as "a certain quality of an individual personality, by virtue of which he is set apart from ordinary men and treated as endowed with supernatural, superhuman, or at least specifically exceptional powers or qualities."[2] Studies of the influence of charismatic leaders, including army officers and politicians, have found a variety of charismatic behaviors: dynamism and energy, self-confidence, deep commitment and motivation, lofty goals, creative and innovative action, defining objectives in ideological terms, expressing confidence in followers and setting high expectations for them.[3]

The previous chapter addressed Herzl's physical appearance. His looks may have impressed people in different ways, but they all agreed on one thing: There was no escaping his charisma. Herzl is portrayed as inspiring involuntary reverence, with a beauty seen as synonymous with greatness. He was hailed as a genius and a man of majesty and vision. Judging by the comments of those who met him in real life, he was irresistibly charismatic. Without this charisma, he would never have accomplished all that he did in such a short span of time.

Mordecai Ehrenpreis saw the longing of the Jews for a savior and Herzl's inexplicable power of attraction as a potent combination. Herzl played the hero in the Jewish collective dream. He was all that the typical Diaspora Jew was not, attracting the Jews with his magnetism:

> "Two thousand years we were imprisoned in the misery of Galut, humiliated, submissive and trampled underfoot. We became bent over, our emotions dulled and our minds twisted. For two thousand years we have been waiting for a liberated Jew to arise, erect, honest and straight-thinking, whose spirit has not been bent and suffocated by the bonds of slavery. Finally the man for whom we hoped and prayed has arrived, the man we saw in our imagination and yearned for. Is it any wonder that he looks to us like a creature from another world? Is it any wonder that the people are attracted to him by some mysterious force?"[4]

---

[1] Reuven Brainin in: *Sefer hacongress* (1923), p. 45.
[2] Max Weber, On Charisma and Institution Building, University of Chicago Press, 1947, p. 48.
[3] Boas Shamir, "Sod hakesher hakarismati," in: *Manheegut upeetuakh manhigut halakhah lema'aseh*, eds. Itzik Gonen and Eliav Zakai, p. 35.
[4] Mordecai Ehrenpreis, *Sefer hacongress* (1923), pp. 190–191.

A correspondent for the Hebrew monthly *Hashiloah* who assures his readers that he is no "mindless disciple" of Herzl, expands on this after attending the First Congress:

> "Although I myself was not overly enthusiastic about the man, there was no ignoring the secret power he wields over the masses. The fact that he had attracted hundreds and thousands of admirers inspired in me a sense of awe and respect. I searched his face over and over again, trying to detect the source of this tremendous power. There was no question we were beholding an extraordinary historical spectacle. The representatives of one of the most stiff-necked peoples in the universe, members of a nation with the least likeliness to bow to authority, stood in the presence of a man of might possessing an iron will, completely enthralled by him, perhaps without even realizing it or understanding why."[5]

The greatest challenge to Herzl's authority arose at the Sixth Zionist Congress, where he proposed establishing a temporary home for the Jews in Uganda. As we shall see, opposition to this scheme led to the most serious leadership crisis of Herzl's career, and one in which his charisma was put solidly to the test.

Herzl's charisma worked equally on Jews and non-Jews. Rabbi Zvi Perez Chajes, the rabbi of Vienna, observes that Herzl's ideas might easily have been treated as the ramblings of a lunatic:

> "As the ambassador of a non-existent state and a people that was not yet nationally unified, his odd proposition, which was mostly tragic but also comic, did not cause a single one of the leaders he met, be it the German emperor, the Turkish sultan, the king of Italy, the pope, or ministers of the British or Russian governments, to laugh with ridicule or pity as one does at a madman. So great was the charm that welled up from his soul, so sublime was the divine beauty of his prophetic vision, so potent was his regal splendor that everyone, young and old, succumbed to him. The king of Italy never missed an opportunity to recall the profound impression that Herzl's visit made upon him."[6]

To leave a lasting imprint on history, however, charisma had to be combined with other factors. On the following pages, we will discuss these additional factors and other aspects of Herzl's persona in a bid to unravel the secret of his success.

High on the list was the political Zionist program that Herzl put together and circulated. The goal was to deliver the Jews from the physical hardships and spiritual malaise that were risk factors for assimilation, as set out in his book *Der Judenstaat* and later *Altneuland*. Herzl acted on many fronts to advance this cause: He embarked on diplomatic forays, organized Zionist congresses, opened

---

5 Ludwipol in: *Luah Ahiasaf*, p. 56.
6 Zvi Perez Chajes, *Sermons and Lectures*, Hebrew Teachers' College, Boston, 1953, p. 159.

a bank and founded the Jewish National Fund. A variety of other skills, together with his renown as a journalist, reinforced his charismatic appeal, which was vital for establishing the Zionist Organization and organizing the congresses.[7]

We shall now turn our attention to three aspects of Herzl's persona that were integral to his charisma: looks, political genius, and the "unity of opposites," i.e., contradictory traits that co-existed in harmony.

Herzl's Looks as a Charisma Booster

Apart from the descriptions of Herzl's appearance, some saw a connection between his looks and his hypnotic effect on people. Recalling his first glimpse of Herzl at the First Zionist Congress, Max Bodenheimer, a leading German Zionist, writes:

> "Herzl was receiving callers in a small reception hall at Hotel Les Trois Rois…At the sight of Herzl, my heart filled with pride and joy. Never had I seen such a handsome man. First I was captivated by his eyes and mouth, which exuded spirit and strength combined with congeniality, gentleness and boundless charm. His gestures were pleasing and refined. Not for naught did they speak of royal bearing. People followed him as if bound by magic cords."

The agronomist Joshua Buchmil, one of the first to join forces with Herzl and a key figure in mobilizing delegates from Eastern Europe for the First Zionist Congress, offers this account of his meeting with Herzl:

> "My talk with Herzl lasted over two hours. His courteous and pleasant tone, his articulateness, his deep, amiable voice, his natural grace – all these immediately captured the listener's heart. His words, the amazing beauty of his entire monumental frame, his incomparably beautiful face bathed in spirituality … The glint of his captivating, hypnotic eyes gripped his interlocutors and did not let them go."[8]

David Shub employs similar terms:

> "The sound of his voice, like beautiful music from the higher realms, exerted a hypnotic power over me. I will never forget those moments…Despite the anxiety that gripped me as I was about to meet him, so soothing was his manner of speech that I felt as if I were sitting and talking with one of my closest friends."[9]

---

7 See the chapter on the First Zionist Congress, pp. 105–126.
8 Bodenheimer in: *Sefer hacongress* (1923), p. 109. Quote from Buchmil, *ibid*, p. 74.
9 David Shub, *Zikhronot levait david*, pp. 20–21.

Nahum Sokolow, editor of *Hatzfira*, spoke of Herzl's "enormous black eyes the likes of which I have never seen before... mesmerizing in their beauty and captivating power."[10]

Mordechai Ben Hillel Hacohen, a contemporary of Herzl, also drew a correlation between Herzl's persuasive powers and physical presence:

> "We arrived in Basel in the morning...I did not rush to attend the meeting of the Jews from my home town...I went to see the unknown, the man who was a mystery in my eyes. As I entered the Congress office, a tall man with a black beard tumbling down to his chest rose from an armchair at the far end of the room and came towards me, his eyes shining like a lightning bolt. Within those few short years, he captured our hearts."[11]

Political Genius

Among the qualities that won over the Jewish masses and contributed to Herzl's mythical status was his political genius. Genius is a quality far beyond the reach of ordinary human beings, which may be one of the reasons it is so admired. Max Nordau, a known cynic, was dismissive of many of the great men of his time but had only reverence for Herzl's brilliance: "He rose to such heights that his acquaintances and friends were left behind, but they foolishly mocked and gossiped about him as he grew taller and they remained small."[12]

He went on:

> "It has often been asked in jest what would have happened to geniuses like Liszt and Paganini if they had come into the world before the invention of the piano and the violin. Herzl provides an answer to this question. He was the 'Liszt' and 'Paganini' born before the invention of the sole instruments through which his genius could be revealed. Herzl was a born statesman of the first degree, without a state, without an organized people behind him, without a single one of the tools essential for practical policy management."[13]

According to historian Benzion Netanyahu, no one understood the secret of Herzl's greatness better than Nordau. In his study of the psychophysiology of genius and talent, in which he ranked different types of genius, Nordau set political genius, and Herzl's genius in particular, at the top of the list. After political genius or statesman, came the scientist and then the poet. By this classification,

---

10 Sokolow in: *Sefer hacongress* (1923), p. 135.
11 Mordechai Ben Hillel, *Olami*, Hapo'alim, Jerusalem 1929, p. 58.
12 Max Nordau, *Zionistische Schriften*, vol. 3, ed. Benzion Netanyahu, Jerusalem 1960, p. 23.
13 *Ibid*, p. 24.

Newton was lower on the scale than Napoleon and Shakespeare was below Cromwell. For Nordau, Herzl represented the political genius of the Jewish people and altogether the highest form of genius to which Jews could aspire.[14]

Mordecai Ehrenpreis also regarded Herzl as a genius, but not just in the political sphere. To Ehrenpreis, he was a polymath genius, "because he encapsulates the whole pageantry of history, because he is the sum of all the cherished virtues of the national soul, and because he combined the bearing of a king with the spirit of a dreamer."[15]

As a journalist, Georges Clemenceau, who went on to become prime minister of France, described Herzl as the kind of genius whose brilliance defied ordinary logic:

> "The Divine Spirit rested on that man Herzl. He saw the Burning Bush on fire. He was a man of genius...Men of genius are rare...Men of genius are recognized by their gigantic proportions, often enclosed in a *cadre* of ordinary existence... Their way of action, of understanding, of discovering the real substance of things and beings is manifested in an altogether personal and original manner. They are beyond ordinary logic, they surpass the level of their contemporaries and are therefore often misunderstood – or, rather, not understood at all."[16]

In addition to genius, Herzl had a phenomenal memory. As Shmuel Pineles, a long-time Zionist activist and founding member of Hovevei Zion, testifies: "He had such fine recall that he was able to address all the Congress delegates by name, even those he had seen but once."[17]

Joy of Opposites

Another layer of complexity was added by the strong contrasts and contradictions that were part of Herzl's character. In Herzl's case, this was not a drawback. All these supposedly conflicting traits worked in harmony and enhanced his magnetism: imagination and practicality; strong leadership and emotional sensitivity; aristocratic mannerisms and shyness; grandiose schemes and attention

---

[14] Benzion Netanyahu, introduction, *Max Nordau to his People: A Summons and a Challenge*, Hozaah Medinit, Tel Aviv, 1946, p. 20.
[15] *Sefer hacongress* (1923), p. 190.
[16] "Clemenceau Remembers Herzl, His Characterization of the Man He Met During the Dreyfus Trial," as told to Pierre van Paassen, in: *Theodor Herzl, A Memorial*, ed. Meyer W. Weisgal, New York, 1929, p. 25.
[17] Pineles in: *Sefer hacongress* (1923), p. 56.

to small details; courage and humility. Nordau saw the multiple facets of Herzl's personality as advantageous. He had intellectual gifts, but it was his prodigious imagination that enabled him to develop a strategy for political Zionism. "'Herzl was a talented writer and an eloquent speaker with a fertile imagination, but at the same time, he possessed an astute and practical mind."[18]

Yehuda Leib Maimon also remarks on these contrasts that created a harmonious whole:

> "His soul was on fire, but his face projected serenity and refinement. He was a man of dreams and lyricism, but also of solid achievement. He was a brilliant feuilletonist, but utterly serious about life. He was sturdy as cedar, but gentle as a reed, stubbornly standing up for his beliefs but willing to consider the opinions of his colleagues and try to reach a compromise. He was sociable, but careful not to become overly intimate, even with those who worked alongside him. He could be high and mighty, and scold both students and friends, but he also knew how to give in. When the Zionist movement called upon him to lead, he knew how to do so infusing his own spirit. He was above partisanship, but made an effort to understand the spirit of each party and its demands. There was a harmony of opposites in his glorious soul... because more than he was splendid in face and form, people were drawn to him by the grandeur and magnificence of his inner being. He was the 'crème de la crème,' a personality at once wondrous and unique."[19]

Mordecai Ehrenpreis comments on this complexity, too:

> "His character was a bale of contradictions. On the one hand, he was innocent as a babe, and on the other he was brimming with sharp intelligence and nothing could escape his eye. He was as gentle and compassionate as a woman but could also be stern and authoritarian, a Bismarck-style dictator. He was a skeptic and a critic, doubting and challenging everything, and on the other hand, he was a man of faith and an enthusiasm capable of boundless devotion. He was a dreamer, his big eyes gazing out into the vastness of eternity, and the next moment he was a pedantic accountant who cared only for facts and figures."[20]

From Diplomacy to National Pride

Some of these contrasts are particularly relevant in our context. The fact that Herzl was a diplomat and a man of the world yet suffused with national pride and Jewish sensitivity, was central to his success. As S. Schwartz tells it, "Herzl was the first Jewish diplomat in the Diaspora who openly projected a

---

18 *Herzl bekhazon hador*, p. 23.
19 Rabbi Yehuda Leib Maimon (Fishman), *Ha'olam*, February 1914, no. 33, p. 220.
20 *Sefer hacongress* (1923), p. 189.

sense of national dignity and self-worth as a Jew."[21] Herzl was not above dispensing with diplomacy if it clashed with his Jewish principles. He refused to kiss the hand of the Pope when he visited Rome, for example, although he was aware that it might turn the Pope against him. Herzl writes: "He received me standing and held out his hand, which I did not kiss. Lippay[22] had told me I had to do it, but I didn't. I believe that I incurred his displeasure by this, for everyone who visits him kneels down and at least kisses his hand."[23]

In his brushes with anti-Semitism when meeting with world figures, Herzl always remained the proud Jew, as attested to by his response to the disparaging remarks about Jews made by the German chancellor Prince Chlodwig of Hohenlohe-Schillingsfurst and German secretary of state Bernhard von Bülow.[24]

Herzl's visit to Palestine in 1898 summoned up another balancing act of diplomacy and Jewish pride: Herzl and his entourage set out for Jerusalem on Friday, October 28, and reached the city towards sundown. Herzl had an infected leg and was running a high fever. His escorts wanted to hire a carriage to take him from the train station to his hotel but Herzl refused, unwilling to publicly violate the Sabbath. He ended up hobbling all the way to his hotel, leaning on two companions.[25]

So Herzl was a cautious diplomat, but when he felt the need to assert his Jewishness, he did so without hesitation. On such occasions, those around him were exposed to yet another dimension of his multi-faceted personality.

The Politician and the Man

Another pair of opposites that dwelled in harmony was Herzl's ability to focus on small details and express concern and human kindness even when preoccupied with matters of supreme importance. A telling incident took place when he visited Palestine at the invitation of the German emperor. After presiding over two spectacularly successful congresses and being received by the great leaders of the world, Herzl's name preceded him as a man of deed and vision, a conductor

---

21 S. Schwartz, *Herzl besifrei yamav*, Hasolel Press, Jerusalem, 1931, p. 33.
22 Berthold Dominic Lippay, the pope's court artist, a native of Budapest. In effect, he misled Herzl: Only Christian believers are required to kiss the pope's hand.
23 *Complete Diaries of Theodor Herzl*, vol. 4, p. 1602.
24 *Ibid.*, vol.2, p. 701. The two statesmen remained cold and aloof. "Do you think that the Jews are going to desert their stock exchange and follow you? The Jews, who are comfortably installed here in Berlin?" Hohenlohe asked acidly.
25 *Zikhronot leveit david*, p. 37. For more, see the chapter on Herzl's visit to Palestine, p. 151.

of global diplomacy who was able to persevere in the face of opposition and ridicule. As he arrived with his entourage on the shore of Jaffa, David Moshe Shub describes a sequence of events that illuminates Herzl's sensitive and caring side:

> "On Wednesday morning I went to the beach to greet them. As I approached, a boat drew up to the shore and our five distinguished guests climbed out…A policeman standing on the beach checking the arrivals one by one and eyeing them suspiciously only glanced at their papers. Dr. Herzl said a few words to him, and he let them go…I was prepared to escort them to town to the hotel when I saw Dr. Herzl standing there, not moving, gazing out toward the sea and the boats bringing more people ashore from the ship. His beautiful, shining eyes were fixed on the ship, as if he were waiting for someone to disembark. I thought he was waiting for his belongings…I turned to him and said we were heading out to the hotel and he needn't worry as his things would be brought to him. He did not reply, however, and continued to look out to sea…
>
> After half an hour, a boat laden with passengers reached the shore. There was a great crush, and the policeman detained each one to inspect their papers as if hoping to find something wrong. Meanwhile, Herzl stood watching the passengers disembark until a woman with a small boy emerged. Herzl hastened over to the policeman and exchanged some words with him. Then he helped the woman down and introduced her to me. 'Mr. Shub,' he said, 'please take care of this woman and see to it that she gets to Zikhron Yaakov.' I did as I was told. Later, when I asked about the meaning of all this and why Herzl had gone to so much trouble for her sake, she told me she did not know this man or who he was, but he was an angel of salvation and wished heaps of blessings on his head! She had come from Rumania to her daughter in Zikhron Yaakov, but she had no travel papers and feared they would not let her disembark at Jaffa. When she saw all these gentlemen on the ship, she did not know they were Jews. But later, when Dr. Herzl lovingly stroked her child's hair and she overheard the words 'Zion' and 'Eretz Yisrael' in their conversation, she realized they were Jews and begged them to help her reach her daughter. This handsome man with the black beard warmly reassured her: 'Do not worry, madam, we will get you to your destination safely.' And the doctor did not forget his promise. In all the hubbub and confusion he remembered the poor thing, and without saying a word, waited for her and brought her ashore. He told the policeman that she belonged to his party and the policeman did not argue: He sensed that this was no ordinary man. It was at that moment that I saw Herzl's greatness, arising from his humility. A man on his way to meet a mighty emperor, whose every thought was focused on preparing for this fateful meeting, still had room in his heart and mind to remember his pledge to a poor woman."[26]

Nahum Sokolow shared another anecdote he heard from David Wolffsohn that illustrates Herzl's sensitive and empathetic nature. It took place when Herzl and Wolffsohn were traveling to Constantinople to see the Sultan:

> "On the way to Constantinople, when the train stopped at a tiny station on the border of Serbia and Bulgaria, the heat was overwhelming…The trip was difficult and exhausting.

---

26 *Zikhronot levait david*, pp. 24–25.

Two people stepped out of the car, a tall man and his friend, of medium height, who looked short beside him. They were walking on the asphalt path along the tracks when the tall man suddenly disappeared.

Theodor, where are you?

One look around and there he was, standing next to the steam engine…engrossed in conversation with the engine man. He held up his arms and beckoned to his companion: Come here, David!

David ran over, grumbling: What are you doing here? Why are you standing out in the hot mid-day sun? But Theodor remained where he was. 'Come over here where I am,' he said in a commanding tone. And we all remember the power of that voice. David approached and stood next to the tall man. From the engine came a blast of hot air mixed with steam and the smell of coal and fuel oil. It was hard to stand there even for a moment. But he insisted:

'Stand here and answer me one question: How much do you think this mechanic earns per month?'

…[Wolffsohn] flinched like a child under the scrutiny of those two big black eyes, enveloped in a dreamy mist. 'His entire wage comes to a hundred francs a month,' he said, 'and he sometimes works sixteen hours a day.'

The tall man stood with one foot on the running board of the train, leaning his head on his hand and shaking it back and forth as he looked at his colleague. 'Did you hear that?'

The break was over…The train began to move, and the two passengers were left behind in this boiling desert, where one could sit and be roasted alive.

The tall one was unperturbed by this slight setback. 'We will send a telegraph to the next station to keep our things. We will get on the next train…Better for this to happen to us than for the train mechanic to be late. So he left.' The tall man plunged deep into thought… 'In our country, this will not happen!' he later told to his friend."[27]

Further evidence of Herzl's sensitivity to the needs of others can be found in accounts of his emotional response to receptions held in his honor and sights he saw while visiting Palestine. His emotion and tears were not perceived as weakness. On the contrary, they were seen in a positive light and only enhanced his charisma. The Jewish orator Zvi Hirsch Masliansky heard from David Wolffsohn about his experience of arriving in Palestine as part of Herzl's delegation:

"Herzl spent the night on the ship's deck while his companions slept in their cabins below. Suddenly Wolffsohn heard a voice calling out to him: 'David, David, are you awake?' He opened his eyes and saw Herzl standing before, dressed as if he were going to meet the king. 'Do you want to see our Mother Zion? ' Herzl asks. 'Come and see the lights winking at us from our beloved Jaffa.' Wolffsohn rose, dressed and went up to the deck. As he stood

---

27 S.L. Citron, *Herzl khayav upeulotav: Lemalut khatzi yovel shanim lepirsum medinat hayehudim bidfus*, S. Shrebrek, Vilna 1921, pp. 101–103 (henceforth: *Citron, Herzl khayav upeulotav*).

beside Herzl leaning on the guardrail, he watched two large teardrops glistening in Herzl's eyes roll down and drop onto his handsome beard."[28]

His meeting with the inhabitants of the Jewish colonies also moved him greatly. Rishon Lezion pioneer Dov Haviv Lubman describes the tears in Herzl's eyes as he looked out at the excited crowd. Avraham Komarov, a teacher, recalls Herzl's tears at the end of his visit to Ness Ziona, when he was escorted by a procession of horsemen from Rishon Lezion and Rehovot:

> "As Dr. Herzl descended from his carriage, eyes riveted on the jubilant young people of Rehovot and the glorious parade that passed before him, teardrops poured from his big black eyes, rolled down his cheeks and seeped into the hair of his black beard like a flower drinking in the morning dew."[29]

If Herzl became emotional at the sight of the colonies of the Baron Rothschild, where the settlers were subject to strict rules imposed by the Baron's administrators, he was even more sentimental in Rehovot, which was an independent colony. Zvi Hochberg, one of the pioneers of Rehovot, tells the story:

> "Herzl was in seventh heaven. For the first time in his life he found himself in the presence of proud young, muscular Hebrews riding on horses and cognizant of their own worth... Tears flowed from Herzl's eyes at the spectacle."

The author Moshe Smilansky, a Rehovot native, also described the event:

> "And then a tremor crossed the face of this enchanting man and in his eyes a tear glittered... His enormous black eyes, deep and melancholy, are all I see, and in them glistens a tear. Could it be?"[30]

A grand sweeping vision coupled with attention to small details was the essence of Herzl's *Der Judenstaat*. Ezriel Carlebach, a journalist who later became editor-in-chief of *Yediot Ahronoth* and *Ma'ariv*, offers a good illustration of the complexity involved: In the midst of writing *Der Judenstaat*, Herzl was investigating a story about lower-class Parisian mothers entering their children in beauty contests:

---

[28] Zvi Hirsch Masliansky, *Kitvei Masliansky: Neumim, Zikhronot umasa'ot*, vol. 3, Hebrew Publishing Company, New York, 1929, p. 255 (henceforth: Masliansky, *Zikhronot umasa'ot*).
[29] *Malki betzion*, p. 94.
[30] *Ibid.*, Hochberg pp. 77, Smilansky pp. 99, 111.

"In the very same hour that his eyes gazed into the distant future and saw salvation which had not yet arrived in a state which had not yet come into being, he raised his eyes, pushed aside the paper, and using the same ink and the same writing style, described the thin, wretched mother who says to the woman next in line that if she had dressed the fruit of her womb in the same flashy rags, her child would have won the prize...1896: The same man, the same nation, the same heart."[31]

Assertiveness and Sincerity Combined

The harmony of Herzl's character was also achieved through a third combination of opposites: dictatorial mannerisms together with sincerity, humility and even shyness. Earlier, we mentioned Avraham Zvi Glicksman's first meeting with Herzl.[32] Glicksman's description of that encounter sheds light on this facet of Herzl's personality:

"As I entered the room, Dr. Herzl rose from his chair and came over to greet me. He shook my hand, welcomed me extremely graciously and pointed to a chair across from his, inviting me to sit near him. Hence I know, and I myself am a witness to the fact, that the claim published in *Vedomosti*, and reprinted in *Hatzfira*... is an outright falsehood, namely that Dr. Herzl was an imperious man and one could more easily speak to the emperor of Austria than to him."[33]

From Glicksman's words it is obvious that Herzl had a reputation for being haughty. Hence his surprise at how easy it was to meet him at his own home and his relaxed, pleasant manner. If one considers that Glicksman was not a prominent figure who could be of value to Herzl but just a Polish Jewish businessman who chanced to knock on his door, Herzl's courteousness is all the more impressive.

In his analysis of Herzl's power, Nahum Sokolow writes that he achieved it not by force but by modesty and simplicity: "He created a special standing for himself among people, winning the hearts of all – the hearts of his people and the hearts of others, the hearts of his followers and the hearts of his opponents. Both camps wholeheartedly respected him. His impeccable manners, his

---

[31] Ezriel Carlebach, "Hamanheeg ha'enoshi," in: *Sefer hadmuyot*, Ma'ariv Books, Tel Aviv, 1959, pp. 92–98.
[32] The exact date of this meeting is unknown but based on the fact it was reported in *Hamelitz* in 1900, it was presumably before that. For more on Glicksman, see p. 30, footnote 38; p. 72, footnote 15.
[33] A. Glicksman, "Sikha im hadoktor herzl," *Hamelitz*, February 1, 1905, no. 86–87.

noble recognition of the importance of tact, which never left him for a moment, his generosity of spirit, these were the sublime weapons he used in his war."[34]

Elsewhere he writes: "Grandeur – that was Herzl's hallmark. This man, with his physical and spiritual beauty, his easy disposition and manners, his brilliance and his humility, did not impose his authority upon us but taught us to be respectful and orderly, and instilled in us love and brotherhood for the sake of the national ideal."[35]

Yosef Eliyahu Chelouche, one of the founders of Tel Aviv, comments on Herzl's shyness: "He extended his hand to us shyly."[36]

In this context, the vast amount of attention paid to Herzl's eyes and facial expression is worthy of note. Much of the magic and mystique that surrounded him was attributed to his eyes, which were said to mirror the contradictions that raged within. Perhaps it was this mix of emotions that so deeply impressed those who looked into them. Yehoshua Barzilai (Eisenstadt), a Zionist activist and author, detected in Herzl's eyes both bottomless sorrow and joy: "What wonderful eyes this man has! All the sorrow of the nation peers out from them, but also magical light that bestows hope and joy on those who behold him."[37] Mordechai Rabinovich, using his pen name "Ben Ami," describes Herzl at the First Zionist Congress as "a prince with a profound and penetrating gaze, both proud and sad at one and the same time."[38] Nordau also writes about his black eyes that projected authority on the one hand, and great human warmth, on the other.[39]

The literature is full of references to the melancholy look in Herzl's eyes. Interestingly, these descriptions associate melancholy with royalty, possibly due to the enigmatic and remote nature of sadness, associated with life in a palace, distant, imbued with respectability yet alluring. Perhaps observers linked the sorrow in his eyes to his concern over the fate of the Jewish people.[40]

In theory, some of these behaviors could be dismissed as diplomatic or political tactics. One could argue that they made for good public relations or helped to boost Herzl's image. Displaying emotion, lack of pretense or any of the other qualities cited here might have been nothing more than a political ploy. However, looking at the way Herzl conducted himself even far from the public eye

---

34 Sokolow, in: *Sefer hacongress* (1923), p. 13.
35 *Herzl bihazon hador*, p. 136.
36 *Malki betziyon*, p. 69.
37 Yehoshua Barzilai, *Kitvei Yehoshua Barzilai Eisenstadt*, Etin Press, Jaffa, 1913, p. 65.
38 *Sefer hacongress* (1923), p. 141.
39 *Ibid*, p. 24.
40 Stefan Zweig writes about Herzl's regal appearance and how it was reinforced by his melancholy eyes. See Chapter 1, footnote 10.

makes it clear that his intentions were pure and his actions sincere. He acted in good faith – not on the basis of some shrewdly coordinated plan. Herzl's genuine sensitivity is what dictated his actions, and not the other way around.

Mordecai Ehrenpreis sums up all these points in a singular declaration of respect and admiration:

> "But the truth is that all these contradictions and opposites were only different manifestations of his extraordinary personality and his rich and multi-faceted soul. Because he was a complete persona who operated by his own rules, with a soul filled with spiritual harmony, like all great souls who drink from the wellsprings of glory... He must be measured by his own standards. For [Herzl], what we call a clash of opposites was the overflow of powerful forces that could not be rolled into one ball. What we call contradiction was the ethical richness of a soul that did not need conventions and lived by its own code of ethics. What we call disjunction was the constant rejuvenation of a giant, steadily conquering new worlds, one by one."[41]

Long-Distance Charisma: Image and Influence

Herzl exerted a magnetic influence on others that went far beyond those in his close circle and those he touched personally. It was a magnetism that crossed distant borders and affected many different Jewish communities. Herzl's name resounded in places where he had never set foot. What was the secret behind this charismatic influence that knew no bounds and affected Jews even from afar?

Herzl's reputation spread throughout the Jewish world, turning him into a living legend. As noted by the artist David Tartakover, "the personality cult surrounding Herzl turned him into a legend in his own lifetime, and he was aware of it."[42] Herzl himself felt the legend taking shape when he was in London, and wrote about it in his diary on July 13, 1896, after speaking at a mass rally in the East End: "I speak for an hour in the frightful heat, great success, succeeding speakers eulogize me. One, Ish-Kishor,[43] compared me to Moses... Now it really depends only on myself whether I shall become the leader of the masses."[44]

Two days later, Herzl appeared in public again and his sense of being transformed into a myth intensified. In his diary he wrote:

---

[41] *Sefer hacongress* (1950), pp. 190–191.
[42] David Tartakover, *Herzl beprofil: Diyukon herzl be'amanut hashismushit,*" Tel Aviv Museum, Tel Aviv, 1979, p. 14 (henceforth: Tartakover, *Herzl beprofil*).
[43] Ephraim Ish-Kishor, a British educator and Zionist activist.
[44] *Complete Diaries of Theodor Herzl*, vol. 1, pp. 418–419.

"As I sat on the platform of the workingmen's stage on Sunday I experienced strange sensations. I saw and heard my legend being born. The people are sentimental; the masses do not see clearly...A light fog is beginning to rise around me, and it may perhaps become the cloud in which I shall walk...This is perhaps the most interesting thing that I am recording in these notebooks – the way my legend is being born."[45]

A legend can be carried far, especially when it contains a message of salvation yearned for by so many. The uniqueness of the political Zionist message and the physical and spiritual attributes of the messenger helped to disseminate the myth and turn Herzl's charisma into an established fact all over the world.

The power of charisma and its ability to influence long-distance was evident on Herzl's visits to faraway places. It was already apparent in the early days of his Zionist odyssey, when he visited Bulgaria after his first trip to Turkey in 1896, and also when he stopped off in Vilna in 1903 on his way back from St. Petersburg to Vienna. Historian Alex Bein writes about his reception in Bulgaria:

"The news that Herzl was traveling to Constantinople to see the Sultan, the Ottoman ruler of Bulgaria and Palestine, was publicized by Reuben Bierer,[46] who heard it from Herzl. The word spread rapidly and Herzl was greeted by close to six hundred cheering Jews."[47]

Herzl writes in his diary about the speeches delivered in his honor and admits to his own astonishment: "In this and subsequent addresses I was hailed in extravagant terms as Leader, as the Heart of Israel, etc. I think I stood there completely dumbfounded...They all pressed about me to shake my hand. People cried '*leshonoh haboh birusholayim*' (next year in Jerusalem)."[48]

If this was the way Herzl was received even before the First Zionist Congress, the welcome awaiting him in Vilna, as the Zionist Movement prepared to open the Sixth Congress there, was many times grander:

"Although his visit was not announced, the news spread by word of mouth and on the day of Dr. Herzl's arrival a great celebration was held. Thousands of well-wishers turned out in their holiday best, thronging the streets to welcome him."[49]

---

45 Ibid., pp. 241–242; *Mitos vezikaron*, p. 128.
46 One of the founders of Kadimah in Vienna and a professor of medicine in Bulgaria.
47 Alex Bein, *Biografia*, p. 158.
48 *Complete Diaries of Theodor Herzl*, vol. 1, p. 368
49 Yitzhak Broides, *Vilna hatzionit veaskaneha: Sefer zikhronot veteudot al peulot hovevei tzion vehatzionim bevilna*, Histadrut Olei Vilna Vehagalil, Tel Aviv, 1939, p. 161 (henceforth: *Vilna hatzionit*).

At the reception held for him, Herzl was called the "greatest son of the Jewish people." One of the leading rabbis of Vilna, Shlomo Cohen, lifted his hands and recited the priestly benediction, and the historian Ze'ev Javitz presented him with a miniature Torah scroll in a carved holder.[50] When it was time for Herzl to leave, the Jews were forbidden to congregate in the streets and bid him farewell at the train station. Circassian horsemen were brought in to replace the police but even their whip lashings did not keep the Jews from pushing their way through to bid Herzl goodbye.[51]

In his diary, Herzl describes how touched he was:

> "The police...forbade all gatherings, even my visit to the synagogue. But later I did drive through tumultuous Jewish streets to the offices of the Jewish Community, where the officials and deputations awaited me in packed throngs. There was a note in their greeting that moved me so deeply that only the thought of the newspaper reports enabled me to restrain my tears."[52]

Herzl's renown also reached far-flung Jewish communities, where admiration for him ran high and he touched the lives of people even without direct contact. There was a combination of factors involved, some the outcome of Herzl's own actions and some resulting from the efforts of others to sing the praises of Jewish nationalism – and Herzl the man. These included:

(a) A primary constellation of followers who knew Herzl personally and created a widening circle;
(b) Letters written by Herzl;
(c) Campaign tours and activities, for public relations and political purposes;
(d) Iconography;
(e) Orators and preachers.

Widening Constellation

The widening circle of Herzl supporters who did not know him personally were nourished by the primary constellation of those who did. People who had met Herzl before the First Zionist Congress, including members of Kadimah, the Jew-

---

[50] *Ibid.*, p. 163; Alex Bein, *Biografia*, p. 451. The mementos are on display at the Herzl Museum in Jerusalem.
[51] Yitzhak Broides, *ibid.*, p. 167.
[52] *Complete Diaries of Theodor Herzl*, vol. 4, p. 1543.

ish Zionist students association in Vienna,[53] and others like David Wolffsohn, Menachem Ussishkin and Yehoshua Buchmil, took part in organizational efforts and helped to enlist Congress participants. Zionist writer and activist Mordechai Ben Hillel Hacohen writes about being drawn in after a visit by Rabbi Shmuel Barabash and the author Yehuda Leib Dawidowicz, who brought him a copy of Herzl's speech to read.[54]

Moshe Schnirer traveled to Vilna at Herzl's behest and persuaded Yitzhak Leib Goldberg to join Herzl's camp: "Isaac Leib has not met Herzl yet but he heard about the man and his deeds from Dr. Moshe Schnirer.[55] Goldberg went on to become an important Zionist activist. According to researcher Gershon Gra, "Isaac Leib and his colleagues returned to Vilna not only with a sweeping plan of action but with real tools that were created at the Congress: the Zionist Movement, the flag and the Zionist shekel."[56] Yehoshua Buchmil, a student from Montpelier, France, was also recruited personally by Herzl: "At the suggestion of Dr. Herzl, and later the actions committee established in Vienna, I agreed to visit Russia to shake up the Jews there and spur them into attending the General Zionist Congress."[57]

Armed with a letter from Herzl, Buchmil traveled from one Jewish community to the next. In Kishinev, he enlisted Dr. Jacob Bernstein-Kogan, a respected Zionist activist (later, an outspoken opponent of political Zionism). In Odessa, Buchmil received another letter of introduction from Moshe Leib Lilienblum, a prominent Hovevei Zion leader.[58] From Odessa, Buchmil made the rounds of other cities in Russia "to drum up support for political Zionism, Herzl and the Congress."[59] He signed up four delegates in Vilna. Deeply impressed by Herzl's vision, they attended the Congress and went on to become key figures in the Zionist movement. Zalman Shazar, later the president of the State of Israel, describes this process of widening circles:

---

53 Among them Dr. Nathan Birnbaum, Dr. Yitzhak Shalit, Dr. Reuben Bierer, Dr. Moshe Schnirer and Engineer Johan Kremenezky.
54 Mordechai Ben Hillel Hacohen in: *Sefer hacongress* (1923), p. 99.
55 Gershon Gra, *Hanadiv haloh yadu'a*, Modan, Tel Aviv, 1984, p. 81.
56 Ibid., p. 86.
57 *Sefer hacongress* (1950), p. 98.
58 At the time, Lilienblum's letter was actually more valuable than a letter from Herzl since Lilienblum was already an established leader and affiliated with Hovevei Zion.
59 *Ha'olam*, no. 33, p. 225; *Sefer hacongress* (1950), p. 75.

> "Attending the First Congress lit a flame for [Berthold Feiwel] that was never extinguished. How beautifully Feiwel spoke about the Congress and about Herzl...Immediately after the Congress, Feiwel returned to his hometown, Brunn, and together with Robert Stricker and Max Hickel established *Jüdische Volksstimme*, one of the first newspapers to hoist the banner of political Zionism, putting themselves at the disposal of their new leader."[60]

The emissaries succeeded in passing on their enthusiasm for Herzl, and although they sometimes aroused unrealistic expectations, those who did attend the Congress came home spellbound. Joseph Luria writes: "They returned captivated by his personality, and were convinced that Herzl believed in the solution he proposed with all his heart."[61] In this way, the circle of Herzl supporters continued to grow and more and more people joined the cause.

The Zionist Congresses became a regular meeting place for hard-core Zionist activists, with new delegates joining each time. Many of the people invited to the First Congress were not necessarily in contact with the organized Jewish community in their home towns, but from the Second Congress, delegates were chosen according to shekel payment in each district, which established a link between shekel payers and their congressional representatives.[62] The Congresses were large gatherings: Journalists and guests were invited, too. When the event was over, participants became agents of change in their communities.

Between one Congress and the next, Herzl organized many private and public gatherings which expanded the ranks of Zionist propagandists. The year between the First and Second Congresses, for example, was spent "organizing and preparing informational material in a way never been done before in the Jewish world. Herzl and Nordau's speeches were studied and learned by heart. Quotes from these bold speeches became mantras that were used like explosives to ignite the movement's fire."[63] As a result, the number of Zionist associations in Russia rose from 25 at the time of the First Congress to 350 by the Second Congress. On the eve of the Third Congress, there were 877 and on the eve of the Fourth Congress, 1,034. In addition, there were 135 Zionist associations in Amer-

---

60 Zalman Shazar, "Berthold Feiwel" in: *Berthold Feiwel ha'ish upoalo*, Hasifriya hatzionit, Jerusalem 1960, p. 13. Feiwel was a member of the Democratic Fraction and later director of Keren Hayesod.
61 Luria, in: *Sefer hacongress* (1897), p. 26.
62 From the Second Congress, the Zionist shekel was introduced as an annual membership fee that granted the right to vote and run for office.
63 Gershon Gra, *ibid.*, p. 89.

ica, and societies were established in Germany, South Africa and other countries.⁶⁴

The circle continued to grow as participants in the Congresses went back to their home communities and reported on their experiences. German-Jewish author Sammy Gronemann attests to the eagerness of the Jewish public to hear such reports:

> "I returned to Hanover and delivered a report on the [Fifth] Congress which seems to have aroused great interest. Other delegates had spoken at our branch before me. Once I invited Goiten, who attended the First Congress, to tell us about those historic days. Arie Moshe Gottesman, who attended the Second Congress in 1898 was asked to speak by the Society for the Cultivation of Jewish Scholarship."⁶⁵

Letters

Herzl's work progressed in stages, all of them accompanied by letter-writing. First he wrote to Baron Hirsch and Baron Rothschild. When he stopped believing that salvation would come from the top, he appealed to the people. He wrote letters to friends in other countries to rally the masses, and waged an incessant campaign to win over newspaper editors, community leaders, rabbis and laymen, politicians and intellectuals, Jews and gentiles. He kept up a running correspondence with them all in the hopes of realizing his Zionist dream.⁶⁶

Herzl's correspondence opened a new chapter in the history of Jewish letter-writing.⁶⁷ The thousands of letters he wrote were an additional tool for managing, organizing and disseminating the message of the Zionist movement. They helped to cultivate his image, and as his biographer, Alex Bein, argues, for anyone seeking to know Herzl the Zionist and Herzl the man, there can be no better source. They follow the sequence of his life almost to his last day, especially from the moment Zionism gripped him.⁶⁸ Herzl saw letter-writing as an art and a seri-

---

64 Report of Oskar Marmorek in: Nahum Slouschz, *Hacongress hatzioni harivi'I*, Tushia, Warsaw, 1901, pp. 17–19 (henceforth: Nahum Slouschz, *Hacongress hatzioni harivi'i*). Growth, however, was erratic. On the eve of the Third Zionist Congress, Dr. Bernstein-Kogan reported that a third of the registered associations were not active, and every month, "societies were born and societies died." Leib Yaffe in: *Sefer hacongress* (1950), p. 19.
65 *Zikhronotav shel yekke*, p. 196.
66 Alex Bein (ed.) Iggrot Herzl, vol. 2 (introduction), Neuman, Tel Aviv, 1958, pp. 7–13 (henceforth: Iggrot Herzl, 2).
67 Ibid., p. 8.
68 Alex Bein (ed.) Iggrot Herzl, vol. 1, Neuman, Tel Aviv, 1945, p. 10 (henceforth: Iggrot Herzl, 1).

ous business. When he needed to write a letter to Meir Cohen, for example, a banker whom he sought to recruit to the Zionist cause, he asked Rabbi Moritz Gudemann to do it.[69] He found it hard to write to Cohen himself:

> "because I do not know him. When I say I do not know him, you must understand: I know nothing about him and what his views are...Do not think I am being absurd, but the same is true for the style of the letter. A letter of appeal must speak to a person's desires, and I need some idea of what those desires are. If not, I shall flounder around and write a confused letter that is not capable of appealing to that desire."[70]

Bein concludes that Herzl followed this rule in all his correspondence. His letters were always attuned to the interests of the person he was writing to, which served as the axis around which everything else revolved: "Herzl does not write letters for their own sake, or simply for the joy of writing or exchanging ideas. He does not write as a philosopher, an author or a lover of conversation. He writes as a man of deed and action, and his letters constitute the vehicle for that...Herzl's letters are a crystallization of his own stubborn will, imbued with self-assurance that was new in the Jewish world and the secret of Herzl's success in his encounters with others."

According to Bein:

> "Herzl believed that genius was the ability to persuade others to adopt new ideas in a way that left them convinced these ideas were their own. Herzl's Zionist letters were much like that: They became his most important tool for sharing his thoughts on the solution to the Jewish problem and moving them from the world of theory into the world of action."[71]

On the extraordinary power of these letters, literary critic Dov Sadan writes: "The more we know about his life and work, the greater the riddle surrounding the man." He is convinced that the key to the riddle lies in Herzl's correspondence. Comparing letter-writing to other modes of expression, Sadan distinguishes between three types of writing employed by Herzl. First are his "public writings," i.e., namely speeches and articles intended for audiences and readers in his own day. Next are his "hidden writings," i.e., the diaries, meant to be read by a future audience, and third are his letters. Sadan attributes great importance to the letters on the grounds that each one is a work of art. He likens the letter-writer to a builder who builds each house to meet the specifications of his client:

---

[69] Rabbi Moritz (Moshe) Gudemann, then chief rabbi of Vienna. For more on Gudemann and Herzl, see pp. 162–164.
[70] *Iggrot Herzl*, 1, pp. 10–11.
[71] *Ibid*, p. 8.

> "It is literally a duel, the battle of the builder who fights with the clay of each and every soul designed to be a brick in his building. What great persistence and precision is needed for this painstaking work...Indeed, studying the letters teaches us that each and every soul addressed in these letters is as important as a brick, or the clay that goes into a brick, and is tested for quality in order to make use of its strength."[72]

Dr. Ehrenrpreis writes about Herzl's letters as a "tailwind" that propelled the whole enterprise and deepened admiration for him:

> "We, who had the rare good fortune to take part in the preparations for the Congress, clearly recognized the great responsibility placed on our young shoulders. We were also grateful for the privilege of toiling shoulder to shoulder with Herzl. That summer was the most enriching of my life. From time to time, as the work progressed, I would receive motivational letters from Herzl in Vienna."[73]

Diplomatic Forays

Perhaps the most influential factor in the spread of Herzl's fame and charisma across such a wide geographical berth was his diplomatic travel and statesmanship. Herzl was convinced that this was the only way to implement his plans. He attached supreme importance to publicizing his diplomatic activities, both to create the public awareness necessary for moving the political process forward and to boost motivation among the Jewish masses:

> "I have got to establish direct contact, a contact that is discernible on the outside, with a responsible or non-responsible statesman – that is, with a minister of state or a prince. Then the Jews will believe in me, then they will follow me. The most suitable man would be the German Kaiser."[74]

Herzl's meetings with world leaders to promote his idea of a Jewish state were new in the landscape of nineteenth century Jewry. With these meetings, Herzl set a historical precedent: He was received not as a lobbyist seeking to ease the sufferings of the Jews but as a proud diplomat who came to discuss the future of his people. The idea of a Jew who looked like a king discussing the Jewish

---

[72] Dov Sadan, "Bein pitaron lekhida (Herzl be'igrotav)" in: *Shivat Tzion 5710*, Hasifriya Hatzionit, Jerusalem, 1950, pp. 354–359.
[73] Mordecai (Marcus) Ehrenpreis, *Bein mizrakh lema'arav*, trans. Moshe Giora, Am Oved, Tel Aviv, 1953, pp. 71–72 (henceforth: *Bein mizrakh lema'arav*).
[74] *Complete Diaries of Theodor Herzl*, vol. 1, p. 312.

question in the royal courts ramped up the Herzl legend. Joseph Luria, the editor of the Yiddish newspaper *Der Yud*, writes:

> "His statesmanship was dynamic, shrewd and brilliant. His activities were veiled in secrecy and sparked the imagination of the people. There had never been Jewish statesmen engaged in Jewish politics before, and Herzl began doing this even before the Congress. In those days, governors or viziers were considered high above the reach of ordinary political activists, so in themselves his meetings with heads of state and cabinet ministers made a profound impression."[75]

Herzl was aware of the impact of his journeys and political meetings on the masses. When he visited Constantinople in 1896 for eleven days and met there with a number of high-ranking officials – although not the Sultan – he made sure to return wearing a Turkish decoration on his chest (Order of the Medijidie) "as visible evidence of the seriousness with which the negotiations were regarded."[76]

When he returned from Palestine after meeting the German emperor two years later, Herzl was sorely disappointed on two counts: his failure to win a charter for the Zionists and the lackluster media coverage of the event. The official German communiqué, for example, summed up the Kaiser's visit as follows:

> "Later the Kaiser received the French Consul, followed by a Jewish deputation which presented him with an album of pictures of the Jewish Colonies in Palestine. In reply to an address by the leader of the deputation, His Majesty remarked that he viewed with benevolent interest all efforts directed toward the improvement of agriculture in Palestine as long as these accorded with the welfare of the Turkish Empire, and were conducted in a spirit of complete respect for the sovereignty of the Sultan."[77]

Herzl's meetings with supreme world leaders left his co-religionists in awe. In his memoirs, Judah Appel, Secretary of the Ohavei Tzion society in Vilna, writes:

> One day in the month of Heshvan 5659 we learned from the banker G. Luria of Pinsk that Dr. Herzl had met in Constantinople with Kaiser Wilhelm. We were all extremely surprised by this news and in my great excitement I rushed to share the glad tidings with the local rabbi.[78] To my astonishment, he was completely unimpressed. 'That is a lie, an outright lie!' he replied coolly. I told him we had received the news from a reliable person whose word

---

[75] *Sefer hacongress* (1923), p. 26.
[76] Alex Bein, *Theodor Herzl: A Biography*, p. 201.
[77] *Ibid*, p. 307.
[78] According to Aharon Hermoni, the rabbi in question was Rabbi Chaim Ozer Grodzinski, the chief rabbi of Vilna. See A. Hermoni, *Be'ikvot habilu'im: Pirkei zikhronot*, Reuben Mass, Jerusalem, 1952 (henceforth: *Be'ikvot habilu'im*).

could be trusted. He answered: 'If so, then he is misleading you unintentionally. To this day, no Jew has ever been received by His Imperial and Royal Apostolic Majesty and to say so is nothing but a fabrication, an *urva parakh* [cock and bull story].' To that, I had no response and I bid him farewell. Upon my return home, I also began to have my doubts. Perhaps the news delivered by Mr. Luria was not true.

Three weeks passed, and I received a letter from Eretz Yisrael written by the son of my Hibbat Zion friend R. Chanoch Henig Ginsburg of Švenčionys who decided to take himself and his family to the Land of Israel. He bought himself land alongside other Vilna Jews who settled in Hadera and sent his eldest son, Aharon Zvi, who was fourteen years old, to study at Mikve Yisrael…This student, Ginsburg, now named Hermoni, would send letters to me from time to time, relaying truthful news from our sacred land. The letter cited above, dated 28 October 1898, consisting of two pages written on both sides, offered a detailed account of the events of that great and momentous day when he and other students working in the fields of Mikve Yisrael were rushed back at the news that Dr. Herzl had arrived. It tells how all the students were dressed in their holiday clothes and Herzl arranged them in rows. The students who could sing (among them Ginsburg) were placed up front and told to welcome the Kaiser with the German anthem…Herzl gave the signal to the young choir, which broke into song. Suddenly the Kaiser pulled his horse aside, rode up to Herzl, leaned over the neck of his horse, held out his hand and asked him: 'How are you?' Dr. Herzl moved closer to the horse, shook the outstretched hand and replied: 'I thank Your Majesty. I am taking a look at the country.' Then the Kaiser whispered something into Herzl's ear, extended his hand again to Herzl and rode off. The Kaiser's wife also nodded her head in greeting to Dr. Herzl.

Upon receipt of this letter, I ran with it straight to the local rabbi. I found him in his study and went up to him: 'Rabbi, do you remember what you said to me when I told you about Dr. Herzl's meeting with Kaiser Wilhelm?' 'Of course, I remember the lies cobbled up by those clowns to make a laughingstock of you.' I pulled out the letter and handed it to him: 'I received this letter today from Eretz Yisrael, written by one of the students at Mikve Yisrael…telling me what he saw and heard with his own eyes and ears. The rabbi is invited to read it and see the truth.

The rabbi read the letter from beginning to end, poring over every word, his face flushed red with excitement. Then he handed me back the letter and said: "Indeed, this time I was wrong! What you said is true and very wonderful. God has done great things for us through His emissary Dr. Herzl. The heart of kings and ministers is in the Lord's hands and whatsoever He desires, they bend to His will. I was wrong and may the good Lord forgive me … 'Rebbetzin!' he called out to his wife in the other room, 'Set the table and let us dine. And also bring fruit for Mr. Appel so that he may bless them and eat. Today is a great day. Listen and you shall be astonished.' We all sat at the table and the rabbi excitedly told his wife the whole amazing story. He also tried to deduce what he thought might be the possible consequences of this meeting."[79]

---

[79] Judah Appel, in: *Reisheet hat'hiya: Zikhronot vekatavim miyamei 'Hovevei Zion berusiya,'* Gutenberg, Tel Aviv, 1896, pp. 464–468.

Iconography

Herzl's portrait played a critical role in building up his persona and influence from afar, as well as spreading the Zionist message. One of the figures who tried to help Herzl win the German monarchy over to the Zionist cause was an Anglican minister, Reverend William Hechler.[80] In April 1896, Hechler contacted Herzl excitedly and told him that the Kaiser had spoken about the Jewish state to his entourage, telling them it was time "to fulfill prophecy" and assist the Zionist movement. Hechler offered to arrange a meeting between them,[81] but Herzl did not want to risk traveling without an invitation. Hechler then asked Herzl for a portrait of himself to show the German leaders.[82]

In the previous chapter, we discussed the profound impression that Herzl's looks made on all who saw him. This magic worked even on those who saw only his picture. Aware of the power of his visual image, Herzl took advantage of this from the earliest days of his Zionist quest. He had pictures of himself printed up and circulated in the tens of thousands. David Tartakover notes that this was not uncommon at the time:

> "Mass distribution of the portrait of a national leader was a widespread practice in the ideological movements of the day...which became possible in the wake of technological advances in photography and the use of stills by newspapers, then the main form of visual communication. Herzl, as an experienced journalist, recognized the vital importance of photography and documentation as an integral part of the Zionist propaganda campaign."[83]

Art historian Haim Grossman agrees that Herzl, a journalist and media man, recognized the value of art and photography in shaping Jewish national consciousness. Understanding the importance of visual images, Herzl willingly posed for painters, sculptors and photographers. He knew it was vital for him to become a household name and that his physical magnetism could envelop him in a "cloud of legend" that would lead the masses in the direction he envisaged. Based on that insight, he asked to be photographed again to recreate a more "authentic" record of his October 1898 meeting with the Kaiser at Mikve Yisrael and allowed Lilien to take the famous portrait of him overlooking the Rhine from the

---

[80] On Hechler, see pp. 129–132.
[81] Hechler proposed that Herzl travel to Karlsruhe, the seat of Frederick I, the Grand Duke of Baden, where the Kaiser was planning to be the following day, with the idea of setting up a meeting with the Duke and the Kaiser himself.
[82] *Complete Diaries of Theodor Herzl*, vol. 1, p. 320.
[83] Tartakover, *Herzl beprofil*, p. 14.

balcony of his hotel. Only someone who visits Herzl's small room at the hotel will appreciate the logistical effort it took to produce this "candid" shot. Towards the same end, he also sat for the Hungarian portrait painter Archduke Joseph Arpad Koopay, the painter and illustrator Hermann Struck, and the sculptor Samuel Friedrich Beer, among many others.[84]

A good example of the importance that Herzl attached to images was the doctored photograph with the German Kaiser. Aharon Vardi desribes the creation of the "first Zionist photomontage":

> "Neither of the two photographs taken by Wolffsohn on this occasion was successful. The better one showed only the Kaiser on his horse and Herzl's left leg. The engineer Josef Zeidner[85] corrected the picture by superimposing on it another photograph of Herzl taken immediately after their return from Mikve Yisrael. This explains the misalignment between the height of the Kaiser on his horse and the figure of Herzl in the 'composite' photograph known to the public."[86]

Tartakover claims that until Herzl's time Jewish iconography consisted only of traditional non-political religious figures such as Moses and Aaron. Then the Herzl legend came along, and although he was political, "his image flooded the Jewish home, emblazoned on everything from decorative pictures and household utensils to consumer products."[87] Others say that this was not a new trend: Before Herzl's day, it was Sir Moses Montefiore whose face appeared everywhere. Sammy Gronemann, for example, introduced Sir Frances Montefiore at a Zionist assembly in Berlin as "the nephew of Moses Montefiore, the first authentic Hovev Zion in modern times, whose picture hangs in Jewish homes throughout the world."[88] In this respect, Herzl became the heir of Montefiore. "Herzl's portrait began to supplant the picture of Moses Montefiore that was never absent in a Jewish home," writes journalist and jurist Mayer Abner.[89] Gronemann describes the sense of pride and joy he felt at seeing Zionist symbols clustered around a portrait of Herzl at the Fifth Zionist Congress.[90]

---

84 Haim Grossman, "Et lekhol khefetz" in: *Et Mol*, no. 176, 2004, p. 11.
85 One of the four delegates who accompanied Herzl on his trip to Palestine to meet the Kaiser, and the only one who had already been to the country before.
86 *Malki betzion*, p. 22.
87 Tartakover, *Herzl beprofil*, p. 18.
88 *Zikhronotav shel yekke*, pp. 157–158.
89 Dr. Mayer Abner, "Zikhronot miyamei hofa'at medinat hayehudim," in: *Ha'olam*, no.33, 1946, p. 233.
90 *Zikhronotav shel yekke*, p. 185.

The role played by Herzl's image, in addition to his writings, is noted by Zionist activist and Anglo-Jewish educator Jacob Koppel Goldbloom:

> "When Herzl's *Der Judenstaat* came out, there were differences of opinion, but it was received with great joy by broad swathes of the Jewish community in East London. The author's picture, which appeared in the Jewish newspapers and a special supplement, was distributed all over the city, and enjoyed pride of place in many homes, among them mine. My awe at the first glimpse of a notebook with Herzl on it will remain with me for life. Gazing at the appeal of his handsome face I said to myself: Here is the man we have been waiting for! He will revolutionize our lives. He will inspire us to liberate ourselves from the yoke of exile and take giant steps on behalf of our people and our country."[91]

Other testimony about the impact of Herzl's portrait, such as that of Haim Kozirovsky, shows that a printed image could sometimes be as effective, if not more, than seeing him in real life:

> "On the day our town received a photograph of Dr. Herzl, the joy of Aaron the shoemaker knew no bounds. Nearly the whole town turned out to see it and Reb Aharon never tired of explaining to everyone that it had been taken in Basel on the Rhine Bridge. The beautiful black beard and the eyes looking far off into the distance, as if peering into the future of his people, made an indelible impression on one and all. People could not get enough of it and kept coming back for another look. Herschel the carpenter made a beautiful frame... Yosel the glazier measured out a piece of glass, and everyone was happy that they could do something for this man who was so close and dear to their hearts."[92]

In his memoirs, Shmaryahu Levin, who attended the Fourth Zionist Congress in London in 1900, writes about his first glimpse of Herzl:

> "I do not have much to say about my first impressions of Herzl. I was not surprised at all, because the image of him I carried in my heart was not at all hazier or paler than what I saw in person. Indeed, the former was possibly more vivid than the latter."[93]

---

[91] Jacob Koppel Goldbloom, in: *Ha'olam*, no.33, 1946, p. 238.
[92] Haim Kozirovsky, "Eikh noda be'ireinu al hadoktor herzl vehatzionut – perek zikhronot," in: *Ha'Olam*, 22 Tammuz 5707 (1947), p. 489.
[93] Shmaryahu Levin, "Mizikhronot khayai," vol. 3, *Bama'arakha*, Dvir, Tel Aviv, 1939, p. 203 (henceforth: Levin, *Bama'arakha*) The Herzl that Levin saw in his mind's eye was probably a combination of the mental image of him on the bridge and his Zionist message. The fact that seeing him in real life made less of an impression may have been due to the circumstances of this first sighting: "I was sitting in a meeting of the Standing Committee...completely absorbed in an argument. Suddenly the door opened and a man walked in, tall and erect, and informed us that the Congress would not be opening in the evening but in the afternoon. Thus we should not wear evening dress but daily attire, as was the English custom. Everyone got up but I continued

Sammy Gronemann tells the story of his visit to an orphanage in Ahlem run by Alexander Moritz Simon. He was accompanied by Baron Börries von Münchhausen, who inquired why there was no picture of Herzl hanging there:

> "We entered the director's room. As customary, we were handed the guestbook to sign our names. Münchhausen, pen in hand, stopped for a moment and asked the director 'Tell me sir, I see you have the portraits of three German emperors up there, along with the portraits of Bismarck and Moltke. So how is it possible that there is not one portrait of any of the greatest heroes of the Jews, from Moses to Herzl?' In the end, Münchhausen donated a portrait of Herzl (an etching by Hermann Struck), which was hung with great pomp and circumstance in Simon's office."[94]

Orators and Preachers

> "Is there anyone in the Zionist world unaware of the importance of the preacher in teaching the masses about Zionism and Zionist settlement?" asked Zalman Shazar, Israel's third president. "Where would Zionism have been in its early years without these Judaism-infused spokesmen? How else would Zionism have been spread in the old country?"[95]

While not insignificant, the role of written material in disseminating the Zionist message had its limitations. Newspapers and books were not always accessible to the Yiddish-speaking Jewish masses, and the number of Yiddish-language publications was small.[96] The synagogue served as the primary venue for social gatherings, exchanging ideas and even news updates. In order to reach his target population, Herzl made use of the *maggid* system, a network of professional preachers and orators who delivered sermons at synagogues, usually on the Sabbath and holidays, but also on weekdays.

Historian Ehud Luz divides the *maggidim* of the nineteenth century into two groups: full-time preachers who excelled at their profession, were hired by the

---

to sit in my chair. The man was gone in an instant. Motzkin nudged my hand and said: Herzl was just here. A quiver went through me. I tried desperately to catch a glimpse of him or his shadow, but I was too late. The man had disappeared. I wanted to see him for the first time as exalted, as towering above the people. Alas! I had seen him without being aware of it! I was upset and furious with myself" (Levin, *Bama'arkha*, p. 204).

94 *Zikhronotav shel yekke*, pp. 50–51.
95 Zalman Shazar, in: Yitzhak Nissenbaum, *Alay kheldi*, 1869–1899, Reuben Mass, Jerusalem, 1968, p. 9 (henceforth: Nissenbaum, *Alay kheldi*)
96 In the late nineteenth century, the majority of Jews in Europe spoke Yiddish. In a census conducted by the Russian authorities in 1897, over 50 million Jews (constituting 96.9% of the total Jewish population in the Russian Empire) declared Yiddish as their mother tongue.

community and paid from the community coffers; and itinerant preachers who received donations from members of the synagogue who came to hear them speak. Many were untrained and their preaching was more a source of livelihood than an ideological mission. The proliferation of this second group led to a decline in the prestige of the *maggid* as an institution. In the Hovevei Zion era, a new class of *maggid* emerged. While the goal of the traditional preacher was to bring his listeners closer to God, and achieved this by quoting from the Scriptures, these new preachers spread a nationalist message and spoke about Zionism, "productivization" and building up the Land of Israel. The audiences consisted not only of members of the older generation but also *maskilim*, supporters of Jewish enlightenment, and passages from Haskalah literature were cited in addition to Scriptures.[97] These preachers became highly effective agents of change, serving as a bridge between Jewish communities across the Pale of Settlement and the intellectual leadership. They infused their sermons with nationalist messages, and were instrumental in helping Hovevei Zion and later the political Zionists increase their outreach.

Miriam Katchensky explores the marketing and public relations strategies employed by the Zionist movement to bring its ideology to the Yiddish-speaking masses in Poland, Russia, and Romania,[98] and shows how the preachers contributed to the leap of Hovevei Zion from theory to action. Documents in the Hovevi Zion archives in Moscow show that Menachem Ussishkin was in charge of a whole network of preachers sent to communities throughout Russia. Rabbi Shmuel Mohilever and his secretary oversaw the work of preachers in the region of Vilna and Belorussia, and the same system operated in other areas.

Facing opposition in the ultra-Orthodox community, the work of the Zionist propagandists was not easy. In trying to prove that there was no clash between Zionism and Judaism, they were heckled and harassed, and ultimately found themselves caught up in an all-out culture war. There were some who openly criticized the rabbis of the anti-Zionist camp and suffered the consequences. One was Chaim Zundel Maccoby (1816–1916), known as the Maggid of Kaminetz, who was forced to flee Russia after the rabbis reported him. As Ehud Luz writes: "Denunciation to the authorities – the popular weapon left over from the wars of the Hasidim and Mitnaggedim – was a Damoclean sword above the *mattifim*;

---

[97] Ehud Luz, *Parallels Meet: Religion and Nationalism in the Early Zionist Movement* (1882–1904), Jewish Publication Society, Philadelphia, 1988, p. 108.
[98] Miriam Katchensky, "Hadrasha beyidish besherut tnuat tzion," in: Yaffa Berlowitz (ed.), *Lesoheyakh tarbut im ha'aliya harishona: Iyun bein tkufot*, Hakibbutz Hameuhad, Bnei Brak, 2010, p. 199, note 1.

more than one of them was arrested on charges of spreading revolutionary propaganda."[99][100]

In his memoirs, Yitzhak Nissenbaum, a traditional orator who became a Zionist propagandist, writes about his cross-country tours at the request of the *murshim*, the district appointees of the Zionist movement in Russia, and his confrontation with the anti-Zionists. In 1900, for example, when the Zionists of Kharkov invited him to speak at the town's main study hall, he discovered that the event had been billed as a memorial service for a rabbi who had died:

> "I stood there shocked and quivering with anger. For this I had been invited? Since when had I become a professional eulogizer? Just then the Zionists came in…They ushered me into my room and told me with a laugh: 'No eulogy. We did not bring you here to eulogize anyone. Speak about Zionist ideology, as you do in other cities. So why did you say I would be delivering a eulogy? Very simple: The largest study hall in town is the *beis midrash* of the Lubavitcher *hasidim*. Last summer, the Lubavitcher rebbe sent out a strongly worded letter to all his followers condemning Zionism. Well, the *rebbe* is sitting here right now! And his followers would never let a Zionist preacher speak at their hall, so we had to fool them…"

Nissenbaum continues the story: "My talk was devoted entirely to answering the Lubavitcher *rebbe*'s charges against Zionism but without mentioning his name…"

The next day, after Nissenbaum spoke again:

> "one of the most high-ranking hasidim – I think it was the '*khozer*' [the official memorizer of the rebbe's Shabbat sermons] – came up to me and told me that my Zionist sermon of yesterday had deeply impressed him and his colleagues. They thought that I was correct in my answers to the *rebbe* and wished to introduce me to him."[101]

This *hasid* appeared the following day to say that the *rebbe* was ill and the meeting was cancelled. However, Nissenbaum was asked to speak a third time. Outrage at his Zionist sermons continued in the *hasidic* community, but after his visits to Bedzin and Sosnowiec, Nissenbaum concluded that the final outcome was positive:

> "On this trip, I saw that the spirit of Zionism left its mark on the *hasidim* and changed their outlook somewhat. But Hasidism had an effect on the Zionists, too, infusing Zionism with some of its mystical devotion and enthusiasm."[102]

---

99 Turned over by informers.
100 Luz, *Parallels Meet*, p. 110.
101 *Aley Kheldi*, p. 159.
102 *Ibid*, p. 154

Nissenbaum was active during the Hovevei Zion era and continued to preach on behalf of the Zionist cause after the birth of political Zionism in 1897. To disseminate the message of political Zionism, *murshim* throughout Russia commissioned preachers and paid them with the shekel dues collected in their districts.[103] According to Reuben Brainin, it was Zvi Hirsch Masliansky who revolutionized Jewish preaching. Masliansky combined his oratory skills and Jewish nationalist ideology, first as a member of Hovevei Zion and later as a supporter of political Zionism, traveling the length and breadth of Europe and then, after emigrating to America, lecturing from coast to coast:

> "In most of his speeches, Masliansky the preacher both admonishes and comforts his audience, expanding their knowledge of Judaism and our history... As he speaks, he knows how to rouse the spirit and capture the hearts of his listeners. He is connected to the audience by thousands of invisible threads and he knows how to dress up words in bright colors. With his rhetoric he touches the emotions of the crowd...His heart is like a wireless transmitter: It sends out and receives sparks from all hearts elated by his words...He feels close to the people and the people feel close to him ... It would be hard for me to paint a portrait of national and Zionist life in Jewish America without Masliansky. Wherever he went, whatever the occasion, he immediately injected a national spirit, set hearts aflutter, strengthened hands and instilled a Hebrew and Zionist atmosphere."[104]

There were other preachers like Masliansky who joined the political Zionist bandwagon. One was Yehuda Zvi Yevzerov, who was recruited by Ussishkin in the early days of Hovevei Zion: "The most prominent preacher in Ussishkin's district was his long-time assistant Yehuda Zvi Yevzerov, who succeeded in persuading many of those he met on his travels to join and contribute to the new movement." When Ussishkin returned from the Third Zionist Congress as the "Zionist appointee of the Yekaterinoslav and Poltava districts and the province of Don," he began to work in earnest and organize lecture tours for Yevzerov.[105]

Yevzerov referred Ussishkin to another preacher, Joseph Zapf, whom he highly recommended: "He is devoted to the idea of Eretz Yisrael, very passionate and industrious, and with his rhetorical skills, he may be of great use. He has con-

---

103 Luz, *Parallels Meet*, pp. 118–123. The Zionist m*urshim* ("authorized officials") were regional leaders appointed by the Greater Actions Committee to oversee propaganda campaigns, shekel dues collection, etc. in specific districts.
104 Reuben Brainin's introduction to Masliansky, *Zikhronot umasa'ot*, 3.
105 Yosef Goldstein, *Ussishkin – Biografia*, vol. 1, Magnes, Jerusalem 2001, pp. 113, 127 (henceforth: Goldstein, *Ussishkin*, 1).

nections in wealthy circles..." Soon after, Ussishkin employed him for some time as an itinerant preacher.[106]

Zapf was scholarly and widely-read, but he was temperamental and difficult to deal with. Louis Lipsky, an American Zionist, described him as a man of great intellect "privately regarded as a high-class schlemiel" with special knack for getting into fights.[107] In 1890, Ussishkin sent Zapf to Kiev, where Sholem Aleichem was a leading Zionist activist. The famous writer had this to say about Zapf's visit:

> "Your Excellency and Royal Highness, Mr. Ussishkin! Terror, pit and trap! Wrath, indignation and trouble! A band of evil angels! Darkness and gloom! Trials and tribulations! God almighty! Until when shall you cause me to suffer? Me, your servant, son of your handmaiden, Sholem Aleichem, I have seen the light...I curse the day this foe arrived, tormenting me and my household...Yesterday this vile Philistine, this Zap, came to see us in Kiev! And now I beg of you, Oh Lord, save me from the clutches of this Zap! Ask him to go to Moscow because he is greatly needed there. Please, have mercy!"[108]

Zapf attended the First and Second Zionist Congresses. After the Second Congress, he was invited to speak before the Jews of Rovno, Uman, Berdichev, Zitomir and other towns, but his heart's desire was to preach in America. He contacted Herzl and offered his services. After the Third Congress, encouraged by Herzl and with the approval of the Actions Committee, he traveled to the United States at the expense of the World Zionist Organization. The precondition for his trip was that he report to Gustav Gottheil and Stephen Samuel Wise of the Actions Committee in America and place himself at their disposal. The American Actions Committee was not pleased, and considered his arrival in the United States a needless intervention on the part of the Viennese committee. Zapf was constantly at odds with the American Zionist establishment, which refused to support him financially, and he basically lived in poverty. Nevertheless, he managed to establish himself as a brilliant speaker and successfully promoted Herzlian Zionism.

There were other Zionist orators and preachers active in America at that time, among them Zvi Hirsch Masliansky, who already had a solid reputation and was accepted by the Zionist establishment. The relationship between Zapf and Masliansky was tense. Klausner recounts that Zapf's sermons after the Kish-

---

[106] Israel Klausner, "Joseph Zaph: Hovev tzion veshaluakh herzl le'amerika," in: *Hatzionut*, vol. 3, 1973, p. 9 (henceforth: Klausner, *Hatzionut*, 3).
[107] Louis Lipsky, *Gallery of Zionist Profiles*, Farrar, Straus and Cudahy, 1956, p. 203.
[108] Israel Klausner, "Sholem aleichem hatzioni," in: Sholem Aleichem, *Leshem ma tzrikhim hayehudim eretz meshelahem*, Dvir and Beit Sholem Aleichem, Tel Aviv, 1981, pp. 166–365.

inev pogrom were full of horrific descriptions that were so shocking the women would cry and faint, and the men would leave the hall fuming. In the end, he stopped being invited to speak at conventions and conferences, began to neglect his appearance and smelled of whisky. Masliansky was more moderate and highly successful. He even founded a major newspaper (which soon closed down due to poor management).[109] Klausner compares Zapf's fate to that of Naftali Hertz Imber, who composed *Hatikvah*. Both were fervent nationalists, both were outside the Zionist mainstream, and both became alcoholics.[110] Zapf lost his standing as a Zionist speaker and towards the end of his life had to make ends meet by working as a courtroom interpreter.

Haim Kozirovsky's reminiscences, published in *Ha'olam*,[111] shed light on the power of these preachers. He writes about his small town, where news from the outside world was long in coming: "We heard about the Dreyfus trial a year and a half afterwards, and the same was true for Herzl and Zionism, of which we learned only after Jews around the world had been talking about it for ages." Kozirovsky paints a colorful picture of the arrival in his hometown of a Zionist preacher. He relates how the bell of the mail coach was suddenly heard on a Friday, sowing confusion among the Jews since the mail was always delivered on Mondays and Thursdays. Who could be coming another day? Maybe a police officer or a customs officer, and that spelled bad news either way:

> "First of all, to head off any trouble, they began to 'burn the *hametz*,' which is to say, get rid of all the '*treif*' stock at the unlicensed taverns. Homeowners began to clean around their houses because dirt could mean fines or even imprisonment. Every other minute they darted out to see what the devil had in his bag. When the coach arrived, sitting inside was a young man with a red beard and a pince-nez on his nose, a velvet hat on his head. He stepped out of the coach and went into the inn. Everyone was annoyed. Who is this schlemiel who appears on *Erev Shabbat* in the mail coach with the bells ringing? He couldn't find an ordinary wagon driver and not upset an entire community? Meanwhile they started to guess who this fellow was. For the *ainikel* [heir] of some *zaddik* he was too young, for a groom he was too old. Then they saw him asking the synagogue beadle to hang signs announcing that 'tomorrow, on Shabbat afternoon, the renowned preacher will speak…' Of course everyone waited with bated breath until the next day to hear what the preacher had to say. That afternoon the study hall was so full that the preacher could barely clear a path to the podium. He wrapped himself in a prayer shawl, arranged his red beard, surveyed the audience, shot a glance at the women's section and began to speak in a pleasant, conciliatory tone of voice: 'My intention is not to preach to you. I came here with a different purpose –

---

109 *Ibid.*, p. 39.
110 Israel Klausner, in: *Hatzionut*, 3, p. 40.
111 The Hebrew-language newspaper of the Zionist Organization, founded in 1906 by Nahum Sokolow.

to bring you good news.' At that point the *maggid* began to describe the existential dangers facing the Jews and the Dreyfus libel in France with such drama that the whole congregation was aghast. Wails arose from the women's section, and the atmosphere was almost Kol Nidre-like…Here the preacher stopped, took out a handkerchief, wiped his forehead, and changed to a soothing tone: 'But now a great man, the finest of our generation, has arisen, a man who feels the pain of his people and demands recompense. He has devised a new way for us to overcome all our pain and suffering, and to become a nation like all the other nations. This man is the eminent Dr. Theodor Herzl, who is already known around the world. His praise is being sung everywhere and he is respected by all. Even kings and ministers have received him. This man called a congress of important Jewish personages and they decided that we must return to the Land of Israel. They established a bank offering shares that each and every Jew will purchase in keeping with his ability, thereby collecting a large sum of money that will enable the acquisition of our land from the Turkish Sultan."

Kozirovsky goes on to report the response of the ultra-Orthodox Jews, who protested loudly, to no avail, and the establishment of an actions committee: "The next day, the whole town was abuzz. Everyone talked only about what had happened yesterday and the committee they had elected. The preacher departed but left a deep imprint on the town, laying the cornerstone of Zionist activity there."[112]

Over time, however, the Zionist preachers lost their appeal. From the mid-1890s, says Ehud Luz, criticism began to mount in the Hebrew press:

"The criticism focused on their inadequate preparation for their task. Their education tended to be superficial; they had only the external trappings of the modern age but were woefully lacking in its true spirit. Many of them, it was charged, were untalented mimics, whose entire stock consisted of no more than 'an anthology of biblical verses and legends, while their education is derived entirely from reading modern literature.' No less damning was the claim that preaching had become one more trade, as *heder* teaching had been in the past…The anarchy that reigned in this area was a source of great concern to the Zionist leadership, which feared its effect on the movement's public image. The regional leaders tried to gain control of preaching activities but were powerless to put an end to the anarchy."[113]

The Zionist propagandists also played a key role in fostering the messianic aura that grew up around Herzl. The decline of the profession is addressed by Ben-Zion Alfes (1850–1940), who writes about his visit to Somme as a Zionist orator:

---

[112] Haim Kozirovsky, "Eikh noda be'ayaratenu al hadoktor herzl vehatzionut," in: *Ha'olam*, July 10, 1907, no. 40, pp. 489–490.
[113] Luz, *Parallels Meet*, p. 121.

"I spoke for about half an hour and it was so quiet in the hall it felt as if everyone had walked out and I was preaching to the wall. But then I looked around and saw everyone sitting in their seats, soaking up my words with great pleasure. If all the orators preached Zionism this way, I thought to myself, we would have hundreds and thousands of new followers every month. So who is responsible for making Zionism despicable to the Haredim? Those pitiful teachers of the 'Hear now, ye rebels' school,[114] who, when they had no pupils, went out to preach Zionism, make themselves some money and talk nonsense. Like comparing Herzl, may he rest in peace, and Moses, and claiming that in some respects Herzl was even greater, thereby chasing many Haredim away. I told the Zionist secretary in Vilna to announce in their bulletins that preaching without certification from the Zionist leadership should no longer be allowed."[115]

In 1901–1902, as the prestige of the propagandists continued to decline, the Zionist leadership voted to end its sponsorship of paid preachers.[116]

---

[114] A play on words quoting *Numbers* 20:10, where "morim" means "rebels" (in the story of Moses scolding the stiff-necked Israelites before he strikes the rock), versus "teachers" in modern Hebrew. Alfes blames the *talmud torah* teachers for the decline of preaching.

[115] Ben-Zion Alfes, "Ma'aseh Alfes: Toldot vezikhronot," in: *Ma'aseh Alfes*, Diskin Orphanage, Jerusalem, 1941, p. 67.

[116] Luz, *Parallels Meet*, p. 122. The Mizrahi movement, established in 1902, continued its Zionist outreach in the Orthodox community using paid preachers.

Chapter 3
Herzl and the Press

> "And Dr. Herzl, father of the new Zionist movement and head of the Congress, stands by the window and surveys the scene, his face aglow, his eyes flashing with steely fire, his intellectual brow radiant with rarefied light, and I instinctively think of the prophet – not the prophet of the desert or the mountains, but the prophet of the electron generation, of journalism and diplomacy..."[1]

The press was instrumental in transmitting the Zionist message worldwide and establishing a public sounding board that put the "Jewish question" on the global agenda. In this chapter we shall see how Herzl made use of journalism – both Jewish and general, both for and against him, to promote the political Zionist cause. We will look at the changes in coverage over time, when they occurred and why, and how the Jewish press affected the dissemination of Herzl's ideas and the development of the Zionist movement. We will analyze who supported Herzl and who opposed him in the world of journalism, and consider what led him in the end to establish a newspaper of his own.

Herzl had a keen understanding of the power of the media. He used it to leverage his ideas and further his aims throughout his Zionist career. Herzl knew that his lofty standing in the prestigious *Neue Freie Presse* (NFP) was a calling card that opened doors for him: It gave him a platform for action and access to people. It was clear to him that without this connection, it would have been difficult to move forward. In a letter to Adolf Stand, a Zionist activist from Lvov, he writes: "It is in fact my journalistic fame that has done much for our Zion project. The project has not been harmed by my newspaper work. On the contrary, the higher my ranking as a journalist, the more I can do."[2]

Herzl's journalistic clout was indeed substantial. Writing about Herzl the journalist, Shalom Rosenfeld looks at Nordau's eulogy at the Seventh Zionist Congress (July 25, 1905). Nordau hails Herzl's political genius as all the more astonishing in that he operated without a state or consolidated national entity, without organizational tools and without sufficient financial backing. Rosenfeld both agrees and disagrees:

> "True, Herzl did not have a state or a unified people behind him, and he did not have an organizational apparatus or money. But he did have one supremely powerful tool whose

---

[1] Nahum Slouschz, *Knesset gedola, o, hacongress hasheyni bebazel*, Tushia, Warsaw 1898, p. 10 (henceforth: Slouschz, *Knesset gedola*).
[2] *Iggrot Herzl*, 1, pp. 147–148.

importance cannot be overstated, a tool that helped him – albeit not the only one – to attain most of the others he needed to transform himself from a prolific, if not particularly brilliant, playwright into a world-famous political leader and statesman within the span of his brief adult life. This one mighty tool, whose power should not be underestimated, is the pen – the pen he began to use at the age of 17 (writing for the largest German newspaper in Budapest, *Pester Lloyd*) and went on to completely master as a reporter, columnist, lead commentator and literary supplement editor of the prestigious *Neue Freie Presse*. With the aid of his pen, his iron will and his phenomenal work output, the doors of emperors, kings, church leaders, intellectuals, prime ministers, politicians and diplomats opened to him, as if by magic."[3]

Herzl's journalistic standing is attested to by the proposal of soon-to-be Austrian prime minister, Count Kasimir Felix Badeni, that Herzl be hired as the editor of a pro-government newspaper established with state backing. "Even before taking office, Badeni's first step was to approach the brilliant and respected journalist Theodor Herzl on this matter, which encouraged Herzl to pursue his own plans for a newspaper," writes historian Jacob Toury.[4] In his diary entry for September 20, 1895, Herzl writes: "Dr. Glogau, Director of the *Presse* Bureau, has just been to see me and has offered me the editorship of a new daily. 'Under certain circumstances, I may be willing to accept,' I told him."[5]

Herzl continued to discuss the offer with Badeni, who had meanwhile become prime minister, but progress was slow. Herzl demanded full independence in editing the proposed newspaper, but "felt more and more clearly that these were not my kind of people and that I could not work with them."[6] Some of the stalling may have been due to the fact that it was difficult for him to leave the NFP, where he enjoyed a special relationship with the editors. Apparently it was a sore point for them and he worried about upsetting them.[7]

Herzl as Media Whiz

Today, Herzl would be called a media whiz. What tools did he have at his disposal in the late nineteenth century? The pen: It did the work of television, radio, computer and ratings combined. In the sphere of communications, Herzl was

---

3 Shalom Rosenfeld, "Doktor teodor herzl itonai," in: *Kesher*, 1977, no.21, p. 2 (henceforth: Rosenfeld, *Kesher* 21).
4 Jacob Toury, "Briyat ha'olam: Itono shel herzl," in: *Zmanim*, 1981, no. 6, p. 54 (henceforth: Toury, *Zmanim* 6).
5 *Complete Diaries of Theodor Herzl*, vol. 1, p. 244 (September 20, 1895).
6 *Ibid.*, p. 259, (November 1, 1895).
7 Toury, *Zmanim* 6, p. 57.

eminently well-equipped: "With his brilliant intuitiveness, Herzl knew this, and alongside his passion for theater, strove with great determination to conquer a field whose importance in his day was second to none – the press."[8] He likened the absence of a newspaper to "the soldiers of the French Revolution [taking] the field without shoes or stockings."[9] Herzl had a keen understanding of the power of the press in promoting national and organizational causes, and did everything possible to harness it for the sake of Zionism. To Dr. Max Emanuel Mandelstamm, an eye doctor and director of the Kiev ophthalmology hospital, Herzl writes: "Without tools, it is impossible to work, and the newspaper is an essential tool. We need it to provide services in high places, where favors are sought, and thereby win services in return."[10]

One such case was the Turkish Sultan affair: The Sultan tried to improve his image in the international press through his interaction with Herzl, while Herzl hoped to obtain a charter for Jewish settlement in Palestine, which proved unsuccessful. Another case involved the Russian interior minister, Vyacheslav von Plehve, "architect" of the Kishinev pogrom, the most documented and photographed outbreak of anti-Jewish violence in the early twentieth century. With Herzl's help, Plehve sought to tone down the negative press coverage of this incident and in return, Herzl obtained an official letter from the Russian government voicing support for the Zionist initiative.[11]

Using the same line of thinking, Herzl published an outline of his political Zionist program in the Jewish Chronicle (JC), the leading Jewish newspaper in England, on January 17, 1896, preceding the publication of *Der Judenstaat* by four weeks.[12] The article was subsequently reprinted in the German-language monthly, *Zion*, which appeared in Berlin, and the Viennese weekly *Oestrreichische Wochenschrift*.[13]

Even in the early days, when Herzl believed he could bring about a Zionist revolution from the top and tried to establish a Jewish state with funding from Baron Hirsch and Baron Rothschild, he grasped the importance of propaganda

---

8 Rosenfeld, *Kesher*, 21, p. 2.
9 Rafi Mann, "Herzl veha'itonut: Mekherev hapladah ve'ad le'iton bekvalim," in: *Kesher*, 1997, no. 21, p. 30, note 56 (henceforth: Mann, Kesher); *Complete Diaries of Theodor Herzl*, vol. 2, p. 631 (April 29, 1897).
10 Letter to Mandelstamm, October 27, 1897, note 1, *Iggrot Herzl*, 3, p. 28; also see letter of October 11, 1897, ibid, p. 18.
11 For more on this, see p. 245.
12 One of the oldest and most important Jewish newspapers in England and the Jewish world, established in 1841.
13 Bein, *Theodore Herzl: A Biography*, p. 158. See also Moshe Ungerfeld, "Melivatay hatzionim harishonim," 3, in: *Ha'olam*, no. 26, 1930, p. 506.

and public relations. In a letter to Baron Hirsch in June 1895, he lists what he needs to move his state-building enterprise forward: "…Beforehand, tremendous propaganda, the popularization of the idea through newspapers, books, pamphlets, talks by travelling lecturers, pictures songs."[14]

Quickly understanding that salvation would not come from the wealthy barons, Herzl turned to the people. Since official Zionist activity (informational meetings or celebrating holidays in the presence of a Jewish flag) was against the law in Eastern Europe, where the majority of European Jews lived, he resorted to other means of disseminating his ideas: letters, preachers, and coverage in Jewish and non-Jewish newspapers. For Herzl, it was important that all journalistic activity be carried out in the open, in compliance with the law, and not underground. He explained this to Avraham Zvi Gliksman:

> "Traveling to a city in Russia with a large Jewish population is indeed essential, but I will only be able to do so after obtaining a permit from the Russian authorities to hold Zionist meetings. As long as we lack such a permit, we cannot speak of, or even think about Poland, because it is absolutely critical that nothing must be done in secret … All that we do and all that we say, without exception, must be carried out in broad daylight, in clear view of writers and reporters who will publish it all in their newspapers for the whole world to see, leaving nothing out. For us, this is a sacred and everlasting principle, and we do not have such a permit yet."[15]

Indeed, newspapers were an indispensable propaganda tool – both for the Jews, to kindle a public debate and win them over to political Zionism, and for the non-Jews, to increase awareness of the "Jewish Question" and promote political Zionism in the international arena.

Herzl's efforts bore fruit: Through journalism, he attracted public attention to his endeavors. After the success of the First Zionist Congress, which was covered by the press, two major newspapers in England, the *Daily Chronicle* and the

---

14 *Complete Diaries of Theodor Herzl*, vol. 1, p. 27 (June 3, 1895).
15 *Tiferet adam*, p. 64. Avraham Zvi Gliksman, a Lodz industrialist who spoke many languages, read about Herzl's scheme and failed to comprehend why the rabbis were not helping Herzl in his bid to rescue the persecuted Jewish masses. Visiting Vienna on business, Gliksman went to the offices of *Die Welt* and asked to meet Herzl. The editor of the paper, Isidor Schalit, sent him to Herzl's home. There he urged Herzl to forget his pride and seek the approval of the great European rabbis: "Because if we win over the rabbis, the pillars of the Torah, then the whole of the House of Jacob will be with us, and once we have millions of working hands then it will be easy to implement this grand scheme." The above was Herzl's response.

Pall Mall Gazette, called for a European conference to discuss the Jewish question.[16] Newspapers also served as a platform for debate with hostile parties.

Herzl initially assumed that the *Neue Freie Presse* would serve as a platform for his Zionist initiative: "This will be done in the pages of the *Neue Freie Presse* for I have a debt of gratitude to this paper to discharge. It sent me to Paris and gave me with the means and the opportunity of acquiring knowledge that is now in the service of the cause."[17] On October 20, 1895, however, he describes how his attempt to mobilize the NFP failed: "Suddenly my decision was made. Win Benedikt for the cause. I went to him and immediately plunged *medias in res* [right into it]. He understood me so well that he made a wry face...I said that I would like best to do it in and with the *Neue Freie Presse*. He: 'You are confronting us with an enormous problem.'"[18]

Herzl then proposed two other options. One was the publication of a small daily paper in addition to the NFP in which he would elaborate his ideas. The other was dedicating a Sunday edition of the paper to the "solution of the Jewish question," and creating a new column for reader responses. The editors of the NFP turned him down, mainly out of fear that their newspaper would be identified as Jewish.

By this time, *Die Welt*, which was written for a Zionist readership, was being published in a weekly format, but Herzl eyed the NFP, a mass circulation daily for German-speakers in general, in a bid to reach an even larger audience. On several occasions, he toyed with the idea of taking over the NFP altogether. In 1898, he offered to buy the paper for two million crowns, but it was just wishful thinking. He did not have a sum at his disposal even close to that. In 1902, when economic circumstances were such that the proprietors might have agreed to sell their shares, Herzl offered to buy Benedikt out. However, receiving no answer to his letter, he concluded that Benedikt was either unprepared to sell or doubtful that he could raise the money.[19]

When the publication of *Der Judenstaat* failed to generate a response, and in some cases, elicited a negative response – from both regular and Jewish newspapers – Herzl felt all the more need for a journalistic outlet to disseminate

---

[16] Hannah Henriette Bodenheimer, *Hatzionim vegermanya hakeysarit*, Kiryat Sefer Ltd., Jerusalem, 1980, p. 70 (henceforth: Bodenheimer, *Hatzionim vegermanya hakeysarit*). Also see the chapter about Herzl's visit to Palestine, p. 131.
[17] *Complete Diaries of Theodor Herzl*, vol. 1, p. 182 (June 17, 1895); Rafi Mann, in: *Kesher* 21, May 1997, p. 24.
[18] *Ibid.*, p. 246 (October 20, 1895). Later, apparently under pressure from the editors of the NFP, Herzl stopped appending his name to his articles in *Die Welt*.
[19] Jacob Toury, in: *Zmanim*, 6, p. 54.

his political Zionist message. In practice, newspapers in those days performed the work of political parties and played a critical role for the Jews in terms of keeping abreast of Jewish communal affairs, relations with the outside world and liaison with the authorities. Newspapers also had global significance owing to the world-wide dispersal of Jewish communities.[20]

Historian Gershon (Getzel) Kressel tries to analyze why the press was so indifferent and suspicious in the early days of Herzl's Zionist quest. In his view, newspapers could not be expected to support initiatives like Herzl's because they lacked the courage to fight for ideas that were not yet fleshed out. It was in the nature of newspapers to be practical-minded and sober, and dismissive of ideas deemed visionary or quixotic. Moreover, newspapers were subject to censorship, so opposition to Herzl may have been a cautionary measure. Nevertheless, Herzl's personality did capture the hearts of some journalists, who dared to swim against the tide: "This was particularly pronounced at the outset, when Herzl first became active. He was opposed and his ideas fought bitterly, but in the end ... they were won over, succumbing to Herzl's personal charm or the challenge of introducing his new ideology in defiance of their bosses."[21]

For all these reasons, Herzl came to the conclusion that the solution was the acquisition of a newspaper or establishing a new one as a mouthpiece for political Zionism. In 1896, a few days after the publication of *Der Judenstaat*, the journalist and writer Saul Raphael Landau came by and offered his assistance: "Dr. Landau proposed to me the founding of a weekly paper for the movement. That suits me, and I shall look into it. This weekly will become my organ."[22]

Herzl's diplomatic ventures delayed further action on the establishment of a newspaper, but when the Viennese papers continued to ignore his ideas, he was spurred into renewing his efforts to buy one.[23] He acquired shares in a paper factory that co-owned a newspaper he hoped to take over with the help of other investors. The idea fell through when the outside funding did not materialize. Herzl quickly sold his stock. At that point, he tried another tack: addressing a conference of the Jewish Colonization Association (JCA) on the necessity of establishing a paper. In October 1896, he wrote to the chief rabbi of Paris, Rabbi Zadoc Kahn, about founding a daily in London and Paris: "In these newspapers, Jewish

---

20 Gideon Kotz, *Hadashot vekorot hayamim*, Hasifriya Hatzionit and Tel Aviv University, Jerusalem-Tel Aviv, 2013, p. 11 (henceforth: Kotz, *Hadashot vekorot hayamim*).
21 Getzel Kressel, *Reisheet tza'aday herzl be'aspaklaria shel ha'itonut ha'ivrit bagolah*, Reuben Mass, Jerusalem, 1943 (henceforth: Kressel, *Reisheet tza'aday herzl*).
22 *Complete Diaries of Theodor Herzl*, vol.1, p. 305 (February 23, 1896)
23 Jacob Toury, in: *Zmanim*, 6, p. 69.

policy will be expressed, for or against Turkey, as dictated by the circumstances...but with no need for the papers to be outwardly perceived as Jewish."[24]

That same day, Herzl also wrote to Jacob de Haas, editor of the London-based *Jewish World*, the second largest Jewish newspaper after the *JC*: "For now, here is a positive suggestion for Lovers of Zion: Establish or purchase a large daily in London in which Zionism can be explained to the clueless masses. My feeling is that such a newspaper will find a readership to keep it afloat only in the East End."[25]

Herzl also encouraged wealthy Jews in Berlin to assist the Zionist cause through the purchase of a newspaper. As in London and Paris, he favored an indirect approach: The papers did not have to be formally identified with the Zionist movement, he told them: "On the contrary, in view of the cowardly aversion to Zionism (which unfortunately exists among the Jews), the wisest course of action would be to slip the idea in through the back door, in a completely innocent way.[26]

As the date of the First Zionist Congress approached, the publication of a newspaper became all the more pressing. On January 3, 1897, Herzl wrote to De Haas asking him to publish a short piece on Zionism as an experiment, to gauge the response.[27] On January 26, he wrote to Willy Bambus about the need for spreading the Zionist idea and stimulating public discourse on the subject. Bambus, a young Zionist leader in Berlin, was the publisher of *Serubabel*, Germany's first Jewish national newspaper, and the editor of a monthly, *Zion*. Dr. Osias Thon, a founder of the Young Israel organization in Berlin, knew of Herzl's efforts and convened a meeting in Vienna in early March 1897 to discuss the establishment of a Zionist daily.[28] On March 12, 1897, Herzl wrote to De Haas again, stressing the importance of publicizing the goals of the Zionist Congress in a wide range of newspapers:

> "The aim of the Congress is to show the world what Zionism is and what it seeks to accomplish. It is critical for the yearning of the Jewish masses for Eretz Yisrael to be articulated in rallies, letters to the Congress, etc. The success of this Congress is vital for Zionism...I ask that you publish the contents of this letter without delay. Please send a comprehensive and detailed report to the *JC* and all the newspapers in England and America in the form of a

---

24 *Iggrot Herzl*, 1, p. 36.
25 Ibid., p. 129. The emphasis was on a daily newspaper, which Herzl felt would be more effective than a monthly. Also see: Rafi Mann, in: *Kesher*, 21, May 1997, p. 28.
26 Ibid., p. 28.
27 Ibid., p. 158.
28 At this meeting, Herzl again spoke about the importance of the Zionist Congress. See below, p. 111.

communiqué. For the *Jewish World*, I think you should write an editorial that illuminates the full scope of importance of this international gathering."[29]

Herzl's difficulties mounted as the Congress drew near. The fiercest opposition came from those Herzl had counted on for help. Not only did they turn their back on him, but they published their criticism in the papers, whereas Herzl had no platform to respond. One of them was Zvi Hirsch Hildesheimer, editor of the *Jüdische Presse*, the weekly newsletter of Esra, an association that promoted Jewish agricultural settlement in Palestine. Hildesheimer had been lined up to speak at the Congress about Jewish philanthropy and its importance for Palestine.[30] Willy Bambus, who was supposed to report on settlement activities in Palestine, also did an about-face, lashing out at Herzl in the same issue of *Jüdische Presse* as Hildesheimer.[31] Herzl tried to appease Bambus by writing him a friendly letter and asking him to refrain from going to the papers, but to no avail.

The publication of Hildesheimer's criticism followed by Herzl's trenchant response became an oft-repeated scenario. In the end, however, the media attacks on Herzl helped to create the public visibility he so desired. It was a kind of biblically-inspired paradox: "And as for you, ye meant evil against me; but God meant it for good" (*Genesis* 50:20). An anti-Zionist treatise written by the Viennese rabbi Moritz Gudemann, a former supporter of Herzl, had a similar effect. Historian Mordechai Eliav writes: "The truth of the matter is that Gudemann's treatise advanced the Zionist cause in that it generated a public debate and allowed the spokesmen for Zionism to publish a crushing rebuttal. Indeed, both Herzl and Nordau replied to Gudemann through the newspapers."[32] However, this pattern only worked in Herzl's favor in the early days.[33] In late 1902, in the wake of the *Altneuland* affair,[34] the face-off between the Ahad Ha'am and pro-Herzl camps received extensive press coverage that worked against Herzl and the Zionist movement.[35]

---

[29] *Iggrot Herzl*, 1, pp. 183–184.
[30] *Sefer hacongress* (1923), p. 421.
[31] *Ibid.* Hildesheimer was one of the first Zionist activists in Germany. In 1884, he founded Esra, a society for Jewish settlement in Eretz Yisrael.
[32] Mordechai Eliav, "Herzl vehatzionut be'enay moritz gudemann," in: *Hatzionut*, no. 7, 1981, pp. 399–425 (henceforth: Eliav, in: *Hatzionut*).
[33] On Ahad Ha'am's attacks in *Hashiloah*, see pp. 225–226; on the attacks of Bambus and Hildesheimer, see pp. 111–112.
[34] See chapter 9, pp. 224–235.
[35] Ahad Ha'am and his supporters, some of whom were members of the Zionist movement, were also negatively affected.

As the Congress drew near, the attacks on Herzl only intensified. Meanwhile another paper, *Jüdisches Volksblatt*, was founded by Dr. Jacob Kohn, an early opponent of Herzl. At this point, Herzl decided that he would no longer rely on the newspapers of others to respond to his detractors and it was high time to establish an independent publication. In his diary, he writes:

> "Several circumstances...make the founding of our own organ a necessity that can be deferred no longer. I asked Dr. Landau what his estimate of the editorial costs would be....- After that I also asked my father whether he agreed, and when he replied in the affirmative, I decided to create the paper which has been talked about so often in the past year-and-a-half and for which the funds could never be raised."[36]

Die Welt

The decision to establish a newspaper was not easy for Herzl. He found himself in a difficult, even impossible position because the paper he worked for, his main source of livelihood and the cornerstone of his journalistic prestige, did not take kindly to his Zionist activity, let alone the idea of a Zionist weekly. Riding on the train to the first Congress, Herzl listed the challenges that lay ahead, which he described as an "egg-dance." One of the "eggs" was the *Neue Freie Presse*, "which I must not compromise or furnish with a pretext for easing me out."[37]

Despite these worries, Herzl founded *Die Welt* before the opening of the First Congress. The paper was financed by Herzl and his family until the Fifth Congress, when he brought in a number of well-to-do partners and transferred ownership to the Zionist Organization.[38]

Saul Rafael Landau served as chief editor for the first eighteen issues, but he and Herzl did not get along and Landau was replaced by Dr. Siegmund Werner. Formally, Herzl kept his distance from the paper so that he would not have to sever his ties with the *NFP* – inevitable if he openly declared his connection to *Die Welt*.[39] Herzl also complied with the *NFP*'s request not to publish articles under his full name. Instead, he signed them using his Hebrew name, Binyamin Ze'ev. Nevertheless, it was a situation that caused him endless distress. On the one hand, he needed the *NFP*, not only as a source of income but to maintain his public image. On the other, he saw his work there as tantamount to slavery.

---

[36] *Complete Diaries of Theodor Herzl*, vol. 2, pp. 545–546 (May 12, 1897).
[37] Ibid., p. 578 (August 24, 1897).
[38] Erwin Rosenberg, *Herzl as I Remember Him*, Herzl Press, New York, 1959, pp. 216–217.
[39] Toury, in: *Zmanim*, 6, p. 63.

On August 21, 1899, upon his return from the Third Congress, he confided in his diary:

> "After a week of tasting freedom once more and being my own master I must return again to my vile servitude at the *Neue Freie Presse* where I am not allowed to have an opinion of my own. It is a question of a measly few thousand guilders which I, being the head of a family, must not give up."[40]

When the first issue of *Die Welt* debuted in June 1897, it was greeted with enthusiasm. The writer Ben-Ami (pen name of Mordechai Rabinovich) writes: "Great excitement at the appearance of this newspaper, and most gratifying and meaningful of all was the fact that it was published in Vienna, a bastion of assimilation."[41]

First and foremost, the paper was intended as a mouthpiece for political Zionism. However, it also served organizational needs, as the journalist Ohad David points out: "Herzl used *Die Welt* as a dual purpose media tool. On the one hand, it published ongoing reports on the activities of the Zionist movement for the consumption of the public at large, conveying the sense that knowledge was shared and the leaders were not detached from the people. On July 2, 1897, for example, the paper reported that the venue of the Congress had been changed from Munich to Basel and explained why. At the same time, it published an exchange of letters between the rabbis and the organizing committee."[42]

When Herzl travelled to Palestine in 1898, his meetings with the German emperor at Mikveh Yisrael and Jerusalem were reported by the NRP. Even if these encounters failed to produce the desired results, the press coverage made waves, boosting the self-confidence of the Jews and building up the Herzl legend.

As the organ of the Zionist movement, *Die Welt* frequently published opinion pieces and promotional material written by Herzl. According to Ohad David, "the language used by Herzl in these articles was emotional and made it very clear who was on the right side and who was hampering the work of the Zionists."[43] Another goal of *Die Welt* was spreading the Zionist message to the non-Jewish

---

[40] *Complete Diaries of Theodor Herzl*, vol. 3, p. 863 (August 21, 1899).
[41] *Sefer Hacongress* (1923), p. 117.
[42] Ohad David, "Melekh hayehudim ke'ashaf tikshoret," *Kesher*, no. 27, 2000, p. 53. In a letter recorded in his diary, Herzl outlines his plan for the newspaper's contribution to political Zionism. See *Complete Diaries of Theodor Herzl*, vol. 2, pp. 549–550 (May 20, 1897).
[43] Ohad David, *ibid*.

public. Herzl's clever use of the paper brought the message of Zionism to the world and kept it on the international agenda. One example was the recruitment of the peace activist Baroness Bertha von Suttner.[44] Isidor Schalit tells the story as he heard it from Herzl (recorded on May 23, 1899):

> "I received a letter from Baroness von Suttner asking me to convince the *Neue Freie Presse* to send her to the Hague Peace Conference for a writers' fee of 1,000 guilders. The publishers refused. So I offered her 1,000 guilders to go on behalf of *Die Welt*. For that, I requested that she interview important figures at the conference and get their views on Zionism. She accepted. In this way, we brought the tidings of Zionism to Europe, which was gathered together, without offending Turkey…"[45]

In practice, Herzl pulled off a brilliant public relations stunt. For the price of 1,000 guilders, albeit not a paltry sum in those days, he brought the news of political Zionism to the most important people in Europe, who read von Suttner. Herzl displayed the same uncanny public relations skills on other occasions in the course of his Zionist journey. Historian Mordechai Naor calls him the "PR chief of the Zionist Organization."[46] He discovered the "poor man's secret weapon" for swaying public opinion and the Zionist movement made use of it from the start.[47]

Naor brings several examples. The Zionist Congress, hastily organized in the first months of 1897 was a PR campaign par excellence.[48] Then there was the establishment of a Zionist bank – the Jewish Colonial Trust; the commissioning of an Arabic language typewriter to be presented to the Turkish Sultan Abdul Hamid II (who reigned in 1876–1909), which ultimately failed; and the publication of Herzl's novel *Altneuland*, which Naor also describes as a PR tool. Through this novel, Herzl wanted to show that the Jewish state would not only be a social and economic success but also a "light unto the nations."[49]

---

44 Bertha von Suttner won the Nobel Peace Prize in 1905.
45 Isidor Schalit, in: *Ha'olam*, no. 14, p. 224.
46 Mordechai Naor, "Herzl keyakhtzan," in: *Kesher*, no. 40, p. 4.
47 *Ibid.* Also see Shlomo Avineri, *Hara'ayon hatzioni legvaneha*, Am Oved, Tel Aviv, 1980, pp. 107–108, note 3.
48 See Chapter 9.
49 Mordechai Naor, *ibid.*, pp. 5–10.

Die Welt in Yiddish

Die Welt targeted German speakers but the majority of the Jews in Eastern Europe at that time spoke Yiddish. There was a need to bring the message of political Zionism to these people, too (the Yiddish press habitually quoted *Die Welt* without attribution).[50] Herzl thus decided to put out a Yiddish edition of the paper, turning to the famous Yiddish writer Scholem Aleichem (pen name of Shalom Rabinowitz). The historian Israel Klausner writes about Scholem Alecheim's brief association with *Di Velt*:

> "Scholem Aleichem wrote sketches and stories for the Yiddish language weekly *Der Jude* published by Ahiasaf, many of them infused with Zionist themes... Die Welt, a weekly Herzl founded in Vienna in the summer of 1897, appeared in German and was therefore inaccessible to the Yiddish-speaking Jewish masses. In 1900, an attempt was made to put out a similar weekly in Yiddish called *Di Velt*...The problem was that the editorial staff sat in Vienna and wrote in Germanic Yiddish. The Yiddish of *Der Jude* was more understandable to the Jews of Poland and Russia. *Di Velt* invited Scholem Aleichem to write for the paper in December 1900 but because he was under contract with *Der Jude*, Di Velt wrote to the publisher, Ahiasaf, requesting permission to employ his services. The publisher objected. So Herzl wrote to Scholem Aleichem himself, and Scholem Aleichem went to his publisher and explained that because it was Herzl who invited him, he could not refuse. The publisher insisted that he was bound by a commitment [to his newspaper], but Scholem Aleichem decided to write for *Di Velt* anyway. When a piece he had written appeared in *Di Velt* (in 1901), the management of Ahiasaf felt that it had suffered a grave injustice. Scholem Aleichem stopped writing for *Der Jude*, and after the closure of *Di Velt*, which was unable to compete with *Der Jude* and caused great financial loss for the Zionist Organization, he found himself the loser on both ends. In April 1901, Scholem Aleichem wrote to Herzl asking for a few hundred guilders in compensation for loss of income..."[51]

Die Welt as a Unifier

The Zionist movement envisioned itself as a home for the world's Jews, with no distinction between east and west. "We are a people – one people," was Herzl's motto.[52] But behind this statement, was a complex reality. The Jews of Eastern Europe, the Ostjuden, and the Jews of Western Europe, the Westjuden, had different cultures and ideologies. The tension between the two groups sometimes

---

50 Kotz, *Hadashot vekorot hayamim*, p. 178, note 21.
51 Israel Klausner, "Scholem aleichem hatzioni," in: *Scholem Aleichem, Leshem ma tzrikhim hayehudim eretz meshelahem*, Dvir, Tel Aviv, 1981, pp. 370–372.
52 Theodor Herzl, *The Jewish State: An attempt at a modern solution of the Jewish Question*, American Zionist Emergency Council, New York 1946, p. 76.

bordered on hostility.⁵³ The writer Saul Phinehas Rabinowitz (known by the Hebrew acronym "Shefer") commented on this disparity between the East European Jews and the young Jews of Western Europe brimming with organizational fervor:

> "We shall not compare the loud-mouthed Galicia youth [Herzl's East European supporters], whose world consists of nothing more than hollow talk and healthy lungs [the ability to shout], to the Westerners, whose views are closer to our own, and who have the organizational resources and education to speak to a group in an orderly fashion..."⁵⁴

This split between East and West was perceived as detrimental to the goals of political Zionism. Herzl needed a united people, and he envisioned the Zionist movement and its institutions as a friendly meeting place for all Jewish sectors. Herzl lay out the primary goal of the movement – the Basel Program – at the First Zionist Congress, and was able to gain unanimous approval for it. The Congress was his first intimate meeting with the Jews of Russia, and he was surprised by their high caliber. In his diary, he describes his encounter with this group as the highlight of the Congress. Up until then, he had corresponded with them and met Russian Jewish cultural figures, but:

> "I took care not to draw any conclusions about the masses on the basis of these cultured persons... we had always imagined them dependent on our intellectual help and guidance. However, at the Basel Congress there appeared before us a Russian Jewry of cultural strength we had not expected. Around seventy people from Russia showed up at the Congress, and we can say with full certainty that they were representatives of the opinions and feelings of the 5,000,000 Jews of Russia. And what an embarrassment for us who thought that we were superior to them! If I were to sum up my very strong impression in a few words, they would be these: they have the inner unity which most European Jews have lost. They regard themselves as nationalist Jews... They are not tormented by any thoughts of assimilating; their nature is simple and unbroken."⁵⁵

Herzl recalls his early confrontation with the skeptics who claimed that the Russian Jews would be his only followers: "If they had said that to me today," he writes after the First Congress, "I would tell them: *dayenu*, that would be enough."⁵⁶

---

53 See Ludwipol's letter on this matter, p. 118.
54 *Sefer hacongress* (1923), p. 288.
55 *Theodor Herzl, Zionist Writings, Essays and Addresses*, Herzl Press, New York 1973, vol. 1, pp. 153–154.
56 Theodor Herzl, *Hacongress habazila'i* (trans. Michael Berkowicz), Ahiasaf, Warsaw, 1897; Katzir, *Kovetz letoldot hatnu'a hatzionit berusia*, Masada, Tel Aviv, 1964, p. 17.

But the road to national unity was long. The sense of solidarity that prevailed in the early days did not last. Arguments erupted over many issues, especially culture and *Gegenwartsarbeit* ("work in the present"), which were mainly being pushed by the East European camp. Herzl sought a newspaper that would provide a sounding board for Zionists of all stripes and create a bridge between the Jews of Eastern and Western Europe. Die Welt was a paper that pledged to give voice to a variety of opinions.

This pluralist orientation was borne out by the employment of Martin Buber and Berthold Feiwel, who had been opponents of Herzl well before the establishment of the Democratic Fraction. Buber was hired as a contributing editor after the emergence of the Fraction, which made no secret of its political opposition to Herzl. Even when Ussishkin broke with convention and attacked Herzl personally over the Uganda proposal, the paper remained open to him: It published his letter criticizing Herzl and calling for a boycott of the Congress resolutions due to its stance on Uganda, to which Herzl appended a rebuttal.[57] The one exception was the paper's response to the wave of vitriol that followed the publication of *Altneuland*,[58] to which we devote a special chapter. Up until this point, the policy of the paper was guided by Herzl's conscious decision to provide a free forum for the articulation of Zionist ideas, even if they conflicted with his own.

Attitude of the Hebrew Press to Herzl and Zionism

At the outset of Herzl's Zionist journey, the Hebrew-language press treated his ideas with skepticism and the attitude was mostly negative and mocking. With the successful conclusion of the First Congress, the thinking about Herzl and Zionism began to change, although there were ups and downs. The shifting attitude toward Herzl in the Jewish papers can be divided into three stages: Stage one beginning with the publication of *Der Judenstaat*; stage two in the days leading up to the First Zionist Congress, and stage three, when the Congress came to a close and the Zionist Organization was born.

Getzel Kressel (1911–1986), a historian of Hebrew-language newspapers, wrote about the attitude toward political Zionism and Herzl in 1896, the year *Der Judenstaat* came out, focusing on the three Hebrew papers active at the time: the two dailies *Hamelitz* and *Hatzfira*, and *Hamagid*, a periodical published

---

[57] *Theodor Herzl, Zionist Writings*, vol. 2, pp. 238–239.
[58] Here the newspaper deviated from its standard practice and refused to publish letters that were critical of Herzl. See p. 230 and footnotes 32 and 33.

weekly for forty years. All of them wrote about settling the Land of Israel and the Hovevei Zion movement "with sympathy and affection," observes Kressel.[59] Sympathy and affection yes, but not active participation. Until Herzl, the wheels moved slowly. Hovevei Zion did not proclaim itself the savior of the physically and spiritually oppressed masses of Eastern Europe, nor of the assimilated Jews of Western Europe – and the press coverage reflected this. Herzl's appearance on the stage via *Der Judenstaat* took the Jewish newspapers by surprise, and they responded accordingly. Below, we shall look at the stance adopted by three papers – *Hamelitz*, *Hatzfira* and *Hamagid*.

Hamelitz

Hamelitz, founded and edited by Alexander Zederbaum, was the first Jewish weekly in Czarist Russia. Notable contributors included Y.L. Gordon, Ahad Ha'am and Lilienblum. After the publication of *Der Judenstaat*, *Hamelitz* wrote favorably about Herzl and his work, and published a review of his book. Having someone as famous as Theodor Herzl, a man of Western culture who was not actively involved in the Jewish world, openly and proudly identifying with his people, was seen as testimony to the immortality of the nation:

> "And the spirit, from whence will it come? Here are dry bones spread over the Valley of Israel. Across the earth, sons have grown alienated and estranged, our hope is all but lost... But here comes the spirit that infuses life into them, and they stand up on their feet... We ask ourselves: Who is this? From the four winds, comes a breath and blows into these parched bones, a lofty spirit from on high awakens our estranged sons and returns them to their people, and they are as dreamers, seeing glorious visions...
>
> Dr. Theodor Herzl is a highly esteemed Ashkenazi author, editor of the *feuilleton* supplement of the largest and most respected German-language newspaper *Neue Freie Presse*, as well as a visionary and a playwright whose work has been performed on stage and brought him honor and respect from every direction. The name Herzl is venerated among kings and ministers. Great nobles and heads of state open their gates to him and greet him with pomp and circumstance. Even Jewish aristocrats, who customarily open their gates only to non-Jews who come to milk them dry and suck their marrow after losing their fortunes and having not a penny to their names – even these small-minded Jews do not disrespect Herzl the Jew, although he is their brother, and are not ashamed of him or embarrassed to be in his company. Indeed, they boast about him after hearing him being praised all day long by the impoverished nobles who feed at their table.
>
> Herzl himself never betrayed his people. The name of Israel did not mortify him. He was not ashamed of the nation of his birth. On the contrary, he and all his friends on

---

[59] *Reisheet tza'aday herzl*, p. 3.

the editorial board of the newspaper where he works are always on guard to defend us from attackers and restore our honor. Yet in spirituality and way of life he has been a stranger to his people. He did not know his brethren and did not walk in the path of Judaism and Torah ... Like a 'captured babe,' he grew up on the knees of European enlightenment ... Most of his life passed without Torah or knowledge of his people and religion. Herzl became a European from head to foot, perfect in every way, educated and enlightened, but with barely a sign of Jewish life, like a dry bone, like a limp limb dangling from the corpse of his people. Can these dry bones live again?"[60]

After noting Herzl's estrangement, the editor of *Hamelitz* goes on to discuss the growing anti-Semitism in Vienna, as a result of which Jews began to despair of integrating in society. This led to a transformation in Herzl the man and his relationship with his people:

"Hopes dashed, with lashing winds and deadly pestilence outside the gate, the sons return to the fortress and nestle in the bosom of their mother, hidden in the shadow of her wings... So Herzl returned to the fold, fully repentant, his soul like hot coals and his heart burning with love for his people... In the place where penitents stand, stand not even the most righteous of saints."[61]

So Herzl, knowing nothing of the mentality of his people, sought a solution for their distress and lay out his solution in *Der Judenstaat*. According to *Hamelitz*, Herzl's advantage over Leo Pinsker, author of *Selbstemanzipation (Auto-emancipation)*, was that everyone knew and respected Herzl, whereas Pinsker was unknown in the West:

"Now the spirit of Pinsker rested on Herzl, although the latter did not know the former ... but with twice as much spirit and even more strength and courage, because of his great talent and all the surrounding bustle of activity. A voice now resounds throughout the camp, among our enlightened and high-born in the West, saying '*Et tu, Brute?* Is Herzl, too, with the Zionists?' But there is no cause here for laughter or mockery, for everyone knows that in the case of Herzl, as is the man, so is his strength...and thus all speak seriously of Herzl and his new book."[62]

After singing this long list of praises, however, the writer wonders whether Herzl's plan is really implementable:

"Herzl has not yet studied what his people think, nor considered their character and disposition. Neither does he know the ways of the Zionists, and this lack of knowledge is em-

---

60 *Hamelitz*, no. 49, March 10, 1896, p. 5.
61 *Ibid*.
62 *Ibid*.

bedded in his proposals ... Very soon he will know who his brethren are, and will see that the time has not yet come for the House of Israel to be built all at once ... because no nation is born in a day, and the rejuvenation of Israel will occur only when the heavenly spirit intervenes... Herzl is wise of heart and he will see..."[63]

It was clear to the readers that the author doubted the feasibility of Herzl's plan. He concludes: "But in the end, it is all a matter of *hilkhata demashikha* [for the messianic era] and just a pleasant dream." In essence, the editor of *Hamelitz* was saying that he did not believe the Jewish people could shake off its troubles, that Herzl's ideas were unrealistic and that implementing them was beyond Herzl's ability. A few months later, the paper expressed similar doubts. Even if a Jewish state were established, "the number of Jews remaining in their home countries would far exceed those in the new state," declared *Hamelitz*. "Very few Jews returned from Babylon in the days of *Shivat Zion*. So Herzl's ideas should be taken as a pleasant dream, or at most an idyll...[64]"

Kressel speculates that this pessimistic tone and public dissociation from Herzl was due to the paper's fear of censorship. He believes the editors were being extremely cautious. On one hand, news about Herzl was covered in the paper, yet the realization of political Zionism was deemed "far away and not worthy of serious discussion."[65] On the whole, coverage tended to be objective in tone, without voicing support for Herzl and his endeavors, presumably to keep the authorities at bay.

Then, writes Kressel, along came a man who burst through the wall of fear, "breaking down the sealed wall of objectivity, and challenging the norm. This fearless man was Yehuda Leib Landau,[66] who sought to fling open the gates of the Hebrew press and let the new winds blow."[67] After Herzl's appeal on the eve of the First Zionist Congress, Landau changed the rules of the game: He wrote an enthusiastic article in praise of Herzl and the Congress that appeared in *Hamelitz* and triggered a change. His article drew an array of responses which essentially put Herzl and political Zionism on the map.

Letters began to stream in from all over the Jewish world. One of them, from Mordecai Zeev Reizen, the rabbi of a Reform congregation in America, described

---

[63] Ibid. After meeting Herzl for the first time, Ussishkin made a similar comment about Herzl not realizing that his biggest war would be with the Jews. See p. 11, above.
[64] *Hamelitz*, no. 152, July 21, 1896.
[65] *Reisheet tza'aday herzl*, p. 7.
[66] Yehuda Leib Landau (1866–1942), rabbi, poet, playwright and Zionist activist, one of Herzl's first supporters.
[67] *Hamelitz*, no. 81, April 21, 1897, signed by Hillel ben Shahar.

how excited American Jews were over Herzl's initiative and program for a Jewish state. But an article brimming with ridicule and contempt for both Herzl and the Congress was also published that year.[68] The writer, Yehuda Leib (Leon) Vintz, complained about the arrogant tone of Herzl's "call to action." Vintz wrote that he could not remain indifferent in the face of what appeared to be empty rhetoric. "Who are these Zionists who will gather for the Congress from all over the world?" he asked. "It is nothing more than a beautiful dream."[69] Herzl's Hebrew language secretary, Michael Berkowicz wrote back to say that he was a partner to the preparations and could testify that delegates from all over the world had been invited to the Congress and they were planning to attend.[70] Yosef Klausner also responded to Vintz. In an article entitled "Stop the mockery," he wrote: "Even if it seems to us that Herzl will accomplish little of what he sets out to do…we still have reason to be proud…that in our day, in these days of impoverishment and small-mindedness, we still have men of spirit and intellect in our midst who are prepared to give of their time and money for the sake of the Jewish people and its salvation."[71]

Influenced by Vintz, the newspaper appears to have gone back to its old doubts: "We must confess that for the most part we regard the proclamations of Herzl and his comrades as over-enthusiasm, bluster and bombast."[72] Meanwhile the debate for and against Herzl continued to rage, and only the success of the First Congress led to a change in outlook. The Congress was covered by Reuben Brainin, who followed Herzl's early work with admiration and zeal. Brainin's articles, along with other commentary in the same spirit, transformed the whole tenor of *Hamelitz*, which now professed deep faith in Herzl and his endeavors.[73]

Hatzfira

Hatzfira was founded by Chaim Selig Slonimski, who later appointed Nahum Sokolow as acting editor. Sokolow, prudent and cautious by nature, already warned in the early 1880s, during the days of Hovevei Zion, against "over- enthu-

---

[68] *Hamelitz*, no. 118–119, June 9, 1897.
[69] Y.L. Vintz, *ibid*.
[70] *Hamelitz*, no. 137, July 2, 1897.
[71] *Hamelitz*, no. 179, August 22, 1897.
[72] *Hamelitz*, no. 158, July 27, 1897.
[73] *Reisheet tza'aday herzl*, p. 9. It was not long before Vintz, too, became an ardent supporter of Herzl. See Kressel 7).

siasm for the Land of Israel, which arouses [hope] in the hearts of defenseless and homeless refugees."[74] He was equally cautious with respect to *Der Judenstaat*. He announced its publication but added a caveat: " [These ideas] must be approached with skepticism – can they be carried out or not – although they themselves may have merit and value."[75] Later, when the book made waves, Sokolow came back to it again, but advised against nurturing delusions. He saw Herzl's initiative as another link in the chain of schemes proposed over the years, such as those of Laurence Oliphant, Paul Friedmann and Baron Hirsch, which had turned out to be little more than fantasies and raised questions about whether a Jewish state was a realistic possibility. "The assumption that the Turks would consent to such a plan beggars belief," he commented.[76] Sokolow's remarks triggered further criticism. Kressel cites the response of Patrikowski, a reporter for *Hatzfira* in London:

> "Herzl's idea was born in a storm of emotion and hysteria and therefore lacks rationality, judgment and moderation. It is highly doubtful, in our opinion, that our moderate Jewish brethren in England will embrace it. One way or the other, Herzl has vigorously stoked the fire of nationalism, which has gained a massive following in recent years...Will this idea lead to a colossal enterprise that will alter the lives of the Jews of the West beyond recognition, or will it become a memory, like other ideas that have cropped up over the generations? Time will tell."[77]

Sokolow continued to caution readers later that year. He compared Herzl's actions to those of children playing with matches who were endangering the "poor man's lamb," i.e., the threshing floor that served the farmer as a source of livelihood. The children were political Zionism and the farmer and the lamb were settlement in the Land of Israel. "That is the essence of Herzl's message and his dream of a Jewish kingdom," he writes. "It is not pleasant to say this, but doing one's duty is not always pleasant."

Via this parable, Sokolow expressed his concern for the fate of the colonies in Palestine in the wake of Herzl's scheme. He believed that the decrees on the colonies were imposed because the Turks were afraid the Jews were trying to establish a state. According to Sokolow, Herzl was not only spreading rumors about founding a state but actually intended to do so:

---

74 Ibid., p. 9.
75 *Hatzfira*, no. 11, January 24, 1896; *Reisheet tza'aday herzl*, p. 10.
76 *Reisheet tza'aday herzl*, p. 10.
77 *Hatzfira*, no. 147, July 14, 1896; *Reisheet tza'aday herzl*, p. 10.

> "One company will build and the other will supervise the builders. The miracle worker also announced that he passed through Constantinople and received a cordial welcome. But what has Herzl's talk accomplished? The spark has already reached the granary. Herzl has innocently handed a sword to the Tugar [Turkish] authorities now threatening the Jewish colonies. So it is our duty to arouse and shake up and inform the public that Dr. Herzl's whole venture is a game... We would advise Dr. Herzl to desist from his prophecy, but if he does not, we shall not cease to do our duty and will let it be known that this eminent dreamer is pursuing his own dream and not that of the people."[78]

Sokolow's article had a tremendous impact, and it reached Herzl's ears through his Hebrew secretary, Michael Berkowicz. Herzl's point- by- point response, translated by Berkowicz and published in *Hatzfira*, emphasized that Herzl's insistence on securing the Jewish state under public law, i.e., gaining international consent, would ensure its viability. This was in contrast to the subversive strategy of Hovevei Zion, which the Turks could sabotage if they saw fit, thereby endangering the whole settlement enterprise.

In his reply, Sokolow again questioned whether political Zionism could succeed and voiced concern that if it failed, this failure could have implications for the entire Jewish people. In any event, he believed that the Jews would overcome because "...the glory of Israel will not lie. In our view, the power of the Jews – the power of thinking and endurance – is stronger and more invincible than any political status that Herzl could dream up."[79] He continues:

> "Even if the society that Dr. Herzl envisions is established and we achieve a state, what will we, a small people among the mighty nations of the world, be known for? We do not oppose the sublime idea of our people possessing a large estate of its own and enjoying autonomy, but to all those who claim this is the only way Israel can be revived, we say: Not only are they not strengthening the national idea, but they are denying it. Israeli nationalism is not territorial. It is not tied to the ground. Our Sages, who knew the spirit of Israel and its doctrines far better than all of us combined, rightly said: 'The Lord blessed be He has shown charity to the Children of Israel by *dispersing them* among the nations.' If all of our people had been gathered together in one place who knows whether any vestige would be left today or whether they would have met their end like other greater and more powerful nations..."[80]

Sokolow thus sharpened the thrust of his disagreement with Herzl, focusing on three points: First, his doubt that Herzl's plan could be implemented and his concern that failure could harm the spirit of the nation. Second, his contention

---

78 *Hatzfira*, no. 218, October 20, 1896.
79 *Reisheet tza'aday herzl*, p. 13.
80 Ibid., ibid.

that even if Herzl established a Jewish state, it would not help the Jews in the way he hoped because the chance of winning significant international standing was small. And third, his ideological insistence that territory was unnecessary and nationhood was not dependent on a state.

Kressel called the clash between Herzl and Sokolow "unbridgeable."[81] Sokolow's views corresponded with those of *Hatzfira*, whose opposition to Herzl continued on the eve of the First Congress. But then the tides turned. Sokolow, who attended the Congress as a journalist, fell under Herzl's spell. He turned into an admirer and devoted supporter of his Zionist doctrine, was appointed Secretary of the Zionist Organization and went on to succeed Herzl as its elected leader. *Hatzfira* became the mouthpiece of political Zionism.

The professional rivalry between *Hatzfira* and *Hamelitz* also seeped into their coverage of Herzl and the Zionist Congress. When the Zionist Congress opened, *Hamelitz* accused Sokolow of hypocrisy. Along with his editorship of *Hatzfira*, he also edited a Polish Jewish newspaper, *Izraelita*, for which he wrote weekly. Another Polish paper then denounced Sokolow for contributing to two papers representing opposing ideologies. He was dubbed "a two-seat editor." What he vetoed in one paper, he supported it in another.[82] *Hamelitz* made mincemeat out of it. It translated a passage from one of Sokolow's articles in *Izraelita* and published it side by side with the same passage as it had appeared in *Hatzfira*.[83] Sokolow was quick to respond. There was no substantive difference in the message, he explained, but only in the style, which had been adapted for different audiences. In part, the change was attributed to the time factor: "One must distinguish between what was written before the Congress and what was written afterwards, because views and opinions have changed for the better. Initially, many Hovevei Zion members were hostile to the Congress but now that the issues are clearer, the language used is different."[84]

Sokolow's reply acknowledges the profound shift in his own outlook. While attending the Congress, he reported in *Hatzfira*:

> "Our readers know that we are not among Herzl's fans ... But in truth I must admit that the man possesses many virtues that make him worthy of leading the party. Dr. Herzl, besides his great talent as a writer, is also a charming man and a man of taste and manners. Tall and comely; black eyes and handsome features; engaging and unassuming; endowed with nobility and spiritual preeminence. With his sparkling black eyes, Herzl looks like a man of imagination and dreams. But he keeps his imagination in check and tries his best to sup-

---

81 *Ibid., ibid.*
82 *Ibid.*, p. 15.
83 *Hamelitz*, no. 202, September 17, 1897.
84 *Hatzfira*, no. 191, September 2, 1897.

press the poetry and prophecy in favor of real life and the hopes and desires of the present."[85]

Kressel describes Sokolow's transformation as the "playful revenge of history." Along comes this "moderate, level-headed editor who called for restraint and reason in the face of Herzl's recklessness who then goes off on wild poetic tangents himself, singing Herzl's praises." After Sokolow aligned himself with Herzl, he turned *Hatzfira* into a political Zionist propaganda tool, "and what Sokolow became for Zionism and the Zionist movement is on record for all to see."[86]

Thanks to Sokolow's change of heart, political Zionism gained a sympathetic journalistic platform that set itself the goal of creating a global Jewish community. Supreme importance was ascribed to establishing ties with Jewish communities around the world, which was accomplished by hiring correspondents from the larger communities to report on a regular basis:

> "We have dispatched writers to all the capital cities with a large Jewish population: St. Petersburg, Berlin, Vienna, Prague, Paris, London, New York... [The newspaper's aims are to] report on what is happening in the world and disseminate knowledge of national affairs, the sciences and current events; to discuss matters of concern to the Jewish people; to act as a beacon and sounding board for public opinion on all issues related to the Nation of Israel across the globe; to bring a round-up of all breaking news, etc."[87]

In the use of on location reporters, it is notable that *Hatzfira* lagged behind other newspapers. Its coverage of the Dreyfus trial was a fiasco, for example, because it had no reporter in France. *Hamelitz*, on the other hand, had a Paris correspondent, Avraham Ludwipol, whose regular "Letters from Paris" column was very popular.[88] In the end, Sokolow hired Ludwipol as the Parisian correspondent of *Hatzfira* and beat *Hamelitz* at its own game.[89] According to Gideon Kotz, Sokolow was the first professional in the sphere of Zionist propaganda. He was among the leading creators of content that we know today as *hasbara*, and identified the press as the ideal tool for disseminating it. Under his editorship, *Hatzfira* became a Zionist organ. When the paper closed in 1906, his condition for accepting the post of secretary-general of the Zionist Organization was the estab-

---

85 *Ibid.*
86 *Reisheet tza'aday herzl*, pp. 16–17.
87 Oren Sofer, *Ein lefalpel! Iton hatzfira vehamodernizatzia shel hasiakh hakhevrati politi*, Mosad Bialik, Jerusalem, 2008, p. 139; *Hatzfira*, no.203, December 11, 1888.
88 Gideon Kotz, in: *Kesher*, no. 33, p. 46.
89 Kotz, *ibid.*, p. 50.

Hamagid

Hamagid commenced its coverage of Herzl[91] copying from Hamelitz which congratulated him on his political initiative.[92] Only later that year (in issues 20 and 21) did the paper raise doubts about the feasibility of Herzl's program: "We do not believe that the time is now ripe for such a grand scheme." What is needed, the paper concludes, is not "striving for a Jewish state but starting small, with the establishment of colonies in the Land of Israel."[93] Austrian Zionists were urged to learn from their Russian and Rumanian brethren who are "founding colonies in the land of our forefathers without noise and fanfare."[94]

Historian Nathan Gelber claims that the paper's opposition to Herzl was due to the fact that its editor, Jacob Samuel Fuchs, had been offended by Herzl. Fuchs sought Herzl's permission to translate and publish *Der Judenstaat* "in order to transmit to the Hebrew reader the excellent content of the pamphlet...which deserves to be known in full to all members of our nation." However, Herzl preferred his Hebrew secretary, Michael Berkowicz, and Fuchs never forgave him for it. Gelber believes this was one of his main reasons for opposing Herzlian Zionism.[95] Also, *Hamagid* did not like the fact that Herzl was assisted by students because many of them had abandoned religion and their behavior was often provocative. The paper was of the opinion that "they cannot be guides to their people as most of them have distanced themselves from the nation, which they disparage and hate."[96] Berkowicz hastened to defend Herzl: "Herzl's call is to the entire nation, not just to students."[97] He also used the opportunity to con-

---

90 Kotz, "Nakhum sokolov vehafunktzia harishmit shel ha'itonut ha'ivrit," in: *Kesher*, no. 2, 1987, p. 23.
91 *Hamagid*, no. 12, September 10, 1896.
92 *Hamagid*, no. 49, December 17, 1986.
93 Ibid., ibid.
94 *Hamagid*, no.20–21, May 27, 1896, p. 88; *Reisheet tza'aday herzl*, p. 17.
95 Nathan Gelber, *Toldot hatnu'a hatzionit begalitzia*, Reuben Mass, Jerusalem, 1958, pp. 292–293 (henceforth: *Tolodot hatnu'a hatzionit begalitzia*).
96 *Hamagid*, no. 20, May 27, 1896; also no. 21; *Reisheet tza'aday herzl*, p. 17, note 31.
97 *Hamagid*, no. 23, 1896, pp. 184–185.

vey an update in Herzl's name about the future location of the Jewish state and its official language.[98]

In his censure of Herzl's plan, Fuchs was joined by one of the leaders of Hovevei Zion in Britain who wrote to say that the Maccabeans[99] also demanded that Herzl set aside the idea of a Jewish state until a more appropriate time: "But Herzl, estranged from Jewish tradition, laughs and ridicules all those who oppose his idea."[100] The editor's advice to Herzl and those of his ilk was "to please study our ancient literature and see that they have departed from the path that leads to happiness."[101] One of the articles in a series that appeared in the paper anonymously, "A flock without a shepherd," was devoted to Herzl. He was accused of appealing only to wealthy Jews while ignoring the wishes of the community. The author concludes that "Herzl is a great writer but not a wise statesman."[102]

Hamagid published the appeal for delegates to the First Congress, prompting the writer Jacob Samuel Trachtman to share his thoughts in an open letter to the editor, "Jewish government or settlement of Land of Israel." Trachtman warns of the danger to the Jewish Yishuv posed by Herzl's initiative and calls on the editor to clarify his position on this question. In reply, Fuchs wrote an editorial entitled "Between the straits" alluding to the pressure Trachtman was putting on him to take a more definite stance. Those who waved the Jewish banner would continue to support settlement in the Land of Israel, he wrote, but

> "they will not cooperate with the political Zionists, who are arrogantly and raucously calling for the establishment of a Jewish kingdom … because the idea of a Jewish state born solely out of the distress and persecution of the people … will never last, or at least not for any length of time, and the result will be 'as vapors and wind without rain.' Yet even if the editor sees no value in political Zionism, he believes that showing good will toward its proponents is important and recommends heart- to- heart dialogue between all the parties. "[103]

---

98 On the location of the state: "He has changed his mind about settling Jews in Argentina and has found no country better able to serve as a home than our Holy Land." On the official language: "He has told me to erase from the book the entire chapter about the lingua franca of the new land. Instead of what he thought heretofore, which is that we will speak the same languages as we do now…Herzl has been convinced that Hebrew will be the language of the land." *Hamagid*, ibid.
99 The Order of Ancient Maccabeans was a society of influential British Jews.
100 *Hamagid*, no. 29, July 23, 1896.
101 Ibid., ibid.
102 *Hamagid*, no. 31, July 23, 1896, pp. 239–240; *Reisheet tza'aday herzl*, p. 19.
103 *Reisheet tza'aday herzl*, ibid.; *Hamagid*, no. 16, 1897, pp. 124–125.

Thus, despite his opposition to political Zionism, Fuchs wholeheartedly supported the Zionist Congress, which he saw as an effective peacemaking tool. On the eve of the Congress, he published an article entitled "Peace be with you."[104] *Hamagid*'s correspondent to the Congress was Reuben Asher Braudes, who Herzl later appointed editor of the Yiddish edition of *Die Welt*.[105] Braudes' impressions of the Congress and his awe of Herzl, along with the all-round positive press coverage of the event, seem to have influenced Fuchs to the point where he changed his mind. He summed up the Congress as "a cornerstone of the building of the House of Israel and a font of peace between the founders of a Jewish state and those engaged in the settlement of the Land of Israel."[106]

Braudes writes about *Hamagid*'s change of direction: "From a newspaper that dispensed skepticism and negativism, warning the pioneers of the Land of Israel not to lend a hand to the Zionists, it became a mouthpiece of political Zionism and eventually the official newspaper of the Galician Zionists."[107]

So putting all the data together, we see that the Hebrew newspapers *Hatzfira* and *Hamelitz* shared a common denominator. Both were initially suspicious of political Zionism and Herzl, and their doubts and opposition were ideological as well as fueled by fear of the Turkish and Russian authorities. However, so impressive were Herzl's diplomatic forays and the spectacle of the First Zionist Congress that they changed their tune and became supporters. *Hamagid* started out praising Herzl and his endeavors, went through a period of uncertainty, and was swept up in the end by the excitement engendered by the First Congress, becoming a spokesman for Zionism. *Hashiloah* was a different case entirely.

Hashiloah

In November 1896, *Hashiloah*, a new Hebrew monthly edited by Ahad Ha'am debuted in Odessa. Herzl and political Zionism were key issues on the agenda. As Ahad Ha'am was a personal and ideological opponent of Herzl, the paper was unsparing in its criticism of him. Ahad Ha'am, hailed as the father of spiritual Zionism, supported the idea of a Jewish conference that would cultivate na-

---

104 *Hamagid*, no. 36, August 26, 1897, p. 289.
105 While Herzl did not know him personally, he appointed Braudes on the basis of what he had heard, i.e., that he was a Vilna Jew who would know how to write for nationalist audiences. See: *Vilna hatzionit ve'askaneha*, p. 169, note 2.
106 *Hamagid*, no. 36, August 26, 1897, p. 289.
107 *Reisheet tza'aday herzl*, p. 21.

tional pride,[108] but bitterly opposed Herzl, who set his sights on a Jewish state.[109] Additional reasons for the discord between the two will be discussed below.[110]

At first, Ahad Ha'am did not criticize Herzl in writing, encouraging his colleagues to do the work for him. Stinging criticism of Herzl was published in the first issue of *Hashiloah* by Dr. David Farbstein and Micah Josef Berdyczewski. Elhanan Leib Lewinsky (who signed his articles "Rabbi Karov") did not hold back either. In the summer of 1897, he wrote this about the impending Congress:

> "I hereby confess my sins: I do not see [the Congress] as *atkhalta degeula* [the start of redemption], nor will it be a high court of justice for Jewish affairs. It will be a meeting like all others. Hovevei Zion has been meeting for forever. Words were said. Many words. But nothing at all was done."[111]

Everything printed in *Hashiloah* was vetted by Ahad Ha'am and bore his stamp. Asked why he did not respond to Herzl himself (before the opening of Congress in July 1897), he replied that he did not wish to add his voice just yet. He was not impressed with Herzl, he said, but *Hashiloah* was not under any obligation to say so. However, after the Congress, which Ahad Ha'am attended as a journalist, he did publish a biting critique. He began with a positive statement about the fact that the Congress had brought together some two hundred Jews

> "who for three days deliberated in public, under the eyes of the whole world, on the establishment of a genuine home for the people of Israel in the land of their forefathers...In so doing, the national solution for the Jewish question burst the barriers of modesty and entered the public domain, laid bare before the world, in language that was loud and clear, head held high. Never since the exile of the Jews from their land had such a thing been seen."[112]

From there on, however, Ahad Ha'am was bitterly critical:

> "Alone I sat among my brethren like a mourner at a wedding and felt it my duty to let it be known: Beware! Danger is nigh! Reactionary politics loom behind the wall. The great excitement of this assembly will end in despair, hopes dashed at our feet...Their eyes gaze with love and admiration upon their fine brother standing on the podium and preaching

---

108 Letter of Ahad Ha'am to Ehrenpreis, May 17, 1897; Yossi Goldstein, *Ahad Ha'am*, Keter, Jerusalem, 1992, p. 242, note 55 (henceforth: Goldstein, *Ahad Ha'am*).
109 *Ibid., ibid.*
110 See pp. 95, 184.
111 *Hashiloah*, vol.2; Mordechai Naor, in: *Kesher*, May 3, 1988, p. 35.
112 Ahad Ha'am, in: *Hashiloah*, vol. 2, no. 6, September 1897.

wonders to his people like one of the prophets of days of yore. He is a false prophet...The salvation of Israel will be brought by the prophets, not by diplomats..."[113]

Ahad Ha'am's article generated a flurry of response and was censured for its negativism. Author and journalist Mordechai Ben Hillel Hacohen published a rebuttal in *Hamelitz* entitled "On recklessness and the ease of tearing down."[114] In his article "Opinions and beliefs," author and journalist Wolf Schur wrote: "Mr. Ahad Ha'am, the master of despair, has spewed words from his lips that will never be forgiven."[115] Moshe Leib Lilienblum also rose up in Herzl's defense. In "Between imagination and the possible," he recommended that Herzl's political Zionist approach be given a chance.[116] Even Marcus (Mordecai) Ehrenpreis, a loyal follower of Ahad Ha'am, came out against him. He charged that Ahad Ha'am misunderstood the tenor of Jewish society and rather than examining Herzl's political idea seriously, endorsed sitting and waiting for the people to achieve spiritual enlightenment.[117] This opposition did not put a damper on Ahad Ha'am. It only fired him up more. As Ahad Ha'am's biographer, Yossi Goldstein, writes:

> "As was his wont, [opposition] only strengthened him. Debate was his elixir of life. He launched into further attacks on Herzl, his ideology and his supporters which appeared in *Hashiloah* and the supplements it put out, and his disdain for Herzl did not cease."[118]

As mentioned earlier,[119] this vilification of Herzl and its counter-response actually promoted the public visibility that Herzl so desperately sought. In the storm set off by Ahad Ha'am, his status as an intellectual icon and the vicious and exaggerated tone of his objections (to the point where even his followers protested) led to a media circus that furthered the Zionist cause. The more Ahad Ha'am inveighed against Herzl, the more exposure Zionism received.

In November 1897, Ahad Ha'am wrote an article entitled "The Jewish State and the trouble of the Jews." In his collected writings, he notes that it was published in *Hashiloah* "in answer to the uproar in the Hebrew press over my little

---

113 Ahad Ha'am, *Kol kitvei ahad ha'am*, Dvir, Tel Aviv, 1947, p. 276 (henceforth: *Kol kitvei ahad ha'am*).
114 *Hamelitz*, February 28, 1898.
115 *Hamelitz*, no. 279, December 29, 1897.
116 *Hamelitz*, no. 229, November 1, 1897.
117 *Die Welt* and *Hashiloah*; see Goldstein, *Ahad Ha'am*, p. 249.
118 Goldstein, *Ahad Ha'am*, pp. 249–250.
119 See p. 76.

piece on the First Zionist Congress." In this article, he again has nothing but scorn for Herzl and emphasizes that even if a Jewish state were established, it would not solve the Jewish problem.[120] One of his criticisms of Herzl is his failure to recognize the difference in outlook and mentality between the Jews of Eastern and Western Europe. In his opinion, the Jews of Western Europe, who had all but forgotten their Judaism, might derive some benefit from Zionism, but to the Jews of Eastern Europe, it would only bring harm: The pull of Herzlian political Zionism would push them away from the spiritual and moral ideals that were already part of their lives.[121]

As we have seen, Ahad Ha'am's views were not popular, but the truth was that his writing kept *Hashiloah* from being shut down. The paper was on the verge of closing for financial reasons, and what kept its backers from continuing to support him was Ahad Ha'am's campaign against Herzl and political Zionism. They felt it was an important mission, and extended their financing for another year.[122] The battle heated up: In 1898, on the eve of the Second Congress, Ahad Ha'am again attacked and mocked Herzl.[123]

Hashiloah continued to serve as a bastion for anti-Herzl ideology, with Ahad Ha'am at the forefront. Goldstein believes it was Herzl's success that sent Ahad Ha'am over the edge, turning his dogged pursuit of the man into a veritable obsession.[124] Later, we will explore the personal rivalry between the two. Meanwhile, one can say that it was probably this combination of ideology and personal antagonism that led Ahad Ha'am to overreact.

After the Second Congress, Ahad Ha'am wrote an article reporting on the congress in which he took the leadership to task for deciding not to pursue a cultural agenda: "It is doubtful that the leaders will consider the voice of the people, namely their aspiration for Jewish settlement and culture."[125] Expanding on his range of anti-Herzl commentary, he wrote "Policy and the Zionist Bank,"[126] protesting regulations that allowed the Jewish Colonial Trust to establish agricul-

---

120 *Hashiloah*, vol. 3, 1, Tevet 5658 (1898); *Kol kitvei ahad ha'am*, pp. 135–140.
121 *Kol kitvei ahad ha'am*, ibid.
122 Goldstein, *Ahad Ha'am*, p. 246.
123 Ibid., p. 250.
124 Ibid., pp. 253–254.
125 Shlomit Laskov, *Khayei ahad ha'am*, Institute for Zionist Research, Tel Aviv University and Hasifriya Hatzionit, Jerusalem 1967, p. 132 (henceforth: Laskov, *Khayei ahad ha'am*).
126 No policies were revised in the wake of this article. Only in 1907 was it stipulated that the money was designated for Palestine only. See *Hashiloah*, vol. 5, no. 5, Iyar 5659 (1899), *Leshe'ailat hayom* 6.

tural settlements anywhere in the world. After the Third Congress he brought this subject up again.[127]

However, all of this was nothing compared to Ahad Ha'am's response to the publication of *Altneuland*. His invective soared to new heights, nearly splitting the Zionist movement. He panned the book and its author, first publishing his review in Russian, then in Hebrew and finally in German in *Ost und West*, a journal for Jewish arts and culture.[128] Shmaryahu Levin came to Herzl's defense in the Hebrew periodical *Hazeman*,[129] and Max Nordau, eager to protect Herzl, castigated Ahad Ha'am in *Die Welt*.[130] Ahad Ha'am's reply to Nordau appeared in five newspapers: *Hashiloah*, *Hatzfira*, *Ost und West*, *Hazeman* and the Russian Jewish paper *Voskhod*. As a result, the ideology of political Zionism was constantly in the news, though sometimes to the movement's detriment.[131]

The Uganda affair provided Ahad Ha'am with another opportunity to blast political Zionism. "The Weepers," which he sent to Klausner, who succeeded him as editor of *Hashiloah*, is a eulogy for the movement:

> "And Zionism, what shall become of it? What brand of Zionism? Baselesque Zionism? It no longer exists. On *rosh hodesh* [first day of] Elul 1897, it was born, and on *rosh hodesh* Elul 1903 it expired, leaving nothing but a name drained of content and a new-fangled program, Zionism reinterpreted. And what of historical Zionism? Don't worry yourselves. It can wait. The time will come…And if a new political genius gets up and wishes to lead you to Zion via a diplomatic shortcut, open the Book of Chronicles and show him the chapter on 'political Zionism' from Uganda onwards. 'Read this, wise man,' you will say. 'Use your wisdom to send the negroes back to Africa. Your predecessor dreamed of taking us there but we shall walk slowly down the long road and cease to preempt the end of days."[132]

Altneuland and Uganda will be discussed further below, but until this point we can say that Ahad Ha'am unwittingly contributed to the positive promotion of Herzl in that his attacks led Herzl's supporters to speak up. On the controversial issues cited above, this was not the case. Here Ahad Ha'am succeeded in driving

---

127 *Hashiloah*, vol. 7, 1–3, Shvat-Nisan 5661 (1901); Laskov, *Khayei ahad ha'am*, pp. 132–133.
128 Laskov, *Khayei ahad ha'am*, p. 210. For more on this, see Chapter 9.
129 *Hazeman*, 12, March 2, 1903.
130 *Die Welt*, March 13, 1903.
131 Yosef Lang: *Daber ivrit! Khayei eliezer ben-yehuda*, Yad Ben Zvi, Jerusalem 2008, p. 436, note 151 (henceforth: Yosef Lang, *Daber ivrit*); Yossi Goldstein, *Ahad ha'am veherzl*, Dinur Center for Research in Jewish History and Zalman Shazar Center, Jerusalem 2012, p. 13 (henceforth: Goldstein, *Ahad ha'am veherzl*).
132 The article, sent in August, was published in *Hashiloah*, vol. 12, 2, September 1903; Goldstein, *Ahad ha'am veherzl*, p. 307.

a wedge between Herzl's long-time allies (members of Bnai Moshe and the Democratic Fraction) and other supporters.

Other Jewish Newspapers

Great Britain

Despite its doubts about the Zionist movement, Britain's Jewish newspaper *The Jewish Chronicle (JC)* was the first to give Herzl a platform for his ideas on the Jewish state. On January 17, 1896, about a month before the publication of *Der Judenstaat*, the paper carried a synopsis of the pamphlet. In the same issue, the editor Asher Myers, was openly skeptical that such a plan could be carried out.[133]

On July 1897, shortly before the First Congress, the paper reported the remarks of Britain's chief rabbi, Hermann Adler, a supporter of Jewish colonization in Palestine, who called Herzl's scheme completely wrongheaded and contrary to the principles of Jewish life, the words of the prophets and Jewish tradition.[134]

However, the attitude of the *JC*, like that of other Jewish newspapers, softened after the First Congress. The *JC* devoted considerable space to coverage of the Congress. It published Nordau's speech in full with photographs of Herzl and Nordau, and the Congress protocols were spread over five densely printed pages. Mordechai Naor notes that the paper's views on political Zionism fluctuated, but from 1907, after the death of Herzl, it became more positive. The editorship of Leopold Greenberg, an admirer of Herzl and considered his "ambassador" in Britain, is cited as a contributing factor.[135]

United States

Political Zionism also made ripples in the United States. In the Hebrew language paper *Hapisga*, Zev Wolf Schur published an emotional appeal to Hovevei Zion in America to hold conventions and elect delegates for the Zionist Congress.[136] As

---

[133] *Khadashot vekorot hayamim*, p. 177. Original in *JC*, synopsis of *Der Judenstaat*.
[134] Rabbi Hermann (Naftali) Adler (1839–1911), was a lifelong opponent of political Zionism. His remarks are quoted by Mordechai Naor, "Herzl ve'emtza'ay hatikshoret," in: *Kesher*, no. 3, May 1988, pp. 32–38.
[135] Mordechai Naor, *ibid., ibid.*
[136] *Ibid.*, p. 37.

in Europe, however, the Reform movement opposed Herzl and its newspapers tore his plan to pieces. In July 1897, the Central Conference of American Rabbis signed a petition against any attempt to establish a Jewish state.[137]

Palestine

In the Jewish Yishuv, there was little press coverage of Zionism in general, and even less of Herzl. *Havatzelet,* a bi-monthly edited by Yisrael Dov Frumkin, was perceived as an organ of the Old Yishuv, which regarded Zionism as illegitimate. In his journal *Hatzvi,* Eliezer Ben Yehuda was careful not to publish anything that might provoke the Turkish authorities. Thus reports from the First Congress did not mention Herzl by name, although a lengthy piece appeared about "Dr. Nordau's speech at the Hovevei Zion convention in Basel."[138] As a supporter of Herzl and political Zionism, such restraint was not easy for Ben Yehuda. He kept abreast of events and was quick to translate the foreign news reports on Herzl into Hebrew for his readers, but he kept the wording vague and avoided Herzl's name for fear of censorship. In one article, for example, he writes: "There in Vienna sits the Eminent Dr. (---), the prophet of a grand ideal."[139]

After the Congress, however, *Hatzvi* filled its pages with reports and commentary that demonstrated a greater willingness to take risks. Even when tempers flared over the *Altneuland* affair[140] and a storm brewed at the Sixth Congress and afterwards over Uganda, Ben Yehuda continued to serve as a loyal commentator for the Zionist movement.[141]

Non-Jewish Newspapers

Great Britain

Thanks to Herzl's efforts, news of the Zionist movement was also circulated by the non-Jewish press in Britain. *The Times* of London ran reports from Reuters, wrote about how the delegates at the Congress greeted Herzl with applause, and published a running debate between two English Jews, Oswald John Simon and

---

137 *Ibid., ibid.*
138 *Ibid.,* p. 36; *Hatzvi,* no. 49, September 17, 1897.
139 *Hatzvi,* no. 38, July 2, 1897, p. 172; Lang, *Daber ivrit,* pp. 352–353.
140 On *Altneuland,* see Chapter 9, pp. 224–235.
141 Lang, *Daber ivrit,* p. 455.

Sephardi rabbi Moses Gaster. Simon claimed that the Zionist Congress did not represent any part of the Jewish people and that reviving Jewish nationalism was not progress but a return to a primitive state.[142] Within two days, Rabbi Gaster published a lengthy reply refuting Simon's arguments. Simon countered with another letter branding Zionism a shameful mistake in which he quoted Rabbi Adler's comments to the *Jewish Chronicle* to bolster his position.[143] In this manner, the British newspapers participated in the Herzlian Zionist discourse and kept a diverse public informed on what was happening in the Zionist arena. This media stir may have been behind the October 1897 proposal put forward by two leading English papers, the *Daily Chronicle* and the *Pall Mall Gazette*, to hold a European conference "for the settlement of the Jewish Question."[144] Other important European newspapers that reported on the Congress joined in: *Frankfurter Zeitung* and *Kölnische Zeitung* in Germany, *L'Echo de Paris* in France and *Pester Lloyd* in Hungary.

After the Fourth Congress in London, Nahum Slouschz reported on the attitude of the British press to Herzl and Congress. He claimed that English public opinion had changed in the wake of the growing success of the Zionist congresses. The very fact that thousands of Jews and non-Jews thronged the conference hall, hanging over the balcony railings, led to a newfound appreciation for political Zionism:

> "*The Times* and all the mass circulation newspapers filed a report from each congressional session, and the weeklies published pictures of the Zionist leaders and the Congress as a whole. With his splendor and impeccable taste, Dr. Herzl charmed the non-Jews as much as the Jews and a number of distinguished newspapers came up with a new name for him: the New Moses."[145]

United States

In London, Herzl told *New York Herald* correspondent Sidney Whitman that *Die Welt* would serve as a platform for the Zionist movement's deep gratitude to Turkey and would gladly report any news beneficial to the Sultan's government.[146]

---

142 Cited in: Naor, pp. 212–213.
143 Cited in Naor's article "Herzl ve'emtza'ay hatikshorot" in: *Miherzl ve'ad ben gurion*, Defense Ministry, 1996, p. 213.
144 *Complete Diaries of Theodor Herzl*, vol. 2, p. 595 (October 17, 1897).
145 Slouschz, *Hakongress hatzioni harivi'I*, p. 11.
146 *Complete Diaries of Theodor Herzl*, vol. 3, p. 863 (August 21, 1899); Kotz, *Khadashot vekorot hayamim*, p. 178.

Leading American newspapers, among them the *Daily Mail*, the *New York Herald* and *The New York Times*, sent journalists to cover the First Zionist Congress. On the eve of the Congress, *The New York Times* reported that Herzl's program was being debated in Europe and the United States, and on the whole, reception was cold. Following the success of the Congress, the paper wrote about Herzl's changed status and the fact that he was being hailed as the "New Moses," as reported in Britain.[147]

The Non-Jewish Press in Jewish Eyes

Evidence of the power of the non-Jewish press in spreading the Zionist message and promoting Herzl can be seen in a comment by the author Moshe Cohen in *Ha'olam*, the Hebrew-language newspaper of the Zionist movement:

> "One day, a story appeared in a Hebrew newspaper about some doctor in Vienna by the name of Theodor Herzl who proposed founding a Jewish state. But truth be told, the Jews did not entirely trust the Hebrew press ... so anyone who wished to lend credibility to some news he heard would add: 'I heard about it from the pharmacist, who read it in the Russian paper.'"[148]

Such a statement emphasized that the news came from a reliable source and could be trusted. Cohen describes the cynicism of journalists writing about Herzl and speculates whether their fear of censorship might have been behind the sneering tone. This dismissive attitude, combined with the fact that the story was in a Hebrew newspaper and not confirmed by another source, led to a certain skepticism among the adult readership. The young people, however, were enthusiastic and welcomed the Zionist Congress as the herald of the Messiah:

> "Only our unlimited faith in Herzl and his towering ability enabled us to withstand all the hardships of those days. In the depths of our hearts lay the serene confidence that in the end Herzl would triumph over all and we were standing on the cusp of the Day of Redemption. The Zionist Congress was in session at the time and the young people were tense to the breaking point. Our nerves were shaken to the core. There, in Basel, the Jewish state was becoming flesh and bone, and we were here, not partners to this act of creation. At last the newspapers arrived carrying the first reports. We devoured every word. In all of it we

---

[147] Mordechai Naor, "Herzl ve'emtza'ay hatikshoret," p. 38.
[148] Moshe Cohen, "Medinat hayehudim be'ayara hayehudit," in: *Ha'olam*, no. 23, February 1946, pp. 221–222.

saw clues and signs. We read and reread, insatiable. Suddenly, one of our friends showed up, euphoric. 'What is it? What happened?' 'Something big and important!'"[149]

Cohen writes about the telegram published verbatim by *Birzhevye Vedomosti*: Today the First Zionist Congress opened in Basel. Just a few words, but how vast their importance! If a Russian newspaper has seen fit to publish this special telegram, it is a sign that something truly momentous has happened."[150]

Jewish Newspaper Circulation

How large was the readership of the Jewish newspapers? How effective were they in spreading the Zionist message? Can we measure their importance by the number of copies that were printed, or perhaps the number of subscribers? Gideon Kotz writes that the circulation figures were not large to begin with, and the fact that "the homes of the editor and distributor became hubs for reading the newspaper for free did not help sales."[151]

The number of subscribers cannot provide us with a realistic estimate of their influence. There were millions of Jews who spoke Yiddish and Hebrew but the total number of readers who subscribed to the important papers at their peak (1897–1898) came to 1,800 for *Hamagid*, 4,000 for *Hamelitz*, 2,400 for *Hayom*, 10,000 for *Hatzfira*, and 12,000 for *Hatzofeh* (published in Warsaw by Eliezer Eliahu *Freedman* from 1903). Kotz emphasizes that the circulation figures for all three Hebrew dailies published in Russia in the early 20th century was lower than for the sole Yiddish paper, *Der Fraynd*, which had over 20,000 subscribers.[152]

So it seems that all Yiddish and Hebrew newspaper subscribers combined did not exceed 70,000. While it is true that one newspaper was read by many people, compared to the number of Jews who lived in Russia at that time, the figures are miniscule. An answer to the question about the extent of readership might be found in Scholem Aleichem's story "Dreyfus in Kasrilevke" which offers a glimpse into the power of the press and how one copy of the newspaper fed an entire village:

---

[149] Ibid., ibid.
[150] Ibid., ibid.
[151] Kotz, *Khadashot vekorot hayamim*, p. 12.
[152] Kotz, "Ha'itonim ha'ivriim harishonim be'eropa: Hebetim kalkali'im ve'irguni'im," in: *Kesher*, no. 29, May 2001, pp. 18–26.

"At the crack of dawn the Kasrilevkians got up and rushed en masse to the post office, but it was closed up tight and even the gates were locked. Little by little, a crowd gathered outside and the street filled with people. The Kasrilevkians wandered up and down, yawning with impatience. They stood there swaying and rocking their bodies to and fro, twirling their ear locks and quietly humming melodies from the *Hallel*...They were all waiting for Zeidel to bring out *Hatzfira*. When at last Zeidel opened the paper and read aloud the stiff sentence that the judges had imposed on Dreyfus the outcry was not against the judges or the generals or the French masses, but against Zeidel...'It cannot be!' Kasrilevke shrieked. 'Stop telling us fairytales!' And Zeidel thrust the paper in their faces. 'Here! Look and see!' ... As hearts flamed and the spirit raged, they stopped waiting for Zeidel to be merciful and come to the *beis midrash*. They began to go to his house. And when they had no patience to go to his house, they accompanied him to the post office to pick up *Hatzfira* every morning, and there, at the post office itself, they read the news."[153]

Haim Kozirovsky, also from a small town, tells a similar story about "newspaper woes":

"Our poor little village was tucked away in the backwaters, in the oily black swamps of Podolia. We had no post office, and it was a seventy-kilometer journey to fetch the mail. Our letters was delivered twice a week by Yitzhak the postman. He was our herald and our lifeline. Newspapers were read in our town by only one person, the Polish pharmacist, a big anti-Semite. So we heard about the Dreyfus trial a year and a half late."[154]

Local Newspapers

In some places, the local Jewish press served as another vehicle for spreading the news of Zionism. Correspondence dating back to March 1896 shows that Leibel Taubish of Kolomyia had written to Herzl on behalf of the local Jewish weekly, *Das Volk*, to tell him how profoundly *Der Judenstaat* had influenced the Jews of his town. Herzl was invited by the paper to submit regular updates on the two Zionist companies whose establishment had been proposed in the book.[155] In the name of the editorial board of the Przyszluc town paper, Dr. Gershon Ziffer wrote Herzl asking for an honest review of his activities and successes and an outline of the Zionist movement's plans for the near future. He also inquired

---

[153] Scholem Aleichem, *Kitvey scholem aleichem*, vol. 5, Tel Aviv, 1950, "Dreyfus bekasrilevke," p. 87.
[154] Haim Kozirovsky, "Eikh noda be'ayaratenu al hadoktor herzl vehatzionut," in: *Ha'olam*, no. 40.
[155] *Toldot hatnu'ah hatzionit begalitzia*, p. 292.

what practical steps the Galician Zionists should be taking to advance the Zionist cause.[156]

As we have seen so far, Herzl's physical appearance, charisma and dissemination of ideas in the media steadily consolidated his image, and his influence began to make itself felt on people near and far. However, he reached the pinnacle of power and glory in the wake of two milestones in his life – the First Zionist Congress in Basel and his visit to Palestine. Over the next two chapters, we will discuss how these episodes helped to build up and enhance his image.

---

156 *Ibid.*, p. 298.

Chapter 4
The First Zionist Congress

> At the First Zionist Congress in Basel, Herzl discovered us and he discovered himself ... We were as dreamers, and he, Herzl, was the greatest dreamer of them all.[1]

On the Eve of the First Congress

Towards the end of 1894, Herzl put the finishing touches on *Das Neue Ghetto* (*The New Ghetto*), a play he hoped would heighten public awareness of the "Jewish problem." The protagonist's call to the Jews to fight for their dignity was essentially an inner cry from the depths of Herzl's soul, conveying a message to Jews and non-Jews alike: The Jewish problem was essentially the world's problem and finding a solution was of paramount importance. However, the play failed at the box office and did not get Herzl's message across. Increasingly restless and agitated, he sat down and penned *Der Judenstaat*, a pamphlet outlining his political Zionist plan. This time, the message came through loud and clear. The pamphlet made waves and lay the groundwork for Herzl's Zionist project. The next step was convening an international Jewish congress.

1897 marked a critical juncture in the history of the Jews. The future looked bleak for Jewish continuity and the prospects of remaining unique as a people. Karl Lueger was now mayor of Vienna. Lueger, a nationalist who blamed the Jews for Vienna's economic decline, ran a campaign that pandered to the lower classes and openly incited against the Jews. Franz Joseph, the Austrian emperor, detested Lueger and barred him from taking office three times. In 1897, however, his appointment was finally ratified.

The anti-Semitic atmosphere in Vienna led to widespread assimilation and even conversion to Christianity as a means of professional advancement. One of the most famous converts of the time was Gustav Mahler. It was only after his baptism in 1897 that he attained his prestigious post as director of the Vienna State Opera. This was the reality in Vienna, then the cultural capital of Western Europe.

In Eastern Europe, amid the tug of war between traditionalists and modernists, the General Jewish Labor Bund was born. The Bund aspired to unite all Russian Jewish workers in a Yiddish-speaking socialist party that vehemently op-

---

[1] Reuben Brainin, in *Sefer hacongress* (1923), p. 44.

posed a national-territorial solution. At the time, the majority of East European Jews were living in the Great Russian Empire.

That same year, another new pathway opened: In August 1897, Herzl initiated and presided over the First Zionist Congress, during which he founded the World Zionist Organization and launched the Basel Program which presented political Zionism and a Hebrew-speaking Jewish state in Eretz Yisrael as an answer to the Jewish question.

Herzl's success in organizing and chairing the Zionist Congress greatly enhanced his reputation and highlighted his charisma. The six congresses held under his leadership became the stage for the unfolding Zionist drama and served as the parliament of the Jewish people. The executive institutions founded at the Congress,[2] and the globe-trotting diplomacy conducted by Herzl and his emissaries, cemented the perception of the Congress as the official representative of the Jews – in the eyes of Jews and non-Jews alike. Herzl had good reason for portraying the Congress as a sign of revival of the Jewish people, after being written off as dead and forgotten.[3] Looking back, he writes:

> "Even if it is given to me to see the realization of all our aspirations, there will be nothing that will gladden me more or fill me with greater enthusiasm that the First Congress at Basel ... That was the first sign of life on the part of the Jewish nation which had been believed to be dead. True, the breath was shallow and short, while the pulse to which we tremulously listened with so much concern and hope was very weak; but we learned to know that our nation was already alive ... For us the First Congress was a crisis which changed our fate and transformed, indeed, revolutionized, the whole world. It divided the history of our Exile into two parts as far as we were concerned: into the part before the Congress and the part that came after."[4]

Herzl went on to preside over five more congresses, which continued after his death, as did the processes that culminated in the establishment of a Jewish state. On the fiftieth anniversary of the First Congress, writer and poet Leib Jaffe, head of Keren Hayesod, reflected on the fulfillment of Herzl's dream: "Everything in the life of our people over the past fifty years ... originated at the First Congress, which harbored within it all the seeds of rebirth that have sprouted and blossomed over time, in our lives and in our land ... "[5]

---

[2] Among them the World Zionist Organization, the Zionist Executive, the Zionist Action Committee, the Jewish Colonial Trust (Jüdische Colonialbank) and the Jewish National Fund.
[3] *The Jubilee of the First Zionist Congress, 1897–1947*, The Executive of the Zionist Organization, Jerusalem, p. 42.
[4] *Ibid., ibid.*
[5] Leib Yaffe, in *Sefer hacongress* (1950), p. 4.

Early Initiatives

The congress idea was not invented by Herzl. In the same way that he was not the first to visualize the establishment of a Jewish state, he was not the first to propose a global gathering of Jews. Earlier proposals arose in response to a worldwide surge of nationalism in the nineteenth century. The phenomenon was largely ignored by the Jews of Europe,[6] but there were a few who were swept up in the nationalist fervor and spoke of bringing together Jews from around the world. None of these efforts succeeded.

Up until the modern era, Jews everywhere were linked by Judaism and religious tradition. With the rise of the Haskalah movement and Emancipation, religion declined as a cohesive force. When modern anti-Semitism reared its head, the Jews of the world needed another organizational and ideological bond through which to address broad Jewish concerns. Alliance Israelite Universelle (also known as Kol Yisrael Haverim or KIAH), established in Paris in 1860, was the first Jewish association formed with that unifying goal in mind. "Blessed be the Lord who has not forsaken His mercy and His truth and created a wonderful society to bring all of Israel together as friends and allies," wrote Rabbi Yehuda Hai Alkalai, on the occasion of its founding.[7] Alkalai spoke of establishing an "assembly of elders" that would assume the role of Messiah ben Joseph.[8] He was convinced that such an organization would have no trouble obtaining a permit from the Sultan and winning worldwide support for the return of the Jews to their homeland.[9] Alkalai was not alone in believing in Alliance and its ability to unite the Jews. Moses Hess, Rabbi Zvi Hirsch Kalischer and other proto-Zionists also entertained high hopes for the organization. However, Alliance failed to become the vehicle for Jewish solidarity it set out to be. In some countries, the Jews bowed out and established similar local organizations.[10] In the 1880s, after the publication of *Auto-emancipation!* calling upon the Jews of the world to unite as a people, Leon Pinsker urged the Alliance and likeminded groups to convene a "national congress," but again without success.

---

[6] Netanyahu, *Khameshet avot hatzionut*, p. 17.
[7] Alex Bein, "Gilgulay hara'ayon shel hacongress hatzioni," in: *Hacongress ha'olami lemada'ay hayahadut*, no. 1, Jerusalem, 1942.
[8] According to Jewish tradition, Messiah ben Joseph will bring the people of Israel material salvation and lay the groundwork for full spiritual salvation by Messiah ben David.
[9] Bein, *ibid*.
[10] This was the case in London in 1871 and Vienna in 1873. See Bein, *Im herzl ube'ikvotav: Ma'amarim veteudot, Gilgulay hara'ayon shel hacongress hatzion*i, p. 60 (henceforth: Bein, *Im herzl ube'ikvotav*).

According to Alex Bein, the term "national congress" was coined in the late 18th century to denote the supreme representative body of a newly sovereign nation. From the days of America's declaration of independence at the First Continental Congress in Philadelphia to the French Revolution, peoples in the throes of liberation used the term for their foundational assemblies or parliaments. Nations throwing off the yoke of oppression in the 19th century convened national congresses and assemblies that became the cornerstone of their national aspirations and bid for self-definition.[11]

In *Auto-emancipation!* Pinsker defined the Jewish problem thus: "National self-respect! Where can we find it? Our great misfortune is that we do not constitute a nation. We are merely Jews, a flock scattered over the face of the earth..."[12] To promote Jewish unity, Pinsker and Hovevei Zion activists organized the Katowice Conference in November 1884 but little was achieved. The foundations were laid for a modest Hovevei Zion society in Russia, but no one dreamed of a congress, let one alone on a national scale.[13]

In the same way that Pinsker's pamphlet did not have anywhere near the impact of Herzl's *Der Judenstaat*, the Hovevei Zion conferences – the Katowice Conference, followed by the Druskininkai Conference in June 1887 – did not bring the kind of change set in motion by the First Zionist Congress led by Herzl. Pre-Herzlian Zionism was inherently sluggish and slow-moving. Hovevei Zion had a double reason for not daring to broach the subject of a Jewish state: first out of fear of the Turkish authorities, with their zero tolerance for nationalist organizing, and second out of fear of the totalitarian regimes of Eastern Europe, where Zionist activity was outlawed.

Moshe Kleinman, editor of the Zionist Hebrew-language journal *Ha'olam*, cites three factors that were holding Hovevei Zion back:

(a) Nationalist spirit was in a state of paralysis – Yearning for Zion and Zionist action were not coordinated. Immigrating to Palestine was beset by difficulties, the volume of immigration was scarcely more than a trickle and the Yishuv was in economic straits.

(b) Lack of resources – Hovevei Zion suffered from a chronic shortage of funding and could barely support the few who moved to Palestine, let alone masses of immigrants.

---

11 Bein, *ibid.*
12 Y.L. Pinsker, "Autoemancipatzia: Kol koreh el bnei amo," in: *Sefer Pinsker*, Hava'ad leyishuv eretz yisrael be'odesa, Jerusalem 1891, p. 63.
13 Bein, *Im herzl ube'ikvotav*, p. 61.

(c) Lack of political and legal support for Zionist settlement – The Ottoman authorities imposed restrictions on immigration, and those who made it to Palestine had their hands tied by rules and regulations.[14]

From the early 1890s, the situation began to change. During this transitional period between Hovevei Zion and the era of political Zionism various attempts were made to establish a global Zionist organization. Max Bodenheimer, a pioneer of political Zionism in Germany before Herzl, was one of the advocates of such an organization. In 1891, he published an article calling on Zionists everywhere to rally together. Another proponent of Jewish unity was the Young Israel society, founded in Berlin that year. In 1893, Young Israel wrote to Zionist organizations around the world proposing a large-scale gathering of Zionists to define the ultimate goals of political Zionism.[15] That same year, Dr. Nathan Birnbaum, editor of *Selbstemanzipation*, raised the idea of a congress for Zionist youth.[16] In September 1893, Birnbaum held a preliminary meeting at his home in Vienna to make plans. A date was set for the intermediate days of Passover in 1894, but due to "lack of funding, organizational experience and a key person to move the project forward," nothing came of it.[17]

In 1895, the Berlin-based Russian-Jewish Scientific Society (Russisch-Judisch Wissenschaftlicher Verein), a society of Jewish students from eastern and western Europe, among them Joseph Luria and Heinrich Loewe,[18] talked about holding a convention of Zionists from all over Europe. Luria submitted a detailed program incorporating lectures and practical workshops, but again the plans remained on paper.

Herzl reshuffled the cards. Apart from his charismatic personality, he was an excellent organizer. Furthermore, as a man of means, he was able to lay out funds from his own pocket. This oiled the wheels for the First Zionist Congress and successfully set the stage for the congresses to come: Political Zionism changed the game.

Herzl and his out-of-box thinking created a new reality. Up until then, Hovevei Zion had pursued the tactic of slow but steady immigration to Palestine. Through the creation of a solid bloc of Jewish colonies, it was hoped that the Turks would change their minds and accept the idea of Jewish settlement in the region as a solution to the Jewish problem. Herzl's approach was different:

---

14 Moshe Kleinman, "Harishonot heenay ba'oo," in: *Sefer hacongress* (1950).
15 Bein, *Im herzl ube'ikvotav*, p. 61.
16 Like "auto-emancipation," the name means "self-emancipation."
17 Ibid.
18 See more on Luria and Lowe in the biographical index.

He insisted on international recognition of the Jews' right to return to their historic homeland in the framework of a political program. Herzl also lay down the basic premise of a home for the Jews as a global issue: "The Jewish State is a world necessity! That is why it will come into being," he wrote.[19] In keeping with this thinking, he opposed illegal immigration to Palestine and believed that settlement should commence only after the establishment of an internationally recognized state. Herzl, unlike his predecessors, was a proud Jew who openly identified as a representative of his people, without fear or feelings of inferiority.

Herzl breathed new life into the Jewish people. The Zionist congresses, the World Zionist Organization and its administrative institutions, the Zionist activity that commenced in their wake and Herzl's ventures in diplomacy – all these fired up the soul of the Jewish masses. They joined the Zionist movement he led, caught up in his dream of a Jewish homeland that would provide an antidote to their troubles.

Birth of the Congress

Alex Bein cites the publication of Herzl's play *"Das Neue Ghetto"* in November 1894 as the first step on the road to convening a Zionist Congress. Herzl, convinced that the Jewish problem was a world problem, turned to theater as a medium for bringing the topic into the public eye. But since it took years for the play to be staged, it was hardly an effective tactic.[20]

A few months later, Herzl tried to convince Baron Maurice de Hirsch to head the political Zionist movement, organize a world Jewish congress and use his wealth to establish a state that would become a refuge for the Jewish masses. Persuading the Baron to meet him in person was not easy. When Herzl first wrote to him in May 1895, he received a negative reply. Instead, he was asked to submit his plan in writing. Herzl persisted, requesting an audience. He worried that the Baron would dismiss him as just another "schnorrer, "but to his surprise, he received an invitation to the Hirsch's home.[21] The two met in early June 1895 but the meeting did not go well. Herzl was nervous and failed to win the Baron over with his grandiose ideas. Herzl left frustrated, feeling he had not ar-

---

19 *Complete Diaries of Theodor Herzl*, June 15, 1895, vol. 1, p. 171.
20 *Im herzl ube'ikvotav*, p. 62.
21 *Complete Diaries of Theodor Herzl*, May 26, 1895, vol. 1, p. 17.

ticulated his thoughts clearly. In the copious notes he had prepared for himself,[22] Herzl wrote:

> "... if the Jews are to be transformed into men of character in a reasonable period of time, say ten or twenty years, or even forty – the interval needed by Moses – it cannot be done without migration. Who is going to decide whether conditions are bad enough today to warrant our immigration? And whether the situation is hopeless? The Congress which you [i.e. Hirsch] have convened for the first of August in a hotel in Switzerland. You will preside over this Congress of notables. Your call will be heard and answered in every part of the world... All the Jewish communities must send delegates, and they will."[23]

Herzl's plans for a second meeting with Hirsch were cut short by the Baron's death in April 1896. Nevertheless, emerging from the Hirsch encounter with fresh insights, he sat down to pen a letter to Baron Edmond de Rothschild. This letter became the basis for *Der Judenstaat*, which was published in February 1896. Herzl and Rothschild met in July of that year. Herzl proposed that Rothschild head the movement but Rothschild, who did not believe in political Zionism, turned him down. At that point, Herzl reached an inevitable conclusion: Salvation would not come from the rich and affluent but from the masses. In a complete about-face, he stopped appealing to philanthropists and turned to the people. Two days after the Rothschild meeting, he wrote to Jacob de Haas, a journalist in London informing him of "his answer to Rothschild's objection: the organization of our masses, without delay."[24] A week later he wrote to David Wolffsohn in the same vein and began to make plans for a Zionist conference.[25]

Herzl realized that a newspaper would be needed to reach out to the Jews and win support for political Zionism. In early January 1897, he wrote to de Haas about founding a Zionist newspaper as a sounding board for his ideas. On January 26, he wrote to Willy Bambus, a leader of the young Zionists in Berlin, on the importance of spreading the Zionist message and making it part of the public discourse.

Dr. Osaias Thon, one of the founders of Young Israel in Berlin, was aware of Herzl's endeavors. At the beginning of March, when he met with his colleagues in Vienna to discuss the publication of a Zionist daily, the importance of holding a Zionist convention came up again and a date was set for August. While Herzl en-

---

22 These notes were discovered by Bein in the CZA.
23 Bein, *Theodore Herzl: A Biography*, p. 126.
24 *Complete Diaries of Theodor Herzl*, July 20, 1896, vol. 1, pp. 430–431.
25 *Ibid*, vol. 2, p. 447.

visaged a glittering Jewish national assembly, the Berlin Zionists headed by Bambus and Hirsch Hildesheimer were thinking of a modest forum at which the settlement societies would continue to discuss their schemes for Jewish colonization as before.[26] These conflicting views led to a blow-up in which Bambus and Hildesheimer quit the organizing committee in anger. Bambus later changed his mind and attended the first two Zionist congresses (thereafter retiring from Zionist activity), but at the time, he ran to the media, arguing that he had only consented to a "planned assembly devoted to a discussion of the manifold tasks of the Palestine aid project." Herzl, stung by the walk-out, accused the pair of intrigue and undermining the Zionist cause.[27] Pawel describes the conduct of Bambus and Hovevei Zion as a flagrant act of disloyalty:

> "Even more difficult [for Herzl] was the betrayal of Bambus and Hovevei Zion of Berlin, who were sailing in one direction and suddenly changed course in mid-stream. They issued a public denial that they had ever considered attending a Zionist Congress, let alone helping to organize one. In their eagerness to preserve their standing and influence in the deeply conflicted Jewish community, they turned their back on Herzl and added their voice to the opposition..."[28]

In addition to the fierce criticism of Herzlian ideology and political Zionism published in *Jüdische Presse*, Bambus deliberately placed a notice in *Allgemeine Zeitung des Judentums* that undercut and weakened Herzl's call for a Congress.[29] In the footsteps of Bambus, members of British Hovevei Zion also dissociated themselves from the Congress after promising to attend. Herzl was infuriated: "Perfidy on the part of Bambus. Today he informs me that he has sent a correction of my Congress announcement to several Jewish newspapers...Bambus gives as a pretext that the Munich Jews are beside themselves and are protesting against the holding of the Congress in Munich."[30] So once again it was an exchange of letters in the press that ironically helped to create the public visibility that Herzl was so eager for.[31]

Undaunted, Herzl only stepped up his activity. After the activists' convention in Vienna in March, he launched into feverish preparations for the Zionist Congress. He worked around the clock and pushed others to do the same. Herzl's first priority, as we saw in the previous chapter, was to get the newspapers to ad-

---

26 *Im herzl ube'ikvotav*, p. 64.
27 *Complete Diaries of Theodor Herzl*, April 24, 1897, vol 2, p. 538; May 9, 1897, vol. 2, p. 544.
28 Ernst Pawel, *The Labyrinth of Exile: A Life of Theodor Herzl*, Farrar, Straus & Giroux, p. 322.
29 Published in Leipzig and Magdeburg.
30 *Complete Diaries of Theodor Herzl*, ibid.
31 See p. 72, above.

vertise the upcoming event. In March 1897, he wrote an explanatory letter to Jacob de Haas, editor of the London-based paper *The Jewish World*:

> "The purpose of the Congress is to show the world what Zionism is and what it seeks. In particular, the yearning of our masses for the Land of Israel must be conveyed through demonstrations and letters to the government ... The success of the Congress, as you can easily see, is critical for Zionism ..."

In the letter, he outlines the Congress agenda and urges de Haas to make haste and publish the contents without delay:

> "Please send the text in full to the *Jewish Chronicle*, as well as all the newspapers in England and the United States ... For the *Jewish World* I think you should make it the lead story and illuminate the importance of this world gathering."[32]

Herzl worried about a poor showing. He feared that instead of a national assembly, the Congress would turn out to be just another local symposium discussing the plight of the Jews. He wanted it to be a foundational event in Jewish history, and worked on two fronts simultaneously: Jewish and international. On the domestic Jewish front, he sent off countless letters and dispatched emissaries to different communities to spread the word and ensure that respectable delegates would attend. On the international front, his working assumption was that drumming up attention around the world would help convince the Jews to participate. As Yosef Luria tells it:

> "It was necessary to create a sense of confidence and excitement surrounding the Congress. Before it, actions had to be taken that would make the people hopeful and show that the Congress was not just another meeting ... but something great and historic. Therefore Herzl made an effort to communicate with world political leaders ... Herzl traveled to Constantinople ... met with the German emperor, visited Paris and London ..."[33]

As noted, Herzl recruited activists to help him. One of them, Joshua Buchmil, writes how he agreed to go to Russia on behalf of the Actions Committee to solicit participants for the Congress.[34] He offers a detailed account of his journey to Kishinev, Odessa, Kharkov, Bialystok and Yekaterinoslav, where he successfully signed up many delegates.

---

32 *Iggrot* 1, chapter 4, pp. 183–184. Also see the chapter devoted to newspaper coverage, p. 75.
33 Yosef Luria, in: *Sefer hacongress* (1923), p. 26.
34 *Ibid.*, p. 75.

Mordecai Ehrenpreis was at the Hovevei Zion conference in Vienna in March 1897, where he met Herzl for the first time. He came away with vivid memories of the man and his power of attraction:

> "The first impression Herzl made on those who saw him was one of grandeur and strength. There was something prophetic in his gaze, something kingly in his appearance. He seemed to be a rare fusion of dreamer and man of action ... When I returned to my safe haven in Diakovar, I saw one thing clearly in my mind's eye: A new chapter had opened in Jewish history. We, who had the rare good fortune to take part in the preparatory work for the Congress, all distinctly recognized the great responsibility placed on our young shoulders, and at the same time we were grateful for the privilege granted to us to work as hard as we could, shoulder to shoulder with Herzl. That summer was the richest of my life."[35]

As the date of the Congress approached, the need for a newspaper mounted. In June 1897, Herzl founded *Die Welt*, which provided a great boost to preparations for the Congress.[36]

First Zionist Congress: Unity and Adulation

The First Zionist Congress was held as planned in August 1897 and enjoyed overwhelming success. Bein lists three achievements: One, the establishment of the Congress as a permanent organ of the Zionist movement; two, the recognition of the Zionist Organization as a bona fide institution; and three, the acknowledgement of a Jewish state as a political solution.[37] These achievements were the start of a process that continued at subsequent congresses, creating the political Zionist infrastructure which led over time to the Balfour proposal in 1917, the United Nations partition plan in 1947 and the establishment of the State of Israel.

Without detracting from the importance of the accomplishments of the Congress itself, Herzl's success in cultivating unity was the linchpin. " ... We have generated the electric current of our unity and desire to strengthen it more and more," Herzl emphasized. "Nobody has a right to divert or draw off part of this current. It would be treason to the whole."[38] In the *Jewish Chronicle*, he made it clear: "We are a people – one people."[39] This became the rallying cry

---

35 *Bein mizrakh lama'arav*, pp. 71–72.
36 On the importance of the press, see pp. 90–92 above.
37 *Im herzl ube'ikvotav*, p. 67.
38 *Sefer hacongress* (1923), p.VIII (Third Congress address, August 15, 1899).
39 First used in the introduction to *Der Judenstaat* (*The Jewish State*, American Zionist Emergency Council, 1946, p. 76)

for Jews everywhere to unite around the political Zionist cause. While Herzl may have thought that the challenges he faced in the early days were external, i.e., convincing the world of the need to solve the Jewish problem,[40] he soon realized that the Jews were not a uniform bloc and he would have to work hard to assemble them under one banner. At the First Zionist Congress, Herzl made it happen. Most of the delegates enthusiastically supported the Basel program and joined in the call for a Jewish state. There was hardly anyone who was not swept up in the excitement. Herzl was justified in feeling as he did after the Congress closed its doors:

> "Were I to sum up the Basel Congress in a word – which I shall guard against pronouncing publicly – it would be this: At Basel I founded the Jewish State. If I said this out loud today, I would be answered by universal laughter. Perhaps in five years, and certainly in fifty, everyone will know it."[41]

This was not empty rhetoric, judging by his explanation of the sense of togetherness he forged at the Congress:

> "The foundation of a State lies in the will of the people for a State ... Territory is only the material basis; the State, even when it possesses territory is always something abstract. The Church State exists even without it; otherwise the Pope would not be sovereign. At Basel, then, I created this abstraction which, as such, is invisible to the vast majority of people. And with infinitesimal means, I gradually worked the people into the mood for a State and made them feel that they were its National Assembly."[42]

A week later, Herzl goes deeper into this aspect of the Congress:

> "Here is the greatest outcome of the Congress: It showed that the Jewish national idea possesses the unifying power to weld people with linguistic, social, political and religious differences into one unified whole. This was vigorously denied until now, but proven at Basel most spectacularly. The raucous political debates that arose everywhere else fell silent at the first assembly of the people. The brothers found each other."[43]

How did Herzl break away from the small-scale leaders' convention mold of Hovevei Zion and organize a congress that became the parliament of a global political movement and went on to dramatically alter Jewish history? It was not by chance. Herzl understood the magnitude of the mission and threw himself

---

40 As Ussishkin was convinced in their first meeting. See *Sefer Ussishkin*, p. 353.
41 *Complete Diaries of Theodor Herzl*, September 3, 1897, vol.2, p. 581.
42 Ibid.
43 Herzl, in: *Die Welt*, September 10, 1897.

into it, body and soul. Without painstaking preparation, he knew the Congress would not achieve its goal. Towards this end, he harnessed all his talent, energy and financial resources to transform it into a foundational event. Herzl cast himself as banker, organizer, scriptwriter and lead actor in the dramatic production of his life, more ambitious by far than anything he had written for the stage. He starred in the show five more times. The Sixth Zionist Congress in 1903 was his curtain call. He died the following year.

In preparing for the Congress, Herzl worked around the clock to eliminate any hitch that could detract from the atmosphere or derail its success. The writer Mordechai Ben-Ami (Rabinovich) describes Herzl's efforts:

> "From the first minute of his arrival in Basel, Herzl completely, with every fiber of his being, acted in the interests of the congress. The rest of the world, for him, literally disappeared. He was involved in even the smallest details, he followed preparations with a keen eye, without letting anything escape his attention, anticipating everything ...
>
> From the first moment in Basel, Herzl displayed greater confidence than in Vienna, and there was not a word more about doubts. The Rubicon had been crossed, and it was time to boldly move forward. This manifested itself in everything that he did and everything he said to me. Nevertheless, in all of the days leading up to the congress he no doubt felt himself on the verge of a decisive struggle and experienced powerful internal anxieties ... I was with him for nearly the entire time, and with every passing day, with every passing hour, he became nearer and dearer to me ... And the closer I got to him, the more his extraordinary, complicated nature revealed itself. And with every hour I could see more and more how deeply engaged he was with his idea and how he gave himself over to it entirely, without thinking of anything else. I had not previously encountered such selfless dedication even among the most ardent of our Hovevei Zion... Such total disregard of self in the service of an idea amazed me."[44]

Ben-Ami's story about choosing the hall for the Congress is an example:

> "On the bridge I ran into David Farbstein whom I had already met in Zurich. He asked me to go with him to look at the hall he had rented for the congress... I went with him. To get to the hall, one had to cross a small garden and make it through rows of small tables where the good residents of Basel drank beer. The room turned out to be quite gloomy and unfriendly, and it smelled like a cheap saloon. This was the Burgvogtei, so well-known to us, and which I do not wish to insult, since we would subsequently spend so many joyous and happy hours there. I spoke decisively against it. But Farbstein maintained that there were no other appropriate quarters, with the exception of one other place, which would require an enormous sum of money. I could not counter this logic, and the hall was rented."[45]

---

[44] Ben Ami, in: *Sefer hacongress* (1950), p. 123. (quoted in: *East European Jews in Switzerland*, eds. Tamar Lewinsky and Sandrine Mayorez, 2013, Ben Ami: Herzl and the First Congress, pp. 240–243).

[45] *Ibid*, p. 121.

But then Herzl arrived and changed the venue. Herzl himself describes the incident:

> "Congress days! Upon my arrival the day before yesterday I went right to the office which the City of Basel has placed at our disposal. It is a vacant tailor's shop. I am having the name of the firm covered with a cloth, in order to forestall any bad jokes. Similarly, in the matter of a hall I am concerned about our not looking ridiculous. Dr. Farbstein of Zurich has hired the Burgvogtei, a large but unsuitable place with a music-hall stage. I asked for suggestions as to how we could make the backdrop for the *saltimbanques* [tumblers] disappear, but ended up by hiring different and more dignified quarters ... "[46]

The hall that was finally hired was the municipal concert hall in Basel, which was considered one of the finest acoustic halls in Europe. Herzl invested much thought in how to create a lofty and festive atmosphere. As he relates after the Congress:

> "One of my first practical ideas, months ago, was that people should be made to attend the opening session in tails and white tie. This worked out splendidly. Formal dress makes most people stiff. This stiffness immediately gave rise to a sedate tone – one which they might not have had in light-colored summer suits or travel clothes – and I did not fail to heighten this tone to the point of solemnity."[47]

Herzl goes on to describe his efforts to persuade Nordau to comply with the dress code he had set:

> "Nordau had turned up on the first day in a frock coat and flatly refused to go home and change to a full-dress suit. I drew him aside and begged him to do it as a favor to me. I told him: today the presidium of the Zionist Congress is nothing at all, we still have to establish everything. People should get used to seeing the Congress as a most exalted and solemn thing. He allowed himself to be persuaded, and in return I hugged him gratefully. A quarter of an hour later he returned in formal dress."[48]

During the Congress itself, Herzl also worked tirelessly to preserve the atmosphere. In his diary, he wrote of the troubles he experienced, the mistakes he made and the huge effort involved in running the event:

> "On the first day I made a number of mistakes; by the second, according to the consensus, I had already become fully equal to the situation ... Everything rested on my shoulders; and this is not just something I am telling myself, for it was proved when on the afternoon of the

---

46 *Complete Diaries of Theodor Herzl*, August 27, 1897, vol. 2, p. 579.
47 Ibid., September 3, 1897, p. 581.
48 Ibid.

third day I left because of fatigue and turned the chairmanship over to Nordau. Then everything was helter-skelter, and I was told afterwards that it was pandemonium. Even before I took the chair, things didn't click."[49]

Indeed, there are many testimonies about the challenges Herzl faced in his attempt to run the Congress in an orderly fashion. For the East European delegates, following the rigid and pedantic rules was difficult, but Herzl's leadership qualities stood him in good stead, and the attendees complied with his requests. He was acknowledged by one and all as a responsible leader. As Max Bodenheimer notes: "Herzl's regal appearance and his opening speech, so impressive and full of wisdom, were a clear mark of his leadership."[50]

Avraham Ludwipol[51] writes about how this impacted on the tense relationship between the East European and West European Jews:

"'Our Western brethren bring with them order, which we, the Jews of Russia, lack,' one of the delegates told me, and his words rang very true ... On Saturday there were four or five meetings, but only one of them was orderly – the one chaired by Herzl. In the morning there was a meeting ... but it ended like all our meetings in Russia. Forgive me for saying this, but I shall say it nonetheless. It began with a quarrel and it concluded ... without achieving a thing ... The last pre-Congress session was held that evening. While the delegates from Russia fought with the political Zionists at these other meetings, in the presence of the progenitor of the Congress, they gave in without a murmur."[52]

Sammy Gronemann also portrayed the East European delegates as having no parliamentary experience. He has this to say about Dr. Lippe, who had been invited to speak as the oldest delegate: "They say that he stood at the train station for days, asking every elderly man arriving for the Congress when he was born, and upon hearing the answer he would add another year to his own age." He offers another anecdote about Dr. Menachem Mendel Sheinkin:

"Typical is the confirmed story about Sheinkin, an old fighter for Zionism from Russia who knew nothing about parliamentary customs and the function of the bell. Sheinkin was amazed by this strange manner of debate in which speakers spoke one after the other, and not all together. He quickly snatched the president's magic tool. Now, when he wanted to make his voice heard, he could do something. The next day, in the middle of someone's speech, he suddenly got up and rang his bell. Dr. Herzl was taken aback: 'Mr. Sheinkin, what is that bell? Get rid of it.' Sheinkin coolly and calmly replied: 'But you have a bell, too, Mr. President." Marmorek the famous bacteriologist, jumped on Sheinkin and grabbed hold of the bell, but Sheinkin resisted, shouting 'this bell is the property of the hotel.'"[53]

---

49 *Ibid*, September 3, 1897, pp. 581–584
50 *Sefer hacongress* (1950), p. 92.
51 A Zionist activist and journalist who wrote for *Hamelitz, Hatzfira, Hashiloah* and *Die Welt*.
52 Avraham Ludwipol, in: Luah Ahiasaf, 1903, pp. 56, 60.
53 *Zikhronot shel yekke*, p. 124.

Herzl the dramatist thus succeeded in pulling off a congress that was attested to by its participants as a formative event in the history of the Jewish people. For the first time since the destruction of the Second Temple, Jews from around the world came together to celebrate their national identity. Herzl's labors created the Congress, and the Congress was his reward. It is hard to overstate the contribution of the Congress, the atmosphere it generated and the way Herzl conducted it, to Herzl's image in the eyes of those in attendance.

The young Zionist leader Leo Motzkin was one of the delegates who was won over. "It was only at the First Congress that Motzkin became a steadfast follower of Herzl," writes Bein.[54] Years later, Motzkin remembers how the crowd went wild for Herzl, basically diverting attention from Nordau, who had spoken eloquently at the Congress and was then at the height of his world fame:

> "Nevertheless, it was plain throughout the Congress that the soul of the Zionist movement was not the brilliant speaker [Nordau] but the dreamer who had been nothing to us only two years earlier. His youthful vigor, his amazing flexibility, his ability to adapt to surroundings that were strange to him in many respects, his skill in calming the huge storms that erupted every moment at the Congress ... All of this made it absolutely clear that he wanted to be, and would be, the leader."[55]

The tremendous impression of the First Congress stayed with Motzkin for years to come. Addressing the Seventeenth Congress in 1931, he said: "How can I stand here without recalling Herzl on the Congress podium, noble and majestic, facing a billowing sea of love and admiration, looking out from on high at the ecstatic audience wildly applauding without stop."[56]

The extent to which the special atmosphere of the Congress contributed to Herzl's stature can be seen from the testimonies below. Ben-Ami writes about how different Herzl looked from the first time they met at the hotel in Basel:

> "Herzl slowly walks up to the rostrum. I stare at him intently. But what is this? This is not the same Herzl whom I had seen to this point, whom I had just seen late the previous evening. Before us there appeared a wondrous, splendid, regal figure, with a deep, distinguished and focused look, proud yet tinged with sorrow. This was no longer the elegant Herzl from Vienna, but a regal descendant of David, suddenly arisen from the grave, appearing before us in all his legendary grandeur and fantastical beauty. The entire audience was overcome with amazement, as though a historic miracle had occurred in front of our eyes. And was it not truly a miracle that had taken place?...In the next few minutes every-

---

54 See Alex Bein's introduction, in: Alex Bein (ed), *Sefer Motzkin*, Zionist Executive Publishing, Jerusalem, 1939, p. 51.
55 *Sefer hacongress* (1923), p. 49.
56 Joseph Heftman, *Herzl bekhazon hador*, p. 58.

thing shakes from enthusiastic cheers, exclamations, applause, and stomping. It seems that the great 2,000-year old dream of our people had come true, that before us stands the Messiah of the House of David."[57]

Looking back on his experience, Reuben Brainin, later Herzl's first biographer, writes:

"The First Zionist Congress in Basel! Simple but superb, modest yet oh so festive. Herzl was there, Herzl the magician, creator of the Congress, a symbol of awakening power, a core of growing strength. He was more than a leader, more than a prophet, more than a politician – even more than a creator. He was the nation itself, with his beauty and dignity, all that was good in us, past present and future – a synthesis of our honorable past and our future glory, a symbol of the eternity of his people."[58]

The jubilant atmosphere of the Congress reached a peak at the closing ceremony. Ehrenpreis recalls the moment:

"Late at night on the third day of Congress, Herzl ascended the podium for the closing session. The excitement that gripped the crowd was beyond description. The entire audience rose to its feet as one, breaking into cheers. A wave of hope and faith swept over all, eyes welled up with tears of joy, people hugged and embraced."[59]

Yosef Luria was another witness:

"Herzl delivered the closing address. He spoke in a sad tone, as he always did at moments of profound emotion, but his manner of speaking was so heartfelt and moving to the core. Herzl's final remarks were simple, without rhetorical flourishes, hyperbole or shrillness, but they were infused with recognition of the tremendous value of the thing he had created. The entire audience shared his feeling that something grand had occurred in the life of the Jewish people, and recognizing this historic moment in all its splendor kindled boundless enthusiasm. The last moments of the Congress restored to him the majesty of the first day. The delegates were loath to leave the hall and say farewell. For three days they had lived the illusion of a Jewish parliament. It had been such a glamorous event, such a celebration, and Herzl had captivated them all. The people had found their great leader!"[60]

Herzl thus succeeded in making his vision of the Congress come true and moving forward on his Zionist journey. Apart from the emotional impact of the Congress that comes through in these testimonies, the gathering also had a practical re-

---

[57] Sefer hacongress (1923), p. 141
[58] Reuben Brainin, in: *Sefer hacongress* (1950), p. 126.
[59] *Bein mizrakh uma'arav*, p. 75.
[60] Yosef Luria, in: *Sefer hacongress* (1950), pp. 161–162.

sult. Many of the leaders and opinion makers who came to Congress as skeptics became believers and joined Herzl from then on.[61]

Herzl's Status in Subsequent Congresses

The First Zionist Congress inspired much hope and expectation. Herzl sought to preserve the excitement of the Congress and keep up the momentum even when he had no sensational news to report. Towards this end, he turned the Zionist Congress into an annual summer event. At the Second Zionist Congress in 1898, again held in Basel, no one was deterred by the fact that Herzl's political endeavors had not yet produced results. At this Congress, Herzl announced his "conquest of the communities" program and the establishment of a Jewish colonial bank, and resolutions were adopted on agricultural settlement and the question of culture.[62] Even the pessimistic Ahad Ha'am, who took a dim view of political Zionism, set aside his objections this time and applauded these resolutions, which enjoyed wide support among the Congress participants.[63]

However, the enthusiasm of the First and Second Congresses was gradually tempered by disappointment when no visible progress was registered on the political level by the time the Third Congress opened in 1899. With a Jewish state not yet on the horizon, an opposition camp began to form. Among its members were leading Russian Zionists. Leo Motzkin complained about the "dictatorial ways" of the Zionist movement and inveighed against the false hopes Herzl had planted in October 1898 when he intimated to the Jews of London that "we are soon to receive the Land of Israel for a return en masse to Zion."[64] Yet with all their grievances, the Russian Zionists remained firmly pro-Herzl. This is borne out by their remarks at a luncheon in his honor after the Congress: "The speeches delivered by the hosts revealed the tremendous love and admiration of the Russian Zionists for the great leader of the Zionist movement."[65] This admiration did not keep them from being skeptical about the feasibility of a

---

[61] Among them, *Hatzfira* editor Nahum Sokolow (see pp. 179–180), and mathematics professor Zvi Hermann Schapira (see p. 197).
[62] "Conquest of the communities" was a program to cultivate Zionist activism among the Jewish leadership and local communities.
[63] Yitzhak Maor, *Hatnu'a hatzionit berussia*, Magnes and Hasifriya Hatzionit, Jerusalem 1986, p. 160.
[64] See pp. 134–135.
[65] Maor, *Hatn'ua hatzionit*, p. 177.

fourth Congress, but once it was announced, their objections melted away. As Nahum Slouschz put it:

> "There have been no harder times for contemporary Jewry than this last year, with troubles of all kinds from expulsion from Romania to famine in the steppes of Russia...All our hopes and trust in the integrity of the human heart and the victory of truth and justice have come to naught... In these times of distress ... the disheartened workers have despaired of reviving the nation and preparing for a more secure future in Zion, and the grand hopes that rang forth on the podium of the First and Second Congress have been stifled by bitterness and profound despair. Belief in the future of our people and the victory of the Zionist ideal as a wondrous cure has also declined ... Spirits are so low that even in the staunchest Zionist camp, we have spent long hours sitting and discussing whether it is worth holding a congress this year ... And as we were deliberating about this and that, a rumor comes from Vienna that our Zionist leaders have decided to convene a national assembly in London, the capital of the world. With the magic word 'congress ...' the slumbering Zionist societies have sprung to life, and the camp is all abustle, as attempts are made to boost the number of shekel-payers ... Every astute Zionist knows that this time, just as last time, the success of the Congress as a major national assembly is of tremendous significance, no less so than practical work."[66]

In the end, the Fourth Congress opened in London in the summer of 1900. Some Russian Zionists were dissatisfied with the gathering, which they felt was basically for show. With a political solution not yet in sight, they demanded that practical work in Palestine begin before the establishment of a state. At the same time, they insisted that the Congress should address matters of culture (see Chapter 8), to which Herzl was opposed.

Out of this clash of wills emerged an opposition camp, the Democratic Fraction, which had 37 members, mostly young Russians studying at universities in Western Europe.[67] Even in the face of rising opposition, however, Herzl managed to preserve the special atmosphere that characterized the First Congress. Indeed, one could say that all the congresses presided over by Herzl were filled with energy and excitement. One exception, perhaps, was the session on the third day of the Sixth Zionist Congress, which we will elaborate upon later.[68] While some delegates who had been at the first congresses may not have experienced the same exhilaration they felt at those earlier events, the thrill never faded entirely.

This emotional response to Herzl and his organizational endeavors did not end with the First Congress. Chaim Weizmann commented that seeing Herzl in person at the Second Congress – Weizmann's first – was unforgettable: "He emit-

---

[66] *Protocols of the Fourth Zionist Congress*, pp. 3–4.
[67] Maor, *Hatn'ua hatzionit*, p. 190. See pp. 222–225.
[68] See p. 255.

ted a kind of radioactive Zionism (radium had not yet been discovered at the time) that electrified those around him and aroused them to action. He had all the qualities that led us to admire him." In this case, however, Weizmann seems to be expressing the sentiments of those around him. Later, he confesses that Herzl was impressive, but "I cannot pretend that I was swept off my feet."[69]

In his book *Or khadash al tzion ta'ir*, Rabbi Yitzhak Yaacov Reines, whose participation in such events began with the Third Congress in Basel, described it as a "spiritual awakening" and a "spectacle wreathed in sanctity." Since hearing could not compare with seeing, he explained, he was doubtful that words alone could convey the splendor and gloriousness of the event and how tremendously it impressed him.[70]

Shmaryahu Levin, attending the Fourth Congress in London, remarked on the linguistic difficulties of the delegates, who were accustomed to meeting in Basel and speaking German:

> "Nevertheless, the Congress profoundly impressed even sideline observers. Firstly, they stood in awe of the prodigious talents of the leader who brought delegates scattered all over the Diaspora to the political hub of the world, imposing upon them order and discipline of which any parliament would be proud ... The Congress left a deep and decisive mark on me. Spellbinding. The presidium on the dais and the regal figure of Herzl conjured up images in my mind of the Sanhedrin and the Great Assembly. For a moment, I forgot our troubles in the world – a nation without a homeland, without refuge or shelter."[71]

Sammy Gronemann, who was at the Fifth Congress, offers further testimony:

> "I sat quietly in one of the back rows, my heart pounding at the sight of the hall and galleries, full to capacity. It was the very picture of a Jewish parliament, not some ordinary gathering...The air was thick with excitement and I was caught up in it. All eyes shone with joy and anticipation."[72]

At the Sixth Congress, Ze'ev Jabotinsky, who had never been to a Zionist congress before, came away mesmerized by Herzl and the whole event:

---

69 Chaim Weizmann, *Trial and Error: The Autobiography of Chaim Weizmann*, Harper & Brothers, New York, p. 44.
70 Yitzhak Yaacov Reines, *Or khadash al tzion*, Possy Shoulson Press, New York, 1946, p. 260. See also: Ge'ulah Bat Yehudah, *Ish hame'orot: Rabbi Yitzhak Yaacov Reines*, Mosad Harav Kook, Jerusalem, 1985, p. 105 (henceforth: *Ish hame'orot*). Rabbi Reines (1839–1915), one of the leading Torah scholars of Lithuania and the founder of the Mizrahi movement, was a supporter of the Uganda program, as we shall see later.
71 Levin, *Bama'arakha*, p. 201.
72 *Zikhronotav shel yekke*, p. 186.

"Herzl made a colossal impression on me, and the word is no exaggeration. There is no other description that fits: Colossal. And I do not easily bow to others. In my whole life, I cannot remember anyone for whom I felt such awe – not before Herzl, nor after. Only in this instance did I feel that I truly stood before a man chosen by fate, before a prophet and a leader par excellence who was worth following come what may. To this day, I can hear his oath echoing in my ears: 'If I forget thee, O Jerusalem …' I believed him. Everyone believed him. And curiously, following the vote, I felt the Congress soar to new and unprecedented heights."[73]

Some people were not swept up immediately but joined the chorus over time. One was rabbi and professor David Neumark. At first he was not a fan of Herzl. He did not like Herzl's looks or the way he ran the First Congress. From the Second Congress, however, he underwent a change of heart:

"Of all the memories that have remained with me from the days of the First and Second Congresses, the most deeply etched in my heart is being a witness to the greatness of Herzl and how he developed, and I am not speaking about internal but external development … Even those who opposed him at first, totally or in part, came to recognize his greatness … I remember how hard it was for me to accept Herzl's authority and to fathom that here was a man who would play an exceptional role in the history of Israel…In my heart, I brushed him off. While everyone admired and looked up to him as an angel of God, and excitedly rose to their feet in his presence, my heart was cold. The shape of his face and his thick beard which everyone saw as a mark of royalty reminded me of the stereotype familiar to Austrians from time immemorial: the travelling salesman … I left the First Congress a heretic … Herzl made no impression on me … This was the image of Herzl I carried with me when I came to the Second Congress. When I went to greet him, I still had that vivid picture of a door-to-door salesman in my mind. But how different he was when I actually saw him! I could not believe my eyes. Here was the same person, the very same beard and mustache, but how changed! From a merchant he had become a glorious king. Every word he uttered, even if I disagreed with him, impressed me deeply. I saw a great man rising from the ranks of the ordinary, climbing up the mountain step by step to reach the heights of history. From one session to the next, Herzl revealed a new face."[74]

---

73 Ze'ev Jabotinsky (1880–1940), founder of Revisionist Zionism and among the foremost liberal thinkers of modern times. See Ze'ev Jabotinsky, *Ktavim: Autobiografia*, Vol. 1, Eri Jabotinsky, Jerusalem 1947, pp. 49–50. According to his biographer Shmuel Katz, Jabotinsky was not only awestruck by Herzl but grasped the deeper meaning of the controversies that raged at the Congress. He believes those days in Basel tipped the scales for Jabotinsky. See *Shmuel Katz, Jabo*, Dvir, Tel Aviv 1993, p. 41.
74 Sefer hacongress (*1923*), pp. 113–115.

Neumark emphasizes that he did not agree with Herzl on many issues and was not happy with the manner in which the congress was run, which he felt violated standard parliamentary procedure. And yet:

> "the more I oppose him, the more that traveling salesman hides, receding into the background and fading away. Behind my façade of attempting to be realistic, I want to hold him there with all my might. I want to see Herzl again as the stereotypical West Austrian salesman. I feel I need this stereotype which is expiring before my very eyes, this ridiculous stock character that lies dead in front of me. I need him to save my soul, which does not and cannot agree to accept the authority of this … I wish I could revive him but my labors are in vain: A prince stands before me. Herzl's countenance radiates beauty and splendor … Again I observe his eyes and face. I am forced to look at them, and almost regretfully I am awed by those eyes as they dream a sublime dream laden with magic and charm, a transformational dream, the dream of a new history. Little by little, against my will and my inner reason, I begin to shed my intransigence. It is true. I began to feel a clear sense that I was witness to the creation of something new, to the birth of a historic figure. My mind is obstinate! I have some serious issues with history and I have evidence that history is blind and perverse. It chooses inappropriate materials for its creations, and insists on doing things its own way. It chose Herzl and fashioned from him a new creature before my very eyes … It grabbed me and forced me to accept the leadership of this merchant. It was a kind of reincarnation… I left the Second Congress in a state of delight mixed with sorrow. I took pleasure in watching history be born, but lamented the loss of my freedom … I was an eyewitness to a new historical construct, globally significant and historic in stature. I rejoice for that opportunity."[75]

An exception to the rule was Ahad Ha'am, who was not smitten by Herzl and remained an unrelenting opponent. At the First Congress, he says he sat there like "a mourner at a wedding feast." But even Ahad Ha'am, who rejected Herzl and political Zionism, appreciated the importance of the Congress for "enhancing the prestige of Jewish nationalism in the eyes of the nations." Ahad Ha'am wrote:

> "The 'Congress of the Zionists,' the battle over which has filled the emptiness of our little world in recent months, has come and gone. Some 200 Jews from every country and every party convened in Basel, who for three days deliberated in public under the gaze of the whole world, on the establishment of a genuine home for people of Israel in the land of their forefathers. In so doing, the national solution for the Jewish question burst the barriers of modesty and entered the public domain, laid bare before the world, in language that was loud and clear, head held high. Never since the exile of the Jews from their land has such a thing been seen."[76]

---

75 Ibid.
76 *Kol kitvei ahad ha'am*, p. 275

From the First Congress, Herzl's political path gradually became clearer and his Basel program began to take off. The Congress was his launch pad. He succeeded in infusing the event with a halo of sanctity, laying the groundwork for a process that culminated in the establishment of a Jewish state. From the standing he achieved there, Herzl moved on to legendary heights. As Reuben Brainin attested:

> "Herzl attained full stature only after his arrival in Basel. Our love for him, our enthusiasm, our hunger for beauty, our yearning for deliverance and salvation – all this came together in Herzl, opening within him secret wellsprings of heroism and faith. At the first Zionist Congress in Basel, Herzl discovered us and he discovered himself. In this atmosphere suffused with love and enthusiasm, he became superhuman and he appeared to us in all his power and glory. We were as dreamers, and he, Herzl, was the greatest dreamer of them all."[77]

Herzl thus accomplished the impossible. If a "Jewish state" was the cornerstone of the Zionist journey, the Congress was a promising marker for the future of Zionist activity. At the end of October 1898, he began to see success. The German Kaiser Wilhelm II invited him to Palestine to grant him the sought-after charter.[78] In the end, it did not happen. Herzl and his entourage returned disappointed to Europe without a charter in hand. However, the journey to Palestine showed that the power of Herzl's charisma also reached across the sea. Many who had heard of him only from afar eagerly met with him, and even ideological foes became admirers. As we shall see in the coming chapter, Herzl was shown great respect by most of the population sectors in Palestine and esteem for him grew by leaps and bounds.

The background for the trip, the trip itself, and its impact and consequences are the subject of the next chapter.

---

[77] *Sefer hacongress* (1950), p. 126.
[78] See pp. 127–140.

Chapter 5
Herzl in Palestine

> On November 2, 1898, a Zionist delegation headed by Herzl was received by the German emperor in Jerusalem; on November 2, 1917, the Balfour Declaration was granted to the people of Israel.[1]

As soon as the Second Zionist Congress was over, Herzl packed his bags and headed for Palestine at the invitation of the German Kaiser, Wilhelm II. One would have hardly expected Herzl to be a welcome guest there. A warm reception by the Turks was also unlikely considering the brutal suppression of nationalism throughout the Ottoman Empire, and certainly the Arab populace had no reason to rejoice.[2] The Orthodox Jews in Palestine loathed Herzl as much as their peers in Europe. Even non-religious Jews were understandably wary in light of the Turkish ban on nationalist organizing and the policy of Baron Rothschild's administrators, who took a dim view of political Zionism.

One would think Herzl would be met with coldness and even hostility. In reality, however, he was greeted with an outpouring of good will. Wherever he turned, he was showered with honor and respect, regardless of the risk. In Palestine, as in Europe, Herzl was hailed as a charismatic leader and his personal magnetism left no one indifferent.

What was the purpose of Herzl's trip?

Background and Objectives

Looking for a way to persuade Sultan Abdul Hamid II to grant him a charter for the establishment of a Jewish state in Palestine, Herzl came up with the idea of approaching the German Kaiser, Wilhelm II, who was an influential ally of the Ottoman Empire at the time. Herzl spoke about it for the first time at his meeting with Baron Hirsch on June 2, 1895. In his diary, he outlines the plan:

---

1 Oskar Rabinowicz, *Fifty Years of Zionism: A Historical Analysis of Dr. Weizmann's 'Trial and Error,'* London, Robert Anscombe & Co., 1950, p. 165.
2 In early 1899, Yussuf Zia al-Khalidi, the Arab mayor of Jerusalem, wrote to the Grand Rabbi of Paris, Zadoc Kahn, expressing worry over Herzl's intentions. Rabbi Kahn delivered the letter to Herzl, and Herzl sent al-Khalidi a reply in March 1899. Pawel, *Labyrinth*, p. 406.

> "I shall go to the German Kaiser; he will understand me ... To the Kaiser I shall say: Let our people go! We are strangers here; we are not permitted to assimilate with the people.[3] First I shall negotiate with the Czar ... regarding permission for the Russian Jews to leave the country ... Then I shall negotiate with the German Kaiser."[4]

Three years later, in October 1898, Herzl was invited to meet the Kaiser in Palestine where he was expected to announce his patronage of Jewish settlement with the blessing of the Turkish sultan. On the following pages we will explore the factors leading up to this invitation and what lay behind the German emperor's willingness to play a pivotal role in furthering the cause of Zionism.

The Kaiser was never a Jew-lover, so it is doubtful he was motivated by any real desire to help them. A more realistic possibility was that he relished the idea of getting rid of them. Writing to his uncle, the Grand Duke of Baden, on September 1898, he took a positive view of Jewish emigration to Palestine, but his anti-Semitic prejudices are documented clearly:

> "In addition, the energy, and the creative powers and abilities of the tribe of Shem would be directed to more dignified purposes that the exploitation of Christians ... I know very well that nine-tenths of all Germans will be deeply shocked ... that I sympathize with the Zionists or even that I place them under my protection when they appeal to me. Nevertheless, I make note of the fact that the Jews killed the Redeemer."[5]

When the German envoy in Switzerland, submitting his report on the First Zionist Congress, predicted that the Jews would take over Palestine after the fall of the Ottoman Empire, the Kaiser responded: "Let the *Mauschels* go to Palestine, the sooner they move off the better."[6] Other considerations may have come into play as well, such as an opportunity to hasten Christian salvation through the return of the Jews to the Promised Land.[7] Perhaps he wanted to be remembered as a modern-day Cyrus the Great. Politics were part of the equation, too. If the Turks agreed to the settlement of Jews in Palestine under the protection of the Kaiser, it would serve German national interests by strengthening Germany's strategic position as a gateway to the East and boosting its competitive edge over

---

3 *Complete Diaries of Theodor Herzl*, May 26, 1895, vol. 1, p. 23.
4 *Ibid.*, June 9, 1895, p. 52.
5 Michael Margalit, *Hakhozeh vehakeysar*, Beit El-Ram Foundation, Department of the History of the Jewish People, Tel Aviv University, Tel Aviv 2007, pp. 106–107 (henceforth: Margalit, *Hakhozeh vehakeysar*); Isaiah Friedman, *Germany, Turkey and Zionism: 1897–1918*, p. 66, Oxford University Press, 1977, pp. (henceforth: Friedman, *Germany, Turkey and Zionism*).
6 Friedman, *Germany, Turkey and Zionism*, p. 59.
7 According to Christianity, true salvation can only be achieved after the Jews return to the Land of Israel and accept Jesus.

the French and British who were vying for regional influence. In addition, Jewish businessmen were leading exporters of German consumer goods. Based on what he heard from his envoy in Turkey, the Kaiser was under the impression that the Turks would not object to him acting as the patron of the Jews and would be prepared to grant the charter they sought.

However, none of this would have been enough to convince the Kaiser if not for the contacts of his uncle, the Grand Duke, with Reverend William Hechler, a representative of the Anglican church in Vienna. Hechler was an eschatologist whose Bible-based astronomy calculations, which he reached long before the publication of *Der Judenstaat*, predicted the onset of the messianic era in 1897.[8] When the journalist Saul Raphael Landau told him about Herzl's book, Hechler took it as a sign from heaven: Herzl was the man who would usher in the coming of the Messiah and advance the messianic cause. Hechler hastened to offer Herzl his help in winning the ear of the Kaiser through his personal acquaintance with the Grand Duke, whom he knew well as a former tutor of the Duke's children. He had already spoken to the Grand Duke about a Jewish return to Palestine back then.

Hechler first visited Herzl in March 1896. Herzl wrote about it in his diary: "The Rev. William H. Hechler, chaplain to the British Embassy in Vienna, called on me. A likeable, sensitive man with the long grey beard of a prophet. He waxed enthusiastic over my solution ... He wants to place my tract in the hands of some German princes. He used to be a tutor in the household of the Grand Duke of Baden, he knows the German Kaiser and thinks he can get me an audience."[9]

Herzl was not sure what to make of Hechler, worried at first that the Germans were making fun of him. However, he soon set his fears aside and went to see Hechler at home, to find out more about the man and see how he could make use of his connections. Herzl describes the visit: "Even while I was going up the stairs I heard the sound of an organ. The room which I entered was lined with books on every side, floor to ceiling. Nothing but Bibles ... Then he spread out before me his [astronomic charts], and finally a map of Palestine. It is a large military staff map in four sheets which, when laid out, covered the entire floor ... He showed me where, according to his calculations, our new Temple must be located ... 'We have prepared the ground for you.'"[10]

---

8 Hannah Bodenheimer, *Hatzionim vegermania hakeysarit*, Jerusalem, Kiryat Sefer, 1980, pp. 63–64 (henceforth: Bodenheimer, *Hatzionim*).
9 *Complete Diaries of Theodor Herzl*, March 10, 1896, vol. 1, p. 310.
10 Ibid., March 16, 1896, pp. 311–312.

While it appears from Herzl's diary that the "groundwork" done by Hechler was planning where the Temple would be rebuilt, according to documents published by Bette and Hermann Ellerin,[11] Hechler was actually referring to a letter he had sent to the Grand Duke a few days after his first meeting with Herzl. It was an eight-page letter that begins by drawing the Duke's attention to:

> "an important book recently published in Vienna. The book is devoted to a topic that I have had the privilege of discussing with you many times, namely the restoration of the Jews to Palestine as proclaimed by the Jewish prophets ... To me it appears that the return of the Jews would be a blessing for Europe ... I am sending Your Excellency three copies of this book."[12]

Hechler went on to reveal the calculations on which he based his belief that the messianic age and the return of the Jews to the Promised Land was near, and cited the benefits that Germany and England would reap if they took the Zionist movement and future state under their wing and proclaimed Palestine neutral territory. In other words, Hechler had "prepared the ground" not only in determining the site of the future Temple. In a letter dated March 26, 1896, Hechler links Herzl and his vision of a Jewish state to his earlier talks with the Grand Duke during his days in Karlsruhe.[13]

> "I told him: I have got to establish direct contact, a contact that is discernible on the outside, with a responsible or non-responsible statesman – that is, with a minister of state or a prince. Then the Jews will believe in me, then they will follow me. The most suitable man would be the German Kaiser. I must be given help if I am to carry out the task. Up to now I have had nothing but obstacles to combat, and they have been sapping my strength."[14]

Hechler turned out to be the right man at the right place and time. He was able to convince the Duke, who then spoke to the Kaiser. These efforts soon bore fruit. On April 14, 1896, Hechler met with Herzl and excitedly reported how the Kaiser, who was in Vienna at the time, discussed the contents of *Der Judenstaat* with his retinue and told them "the time had come 'to fulfill prophecy.'"[15] A week later, on

---

11 Hermann Ellerin (ed.), *Herzl, hechler, hadukas hagadol mebaden vekaisar germania 1896–1904*, Bank Elran Publishing, Tel Aviv, 1961, p. 1 (henceforth: Ellerin, *Herzl*).
12 Margalit, *Hakhozeh vehakeysar*, pp. 66–67.
13 Bodenheimer, *Hatzionim*, p. 71; a photocopy of the letter appears in Ellerin, *ibid*.
14 *Complete Diaries of Theodor Herzl*, March 16, 1896, vol. 1, p. 312.
15 *Ibid*, April 14, 1896, p. 319.

April 21, 1896, Hechler summoned Herzl to Karlsruhe to meet the Duke.[16] On April 23, they sat together for about two and a half hours. Scholars differ on the results of that encounter. According to Hannah Bodenheimer, the Duke was tremendously impressed with Herzl and he became "the first non-Jewish Zionist in Germany and an indefatigable warrior for the Zionist cause."[17] Alex Bein also sums up the visit as a great success for Herzl and the Zionist movement, claiming that this initial achievement encouraged Herzl and gave him the courage and motivation to continue on the political path.[18] Ernst Pawel reaches a different conclusion: "Objectively, the results of the audience were minimal. Though he turned down Herzl's request for introduction to the Kaiser and the Russian Czar, the Grand Duke graciously granted him permission to keep him informed about the progress of the enterprise."[19]

In retrospect, it appears that Bodenheimer and Bein were right: The Duke did help Herzl and the end result was productive. In the forty months between Hechler's visit to Herzl and the invitation of the German Kaiser, Herzl continued to cultivate his ties with the Duke employing Hechler as the intermediary, as attested to by the correspondence between them.[20]

In addition to the joint efforts of Herzl and Hechler, the Duke was increasingly influenced by the growing public visibility of the Zionist cause. The establishment of *Die Welt* and the successful congress in Basel brought the Zionist endeavor closer to his heart, to the point where he was prepared to lend Herzl a hand.[21]

Bodenheimer believes that the Grand Duke was swayed by the atmosphere of international support for the Zionist idea. In October 1897, after two leading British papers, the *Daily Chronicle* and the *Pall Mall Gazette*, proposed a European conference on the Jewish question, Herzl felt he had a "talking point" for requesting an audience with the German Kaiser.[22] On October 22, against the backdrop of the sensation created by the First Congress, Herzl wrote to the Grand Duke outlining what had been decided there and asked for the Duke's assistance

---

[16] In a twist of fate, the Baron Hirsch, upon whom Herzl hung high hopes and planned to meet again, died that day. In his diary, Herzl wrote: "A curious day. Hirsch dies, and I make contact with princes," *Complete Diaries of Theodor Herzl*, April 21, 1896, vol. 1, p. 323.
[17] Bodenheimer, *Hatzionim*, p. 156.
[18] Bein, *Theodore Herzl: A Biography*, p. 197.
[19] Ernst Pawel, *The Labyrinth of Exile: A Life of Theodor Herzl*, New York, Farrar, Straus & Giroux, 1989, p. 283.
[20] Margalit, *Hakhozeh vehakeysar*, vol. 2, Letters 1896–1904, pp. 78–152.
[21] Pawel, *Labyrinth*, p. 361.
[22] Bodenheim, *Hatzionim*, p. 70.

in promoting a conference of the Great Powers to discuss a territorial solution for the Jewish problem. He appended a note which he requested that the Duke pass on to the Kaiser. Saying he feared that long explanations in writing might not interest the emperor, he proposed that they meet in person.[23] In December 1897, Herzl received a reply through the Duke informing him that the Kaiser would not see him but would be prepared to read his report on the Zionist Congress. Herzl sent it to Hermann von Lucanus, the head of the Kaiser's office, but never heard back.

In March 1898, the papers reported that the German Kaiser was planning a journey to the Holy Land to dedicate the Evangelical Church of the Redeemer near the tomb of Jesus. Hearing of this, Herzl stepped up his efforts and together with Hechler continued to pressure the Grand Duke. Finally, something moved. On June 5, Hechler informed Herzl of the Duke's proposal that he approach Philip Eulenburg, the German ambassador to the Austro-Hungarian Empire, and tell him in the Duke's name that Zionism might be useful to Germany. The Duke did not stop there: On July 28, he wrote a long letter to the Kaiser himself. The first part of the letter describes his introduction to Herzl and the Zionist movement. He confesses that he was initially skeptical, but eventually concluded that this "interesting" movement, its colonies in Palestine and its industrious efforts to establish an "Israelite state" warranted a certain amount of attention. In view of the Kaiser's upcoming journey, the Duke suggested that Count Eulenburg, the German ambassador at Vienna, be given the task of exploring the Zionist idea and the possibility of incorporating it in Germany's long-range policy aims.[24]

The second half of the letter touches on Hechler's proposal that the Sultan cede territory in the region where the "original Ark of the Covenant" was thought to be located."[25] After receiving an encouraging response to the letter, the Grand Duke invited Herzl for a meeting. In September 1898, as soon as the Second Zionist Congress ended, Herzl went to see him. The Duke told him about the letter he had written to the Kaiser and confided that through the auspices of the ambassador in Constantinople, Marschall von Bieberstein, the German government had already been informed that the Turks took a favorable view of Zionism. The Duke's proposal did not fall on deaf ears: The Kaiser appointed Eulenburg his personal assistant on Zionist affairs and Herzl turned his attention to setting up an interview with Eulenburg. On September 14, Herzl received a telegram

---

[23] *Complete Diaries of Theodor Herzl*, October 17, 1897, vol. 2, pp. 595–597.
[24] Ellerin, *Herzl*, p. 13; Pawel, *Labyrinth*, p. 361.
[25] Ellerin, *ibid*; Pawel, *Labyrinth*, p. 283.

from Eulenburg inviting him to his palace in Vienna. At the meeting which took place two days later, Herzl acquainted him with the Zionist project, emphasizing that the goal of the movement aligned with German interests. Since Germany was in an influential position vis a vis Turkey, he hoped that Germany would assist in furthering this common goal. Eulenburg promised to look into it and recommended that Herzl speak to Bernhard von Bülow, the German foreign secretary, the following day. On September 17, Herzl and Bülow met, but this meeting was less successful than the one with Eulenberg. Herzl describes it as follows:

> "Bülow received me in his living quarters ... He greeted me with captivating kindness ... At this I grew weak. I had confronted Eulenburg, who had received me coolly, with resoluteness, and my words had been iron-like and clear. In Bülow's presence I unfortunately became a vain writer and strove harder to make polished *mots* [phrases] than to talk seriously to the point ... After the conversation I had the delayed reaction *d'avoir ete berce et roule* [that I had been properly taken in] ... Then I left, and know even on the stairs that nothing was going to come of it – either because I had committed some blunder, or because he does not consider it expedient."[26]

Nevertheless Herzl remained hopeful, as both Bülow and Eulenburg had promised that the German government would broach the matter of Zionism with the powers that be in Constantinople.[27] At the time, Herzl was in the midst of various projects, among them the establishment of the Jewish Colonial Bank, which required him to travel around Europe. From Vienna, he went to France, Holland and England. While juggling all this, he kept the German channel open in his bid to gain a hearing with the Kaiser. In Paris, he booked into the Hotel Castille on rue Cambon. In the same room he used as a correspondent of *Neue Freie Presse*, and on the same desk on which he penned *Der Judenstaat*, Herzl wrote a letter to Eulenburg explaining the advantages of a Jewish state for Germany and Turkey. He concluded on this note:

> "The journey to the Holy Land is now grandly conceived as a pilgrimage on the part of His Majesty. But it can turn out to be more: it can attain to the significance of a historic turning-point in the Orient, if the return of the Jews is initiated ... Commending the cause which I represent in all humility to Your Excellency's benevolence."[28]

---

26 *Complete Diaries of Theodor Herzl*, September 18, 1898, vol. 2, pp. 665–668.
27 Bodenheimer, *Hatzionim*, p. 72.
28 *Complete Diaries of Theodor Herzl*, September 18, 1898, vol. 2, pp. 671–672.

Herzl's letter achieved its aim. A week later, he received a surprisingly positive response from Eulenburg:

> "I have only good news for you ... His Majesty the Kaiser has shown complete and deep understanding of the movement headed by you. Convinced of its righteousness, I was a zealous exponent of your cause; my friend Bülow is of the same mind and this might be of great significance for your cause. Following my exposition, His Majesty has declared himself ready to intervene with the Sultan and as far as possible to present your case urgently and vigorously. In this, the Kaiser will be supported by Secretary of State von Bülow, who will accompany him...The Kaiser does not wish to receive you before his trip, so as not to give rise to interpretations and presumptions that will only do harm, but he is willing to receive a deputation of Zionists in Palestine. If you lead such a mission, you will have an excellent opportunity to convey your thoughts to him personally."[29]

In a postscript to the letter, Eulenburg wrote:

> "I have just had another thorough conversation with His Majesty regarding your letter. His Majesty has instructed me to inform you that your confidence in H.M.'s interest to further your cause and to protect the poor and oppressed Jews, is not misplaced. His Majesty would discuss the matter with the Sultan in a most emphatic manner and will be pleased to hear more from you in Jerusalem. The Kaiser has already issued orders to the effect that no obstacle is to be placed in the way of the [Zionist] delegation. In conclusion, H.M. wishes to tell you that he is very much prepared to undertake the protectorate in question."[30]

Eulenburg expressed the hope that Herzl would arrive in Palestine at the appointed time and declared that the Kaiser would be disappointed if he did not see him there. He suggested that Herzl travel first to Constantinople while the Kaiser was in town, although the "center of gravity" would still be Jerusalem. He appended a detailed itinerary for the Kaiser and his entourage in Constantinople, Haifa and Jerusalem, and ended with an invitation to Herzl to visit him privately at his estate outside Berlin for further information.

Herzl was certain that this invitation signified a genuine turn in the history of the Jewish state-to-be, and that his vision would soon become a reality. At a mass rally in London on October 4, 1898, his tone was prophetic:

> "I shall not paint for you a picture of the return to Zion, which will commence shortly. I promise you that day is not far off. I know whereof I speak. Never have I spoken with

---

29 Bein, *Theodor Herzl: A Biography*, 280.
30 *Ibid.*

such confidence. Today I say to you: The time is drawing near when the people of Israel will get up and leave their homes."³¹

On his way back from London to Vienna, Herzl visited Eulenburg in Berlin. Eulenburg repeated what he had told Herzl about the Kaiser's enthusiasm and commitment to the Zionist idea and expressed his confidence that the Sultan would cooperate. On October 9, 1898, he again met the Grand Duke in Potsdam, who confirmed that the Kaiser was waiting to see Herzl in Constantinople and receive his delegation in Jerusalem. Again, Herzl was assured of the Kaiser's certainty that the Turks would respond favorably to his request. The rest of day, however, turned out to be a disappointment. Herzl asked to speak with Bülow and the German chancellor, Hohenlohe, to discuss the details of the meeting with the Kaiser. When he went to see them at noon at Bülow's request, the two of them received him with undisguised coldness and skepticism.³²

Herzl writes: "Hohenlohe looked at me with his dim, blue, old man's eyes in anything but a kindly fashion. From him, too, I heard the first anti-Semitic remark in these exalted circles: 'Do you think that the Jews are going to desert their stock exchange and follow you? The Jews, who are comfortably installed here in Berlin?'"³³

As Herzl tells it, Bülow seems to have found himself in an awkward position, as the conversation moved from an anti-Semitic quip to a cross-examination about how much territory was being sought. Herzl explained that it would depend on the number of Jewish immigrants, stressing that the Jews would purchase the land.

Hohenlohe went on: 'And you want to found a state there?' Herzl: 'We want autonomy and self-protection.' Hohenlohe: 'What does Turkey say to all this?'"

In his diary, Herzl records his thoughts:

"*Je le croyais mieux renseigne* [I had believed him better informed] ... [I] replied: The Grand Duke told me that favorable reports had come in from Herr von Marschall [the German envoy in Turkey]. Bülow, who had been sitting in the corner of the sofa next to Hohenlohe's armchair, with his lips pursed tight and his eyes deliberately vacant, interjected: 'I don't know anything about that, I've seen nothing from Marschall on the subject.' I did not

---

31 Vardi, *Malki betzion*, p. 10. The speech was translated into English and published in the *Jewish World*, on October 7, 1898. Herzl's predictions cost him dearly: He was accused of sowing false hopes in the masses.
32 Vardi, *Malki betzion*, pp. 10–11.
33 *Complete Diaries of Theodor Herzl*, October 9, 1898, vol. 2, p. 701.

allow myself to be disconcerted, and said: 'I have reports that the sentiment is favorable. I recently telegraphed to the Sultan and he replied.'"[34]

Herzl, puzzled by the whole exchange, asks: "But why the depressingly cool behavior of Hohenlohe and Bülow?" He goes on to offer two explanations: "Either they are at odds with their Imperial master, but do not dare as yet to stand up to him. So for the present they treat the matter with dilatory coldness, in order to trip it up at the proper moment and bring the whole thing to the ground. Or is it merely the official face of diplomacy?"[35]

The meeting ends with Herzl inquiring: "Where will the Kaiser receive me? In Constantinople and in Jerusalem?" To which Bülow replies: "In any case only once!"[36]

Perhaps Herzl was wrong to answer Hohenlohe's question so hastily, citing Marschall's favorable reports. He apparently assumed that Hohenlohe knew more than he did and was testing him. Under the circumstances, Herzl might have been better off not volunteering the information from the Grand Duke and letting Bülow answer, because if Bülow did not know of Marschall's reports, Herzl was putting him in a bad light. After all, Bülow was the foreign secretary, so one would expect him to be informed of such matters. This might explain Bülow's coolness toward Herzl. Even if Bülow did know and was only pretending not to, Herzl would have been better off not confronting him. Moreover, Bülow might have objected from the start, but did not want to openly oppose the Kaiser. Being in the company of Hohenlohe in an atmosphere permeated by anti-Semitism may have helped to solidify this negativism. One way or another, the meeting with Bülow and Hohenlohe put something of a damper on his jubilant morning with the Grand Duke and the excitement over his upcoming travels.

Journey to Palestine

On receiving an invitation to meet the Kaiser in Palestine, Herzl writes: "I read the letter in the carriage, and at first was almost dazed by it. The colossal achievement which it represented at first had an unpleasant effect on me. I saw at once the grave consequences which this can have for me at the *N. Fr. Pr.* If, after the expiration of my leave, I go to Palestine instead of reporting for duty at the

---

[34] *Ibid.*, pp. 701–702.
[35] *Ibid.*, p. 703.
[36] Ibid. In fact, they met twice – in Constantinople and Jerusalem.

office, this could quite simply cost me my job. On the other hand, I cannot disregard the Kaiser's wish, which really is a command."[37]

For Herzl, the invitation posed a serious dilemma. On the one hand, the journey offered the possibility of a breakthrough for political Zionism and the charter for which he had worked for so long. On the other, it was hard for him to be away from his workplace and family for such an extended period. When Herzl broke the news to his editors, they were not pleased: "I foresee difficulties for the *Neue Freie Presse* arising from this," said one of them. "After all, he invited you as a Zionist."[38] Parting from his parents, and especially his children, was difficult for him. In his diary he writes about the cumulative effect of being away from home so often, after spending so much time that month promoting the Zionist cause in Europe:

> "Taking leave of my loved ones was quite hard this time. I could very well stay in my beautiful house, with my lovely children, whose rosiest childhood is passing without my enjoying it; who are growing up without my observing the delightful details of their development. And I am undertaking such a long journey, one that may not be without danger. I have even been warned that an attempt on my life might be made in Palestine ... But it is my duty to go."[39]

He was not indifferent to the threats on his life: "It affected me deeply at parting that my good parents cried. They would be the only inconsolable ones if I did not come back. It would be no comfort to my poor old parents that I would then be a figure in world history."[40]

In the end, however, his sense of duty and the great prospects that lay ahead took precedence over anxiety and personal concerns. Despite fears over how his editors would react (especially so soon after being away from Vienna for the Second Zionist Congress and his traveling so frequently in connection with the Zionist bank), and despite not wanting to be away from his children and parents, Herzl began to prepare for the trip.

Herzl set out on a journey that seemed infinitely promising: His dream of a Jewish state was on the verge of coming true. He and his associates reached Constantinople. There, after a nerve-wracking wait, he met the German Kaiser. "Just

---

[37] *Complete Diaries of Theodor Herzl*, October 2, 1898, vol. 2, p. 675.
[38] *Ibid.*, October 11, 1898, p. 707.
[39] Eliezer Ben Yehuda had sent a warning that the Turks might try to assassinate him while he was visiting Palestine. The message was conveyed through the editor of *Die Welt*, Dr. Siegmund Werner. Vardi, *Malki betzion*, p. 13; *Complete Diaries of Theodor Herzl*, October 14, 1898, vol. 2, pp. 709–710.
[40] *Ibid.*, p. 710.

tell me in a word what I am to ask of the Sultan," said the Kaiser. To which Herzl replied: "A Chartered Company – under German protection." The Kaiser agreed. Herzl and his colleagues then sailed from Constantinople to their next destination – meeting the Kaiser in Jerusalem. They were brimming with confidence that the Jews would soon have a state.

But the journey was not a success. That same evening, at a banquet at the Sultan's palace, something happened to change the Kaiser's friendly attitude. The Sultan had apparently responded negatively to his overtures and as a guest, the Kaiser felt he could not press him further.[41] So when the Kaiser received the Herzl's deputation in Jerusalem, he brought with him no news of a charter. Herzl delivered his speech, but the German monarch acted as if he were not the one who had invited Herzl to Palestine and they had never met in Constantinople to coordinate their positions. By the end of this lengthy expedition, so filled with expectations, the delegation returned home mostly empty-handed, apart from the experience of visiting the Holy Land and the Kaiser's assurance of his continued interest.

The visit may not have been a diplomatic triumph, but it was important for other reasons. Herzl returned to Europe with new and profound insights about Palestine and its inhabitants, some of which found their way into his second book, *Altneuland*. Herzl's journey was also significant in that it changed the public mindset: The fact that a Jewish leader had talked politics with the leader of a country as powerful as Germany was a historic precedent even if no charter from the Turks had come out of it. In retrospect, Herzl consoled himself over the failure of the summit: "The fact that the Kaiser has not taken over the protectorate is of course excellent for the later development of our enterprise ... For the protectorate would have been a clear immediate advantage, but not a long range one. We should later have had to pay the most usurious interest for this protectorate."[42] From this comment, he seems to have realized that the English option was a better one, and if he had accepted the protection of the German emperor, there would have been a clash.

Why did the Kaiser renege on his original commitment? Initially he seems to have been won over by the Grand Duke and Count Eulenburg and had every intention of helping Herzl. Both Eulenburg and the Grand Duke attest that the Kaiser tried to speak to the Sultan on two separate occasions but could not get through to him. In 1901, Eulenburg told Herzl that that the Sultan had "rejected the Kaiser's suggestion so brusquely that it was not possible to pursue the matter

---

41 Vardi, *Malki betzion*, p. 15.
42 Bein, *Theodor Herzl: A Biography*, p. 308.

further." In 1902, the Grand Duke related to Max Bodenheimer that the Kaiser had twice attempted to raise the issue at dinner, but the Sultan had demonstrated "a complete and ostentatious lack of understanding."[43]

The Turks may have misled the Germans. In talks with Marschall von Bieberstein, the German ambassador, they did not state that granting a charter to the Jews under the protection of the Kaiser was out of the question, but when the Kaiser arrived in Constantinople, he discovered that the Turks were against it. Herzl was convinced that von Bülow was responsible for the Kaiser's change of heart.[44] Herzl's presumptions may not have been far-fetched. As Bein tells it:

> "No one then is to be blamed for the collapse of the protectorate idea; if any blame attaches it is to the Machiavellianism and court flunkeyism of Bülow, who permitted the Kaiser to make promises which were later to be broken."[45]

Michael Margalit offers a different explanation: "We believe that the Kaiser, who did not wish to be seen as someone who broke his promises, insinuated that Bülow was the leading opponent...and Bülow was not the type of man who would dare to challenge the Kaiser ... Bülow was the indentured servant who pulled the chestnuts out of the fire, but the decision was Wilhelm II's."[46]

However, it is worth bearing in mind that Bülow was the secretary of state, and it was his job to consider Germany's interests in Europe as a whole. He knew that France and Russia would not sit quietly if Germany helped to establish a Jewish state under its protection, which would have tilted the balance against them.[47]

Looking back In October 1900, Herzl wondered if perhaps he himself had been at fault, for not showing up at the reception organized by the Jews of Jerusalem in honor of the Kaiser:

> "The memory of some mistakes that I have made keeps tormenting me. My greatest mistake so far was not waiting for the Kaiser at the entrance gate of the Jews. At that time, I thought it would be better not to, because then he might have regarded that reception as the one to which he had ordered the Zionist deputation, and I wished to have a special solemn audience of our own. However, for the Kaiser, who has a penchant for symbolic acts, it would have been the right thing if I, whom he regarded as the head of all Jews, had waited for him

---

43 Friedman, *Germany, Turkey and Zionism*, p. 76.
44 Pawel, *Labyrinth* p. 365.
45 Bein, *Theodore Herzl: A Biography*, p. 309.
46 Margalit, *Hakhozeh vehakeysar*, p. 49.
47 Friedman, *Germany, Turkey and Zionism*, pp. 82–83.

at the threshold of our city of Jerusalem and greeted him there. That is when he may have turned away from me. I realize this only now."[48]

In any case, it seems the chances of success were slim from the start since the Turks consistently said no to such initiatives.

Secrecy of the Mission

Herzl tried to keep his visit to Palestine under wraps. He was accompanied by a party of four: his right-hand man David Wolffsohn, a businessman; Max Bodenheimer, a lawyer; Dr. Moritz Schnirer, a physician; and Josef Zeidner, an engineer and the only one who had been to Palestine before, as a representative of the Ahva land purchase society. Herzl instructed them not to discuss the trip with anyone. Taking leave of his close friends, Herzl remained closemouthed, not even saying in what direction they were heading.[49] Seidener later wrote that they pretended to be journalists and Herzl asked them not to tell a soul about the destination or purpose of their expedition.[50] Indeed, very few residents of Palestine knew of Herzl's forthcoming visit.[51]

Moshe David Shub wrote about Herzl's trip to Palestine in his memoirs. He received a telegram in German from David Wolffsohn informing him of his arrival in Jaffa on Wednesday morning with four friends. Shub was asked to come meet them. To the telegram, Wolffsohn appended a Hebrew phrase in English letters: "*awal hadavar jehe besod gadol,*" i.e., but the matter must be a big secret.[52]

Shub revealed the secret to Dr. Hillel Yaffe, who was chairman of the Hovevei Zion action committee in Odessa, but Yaffe did not believe him: "He said I must be mistaken."[53] The Jews living in Palestine who heard of the visit assumed Herzl was arriving as a journalist. Nobody had any idea he was on a Zionist mission. *Hamelitz* described Herzl and his party as correspondents for the European newspapers.[54]

The truth of the matter is that Herzl wanted the publicity, but not in real time, fearful that it would create a needless stir that would only sabotage his ef-

---

48 *Complete Diaries of Theodor Herzl*, October 5, 1900, vol. 3, p. 981; Vardi, *Malki betzion*, p. 26.
49 Vardi, *Malki betzion*, p. 28. Also see p. 13, note 1.
50 J. Seidener, in: *Sefer hacongress* (1923), p. 162.
51 Vardi, *Malki betzion*, pp. 13, 63, 65.
52 Shub, *Zikhronot levait david*, p. 33.
53 Ibid., p. 6.
54 Vardi, *Malki betzion*, p. 18; *Hamelitz*, no. 240.

forts. David Yudelevich, a veteran educator and one of the founders of Rishon Lezion, asked Herzl if he could send a cable to Europe but Herzl asked him to wait: "There is a great difference between telegraphic news that reaches Europe immediately and a report filed two weeks later."[55]

Why the secrecy? Herzl probably worried about incurring the wrath of the Turkish authorities, who might respond in a way that could impinge on his work. Moreover, an enthusiastic welcome from the colonists could result in a backlash against them from both the Turks and the Baron's administrators.

Herzl's Charisma in Palestine

Herzl's good looks continued to awe everyone who crossed his path in Palestine. Herzlian charisma remained undiminished, even across the sea. If there was any negative talk about Herzl it did not detract from the impression he left on people. Whether he was recognized or not, all were captivated by his beauty and the impressive figure he cut.

On Herzl's arrival in Jaffa, Moshe David Shub writes: "I was about to lead [the guests] to their hotel when I saw Dr. Herzl standing there gazing out to the sea ... with his beautiful, luminescent eyes."[56] Another Jew from Jaffa who was present at the time, was also struck by his appearance:

> "I saw Herzl only after he had ... climbed into his carriage. Seeing his proud regal figure, like a king, with his long black beard and beautiful eyes turned toward the spot where a group of Jerusalem Jews stood, my heart began to quiver and tears rose to my eyes ... When he sat in the carriage and drove off, the Jews lifted their eyes to the heavens and loudly recited the *shekhiyanu* prayer."[57]

Residents of the colonies felt the same way. In Rishon Lezion, Herzl reached the administration building where he was met by David Yudelevich, a Bilu member and long-time educator: "I opened the door. The first to enter was a tall, handsome man with a black beard and two immense eyes, black and sparkling, looking straight ahead. Panic struck. I realized it was Dr. Herzl."[58]

---

55 *Ibid.*, p. 83.
56 Shub, *Zikhronot levait david*, p. 34.
57 Vardi, *Malki betzion*, pp. 63–64.
58 *Ibid.*, p. 81.

Herzl's visit to Mikveh Yisrael is remembered thus:

> "All the teachers and students stood dumbfounded, gazing into this man's face as if watching a splendid drama. And I, too, could finally observe him from close quarters. Every movement testified to his majesty and grandeur. His garb was simple. Even on a day like today he was dressed like a tourist. His suit was yellow, with a white English hat on his head, emphasizing all the more the blackness of his eyes and the handsome beard that lent such wonderous charm to his face. Simply put, the divine presence rested upon him."[59]

The Baron's administrators, as we said, were no fans of Herzl. His visit to Palestine should have been met with animosity. But even in this case, Herzl's mysterious power seems to have worked its magic and broken down their resistance. Apart from paeans to his physical beauty, many recalled his effect on them. Eliyahu Ze'ev Levine-Epstein, who knew Herzl from Vienna, tells of the letter he received from Shub when Herzl was in town describing how the farmers of Rishon Lezion and the Baron's administrators would not let him leave. He finally gave in to their pleading and stayed overnight. It was yet another sign that something new was in the offing:

> "Even the Baron's administrators, who would curse and belittle Herzl every time they heard his name, begged him to stay and showered him with respect ... It was not as though they had received orders from Paris [home of the Baron Rothschild]. That moment, I saw in my mind's eye a marvelous spectacle: The Baron and Herzl united on everything concerning Zionism. My brain seethed and my heart pounded."[60]

The writer Dov Haviv Lubman describes the excitement of the chief administrator of the colonies, Yosef Haim Hazan, at the news of Herzl's arrival:

> "He was in such a state of confusion that he went out to welcome the delegation wearing a shoe on one foot and a sandal on the other. He was pale, his knees knocking in fright. He knew that Herzl's publicly proclaimed views were not to the liking of Paris, and he might be reprimanded if he received him officially in the Baron's name. Yet upon meeting him, he was smitten by his ineffable glory and stood trembling like a slave before his master, hanging on his every word."[61]

Here is more on Herzl's charisma and its impact on the staff and students of Mikveh Yisrael:

---

59 Aharon Hermoni, in: Vardi, *Malki betzion*, p. 136.
60 Vardi, *Malki betzion*, p. 118.
61 *Ibid.*, p. 74.

"As he observes us, a smile of pleasure crosses his face. The students look down, unable to withstand his penetrating glance, and many of them blush ... Here, too, Herzl has won his rightful place: He is no longer a guest standing before us but our master and leader. Less than five minutes have passed since his arrival and all of us – the students, teachers, office staff and supervisors – are ready and waiting to follow his orders. Our headmaster, known throughout the land for his fearlessness and love of law and order, stands by the honorary arch next to a giant plough and waits with bowed head for directives from Herzl, the Viennese doctor who came here without authorization from the supervisors of our school in Paris ..."[62] I also remember how after the procession, a cluster of teachers stood around Herzl in the schoolyard and our headmaster, known for his opposition to Zionism, raised a glass of wine and proclaimed: 'To Zionism and Herzl's victories! Long live Zionism.'"[63]

Moshe Smilansky writes about meeting Herzl in Rehovot:

"We all dismount from our horses. The door of the carriage reopens and out leaps a tall fellow with a square black beard ... [and] big, deep-set black eyes suffused with melancholy. Brow and face drenched in sorrow. Even the hint of a smile on his lips comes from sorrow... His face left me enchanted. I, who had never been afraid in my life, grew weak-kneed."[64]

The residents of Jaffa and Jerusalem also responded with unprecedented enthusiasm. "Not only did he win the hearts of the Kaiser and his deputies," writes Dr. Hillel Yaffe, "but also the hearts of the people, who saw him as their leader and representative in the land of the forefathers."[65] Mordechai Ezrahi-Krishevsky remembers Herzl's visit to Jerusalem:

"I was a teacher in those days at the Alliance school in Jerusalem ... When Herzl came to Jerusalem, the teachers were warned to keep their distance from him, but I had not sold my soul to Alliance and went to see him ... Herzl's presence in the city was palpable. Men and women thronged the lane where he was staying and rejoiced if they were able to catch a glimpse of him."[66]

Itamar Ben-Avi also recalls his sighting of Herzl in Jerusalem:

"Can anyone imagine my excitement at hearing suddenly that Herzl was in Jerusalem? My idol in Jerusalem! I walked downtown, toward the place where he was staying ... Herzl did not come out that day, or if he did, it was earlier ... Dejected, I turned to walk home ... Still mourning my fate, a felt a light tap on the shoulder. It was Dr. Heinrich Lowe ... He asked

---

62 Aharon Hermoni, in: Vardi, *Malki betzion*, pp. 136–137.
63 *Ibid.*, p. 138.
64 Moshe Smilansky, in: Vardi, *Malki betzion*, p. 111.
65 Dr. Hillel Yaffe, in: Vardi, *Malki betzion*, p. 67.
66 Vardi, *Malki betzion*, p. 176.

me: 'Where are you going'? 'Home.' 'But don't you want to see Herzl?' I barely had time to answer him when he grabbed my arm ... The door opened and who emerged? Herzl, the man of my dreams, in all his splendor. I will never forget that moment. Tall, head held proud and erect, a long black beard, such a solemn look but at the same time so engaging, the mirth of the gods on his lips ... Dr. Lowe, who was by my side, kept whispering in my ear with childlike wonder: 'So what do you say? What do you think of this Herzl? Exquisite! A king ... the very image of a god."[67] The hordes of tourists and the army officers and all the passersby – everyone stopped to look at him, to take in this delightful spectacle: Herzl with his Eastern beauty, eyes like bottomless pools, black Assyrian beard ... [68]What a wondrous thing it was: Jerusalem in those days was so remote from Zionism of any kind, but Herzl was a sight that no one could ignore ... Just to see him walking. I have seen many exalted and illustrious people. I have seen princes and kings and some of the grandest emperors, but a phenomenon like Herzl I have never seen in my life. Divinity incarnate. A messianic vision revealed. We could not take our eyes off him. We were transfixed by his every move, as the crowd in front of us split down the middle."[69]

The power of Herzl's charisma is further attested to by Moshe David Shub, who found the contemptuous attitude of Jerusalem's ultra-Orthodox Jews profoundly disturbing:

"It is interesting how many of Herzl's opponents, after seeing him once, turned into supporters and admirers. While he was in Jerusalem, I met two of his well-known detractors on the street ... Knowing that I was a devotee of the doctor, they asked me jokingly: 'Nu, how is your rebbe?' 'I can assure you that if you meet him and exchange a few words, you will change your tune!' I replied. 'Fine,' they said. 'Go ahead and introduce us.' We set a time. Dr. Herzl received them in his chambers. When they left, I asked them: 'So, my dear fellows, what do you say now about my rebbe?' ... 'There is no doubt about it. The man is a marvel,' they answered. These men, who were among the leading figures of Neturei Karta in Jerusalem, became Herzl enthusiasts even without being Zionists."[70]

---

67 Itamar Ben-Avi, in: Vardi, *Malki Betzion*, pp. 149–151.
68 Ibid., p. 154. Two additional testimonies of people who saw Herzl in Jerusalem are worth noting. Zalman Ben Tovim writes: "My first glimpse of the Zionist president was of him walking slowly, leaning on the arms of his colleagues. His towering height, his noble visage, the black beard that further enhanced his charm. I was filled with awe and tingles ran down my spine. I found myself utterly wonderstruck at the sight of this president of Israel in all his splendor and majesty." Zvi Grayevsky, a Jerusalem-born writer, offers this account: "I can still see him today in all his beauty, glorious and magnificent. Herzl, the great leader and builder of the Zionist movement, the reviver of dry bones, so proud and tall, his beaming face full of light, evoking gladness and sorrow at one and the same time" (*ibid.*, p. 164).
69 Ibid., pp. 149–153.
70 Shub, *Zikhronot levait david*, pp. 20, 21, 41.

Through the force of his personality, Herzl was able to soften people's resistance and create an atmosphere of veneration wherever he went.

Herzlian Charisma and its Long-Range Impact

As we have seen, Herzl's charisma "sprouted wings" and continued to work in his favor on distant shores. The Jews of Palestine had heard stories about Herzl's activities in Europe and were tremendously excited when he landed in their midst. In his memoirs, Aharon Vardi devotes a whole chapter to "guests in Jerusalem," among them the German Kaiser and his wife. Another one, of special importance, was Theodor Herzl:

> "This magnificent guest, who draws the eye of everyone who sees him…and warms the cockles of every Jewish heart, is Theodor Herzl! Hurrah! At long last, an opportunity to see this person, whom we have heard so much about and whose name works like a charm to stir the hearts of tens of thousands … People could scarcely believe their eyes: Here was the flesh-and-blood man standing before them! He was the talk of town, and everyone wanted to catch a glimpse of him, but more than the masses who ran out to greet him were seeking a savior or sage, they wanted to see the dashing figure."[71]

David Yudelevich of Rishon Lezion recalls his astonishment at hearing that Herzl was on his way. Until then, he had only known him from afar, from his journalistic writing and his resounding influence on the Jewish world:

> "I stand there in sheer disbelief. Herzl here?! I fix my gaze on the glittering eyes of the man whose name has enthralled me night and day. For four years, I have devoured with extraordinary spiritual gusto every word he has written or spoken, all that has been said or written about him, for or against, delighting in his hopes, feeling his pain, and here he is, large as life, in front of me."[72]

---

71 Vardi, *Malki betzion*, pp. 158–159.
72 Yoram Majorek (ed), *Im herzl leyirushalayim*, Central Zionist Archive press, Jerusalem 1988 (henceforth: Majorek, *Im herzl leyirushalayim*, p. 34. In Ness Ziona, people danced in the street upon hearing that Herzl was coming. Efraim Yehuda Komarov, one of the early pioneers, relates how he rang the great bell to announce Herzl's arrival in half an hour: "These tidings, which came as a surprise, without prior knowledge of [Herzl's] journey to Palestine, deeply affected people emotionally. In a burst of joy, they danced around the bell." This is confirmed by another town resident: "Each of us felt indescribable spiritual joy…This was no small matter: We had been granted the privilege of seeing in person this great man whose lofty vision aroused us from our slumber and blew life into our desiccated bones." See Zvi Hochberg in: Vardi, *Malki betzion*, p. 95.

Another vehicle for the spread of Herzl's charisma outside Europe was the widespread dissemination of his portrait in the Jewish community. When Moshe David Shub went to Jaffa port to await Herzl and his deputation, curious crowds began to form there, hoping to catch sight of him. "One person even whispered in my ear ... 'That is Dr. Herzl, isn't it?' He recognized Herzl from the pictures that had been distributed around the country."[73]

Dov Haviv Lubman writes about meeting Herzl in Rishon Lezion on his way home from working in the vineyards:

> "I chanced upon two carriages full of elegantly dressed gentlemen wearing cork hats, as was the custom among tourists. They asked to halt the horses, half rose from their seats, doffed their hats and wished me a hearty '*shalom aleichem*.' Among them was a winningly handsome man who glanced my way with the most beautiful eyes. Immediately the portrait of Dr. Herzl sprang to mind."[74]

Aharon Zvi Hermoni (Ginzburg), then a 14-year old student at Mikveh Yisrael, tells of his frustration upon hearing that Herzl had been there in his absence:

> "Guess what!' says my good friend Haim. 'Who do you think was here an hour ago? You will never guess ... Dr. Herzl. Yes, the man himself. Why is your mouth hanging open? No, I am not joking' ... Mindboggling ... If I weren't so ashamed, I would lay down and cry. Herzl was here and I missed him!"[75]

His friend consoles him that Herzl would be back in two days, and goes on to describe the scene:

> "The headmaster's carriage pulled up. It stopped in front of the winery and the headmaster's wife climbed down, but before her a black-bearded gentleman jumped out attired in the tropical dress of a tourist ... We were transfixed by this gentleman ... so dignified, so refined and modest. Such masculine beauty! He stood tall and erect, with big black eyes flashing but filled with gentle warmth. His long black beard framed a Semite face... a handsome Oriental prince in European dress. Even the Arab laundress who was watching through a little window cried out: 'Oh look, what a prince, as beautiful as an angel of Allah'...Exactly! I had seen his picture in the newspapers and on postcards, but I never imagined him so fine and princely. Out of a storybook!"

In short, although Herzl did not achieve his declared aim and return with a charter in hand, his trip to Palestine could be crowned a success. Herzl captured the

---

73 Shub, *Zikhronot levait david*, p. 24.
74 Vardi, *Malki betzion*, pp. 73–74.
75 Aharon Hermoni, *Be'ikvot habilu'im: Pirkei zikhronot*, Jerusalem: Reuben Mass, 1952, p. 62.

hearts of all who turned out to see him and the experience of the visit buoyed his spirit. Sailing back to Europe, he began to write his second book, *Altneuland*, while leading the Zionist movement on its path to founding a Jewish state.

Response of the Local Inhabitants

Considering the demographic make-up and who was governing the country at the time, one can understand Herzl's interest in keeping the news of his visit secret from the vast majority of the local populace. Palestine was inhabited by a mix of Arabs and Jews, some of them subjects of the Ottoman Empire. However, internal affairs in many of the Jewish colonies were overseen by administrators of the Baron Rothschild, who were among the opponents of Herzl in Palestine for reasons that we shall discuss below.

The Turkish Authorities

Herzl knew that the Turkish authorities frowned on nationalist organizing of any kind and took a dim view of his efforts to win a charter from the Sultan to establish a Jewish national home. Aharon Vardi writes about this:

> "Under the singular conditions in Palestine, of course, not a hint of Zionist activity could be pursued. In Constantinople, Zionism was viewed with suspicion from its inception. Orders were given to keep track of its movements in Palestine and to try offenders as insurgents with all the force of the law. In some communities, the Jewish leadership was assembled and warned of the dangers of Zionism. The Hakham Bashi of Turkey, Rabbi Moshe Halevi, also issued such a warning. The latter, by the way, used to spit when someone mentioned Herzl's name.[76] Confirmation for this comes from Dr. Aharon Meir Masie: 'Once the pasha, Tawfiq Bey, who was a private patient of mine and remained a friend, showed me articles from overseas Zionist newspapers and asked me if I were also involved. 'The Yishuv's hands are clean,' I told him. 'So be aware,' the pasha said. 'If the opposite of what you say turns out to be true, I will not be in a position to help.'"[77]

While Herzl was in Palestine, the Ottoman authorities provided him with an escort, Mendel Kremer, a Jerusalem pharmacist who also worked for the Turkish secret service:

---

[76] *Complete Diaries of Theodor Herzl*, May 19, 1901, vol. 3, p. 1114.
[77] Vardi, *Malki betzion*, p. 179.

"This fellow was assigned the task of keeping track of Herzl during his stay in the country – at the request of the Jerusalem Pasha, on instructions from the government in Damascus.[78] In his pocket, he carried a warrant for Herzl's arrest that could be acted upon if he committed even the slightest offense. Kremer later claimed he was a supporter of Herzl and gave Herzl the paper as a souvenir before he left Palestine. Evidence of Kremer's sympathies can be seen in the fact that after the meeting with the Kaiser in Jerusalem, when Herzl and his associates reached the camp gate, the Turks refused to let them leave, saying they had not received the proper orders. 'Suddenly a man appeared out of the crowd of thousands, exchanged a few short words with the soldiers, and they immediately untied the ropes and flung open the gate. That man was Mendel Kremer.'"[79]

It was sensible for Herzl to be cautious in his dealings with the Turks, and he had good reason after being warned of a possible assassination attempt.[80] Yet he was not deterred from interacting with the Turks, and his personal charisma stood him in good stead. While touring Jerusalem, Herzl decided to climb to the top of David's Citadel, then a Turkish army barrack, without prior coordination or a permit, his heart set on seeing the view from above. His companions were fearful and tried to dissuade him: "Herzl would not listen. 'We will go!' So we did, and then lo and behold: As we ascended the stairs to the tower with Herzl in the lead, the officers at the gate rose to their feet and greeted us. One of them asked in French 'Your request, monsieur?' 'To see the city from the citadel.' 'With pleasure.' And so we went up, all of us spellbound."[81]

The Jews of Jaffa lived in fear of the Turks. Yosef Eliyahu Chelouche writes that the leaders of the Sephardic community debated whether or not to meet with Herzl. Some argued that it was too risky because of the close watch being kept on the residents: "We exercised great caution when we went to see Herzl, arriving at his hotel one by one, so they would not notice us."[82] When they reached their destination, it turned out that Herzl and his entourage had already left for the train station on their way to Jerusalem. Not giving up, Chelouche and his party continued to the station to bid Herzl farewell. When they got there, Herzl turned to Chelouche and inquired whether if the people lined up behind the fence were Jews. Learning that they were, Herzl asked to extend his greetings and urged them to disperse so as not to provoke the Turkish authorities.[83]

---

78 *Ibid.*, p. 18, footnote 1.
79 Bodenheimer, *Hatzionim*, p. 51.
80 See p. 137 above, footnote 39.
81 Vardi, *Malki betzion*, p. 15; Majorek, *Im herzl leyirushalayim*, p. 62.
82 Vardi, *Malki betzion*, p. 68.
83 *Ibid.*

In Jerusalem, where the Turks were even stricter, the Jewish community worried about backlash from Herzl's participation in a public reception in honor of the Kaiser. The educator Ephraim Cohen-Reiss writes:

> "At a time the Turkish government was showing signs of animosity toward Zionism, his attendance was a worrisome problem ... [Rabbi Yaakov Shaul Elyashar] had been warned by Rabbi Moshe Halevi of Constantinople not to arouse any suspicions that he or the community were in favor of Herzlian Zionism because the Sultan was absolutely opposed to the movement, and this could endanger the Jews of Turkey."[84]

Rumor had it that Rabbi Halevi urged Rabbi Elyashar, the chief rabbi of Palestine in 1893–1906, to declare a ban on Herzl, but Cohen-Reiss says this was not true.[85] According to Cohen-Reiss, Tawfiq Pasha, the Turkish intermediary who coordinated the Kaiser's visit to Jerusalem, boasted: "We settled our accounts with the Armenians in three days. With the Zionists we will do it in three hours."[86]

Despite these concerns, no Sephardi ban was imposed on meeting with Herzl. Among Herzl's visitors was the Sephardi chief rabbi, Rabbi Yaakov Meir, who explained that the rabbinate had decided against acknowledging him publicly so as not to bring down the wrath of the Turkish authorities.[87] The leaders of the Zionist movement in Jerusalem grappled with the same issue. Haim Michal Michlin writes:

> "To our regret, we could not hold a reception for the leader. Thousands of eyes were scrutinizing every move we made, especially anyone who was a Turkish subject. Bitter would be the fate of those who attracted the eye of one of their spies or secret police and were found to have any discourse with Herzl. But one by one, we went to his lodgings, sneaking in like thieves, for the privilege of shaking the leader's hand or having him glance our way."[88]

The Arabs of Palestine

One would have expected the Arab inhabitants of Palestine to oppose Herzl's visit. In general, they did not welcome Jewish settlement in the country, and

---

84 *Ibid.*, pp. 169–170.
85 *Ibid.*, p. 170.
86 *Ibid.*, p. 171.
87 Ibid., p. 28.
88 *Ibid.*, p. 167. Haim Michal Michlin (1867–1937), a builder of Jerusalem neighborhoods who maintained ties with Herzl and sold shares of the Jewish Colonial Trust despite the government prohibition.

had no reason whatsoever to welcome Herzl. Nevertheless, he was accorded the utmost respect. According to Mordechai Ezrahi-Krishvesky, they were awed by his regal looks: "'*Malik al-yahud*' [king of the Jews], they would whisper among themselves, and if they compared him with Kaiser Wilhelm, Herzl would tip the scales."[89]

Itamar Ben-Avi also writes about how taken the Arabs were with Herzl's appearance. Walking in the streets of Jerusalem, the Arabs would point him out as "*akbar al-yahud* – the greatest of the Jews."[90] Moshe Smilansky records a similar response among the Arabs of Rehovot: "'*Malik al-yahud!*' murmur the Arabs standing between the trees as Herzl goes by."[91]

The Jews of Palestine

For the most part, the Jews of Palestine took a cautious view of Herzl. Smilansky has a simple explanation: "Outside of Eretz Yisrael, everyone knew who Herzl was. The new Zionism had already won hearts. But we did not know Herzl yet, and Zionism was still suspect in our eyes."[92] There were also ideological reasons for this anti-Herzl stance. Generally speaking, the Jews of Palestine fell into two main groups: members of the Old Yishuv and the pioneers of the *moshavot*.

The Old Yishuv

The Haredi Jews of the Old Yishuv were hostile towards Herzl for much the same reasons as the Haredi communities across Europe.[93] *Hahavatzelet*, a newspaper with a Haredi readership, reports from Jerusalem:

> "On the eve of Shabbat, the 13th of Heshvan, the celebrated Dr. Herzl and his retinue reached Jerusalem. His official purpose was to report for the newspaper *Neue Freie Presse*, of which he is an editor, on the spectacle of the visit of the Kaiser and his wife to Jerusalem and environs ... But [Haredi sources] said that his hidden purpose in coming to Jerusalem was to violate the strict prohibition, punishable by death, that applies only to Jerusalem and nowhere else, against going up to the Temple Mount – a sin which according to

---

89 *Ibid.*, p. 177.
90 *Ibid.*, p. 154.
91 *Ibid.*, p. 113.
92 *Ibid.*, p. 104.
93 See pp. 169, 191–192, 196–198, 202–205, 214–216.

most *halakhic* authorities warrants the death penalty even today. And indeed, he did carry out this act."[94]

In the same paper, we find a detailed account of the incident sent in by a resident of Jaffa:

> "Many Haredi Jews have asked me to denounce those who desecrated the Sabbath when His Majesty the Kaiser departed for Jerusalem. Mr. David Shub, who claims to belong to the pious camp, traveled to Jerusalem with Dr. Herzl... and they were accompanied by Mr. Niego, the administrator of Mikveh Yisrael. The [train] cars leaving at that time were full, so they waited for half an hour. More cars were added to the line for a special trip, and many Jews were at the station who were also planning to board ... They were told that the train would not reach Jerusalem until an hour after sunset, so they sold their tickets and decided not to go. One of these passengers approached Mr. Neigo and told him: 'If you go you will publicly desecrate the Sabbath.' He hastily bid [Mr. Neigo] farewell and returned to town, and only [Mr. Neigo] and Mr. David Shub, who had been told by many people not to travel lest he violate the Sabbath, refused to listen and boarded the train. Astonishingly, Reb Yudelvich, the teacher from Rishon Lezion, went along, too ... These are our religious teachers and Zionism's finest."[95]

---

[94] *Hahavatzelet*, November 6, 1898, p. 35.

[95] *Ibid*. This charge of Sabbath desecration needs further elucidation: There is no question that the paper was wrong, at least with respect to Neigo, who claims he did not travel to Jerusalem that day because he had to stay with his charges at Mikveh Yisrael over the weekend. See *ibid*., p. 140. Looking at various accounts of what happened on Friday, October 28, 1898, it seems the train was indeed delayed and arrived in Jerusalem in the late afternoon, but Herzl and his colleagues walked from the train station to the hotel and did not violate the Sabbath. Other reports on the train delay do not indicate arrival after sundown. Shub writes that the train pulled in close to sundown but before the start of Sabbath (Shub, *Zikhronot levait david*, p. 37). According to Vardi, the hour was late "and the inhabitants of Jerusalem had already finished their Sabbath eve prayers" (Vardi, *Malki betzion*, p. 23), but it was customary among some Jews to welcome the Sabbath early, when it was still light outside, and then recite the *Shma* in their homes after sunset. If that was the case, they could have finished praying by then. Also, one must consider how long it took Herzl, who was not feeling well, to walk from the train station to the center of town. Eliyahu Ze'ev Levine-Epstein's account does not mention any outright Sabbath desecration: "Later Friday afternoon I waited for the train, which always arrived before sundown, but unfortunately only the Kaiser's administrative staff and the military orchestra disembarked. Herzl's train was late (Vardi, *Malki betzion*, p. 120). Teacher and journalist Zalman Ben-Tovim writes about the Jews of Jerusalem who went out for a walk after their Sabbath meal to catch a glimpse of the Kaiser and his entourage: "And suddenly there was Dr. Herzl coming down Jaffa Road with his colleagues. They had just left the train, which had been delayed and pulled into the station as the holy Sabbath was ushered in" (Vardi, *Malki betzion*, p. 23, 170). According to this account, Herzl was on Jaffa Road when the Sabbath began. Assuming it took over half an hour for Herzl to get there, with his high fever and leg infection, leaning heavily on Shub and Wolffsohn, and he was seen on Jaffa Road at the start of the Sabbath, then the train clearly reached the station be-

Rothschild's Administrators and the Colonists

The inhabitants of the *moshavot* (Jewish agricultural colonies) had different reasons for opposing Herzl. Firstly, most of the *moshavot* were financed by Baron Rothschild and managed by his administrators, who upheld his policy of opposition to political Zionism. According to Dr. Hillel Yaffe, nearly all of them viewed Herzl with contempt and would not allow the colonists to organize a reception in Herzl's honor "because they say he is frightening the government with his publicized schemes and demand that an international agreement must be reached openly."[96]

Rothschild's officials were known for their strictness and hardline policies towards the colonists. In the spirit of their anti-Zionist views, they prohibited the sale of the Zionist shekel in the moshavot. As Vardi tells it: "All day long they sputtered and cursed Zionist propaganda. There was this group, on the one hand, and the Hovevei Zion of Jaffa on the other, with their opposition to Herzlian Zionism being the only thing they had in common."[97]

Brought together by their antipathy for political Zionism, members of Hovevei Zion in Jaffa joined the Baron's administrators in their fight. One would thus presume that neither group would welcome Herzl. Initially the colonists were apathetic towards political Zionism, writes Vardi, and even the young people were not fired up over the idea of Jewish statehood. In the end, however, it was not love of Zionism but hatred of the establishment that won them over: "We young people were attracted to Zionism out of contrariness, because the administrators we despised were against it."[98]

True, Herzl had supporters in Palestine and some of them attended the Zionist congresses,[99] but on the whole, the future for political Zionism did not look

---

fore sundown and no Sabbath desecration occurred. Shub also responds to the newspaper's accusation that Herzl had come to Palestine with the intention of committing a mortal sin: "The same newspaper reported that we visited the site of the Temple – which is an absolute lie. Dr. Herzl did not go there because I told him it was prohibited and in Jerusalem it was seen as a grave transgression" (Shub, *Zikhronot levait david*, pp. 37–38).

[96] Vardi, *Malki betzion*, p. 65.
[97] Ibid., p. 104. An unnamed doctor from Rishon Lezion warned that Zionism was a dangerous ideology that was solely interested in publicity. "Any resident of Eretz Yisrael who purchases the shekel is sinning against himself and the nation," he declared.
[98] Ibid., p. 104.
[99] Delegates included Wilhelm Gross (author of the first letter to Herzl in support of Zionism, written in 1896), Ephraim Cohen-Reiss, David Yellin, Dr. Yosef Yermans, Yechiel Michal Pines, Ze'ev Yavetz, Avraham Mani, Eliezer Ben-Yehuda, Heinrich Loewe and Dr. Lazar Grunhut. See Vardi, *Malki betzion*, p. 55.

bright. One would think that Herzl would skip visiting the colonists and do his best to avoid encounters with Rothschild's administrators, government officials and the local Arabs. It turned out that this was not the case. In practice, Herzl was feted by the locals, who also fell under the spell of his personality, handsome looks and charisma. Vardi describes his royal treatment:

> "Herzl arrived in Eretz Yisrael unannounced and no one came to greet him at the gates of Jerusalem ... The Jewish leaders stayed away, some out of opposition to Herzl and some out of fear of the secret police. But lo and behold! The moment he set foot on the soil of the colonies, dread of the government and Rothschild's bureaucrats seemed to melt away. A Zionist awakening ensued, the likes of which had never been seen before. Even the bureaucrats themselves had to say amen. What was going on here, for Rishon Lezion, the apple of the Baron's eye, to hold an assembly on a weekday, with men, women and children turning out to honor a man who was not the Baron or any relation to him? The people received him like a prince, and the same was true for Wadi Khanin and Rehovot. The winds of freedom began to blow and have hung in the air ever since. Even in Jerusalem itself, where the authorities are more vigilant, there were people who came out to kiss the hem of his garment and say *shekhalak mekhokhmato leyiraiyav* [a blessing recited upon seeing a sage]."[100]

Back to Europe

In early November 1898, Herzl returned disappointed from his trip to Palestine. His hopes for the establishment of Jewish state, which had seemed so certain after his audience with the Kaiser in Constantinople, were dashed after their encounter in Jerusalem. Even so, the very fact that he had met with the Kaiser could be hailed as an unprecedented political achievement. Herzl continued his travels and efforts to expand and consolidate the Zionist movement but did not know at the time that his problems in securing a charter for the Jewish state would be compounded by challenges at home.

The second half of this book will focus on the wall of opposition that Herzl faced and how he coped with the numerous obstacles that crossed his path. His image as a leader, which gradually evolved, as we have seen in the previous chapters, was frequently put to the test. On the following pages we will take a closer look at the actions of those who opposed Herzl both inside and outside the Zionist camp and what motivated them, as well as Herzl's response and how he held up over time, from one Zionist congress to the next – until his death.

---

100 *Ibid.*, p. 56.

Part 2: **Zionist Journey**

Chapter 6
Opposition to Herzl

> *It was into this dull atmosphere of decline that Herzl's 'Judenstaat' broke with the effect of a thunderbolt.*[1]

From the pinnacle of glory at the First and Second Congresses and a sense of accomplishment at having met with the Kaiser (if not satisfaction with the results), Herzl returned to the daily grind. He was forced to contend with ruthless opposition within the Zionist Movement and a wide range of grievances from without.

In the following chapters we will look at his opponents – Jews of Eastern and Western Europe, ultra-Orthodox, Zionists, Hovevei Zion and others. We will look at those who never joined him and those who joined and left. We will probe Herzl's response to them: when he took their objections in stride and when he took advantage of the attacks on him to respond and generate the publicity he needed to leverage and promote the goals of Zionism. We will explore how he dealt with different types of resistance with the help of his personal charisma and power of endurance, and how his temperament and demeanor stood him in good stead when crisis loomed, leaving even his opponents deeply impressed.

The atmosphere of uncertainty and indecision that pervaded the Jewish world in these early days of Zionism had much to do with the weakness of Hibbat Zion. The movement raised funds for the purchase of land and encouraged Jewish colonization in Palestine, but its operational methods were slow and cumbersome, and success was negligible. It avoided flaunting Jewish nationalism out of fear of the Ottomans in Palestine and Russian decrees, and ultimately failed to excite the masses. Its ability to raise money to help the pioneers was limited, and it was clear that salvation for the Jews of Europe did not lie here. Herzl criticized the movement's strategies and foot-dragging. Moshe Kleinman, editor of *Ha'olam*, called Herzl's criticism cruel yet painfully true: "because if we tally up what the Hovevei Zion have done, it will take a thousand years to achieve our goals."[2] Herzl disapproved of Hibbat Zion's policy of buying up land and building new colonies without obtaining a charter, and called for halting further colonization until a Jewish state was publicly recognized. To many members of Hibbat Zion, Herzl's schemes were thus objectionable in that they posed a "genuine danger to the cause."[3]

---

1 Bein, *Theodore Herzl: A Biography*, p. 179.
2 Kleinman, in: *Sefer hacongress* (1950), p. 21.
3 Buchmil, in: *Sefer hacongress* (1923), p. 72.

Leib Yaffe explains this further: "Hibbat Zion was afraid to stick its neck out at the time ... The Hovevei Zion were alarmed by Herzl's proud and fearless call and the public campaign he was waging in the full light of day. This new fellow who suddenly came from a faraway world, preaching their cause with naiveté and daring, oblivious to reality or obstacles, was strange and suspect in their eyes."[4]

Yaffe spells out the concerns of Hibbat Zion one by one. The bottom line was that without knowing whether Herzl's ideas would lead anywhere, he posed a tangible danger to the little that had been achieved with such painstaking effort. The first concern was that political Zionism would provoke the Turks into banning Jewish immigration and imposing harsh decrees on the pioneers. The second was that the Baron Rothschild, an opponent of Herzl, might halt his philanthropic aid to the Yishuv. Yet another concern was that the Russian government might shut down the work of the Odessa Committee. Last but not least, it was feared that Jewish nationalism would lead to the abandonment of Jewish values because the head of the movement was not a religious Jew.[5]

Yet fears aside, Hibbat Zion's policies had not brought salvation to the Jews. What was needed then was a dramatic upheaval that would infuse the Jews with new life and inspire them to embrace Jewish nationalism. Herzl launched a double transformation: in the Jewish people, via a process that began with the publication of *Der Judenstaat*, the convening of Zionist congresses and the establishment of the Zionist Organization; and in the world's leaders, via vigorous diplomacy. Herzl accomplished this feat through hard work, all the while juggling outside opponents and relentless bickering within the political Zionist camp. Some of this opposition he tolerated and some he had no choice but to fight, but his personal charisma played a critical role throughout.

The chronicle of opposition to Herzl can be divided into three stages:

Stage one: From the publication of *Der Judenstaat* in February 1896 until the call for the First Zionist Congress in April 1897. At this stage, only a minority was enthusiastic, while the majority treated him with suspicion and disdain, if not outright opposition.

Stage two: After plans for a Congress were announced, opposition mounted. Doubt and ridicule were replaced by objections based on lack of faith in the viability of the program and fears that Herzl and political Zionism would do harm.

Stage three: The success of the First Congress, the establishment of the Zionist movement and its organizational apparatus, and Herzl's diplomatic overtures.

---

4 Yaffe, in: *Sefer hacongress* (1923), p. 284.
5 *Ibid*.

All of this changed the picture. Enemies became lovers and the apathetic became admirers. Nevertheless, opposition to Herzl persisted in different forms and levels of intensity.

Who were Herzl's opponents and how did he respond to their outpouring of scorn and hostility? From where did he derive the emotional strength to continue his leadership role in the face of such contempt? On the following pages we will look at how Herzl's leadership skills helped him over the hurdles placed in his way by his adversaries, sometimes showing tolerance and sometimes battling his opponents head on. Finally, we will examine the durability of his charisma under crisis. We will study the torrent of negativism – the derision, the distortion of his words and the antagonism, some of it personal and some of it ideological. There were those who opposed Herzl out of ignorance and others out of hatred. Sometimes the opposition was based on lack of understanding. Being a complex, larger than life person almost invariably led to misunderstandings and misrepresentation.[6]

The mockers came first. Herzl writes about them: "One of the major battles I shall have to fight will be against the self-mockery of the Jews. This readiness to scoff represents, at bottom, the feeble attempts of prisoners to look like free men. That is why this mockery actually touches me."[7]

In 1896, in a speech to the Maccabean Club of London at the outset of his Zionist career, Herzl addresses this point:

> "Not this: My arguments were not opposed, they were simply disregarded. Many people read in a book not what is printed there, but what they themselves read into it. And those who know only the title were the most irate in offering judgment! The Jewish State! What madness – or should one say, what folly? Is this the joke of a comedian who wants to give the world a good laugh at the cost of his own unhappy people?
>
> The number of disparaging remarks was past counting. I have saved some of them. One day they will be a nice memorial for their authors should the Jewish State come into being. What sustained my philosophical attitude was the fact that the critics contradicted one another even more sharply than they contradicted me. With my pamphlet I stood, as it were, in the middle. One critic pronounced me a foolish optimist, another said I was a timorous pessimist. One moment my plan was a castle in the air, the next moment it was a shrewd business scheme …
>
> Of course, people were concerned with me personally, and the story went around that I wanted to become the King, or a Minister, of the Jewish State. To many, yet another view seemed plausible: that I was angling for a Jewish position abroad, perhaps that of ambassador to Vienna."[8]

---

6 On Herzl's genius, see pp. 39–40, above.
7 *Complete Diaries of Theodor Herzl*, vol. 1, pp. 106–107.
8 Herzl, *Zionist Writings*, Herzl Press 1973, vol. 1, p. 35.

Two years later, in an address delivered in Berlin, Herzl describes how he was ridiculed by the Berlin journalist Albert Klausner: "When *Der Judenstaat* was published Herr Klausner opined: 'If these are the ideas of an individual, they are the ideas of a madman!'"[9] Nevertheless, Herzl did not allow such responses to stand in his way.

From the time Herzl set out on his Zionist journey until the day he died, he knew there would always be people who would distort his words. Berl Katznelson observes: "In the context of Zionism, we frequently encounter the distortion of Herzl's character out of malice or ignorance."[10] A few months before his death, Herzl wrote to a young doctor from Geneva: "I am accustomed to having my words twisted in the most perverse way, and without a doubt, they will be twisted now yet again.[11]" Nahum Sokolow lamented the posthumous falsification of Herzl's image: "It is hard to accept that the legend of Herzl is being trampled like a doormat ...The tragedy is that this distortion clings like a skin ... Is there no one left who knew our first leader? Has the time come already to make a travesty of Herzl and the story of his life?"[12]

Herzl's awareness of the hurdles and his ability to accept and cope with them were one of his most important skills as a leader. There seems no question that the magnitude of the enterprise and Herzl's sense of mission were also a driving force.[13]

Opposition to Herzl: A Timeline

Let us begin by building a "timeline of opposition" to Herzl, charting the obstacles he faced and his solitude from the end of his Paris period and completion of his play *The New Ghetto* on November 11, 1894, up until the conciliation meeting of the Va'ad Hapoel in Vienna on April 11, 1904.

The first to declare Herzl's ideas insane was his friend Friedrich Schiff, a doctor and journalist based in Paris. Herzl asked Schiff to replace him on the newspaper during the three weeks he shut himself up to compose his letter to the Rothschilds (which would later become *Der Judenstaat*). Three weeks later, on

---

9 Ibid., p. 211.
10 *Bekhavlei adam*, p. 68 [Berl Katznelson, *Revolution and Roots: Selected Writings and Letters*, ed. Avinoam Barshai (Tel Aviv, 1966) [Hebrew].
11 He is referring to the Uganda crisis; quoted in Georges Yitshak Weiss, *Herzl, Kriya khadasha*, 2008, p. 19 [Hebrew].
12 Sokolow, *Hatzofe levayt yisrael*, p. 411.
13 This subject will be developed further in Chapter 11.

June 17, 1895, Herzl wrote Schiff a note asking him to come over the next day because he had some important news. When the curious Schiff arrived, he was shocked by what he saw and certain that something terrible had happened. Herzl, who was always impeccably groomed, was a mess. His hair was wild, his clothing disheveled and his eyes feverish. Herzl handed Schiff the manuscript. This is Herzl's account of his response:

> "While he was reading it, he suddenly burst into tears. I found this emotion natural enough, because he was a Jew: after all, I, too, had wept at times during the writing of it. But to my consternation he gave me an entirely different reason for his tears: He thought that I had gone mad, and since he was my friend, my misfortune made him very unhappy. He ran off without saying another word. After a 'sleepless night he returned, and pressed me hard to drop the matter ... "[14]

A year later, when Herzl reminded Schiff of that evening, Schiff replied: "Well, so perhaps I was wrong."[15] Schiff suggested that Herzl submit his "crazy plan" to Nordau, who was also a psychiatrist, and ask him if it was the work of a sane person. It was a proposal that had left Herzl shaken.[16] But Herzl was sure he had not lost his senses. Despite the emotional turmoil he had been through, he says he was tremendously reassured by the fact that Schiff, who had come to him with a list of expenses for those three weeks, kept making mistakes in his calculations whereas he was able to add up the figures in his head.[17]

Nordau and Herzl had known each other since Herzl's journalistic posting in Paris. They had spoken several times about the Jewish question and concurred that one of the factors that kept them loyal to the Jewish people was anti-Semitism. Herzl hoped that since they agreed on this point, Nordau would also agree with his conclusion. Nordau, however, reached the opposite conclusion: "The Jews will be compelled by anti-Semitism to destroy among all peoples the idea of a fatherland."[18]

In November 1895, Herzl completed his four-year stint in Paris and returned to Vienna. Two months later, he went back to Paris to spread his message and succeeded in winning Nordau over to the political Zionist cause. Anna and Maxa Nordau (Nordau's wife and daughter) tell the story:

---

14 Herzl , *Zionist Writings*, vol. 1, p. 18
15 *Complete Diaries of Theodor Herzl*, vol. 1, p. 425.
16 Pinhas Blumenthal, *Ein zo agada: Dyukono shel khozeh*, Am Oved, Tel Aviv 1964, p. 133.
17 *Complete Diaries of Theodor Herzl*, vol. 1, p. 117.
18 *Ibid.*, p. 196.

"Herzl came to see Nordau, and read his book to him. His first words were: 'Schiff says that I'm insane.' For three consecutive days he came back reading, explaining, arguing. Max Nordau listened, answered, discussed. The idea pierced him like a sword of light. The air vibrated about those two. Herzl, the younger of the two, with his handsome Assyrian head, was anguished, fevered, uplifted by his faith and his ardor. The older man watched him out of the grey eyes which burned in his white-bearded face. He curbed himself, but he was overcome and impressed. At last he rose and opened his arms to his trembling friend: 'If you are insane, we are insane together. Count on me!' Thus the Jewish State was born."[19]

Even before that, during the three weeks he spent writing to the Rothschilds in Paris, Herzl sent a letter to the rabbi of Vienna, Moritz Gudemann, trying to enlist his support. In the letter, he set out his plan and asked Gudemann to read it to Rothschild. The exchange of letters bore fruit: On August 17, Gudemann and Herzl met in Munich. Gudemann, carried away by Herzl's vision, exclaimed: "It is as if I saw Moses in the flesh."[20] Before they parted, he said: "Continue to be that which you are. Perhaps you are the one who has been called by God."[21] Despite Gudemann's outward enthusiasm, he had doubts about the feasibility of the plan. Herzl did not know that Gudemann had written a postcard to his wife that same evening saying: "Herzl is a poet. His plan, however interesting, cannot be implemented."[22]

Later, as the Zionist idea gained momentum and the First Zionist Congress drew near, Gudemann retracted his support and joined the opposition camp. In April 1897, he published a pamphlet entitled *Nationaljudentum (National Judaism)* in which he came out against political Zionism. His claim was that Judaism and Jewish nationalism were irreconcilable. Herzl reminded him that when he gave him the galleys of *Der Judenstaat*, the rabbi had praised the book. On February 2, 1896, Gudemann wrote: "I have read it all and find absolutely nothing to object to." Herzl attributed Gudemann's change of heart to pressure from affluent Jewish community leaders.[23]

---

19 Anna and Maxa Nordau, *Max Nordau: A Biography*, The Nordau Committee, New York 1943, pp. 118–120.
20 *Complete Diaries of Theodor Herzl*, vol. 1, p. 233; Pawel, *ibid.*, p. 183; Bein, *Theodore Herzl: A Biography*, p. 150.
21 *Ibid.*
22 Amos Elon, *Herzl*, Am Oved, Tel Aviv 1977, p. 184 (henceforth: Elon, *Herzl*).
23 Bein, *Theodore Herzl: A Biography*, p. 220. Analyzing Gudemann's remarks, Mordechai Eliav says Gudemann was implying that he and Herzl had misunderstood one another: Gudemann thought Herzl's intention was to join the fight against anti-Semitism, not play savior to the Jews by founding a state. Herzl did not accept this. He reminded the rabbi that when the three of them – Herzl, Gudemann and the banker Gustav Cohen – met, Gudemann had excitedly likened Herzl to Moses. Gudemann claimed in his memoirs that he had simply been taken by

Robert Wistrich also believes there was a misunderstanding here: "The truth of the matter is that Herzl seems to have been fundamentally wrong in his reading of Gudemann's thoughts, no less so than Gudemann in misreading the intentions of the Zionist leader. Each hoped to make use of the other to advance goals that ultimately conflicted."[24] Herzl wanted to build himself up with the help of Gudemann's connections and prestige, and Gudemann thought that Herzl could fill the void created by Rabbi Dr. Joseph Samuel Bloch's departure from the Austrian parliament, taking his place in the battle against rising anti-Semitism.[25]

Moshe Ungerfeld offers a different explanation in the Hebrew weekly *Ha'olam*. He describes a meeting of Jewish community leaders in Vienna to discuss the growing assimilation problem:

> "These were the days of Franz Joseph, and for every Jew who crossed the threshold of the church and was baptized with holy water, all the gates swung open and the path was paved to government positions and every high honor ... The leaders of the community met to discuss how to plug the dike ... A ball was organized for influential members of society to which representatives of newspapers with Jewish publishers were invited. Among the attendees, a certain tall fellow with a fine face, a handsome black beard and an air of majesty, drew all eyes. He arrived accompanied by his mother. Some guessed that he was a liberal Catholic and some that he was a baptized Jew. To many others, he was a complete enigma ... The ball was opened by Rabbi Dr. Isaiah Gelbhaus, a great scholar of distinguished lineage and an eminent writer ... After his remarks, this wondrous fellow walks over to him and introduces himself as the representative of the *Neue Freie Presse*."[26]

Herzl complimented Gelbhaus on his outstanding talk, informed him that he had a solution for the problem of assimilation and suggested they meet. A few days later, at Gelbhaus's home, Herzl read him selections from *Der Judenstaat*, which had not yet been published. Gelbhaus proposed that he meet Dr. Joseph Samuel Bloch, proprietor and editor-in-chief of the newspaper *Wochenschrift*.

---

surprise and responded without thinking. After that, he published his anti-Zionist polemic in which he called Zionism a perversion of history. He denied having written it at the behest of Vienna's Jewish elite. According to Eliav, Gudemann knew very well that the rich Jews felt this way and therefore Herzl's version was more reliable. Mordechai Eliav, "Herzl vehatzionut be'eynay Moritz Gudemann," *Hatzionut*, 7, pp. 399–425.

24 Robert Wistrich, "Hatzionut umevakreha hadati'im bevina shel shalhay hame'ah ha-19," in: *Tzionut vedat*, eds. Shmuel Almog, Jehuda Reinharz and Anita Shapira, Mercaz Shazar, Jerusalem 1994, p. 186 (henceforth: Wistrich, "Hatzionut umevakreha").
25 Ibid.
26 M. Ungerfeld, "Melivatay hatzionut harishonim," in: *Ha'olam*, 26, 1930, p. 506.

Herzl was excited: He knew the power of Bloch and his influential paper. Bloch, who also recognized the importance of Herzl's idea, was willing to get together. To this meeting, Bloch also invited the chief rabbi of Vienna, Rabbi Gudemann.

Gudemann did not stand on ceremony and came to Bloch's house, not wanting the meeting to take place at his own home or office at the Jewish community house lest someone think he was negotiating officially with Herzl, which would infuriate the lay leaders. Gudemann and Bloch agreed to support Dr. Herzl "as long as he does not write anything about it in the newspapers without their permission. He could publish and distribute his book, but the main thing was not to let anything leak to the papers about this new movement before consulting with them." Herzl consented. After *Der Judenstaat* came out, Bloch stood by his word and reported the event on the front page of his newspaper. He reviewed the book favorably, but beyond that took no further action. Herzl, who saw that Bloch and Gudemann's strategy would bury his idea alive, decided to go public. An article by Herzl was published by the *Jewish Chronicle* in London with immediate effect:

> "Then one day the London Rothschilds became enraged by an article published in one of the English newspapers and signed by Herzl. In this article, it was suggested that as global anti-Semitism grew, so too would Jewish national recognition grow, along with the movement for establishing a Jewish state in the Land of Israel."

In this article, Herzl also alluded to his new plan and remarked in passing that even personalities as distinguished as Rabbi Gudemann had responded favorably and promised to help. In the wake of this comment, the London Rothschilds reprimanded the Vienna Rothschilds for allowing their chief rabbi to support this dangerous movement and Rabbi Gudemann was summoned by Rothschild and personally taken to task. Gudemann himself regarded the article as a violation of his "contract" with Herzl and cut off all relations with him. Right after that, he sat down and wrote his pamphlet against Herzl and Zionism, *National Judaism*, in which he brought "decisive historic evidence" to show that Judaism had never been national in character but only religious. Thus the Jews of Germany were Germans of the Mosaic faith, the Jews of France, Frenchmen of the Mosaic faith, and so on. Bloch, on the other hand, did not come out publicly against Herzl until Herzl began to publish *Die Welt*, which Bloch regarded as serious competition against *Wochenschrift*. It was only then that he turned hostile to Herzl and the Zionist enterprise.[27]

---

27 *Ibid.*

Herzl's first days in Vienna after returning from Paris were very difficult. On the one hand, his standing at *Neue Freie Presse* was solid. He had come back from Paris after a trial period and had done so well that his editors rewarded him with the prestigious post of literary editor. On the other, his embrace of Zionism placed him in a difficult position because the overwhelming majority of Viennese Jews were against him. Leib Yaffe describes his predicament in those days: "Herzl was forlorn and isolated at the start of his journey. His plan was treated like a pretty thought, if not foolish or insane. His friends predicted that his fate would be either ridiculous or tragic."[28]

In Vienna, however, Herzl also found budding circles of support. First and foremost were his parents, who provided both moral and financial backing. Herzl was deeply attached to his parents. His mother instilled in him the confidence that he was destined for greatness, and his father stood by him, physically, emotionally and financially. When he composed *Der Judenstaat* in a state of near frenzy, scribbling on bits and pieces of paper, his father put the pamphlet together in an organized fashion. His father's encouragement and financial help were also indispensable when he founded *Die Welt* and the Jewish Colonial Trust.

The second tier of support came from a handful of Vienna Zionists. David Isaiah Silberbusch writes about Herzl's early appearance on the scene:

> "Members of Hibbat Zion everywhere were thirsting for a new word, not yet knowing what it was ... when suddenly, like a note dropped from the sky, a rumor began circulating that a new word had entered the lexicon of the Jews thanks to none other than a radically assimilated Jew ... A Jewish state. That was the word ... It was a word of tenfold value to us, the veteran Zionists of Vienna ... In the wall of assimilation that we had unsuccessfully sought to breach, a gaping hole suddenly opened, and that hole was the work of one who had been among the wall's fiercest defenders. The man now raising the banner to guide the nation to Zion had been a solid pillar of assimilation. He was one of the most popular editors of the *Neue Freie Presse*, beloved for his entertaining fare and small-talk mixed together with lofty ideas. We are speaking of the young writer, Theodor Herzl."[29]

Silberbusch, let us remember, was describing the response to Herzl of a very small group of Viennese Jews. The Zionists of Vienna, among them members of Kadimah, a Jewish fraternity and dueling society, were particularly enthusiastic, warmly embracing him as their leader.[30] Erwin Rosenberger, a student in

---

28 Yaffe, in: *Sefer hacongress* (1923), p. VII.
29 D.I. Silberbusch, *Mipinkas zikhronotai*, Hapoel Hatza'ir Press, Tel Aviv 1936, pp. 206–207.
30 *Ibid.*, pp. 205–217; Bein, *Theodore Herzl: A Biography*, p. 185.

Vienna and later the editor of *Die Welt*, recalls Herzl's first meeting with the Jewish students at the University of Vienna:

> "It was on February 8, 1896 that I first saw the man who was to influence so greatly the course of my life. That evening, Dr. Theodor Herzl appeared as guest at a lecture in the clubroom of the Judische Akademiche Lesehalle, the Jewish students' society, in Vienna's 9th District ... This day was a memorable one for him; it was memorable and heavy with consequences for us students, too – indeed, for all of Jewry, when one considers the important role played in the Zionist movement by the Jewish students of Vienna ... He began to speak at once in the middle of the room rather than on the podium; it was like a friendly private conversation and yet like a kind of official platform speech. Standing nearest him were Dr. Jacob Kohn and Isidor Schalit ..."[31]

According to Rosenberger, Herzl talked to them about *Der Judenstaat* and his Zionist vision. Isidor Schalit shares the story of how he bumped into Herzl's publisher Max Breitenstein in the street and was given the galleys of *Der Judenstaat*:

> "I was in a great hurry as I walked down Wahring Street and in my haste I bumped into someone and knocked him over. It was Dr. Breitenstein the bookseller. I had met him as a member of the Austrian Israelite Union ... and now this unfortunate thing happened. I had pushed a Union old-timer into the dusty road. Young people in those days still had respect for the elderly ... I picked Dr. Breitenstein up from the ground, brushed him off and mumbled a profuse apology. 'Alright now, that's enough. It wasn't your fault! Here, I have something that will surely interest you,' he said, as he thrust a bundle of papers into my hand and disappeared. They were printer's galleys. In those days they did not know how to do proofing with a hand press as we do today. The typesetter would take a sheet of damp paper, lay it flat over the composing stick and brush vigorously. Anyhow, I began to read what he had given me: *The Jewish State: An Attempt at a Modern Solution of the Jewish Question* by Theodor Herzl. His words struck a chord in my heart. Throughout the duel, my mind was totally preoccupied ... We returned to the *sukkah* [clubhouse] triumphant and amid the din of our victory celebrations, I started to read aloud. A great hush settled over the room, as if it were a sanctuary, and then such whoops of joy erupted, the very foundations shook. I had to go see Breitenstein to find out more about this Dr. Herzl, an editor for *Neue Freie Presse*, who resided at 9 Pelikanstrasse. I hurried over there. 'What you, Herr Doktor, have written is what we have dreamed of, the dream of so many. It is the thing we have been seeking for years but never found ... a Jewish state. Please, sir, come and be our leader, and we will do everything humanely possible to make it happen.' Herzl accompanied me immediately to the Kadimah club."[32]

Schalit's version of the story thus differs from that of Rosenberger.

---

31 Erwin Rosenberger, *Herzl as I Remember Him*, Herzl Press, New York 1959, pp. 11–14.
32 Isidor Schalit, in: *Ha'olam*, 33, 1946, p. 219.

Another Herzl supporter was the lumber merchant and banker David Wolffsohn, who took over the helm of the Zionist movement after Herzl's death. For Wolffsohn, *Der Judenstaat* was a life-changer: "When I had read it to the end, I felt that I had become another man. The broad perspectives, and the faith, strong as a vision, which speaks from every line of the *Judenstaat*, [have] opened before me a new world ..."[33] Members of other Zionist societies in Europe felt the same way. They wrote to Herzl urging him to assume the mantle of leadership and steer the Jewish people towards a state.

These pockets of support were important, but far from sufficient. Herzl, who needed an appreciative audience, found himself confronted in Vienna by a vast anti-political Zionist front that mocked and ridiculed him. In his autobiography *The World of Yesterday*, Stefan Zweig writes about the response to *Der Judenstaat* among the Jews of Vienna:

> "I was still in the *Gymnasium* when this short pamphlet, penetrating as a steel shaft, appeared; but I can still remember the general astonishment and annoyance of the bourgeois Jewish circles in Vienna. What has happened, they angrily, to this otherwise intelligent, witty and cultivated writer? What foolishness is this that he has thought up and writes about? Why should we go to Palestine? Our language is German and not Hebrew, and beautiful Austria is our homeland. Are we not well off under the good Emperor Franz Josef? Do we not make a decent living and is our position not secure? Are we not equal subjects, inhabitants and loyal citizens of our beloved Vienna? Do we not live in a progressive era in which in a few decades all sectarian prejudices will be abolished? Why does he, who speaks as a Jew and who wishes to help Judaism, place arguments in the hands of our worst enemies and attempt to separate us, when every day brings us more closely and intimately into the German world? The rabbis thundered passionately from the pulpits, the head of the *Neue Freie Presse* forbade the very mention of the word Zionism in his 'progressive' newspaper. Karl Kraus, the Thersites of Viennese literature, the master of invective, wrote a pamphlet called 'The King of Zion,' and when Theodor Herzl entered a theatre, people whispered sneeringly: 'His Majesty has arrived!' At first Herzl could rightly feel himself misunderstood – Vienna, where he thought himself more secure because had been beloved there for so many years, not only deserted him but even laughed at him."[34]

Herzl's reaction is interesting. Rather than taking offense or wallowing in self-pity, he contemplates their arguments. When his friend Friedrich Schiff teases him, asking in jest if he thinks he invented the dirigible airship, Herzl writes in his diary: "Hm, perhaps I did! I thought to myself, and kept silent."[35] Herzl thus sheds light on how his mind works: Schiff pokes fun at him but instead

---

33 Bein, *Theodore Herzl: A Biography*, p. 183.
34 *The World of Yesterday*, pp. 103–104.
35 *Complete Diaries of Theodor Herzl*, vol.1, p. 108.

of being insulted, Herzl ponders the remark and wonders whether there could be some truth in it.

Opposition in Western Europe

In 1896, following the publication of *Der Judenstaat*, Herzl launched his political campaign. In June of that year, he commenced the diplomatic forays that continued until his death in July 1904. Soon after that he started planning an international convention – the First Zionist Congress. At this stage, opposition began to emerge from different corners. According to historian Yosef Salmon, Herzl initially thought that funding for the Zionist enterprise would come from the Rothschilds and he could win public support through the rabbis. It did not take long for him to realize that the situation was more complex than that and the great challenge that lay ahead was not so much convincing the world as convincing the Jews. Herzl's first appeal was to Rabbi Gudemann, the chief rabbi of Vienna, who was receptive at first but caved in soon enough to the pressure of the Viennese religious establishment and turned his back on him.[36] Until Gudemann's death in 1913, all the rabbis of Vienna shared this negative view of Zionism.[37]

Herzl's overtures to the chief rabbi of England, Rabbi Naftali Zvi Adler, were likewise rebuffed. In Britain, opposition to Zionism was wall-to-wall.[38] The Anglo Jewish community was afraid of political Zionism. The Hovevei Zion in England initially welcomed Herzl, but then made their support contingent on a pledge that he would not criticize the strategy of the movement and would lend his blessing to slow-paced settlement in Palestine prior to obtaining a charter. Herzl refused: He was interested only in settlement that could be protected by a "Jewish army," he declared. This response led to a rift with Hibbat Zion in Britain. Colonel Albert Goldsmid, a Rothschild loyalist, advised against "speaking too loudly" about the national idea, and wrote a letter to Baron Nathaniel Rothschild warning him against Herzl and his plan.[39]

While the chief rabbi of France, Rabbi Zadoc Kahn, an active member of Hibbat Zion, was sympathetic to Herzl and his cause, this never became outright

---

[36] See above, pp. 162–164.
[37] Wistrich, *Hatzionut umevakreha*, p. 187.
[38] Yosef Salmon, Im ta'iru ve'im te'oreru: Ortodoxia bemetzaray haleumiut, Shazar Institute 2006, p. 245, note 32. See also: Stuart A. Cohen, "Mini'im umotivim dati'im behitnagdutam shel yehudim be'anglia letzionut hamedina, 1895–1920," in: *Zionut vedat*, pp. 200–201.
[39] Bein, *Theodore Herzl: A Biography*, p. 207; Pawel, *Labyrinth*, p. 307

support. Herzl did not believe that the Jews of France were behind him and made little effort to win them over. Kahn felt that the loyalty of French Jews should be to France, and thus veered away from political Zionism.[40]

In Germany, too, the rabbis were among Herzl's early opponents, though not the only ones. Yaakov Zur notes that opposition to political Zionism in Germany crossed ideological bounds and extended to every streams of Judaism from Reform to ultra-Orthodox. The attack on the Zionist movement came from all sides.[41] Adolf Bohm pronounced the Orthodox Jews of Germany no less hostile to Zionism than the assimilated Jews.[42] Rabbi Dr. Isaac Breuer, later a founding member of Agudat Yisrael, went so far as to describe Zionism as "the most dangerous enemy the Jewish people has ever known."[43] This did not deter Jews from the Orthodox or assimilated world from joining the movement, but the ones who did were mainly young people with no political power.[44]

Paradoxically, hostility to Herzlian Zionism became a common cause for the Reform and Orthodox congregations across Western Europe. At the height of preparations for the First Zionist Congress, which was supposed to be held in Munich, Haredi and Reform rabbis joined forces in an anti-Zionist campaign that forced Herzl to relocate the congress to Basel. Herzl named them the "Protest Rabbis."[45]

Opposition in Eastern Europe

The Jews of Eastern Europe were more traditional than those of Western Europe, and political Zionism could be more readily absorbed because the Jewish community did not enjoy the civil liberties granted in Western Europe. For this community, Herzl's "Jewish state" was a promise, not a threat. Yet even here, he had opponents. Roughly speaking, the attitude toward Herzl fell into three categories:

---

40 Salmon, *ibid.*, note 35.
41 Yaakov Zur, "Ha'ortodoxia hayehudit begermania veyekhasa el hatzionut," in: *Zionut vedat*, p. 127 (henceforth: Zur, *Zionut vedat*).
42 Yaakov Zur, "Bein tzionut ve'ortodoxia begermania," in: *Hatzionut umitnagdeha ba'am hayehudi*, eds. Haim Avni and Gideon Shimoni, Hasifriya hatzionit, Jerusalem 1990, p. 75.
43 Isaac Breuer, *Judenproblem*, O. Handel, Halle (Saale) 1918, p. 75; *Hatzionut umitnagdeha*, ibid.
44 Zur, in: *Zionut vedat*, p. 131
45 Herzl, *Zionist Writings*, vol. 1, pp. 119–124.

(a) Haredi Jews who rejected Zionism from the outset and never accepted it – They saw Zionism as the successor of the menacing Enlightenment movement which had caused much disruption in the Orthodox world, or believed that the goals of Zionism went against the Torah and the teachings of its sages;

(b) Haredi Jews who were initially attracted to political Zionism and later withdrew from it. Members of this group included Rabbi Eliyahu Akiva Rabinovich of Poltava and Yehuda Leib Tsirelson of Priluki,[46] who attended the first Zionist congresses, but quit in the wake of the kultura controversy. Some became bitter foes of the movement;

(c) National Haredi Jews who supported political Zionism and were prepared to fight for it.

We will not elaborate here on the first category of Orthodox Jews, but on those who embraced Zionism but then split in different directions, some leaving the movement and others remaining.[47] The National Haredi Jews were supportive of Herzl and political Zionism. Among them were a number of rabbis – Rabbi Shmuel Mohilever (whose views were particularly influential) and later Rabbi Shmuel Yaakov Rabinowitz of Aleksot. They belonged to a small rabbinic minority that saw political Zionism as a means of saving the Jews from the torments of the Russian government. As Salmon puts it: "The Zionist argument was diverted from its cultural and spiritual core, and translated into a platform that could solve the existential problems of the Jewish people."[48]

This group constituted Zionism's great hope: In it lay the potential support of the religious masses in Eastern Europe. For the most part, however, these hopes were dashed. The participation of the ultra-Orthodox in the first congresses and their subsequent exodus will be discussed in the chapter devoted to the culture debate. But to answer the question of why they joined the Zionist movement in the first place, under the leadership of a man who was not an observant Jew, we must return to the relationship between Haredim and non-Haredim in the Hibbat Zion era.

The Haredi stance on political Zionism and the Hovevei Zion followed a similar trajectory. In both cases, the community moved from support to opposition. At first the Hovevei Zion enjoyed the blessing of the rabbis, but this changed in the wake of the Gedera Bilu dispute,[49] the *shmitta* dispute,[50] and even more so

---

[46] Salmon, *ibid.*, p. 40. See pp. 193–194 on the culture debate.
[47] Salmon, "Tzionut ve'anti-tzionut beyahadut hamesoratit bemizrakh europa," in: *Zionut vedat*, p. 34.
[48] *Ibid.*, p. 40.
[49] The Gedera controversy occurred in 1887 when the Bilu pioneers set up camp on the Sabbath, constituting a public desecration of the Jewish day of rest. Members of the Old Yishuv de-

the refusal of Ahad Ha'am and the Bnai Moshe society to accept Jewish law as the sole norm for a Jewish national collective on the grounds that it only applied to a certain sector.[51]

In theory, Herzl's entry should not have altered the picture. The Haredim should have boycotted him based on their experience with Hovevei Zion. Yet despite the programmatic approach of *Der Judenstaat*, which was foreign to the religious Jews of Eastern Europe, and the rabbis' knowledge that they would not have a say on policy matters in the Zionist movement and a future Jewish state, they did not reject Herzl out of hand. On the contrary, he received dozens of telegrams from rabbis in support of his call for a Zionist congress.[52]

The First Congress was held in Basel under West European hegemony, which posed a hefty challenge for the East Europeans for a number of reasons. First of all, the Jews of the East felt inferior to the West European Jews and were suspicious of them.[53] Second, they were not familiar with the local customs. Third, the congress was largely conducted in German, which many East European Jews did not speak. Fourth, the trip was expensive, which kept many Russian rabbis away. And fifth, they were deterred by the presence of Ahad Ha'am devotees and members of Bnai Moshe. Rabbi Reines, later one of Herzl's most ardent supporters, did not attend because of Herzl's perceived irreligiousness. The voice of the religious Jews of Eastern Europe was hardly heard on the podium of First Congress, and the opening speech by Dr. Karpel Lippe of Jassy, the oldest delegate, was even anti-religious. The atmosphere was so hostile that one of the Russian delegates hid to pray *mincha*.[54]

Even so, the Zionist movement captured the hearts of many traditional Jews. There are several possible reasons. Historian Jehuda Reinharz believes the alliance was made possible by the "pure Zionist approach" adopted by the Haredim during the conflict with Hovevei Zion, i.e., concentrating on Zionism as an eco-

---

clared that it was better that the Land of Israel remain unsettled than become a home to Sabbath desecrators.
50 The *shmitta* controversy arose in 1888 over the observance of the sabbatical year, when the Torah commands that agricultural lands lie fallow. Fearing that no farming for a whole year would lead to the economic collapse of the colonies, Rabbi Shmuel Mohilever and other rabbis came up with a strategy called "*heter mekhira*" in which the land would be sold to non-Jews for two years, thereby allowing the farmers to work during shmitta. Rabbi Yehoshua Leib Diskin, Rabbi Shmuel Salant and others objected to this arrangement.
51 Salmon, "Tguvat hakharedim bemizrakh europa latzionut hamedinit," in: *Hatzionut umitnagdeha*, pp. 52–55 (henceforth: Salmon, "Tguvat hakharedim").
52 Ibid., p. 56.
53 See letter of Saul Pinhas Rabbinowicz (aka Shefer), p. 176.
54 Salmon, "Tguvat hakharedim," p. 56.

nomic and political solution for East European immigrants. This approach aligned with Herzl's interest in steering away from culture issues.⁵⁵ Ehud Luz, on the other hand, attributes it to Herzl's carefulness not to offend religion in any way and to treat the religious leaders with respect. On top of that, he cites Herzl's motto at the First Zionist Congress: "Zionism is a return to Jewishness even before there is a return to the Jewish Land."⁵⁶ Salmon also comments on the use of this phrase: "The Zionist Organization won the hearts of many traditional Jews. Religious Zionists obscured the world view of the Zionist leadership, highlighting statements that had little basis, such as the orphan sentence in Herzl's congress speech about Zionism being a return to Judaism."⁵⁷ Rabbi Rabinowitz of Aleksot interpreted the remark literally: Zionism was first of all a return to Judaism because Zionism would bring back many freethinkers who had abandoned Judaism.⁵⁸

It is hard to accept the arguments of Salmon and Luz, which imply that Herzl's remarks were deliberately slanted to mislead the religious public and win them over to Zionism. Obviously Herzl was not saying that the return to Judaism was a return to a life of Torah and religious commandments. He also made it clear that Zionism was not out to intervene in anyone's religious beliefs. At the First Congress, he assured the assembled crowd that "Zionism is not intending to do anything that would harm the religious belief of any aspect that is within Judaism."⁵⁹ What he meant to say, therefore, was that all streams of Judaism were welcome to operate under the political Zionist umbrella and advance their cause according to their proportional strength in the movement.

Gaining the support of the religious community also presumably had much to do with Herzl's unique persona. As Luz writes:

> "'Herzl, a legend in his own lifetime who symbolized the latent yearnings of all walks of the people, found his most ardent admirers among the observant Jews of Eastern Europe.' To his followers he was a penitent who had left assimilated society, the 'severed limb of the Jewish people,' with the goal of redeeming them. Even those who were hostile to Zionism because of its leaders made an exception in Herzl's case on the grounds that he was a *tinok shenishba* (evoking the Talmudic principle of the captive child who received no Jewish education and thus sins inadvertently) and were completely mesmerized by him."⁶⁰

---

55 Jehuda Reinharz, "Tzionut ve'ortodoxia: Nisu'im shel nokhut," in: *Zionut vedat*, pp. 151–152.
56 Luz, *Parallels Meet*, p. 140.
57 Salmon, "Tguvat hakharedim," p. 58.
58 Raphael, *Ish hameorot*, p. 95.
59 Herzl, *Kitvei Herzl be'asara krakhim*, vol. 7: *Bifnay am ve'olam*, Hasifria Hatzionit, Jerusalem, 1961, p. 130.
60 Luz, *Parallels Meet*, p. 140.

Shmaryahu Levin's testimony supports this view. In his memoirs, Levin describes the great impression Herzl made on a sober-minded man like Rabbi Shmuel Mohilever, perhaps all the more so because of his detachment from Judaism:

> "Rabbi Shmuel Mohilever made a supreme effort to reach out to me, and since Grodno was close to Bialystok, I visited him frequently. On these occasions, I could not help noticing what a profound impression Herzl and his tidings made on this great and pious scholar, a man of deep faith for whom Herzl's world was truly foreign and the converse of his own. This was the same man, by the way, who fought against Pinsker because of his secularism ... I was interested to know if the rabbi would treat Herzl the same way, and make the same demands he had made on Pinsker. I saw it with my own eyes: Herzl's influence on him was miraculous. The elderly rabbi had not yet made up his mind whether or not to heed Herzl's call, or whether he would join him without reservation, but it was clear that Herzl's estrangement from Judaism impacted on him deeply: Along comes a stranger, unfurls the banner of national liberation and leaves this devout and scholarly man of faith in awe. In his eyes, Herzl and his prophecies were a sign of the times, a sign of grace."[61]

Nevertheless, Herzl's persona only drew in the religious nationalists. Haredim from other streams who jumped on the political Zionist bandwagon ended up leaving the movement and fighting against it over the culture issue that split the Zionist camp.

United States

The political Zionist platform that bore Herzl's name also reached the United States. In the Hebrew newspaper *Hapisga,* Zev Wolf Schur published an impassioned plea to Hovevei Zion in America to "hold assemblies and choose delegates to the Great Assembly [the Zionist Congress]."[62] But in America, like Europe, the Reform movement responded with fury. Herzl was mercilessly attacked in the movement's newspapers and in July 1897 the Reform rabbinate released a statement denouncing the idea of a Jewish state.[63]

Despite the geographical divide, however, Herzl and political Zionism succeeded in the United States. On the question of whether America and the nature of Jewish life there were conducive to Zionism, at first glance Aryeh Goren says no. He argues that precisely because life was so comfortable for the Jews, the Zionist solution did not stand much chance. To emphasize this point, he cites

---

61 Levin, *Bama'arakha,* pp. 122–123.
62 Mordechai Naor, *ibid.,* p. 37.
63 *Ibid.*

the comment of the nineteenth century American novelist Herman Melville: "We Americans are the peculiar, chosen people – the Israel of our time; we bear the ark of the liberties of the world."[64]

As part of the American experience, America pledged the "inclusion" of its Jews. It was an invitation, but also very much a potential demand for assimilation. Figures like the American Jewish banker Jacob Schiff expressed concern that the Zionist movement would cause a flare up of anti-Semitism in America. Zionism in America thus encountered a rocky start. Two out of the three main denominations of Judaism – Orthodox and Reform – immediately came out as strong opponents, whereas the Conservative movement was friendlier.[65]

Nevertheless, America differed from Europe in that some Reform rabbis did voice support for political Zionism. A prominent example is Rabbi Gustav Gottheil of Temple Emanu-El in New York, who declared in 1893 that the Palestine was no longer the land of the Jews. Four years later, he changed direction, becoming an outspoken advocate of Zionism, a loyal follower of Herzl and vice president of the Zionist Organization of America. There were other Reform rabbis like him, albeit not many, and together they formed a group known as Converts to Zionism.[66]

The Zionist Movement in the Eyes of the Masses

Up to now we have looked at how the rabbinic and lay leaders of various communities responded to Zionism. What we need to consider at this point is the extent to which the rabbis and community activists truly represented the Jewish masses. On the one hand, the conventional wisdom is that Zionist sentiment was greater in Eastern Europe than Western Europe. On the other hand, the Zionist movement at its peak managed to attract only a small minority of East European Jews. Could it be that these claims of support or opposition come from a tiny vanguard who took the liberty of speaking in the name of a whole camp?

The abundance of testimony about the frenzy set off by *Der Judenstaat* and Herzl's audience with global leaders also requires examination: Is newspaper

---

[64] Aryeh Goren, "Hatzionut umitnagdeha beyahadut amerika," in: *Hatzionut umitnagdeha ba'am hayehudi*, p. 354.
[65] Evyatar Friesel, "Mashma'ut hatzionut vehahashpa'a al yahadut amerika," in: *Zionut vedat*, pp. 216–220.
[66] Jonathan Sarna, "Mumarim letzionut betnu'at hareforma ha'amerika'it, in: *Zionut vedat*, pp. 223–224.

coverage an accurate index? Did the press reflect public opinion or attempt to shape it?

While we cannot provide a definitive answer to this, we do have testimony from which we can learn about the mindset of the masses. Stefan Zweig's comments above, for example, emphasize the negative attitude in Vienna toward Herzl's political Zionism.[67] As a German-born jurist and Zionist activist who married an East European woman, Sammy Gronemann was intimately acquainted with the spirit of the times:

> "Jewry split into two camps: Zionists and non-Zionists. All the other distinctions suddenly seemed ridiculous and old-fashioned. But it was only one little group, at least in Western Europe, that assembled under the unfurled banner. The vast majority of Jews in every other country opposed the new ideology. Orthodox and liberal, conservative and reform – they all screamed and scoffed at the Zionists who were gripped by foolishness ... In those days I myself protested this new ideology with all my might. For a German Jew, one must remember, having one's entire outlook turned upside down was a complicated surgical procedure."[68]

Gronemann explains why East European Jews found it easier to join the Zionist movement: "The Jews of the East... were familiar with Jewish folk culture and grew up in an aura of Judaism that our Jews [the German Jews] could no longer grasp."[69]

Gronemann's theory was not unfounded. In the eyes of West European Jews, Herzl's doctrine endangered the prospects of integration in their home countries, which was never an option for the Jews of Eastern Europe. This community was still largely observant and close to Jewish tradition to one extent or another, which made it easier to identify with Hovevei Zion and then political Zionism. Nevertheless, the distinction between East and West in this sphere was not clear-cut. In Western Europe, we find Zionist activists who went on to assume leadership positions, like Heinrich Loewe, Max Bodenheimer and Nathan Birnbaum, who worked on their own and recruited others to the Zionist cause even before Herzl arrived on the political Zionist stage, and when he appeared, immediately pitched in to help him. At the same time, there were East European Jews who fought political Zionism tooth and nail. Among them were Hovevei Zion leaders who rejected Herzl and his approach. They saw him as a gatecrasher whose ideas jeopardized their achievements. Even in the Vilna branch of Hibbat Zion, which was considered a Zionist stronghold, there were members who de-

---

67 See above, p. 167.
68 Gronemann, *Zikhronot shel yekke*, p. 96.
69 Ibid., p. 97.

clared war on him.[70] As the First Congress drew near, some Hovevei Zion in Eastern Europe[71] sounded a warning call against it, but once they understood it was a fait accompli, they jumped on the bandwagon: In July 1897, Saul Pinhas Rabbinowicz (aka Shefer), a Hovevei Zion leader in Russia, wrote:

> "In retrospect, it would have been preferable if the Congress had not come into being, but now that it has, we must sweeten the bitter pill and strive to prevent any harm or damage to the existing colonies and our future endeavors."[72]

Herzl's initiative roused Hibbat Zion from its slumber and lackadaisical pace, infusing it with the spirit of combat. The movement attempted to restrain Herzl and subdue the flames of public nationalism he so assiduously built up. Toward this end, Hovevei Zion in Eastern Europe sought to join forces with their counterparts in Western Europe. Shefer writes: "Meanwhile, I have begun to think about how we can win the hearts of the Westerners, convincing them to adopt our view, speak as we do, and unite as a single party. Otherwise we will not succeed in standing up to the loudmouthed youth of Galicia [Herzl's East European supporters] whose world consists of nothing but rhetoric and healthy lungs ..."

In his letter, Shefer spells out the mission of the party he wished to establish, stressing that its power depended on cooperation with its allies in Western Europe:

> "Again I want to say that all our work must be aimed at creating a unified party with a message that will be heard, and this is only possible if we are joined by Westerners who think much like we do, and have the organization and training to speak clearly as a group. Only this way can we assure that the outcome of the Congress will benefit the real Lovers of Zion, by which I mean love of Zion in the practical sense, carried out with forethought, agility and caution, not shouting at the top of one's lungs without looking at both sides of the coin."[73]

One can easily see from Shefer's remarks that Herzl and political Zionism were not considered "real" Zionism. It was Hibbat Zion that was regarded as authentic. This was the thinking in Eastern Europe up until the First Zionist Congress.

To summarize, many Hovevei Zion ended up completely charmed by Herzl and became devotees of political Zionism. While one would have thought his extraordinary success at the First Congress would guarantee a firm wall of support

---

[70] Yosef Eliash, *Zikhronot tzioni merussia*, Hasifriya Hatzionit, 1956, p. 67.
[71] See *Sefer hacongress* (1950), p. 178.
[72] Shefer, in: *Sefer hacongress* (1923), pp. 284–285.
[73] *Ibid.*, p. 287.

for his Zionist quest, the reality was otherwise: His path was not strewn with roses. Steadily mounting opposition in the Zionist Organization forced him to diffuse his energies and grapple with forces that eventually sapped his strength. The reasons for this opposition, how Herzl dealt with it, and the price he paid, will be addressed in the following chapter.

Chapter 7
Opposition to Herzl in the Zionist Movement

On the Eve of the First Congress

Before the First Zionist Congress opened its doors, Herzl's opponents worked tirelessly to undermine his efforts, but Herzl was no match for them. He persevered and went on to preside over this congress – and five more – before his death. Nevertheless, the Zionist congresses and institutions founded in their wake created a wide berth for action among those who opposed him.

Opposition to Herzl took many guises. First, there was the gentle, even friendly opposition, such as that described by Ze'ev Jabotinsky in his autobiography. Recalling the Sixth Congress, a first for him, Jabotinsky relates how he met Dr. Weizmann, "a tall, lanky fellow with a triangular black beard and a shiny bald pate whom I was told was head of the 'opposition.' I sensed right away that I, too, belonged in the opposition without yet knowing why."[1] A possible explanation is that Jabotinsky, a born dissident bubbling with youthful exuberance, was bothered by the staid formality imposed by Herzl in the congress halls and joined the opposition as an outlet for his rebellious streak. Louis Lipsky says something along the same lines about the mathematician and Zionist activist Leo Motzkin, one of the ringleaders of the Democratic Fraction: "He believed that if opposition did not exist, it should be created, because one-sidedness was a dangerous thing."[2] Motzkin went on to fight Herzl bitterly on a multiple issues. At the same time, deep down he remained an inveterate admirer of Herzl. Alex Bein states that in his Zionist outlook he was closer to Herzl than most of the Democratic Fraction: "Motzkin, a leader of the opposition against Herzl at the Zionist congresses, admired him from the depths of his heart and was one of the most faithful followers of his Zionist doctrine. It is no wonder that Herzl's death in July 1904 left Motzkin shaken to the core. On the way to the leader's funeral in Vienna, when a travel companion pointed out that his necktie was askew, Motzkin sighed mournfully: 'Who cares anymore? When Herzl was alive, I always fussed over my appearance before leaving for the Congress so as not to offend the President's aesthetic sensibilities or mar the festive atmosphere. But now?' ..."[3]

---

[1] Jabotinsky, *Autobiografia*, pp. 48–58.
[2] Louis Lipsky, *Dmuyot batzionut*, p. 94.
[3] *Sefer Motzkin*, 1939, ed. Alex Bein, Zionist Executive and World Zionist Organization, Jerusalem 1939, p. 69.

Herzl faced an opposition that was fierce and hostile, and as we shall see, motivated by personal resentment. Some of this opposition waned over time in response to trends and developments in the Jewish world and beyond. In general, opposition toward Herzl in the Zionist movement could be categorized as either moderate or radical.

First Category: Friendly Opposition

This category includes people who actually met with Herzl and interacted with him at Zionist functions. They can be divided into a number of subcategories:

From Opposition to Support

Some people were negative at the outset but succumbed to Herzl's charms upon closer acquaintance. Many members of this group were affiliates of Hovevei Zion who regarded him as unfair competition and a threat to the organization's achievements in Palestine and Russia. They pronounced him a reckless daredevil whose antics would only provoke the Ottoman authorities and make life more difficult for those devoted to improving the lot of the Yishuv.[4] After meeting Herzl in person these fears were largely dispelled, and they respectfully bowed to his authority. This was the case with Menachem Ussishkin, for example, who was highly skeptical and initially refused to meet him altogether. As soon as he did, he changed his tune and placed himself at Herzl's service,[5] although he later fought against him tooth and nail on Uganda. Even Hermann Schapira, who came up with the idea of establishing the Jewish National Fund, opposed political Zionism until he met Herzl. Leib Yaffe describes how he and a group of pro-Herzl students visited Schapira in Heidelberg, where he was a professor of mathematics: "Schapira received us courteously but coldly... Like many Hovevei Zion, he was alarmed by Herzl's bold demands. In his view, the talk about a Jewish state could only do harm ... but at the Congress, Schapira was won over, like many other skeptics and opponents."[6] The same was true for Nahum Soko-

---

4 Leib Yaffe, see p. 158 above.
5 *Sefer Ussishkin*, pp. 352–354.
6 *Sefer hacongress* (1923), pp. 224–225.

low.⁷ These were people who changed their mind after taking part in the First Congress, where they became fans and supporters.

Some were not smitten upon meeting Herzl for the first time but fell under his spell as time when on. One was David Neumark. At the First Congress, he sneered at Herzl, whom he said reminded him of a traveling salesman. However, little by little, Neumark was drawn in, to the point where he was awed by Herzl's majesty and mourned his death as a personal and national calamity.⁸

Another case, similar in some respects but not all, was that of Joseph Cowen, one of the founders of the British Zionist movement. He attended the First Congress as a guest at the urging of Israel Zangwill but was plagued with doubts about Zionism and Herzl. He feared that the "bride was too beautiful." He found Herzl overly self-assured and was disturbed by the fact that he had a ready answer to every question, no matter what. He worried that political Zionism was unrealistic and came away from his first encounter with Herzl convinced that with all his outward charm, the man was either a dreamer or a madman.⁹ Later, he confessed that although Herzl had been very gracious towards Zangwill and himself, and they had conversed on several occasions, he could not rid himself of his fears and misgivings. Furthermore, Herzl was so full of humor and jest that Cowen wondered if he weren't living in some fantasy or magical dreamland. Herzl also spoke about Judaism and the Jews very differently than he had ever heard before. So it was a slow process for Cowen. At a certain point, he concluded that Zionism was a glorious but impossible dream. Only by the Third Congress, which he attended as a delegate, was he fully confident in the path of Herzlian Zionism. After Herzl's death, he wrote about feeling that "all our hopes have been lost."¹⁰

Respectful Opposition

Whereas there were some who switched sides from opposition to support, there were others who were part of Herzl's social circle and knew him well but disagreed with him ideologically. Yet this did not diminish their respect for him. They saw him as the father of political Zionism and instrumental in breathing new life into the concept of Zionism. Members of the Democratic Fraction fell into this category, among them Martin Buber, Berthold Feivel, Ephraim Lilien,

---

7 See above, pp. 86–91, on the chapter about Herzl and the press.
8 See above, pp. 124–125; *Sefer hacongress* (1923), p. 19.
9 *Sefer hacongress* (1950), p. 153.
10 *Ibid.*

Leo Motzkin and Yehiel Chlenov. They did not see eye on eye on a wide range of issues, from *Kultura*,[11] *Altneuland*[12] and Uganda,[13] to his authoritarian leadership style. Nevertheless, they continued to honor and admire him, and could not imagine the Zionist movement without him.

According to the American Zionist leader Louis Lipsky, Motzkin and his colleagues regarded opposition as an *apriori* necessity. The whole purpose of the Democratic Fraction was to defy Herzl and make him uncomfortable. They sought to exploit their collective power to criticize and flex their muscles, but without posing a genuine threat because it was clear to them that the Zionist movement was nothing without him.

Myriam Schach, a French Zionist, also commented on this subject:

"The opposition was very fiery and fierce, which raised the question of why these cantankerous 'contenders for office' did not bring down the 'government' they so disliked. Parliamentary law gave them the means to do so. For a brief period, Herzl taught my colleagues to think in 'parliamentary' terms although most of them had never seen a parliament in their lives! Since it was a strictly secret ballot, they could have simply refrained from a 'vote of confidence.' True, they were only a minority, but Herzl needed the influence of a united Congress behind him for negotiations with the 'outside world.' So what was it that held the opposition back? The answer is that none of the parties or their leaders were willing to take upon themselves a regime change that involved so much responsibility and so few resources.

In this context, I surprised one of the top 'heirs' (as the leaders of the Fraction were known in Herzl's close circle) with a question: 'If Herzl decided one day he was leaving after growing sick and tired of all the unjust and shameful attacks on him, and you were offered a chance to replace him, what would you do?'

-We would run for our lives!

-So why are you so interminably critical of him?

-But hasn't that always been the purpose of opposition? Disraeli and Gladstone were subjected to even harsher criticism, worse than ours ...'

Many thanks for including Herzl in that grand company, I replied, but a serious party in England never attacks the government if it cannot offer an immediate alternative, whereas you want to play at learning how to command before you have even served. It's a sterile, pointless game if not successful, and dangerous if it is..."[14]

Schach goes on to describe how the Fraction members never tired of mocking Herzl for hobnobbing with the royals and strutting down ministerial halls:

---

11 See pp. 198–204.
12 See pp. 224–235.
13 See pp. 236–271.
14 Myriam Schach, *Asher itam hit'halakhti*, translated by K.A. Bertini, Dvir, Tel Aviv 1951, pp. 41–43 (henceforth: Schach, *Asher itam*.

"Yet they knew perfectly well that losing such privileges would rob their leader of all prestige in the eyes of the Zionist public and the entire world. And since both sides wished, above all, to avoid any visible rupture, the Standing Committee always ended the most heated of arguments with a 'closing prayer' and an 'ode to peace.' The General Assembly (the plenum) would pass all motions unanimously! The Congress would approve them, too – until Uganda ... A vote of confidence in the leader would end with all the delegates rising to their feet in unending applause, the beloved leader perceived as synonymous with [Zionism] itself."[15]

As Schach notes, this was the custom until Uganda. At that point, Ussishkin's people proposed taking over the leadership from Herzl, as we shall see in Chapter 10.

Opposition Spurred by Personal Rivalry

In this group were the "frustrated leaders" – charismatic figures with leadership ability who recognized Herzl's power and respected it, but because they were born leaders themselves, chose to sit in the opposition. They challenged him both on ideological grounds – *Kultura* and *Gegenwartsarbeit* ("present-day work") – and because of his leadership style, at the Congresses and in the intervals between them. At the top of the list were Chaim Weizmann and Menachem Ussishkin, whose lust for leadership turned them into provocateurs.

These three groups of opponents belonged to the category of homegrown opposition. Even in the opposition, they treated Herzl with respect and habitually bowed to his authority. But there was another category of opposition whose bite was much fiercer.

Second Category: Radical Opposition

"Two kings cannot serve with one crown"[16]

In this category are people who were never enamored with Herzl at any stage, even after interaction with him. They seem to have been a special breed, gifted individuals who could not find a niche for themselves under Herzl and ended up opposing him. Notable examples:

---

15 *Ibid.*, p. 44
16 Babylonian Talmud, *Hulin*, 60b.

Nathan Birnbaum

Nathan Birnbaum, known by his literary pseudonym Matityahu Akher (the other Matityahu), founded the Zionist students' organization Kadimah in Vienna in 1884 and served as the spiritual mentor of some of the Zionist greats. Here he is remembered by David Isaiah Silberbusch:

> "Back in the early 1880s, Birnbaum reached the conclusion that political Zionism was the solution to the Jewish problem. It was he who coined the word 'Zionism' in its political connotation. When Herzl arrived in Vienna with *Der Judenstaat*, the students of Kadimah took him as their leader in the hope that he would guide them toward the realization of the Zionist dream. Birnbaum was frustrated. He watched the idea he had conceived and cultivated, and the organization he headed, handed over to the new man in town. He was a doctor of law and a brilliant intellectual who was having trouble providing for his family. When Herzl stepped in and began to finance Zionist organizational activity, Birnbaum expected that the Zionist movement under Herzl would recognize him as a pioneer of the movement and he would be given a job and a salary. At the First Congress, his friends pressed him to accept the position of Congressional Secretary. Birnbaum felt uncomfortable with this and turned down the appointment. His friends, suspecting his refusal was political, were furious with him. One of them, Shlomo Schiller, declared: 'It would be a mortal sin to let Birnbaum shirk his duty.' Dr. Maltz of Lvov chimed in: 'We must force Birnbaum to accept the nomination, since without Birnbaum we would not have Herzl today.'[17]
>
> It seems enough to mention the names of just a few of these unique individuals, who over the years earned a reputation for their brilliance in the Jewish community: Dr. Mordecai Ehrenpreis, Dr. Osias Thon, Dr. Yehuda Leib Landau, Dr. David Neumark and Shlomo Schiller. Suffice it to say that all of them acknowledged Dr. Nathan Birnbaum as their spiritual leader."[18]

At his colleagues' urging, Birnbaum accepted a paid job as secretary of the World Zionist Organization but it was a position that invariably led to conflict and Birnbaum found himself unemployed: "The man who was once a leader and walked erect at the head of his flock was now shunted aside like a sickly lamb left out in the field to die."[19] He never managed to find his niche in the Zionist movement and finally left it. He turned religious and went on to become one of the leaders of ultra-Orthodox community.[20] In his memoirs, Mayer Abner muses on the relationship between Herzl and Birnbaum:

---

17 Silberbusch, *Mipinkas zikhronotai*, p. 221.
18 *Ibid.*, p. 205.
19 *Ibid.*, pp. 223–224.
20 See Birnbaum's book *Am hashem: Mivkhar ktavim umasot*, Netzakh Books, Bnei Brak 1977; Eliezer Schweid, "Mul 'She'elot kiyum hayahdut': Lekheker haguto shel natan birnbaum al hatzionut," in: *Hatzionut umitnagdeha ba'am hayehudi*, pp. 301–319.

"It was at the First Zionist Congress in Basel. I look around and there is Nathan Birnbaum sitting in the small auditorium of the Municipal Casino, maybe in the fifth row, while Herzl is on the podium, presiding over the Congress. At that moment it occurred to me that peaceful, amiable relations between the two were not possible. From Birnbaum's perspective, Herzl was nothing but an upstart who had snatched the crown off his head. Until then, Birnbaum had been our acknowledged leader and everything in the world that had to do with Zionism was the fruit of his labors ... This tension, between Birnbaum the trailblazer and Herzl who shone with the aura of true leadership, created a special set of circumstances known as the Birnbaum problem. Appointing Birnbaum as the first general secretary of the Zionist Organization was not a worthy solution ... The future would prove that this appointment could never last long ... And that, in effect, ended the Zionist chapter in Birnbaum's life."[21]

Birnbaum's frustration at being deposed is summed up by Abner: "Who ever heard of such a thing? A king toppled from his throne becoming the servant of the person who deposed him and now wears the crown on his head?"[22]

Ahad Ha'am

Writer and thinker Asher Ginsberg, known by his nom de plume Ahad Ha'am (One of the People), was hailed as the "prophet of spiritual Zionism." As the spiritual leader of the Hovevei Zion, he was a bitter opponent of political Zionism in general and Herzl in particular. That battle was an ideological one, fought over the fundamental role of Zionism. Ahad Ha'am argued that the Jewish people needed an infusion of spirit, not a political solution. He famously remarked that the salvation of the Jews would come from the prophets, not diplomats.[23]

However, the dispute between Ahad Ha'am and Herzl was not only over spiritual matters. Herzl, who was not well-versed in the customs of East European Jewry, erred in not inviting Ahad Ha'am to the Zionist Congress personally. If he had, Ahad Ha'am might have toned down his criticism. Ahad Ha'am attended the Congress nonetheless – as a journalist, not a delegate – and from then on never missed an opportunity to lash out at Herzl and his ideology.

Ahad Ha'am regarded Herzl as a rival and was not happy with change of direction in the Jewish world. Because of it, he lost his finest students, who joined Herzl's camp and worked enthusiastically to promote the cause of political Zionism against the wishes of their master (whom they continued to admire). Ahad Ha'am's opposition turned ugly at times, and he was constantly spoiling for a

---

21 Mayer Abner on Nathan Birnbaum, *Sefer hacongress* (1950), pp. 301–320.
22 *Ibid.*
23 Ahad Ha'am, Yalkut katan, *Hashiloah*, 1897, p. 568.

fight in the hopes of bringing his disciples back to spiritual Zionism and splitting the Zionist movement. This was the strategy he adopted in the debates over *Kultura*, the Jewish bank and the *Altneuland* affair, and last – but certainly not least in terms of malice – on the question of Uganda. We will take a closer look at all these issues in the coming chapters.

Davis Trietsch

Davis Trietsch, a Zionist activist and member of the Democratic Fraction, rejected Herzl's political approach. As a long-time promoter of Jewish colonization, even before Herzl's day, he was an advocate of building up clusters of settlement in the vicinity of Palestine, in places like el-Arish and Cyprus. The idea came to him in 1893, after leaving Germany for the United States. Witnessing the hardship of the Jewish immigrants in New York, he concluded that the Jews should be settling in areas closer to Palestine. In 1896, Trietsch read about Herzl's *Der Judenstaat* in an Austrian newspaper. Inspired, he traveled to Basel for the First Zionist Congress. There he read an article by Nathan Birnbaum, published in 1894, calling on Jews to settle in Cyprus and locations like Sinai.[24] Trietsch unveiled his plan to Herzl, only to be turned down. Herzl said he "had given careful consideration to this interesting proposal," but did not think the time was opportune to discuss it, "as we have better prospects in view."[25]

Upon his return to America, Trietsch stepped up his activity in the Zionist movement. So devoted was he to the cause that he gave up playing chess, which he loved and played on a championship level.[26] In 1899, he arranged for 11 Ukrainian Jewish miners to establish a colony in Cyprus, but the scheme fell through.

At the Third Zionist Congress, Trietsch tried to convince Herzl to support his Cyprus plan, but without success. "It was all in vain," writes Bein. "The Hovevei Zion would hear nothing of any plan relating to another land than Palestine, even if it lay as close to it as Cyprus."[27] Therefore when Herzl met with the British to discuss Jewish colonization in the Sinai Peninsula, Trietsch was furious: He saw it as his scheme from which he was being left out. At the Uganda Congress, Trietsch viciously attacked Herzl, claiming he had done nothing for the past six

---

[24] Mordechai Eran, "David Triesch, Ha'ish upoalo hatzioni 1870–1935," MA thesis, Hebrew University of Jerusalem, 1999, p. 4.
[25] Bein, *Theodore Herzl: A Biography*, p. 412.
[26] Eran, *ibid*.
[27] Bein, *Theodore Herzl: A Biography*, pp. 412–413.

years apart from chasing momentary success. Bein describes the stand-off between Trietsch and Herzl:

> "The clash ensued not because of any specific criticism against Herzl's grand colonization schemes, but because of the tone of the criticism. It was a savage personal attack, in which [Triesch] accused Herzl of making thoughtless decisions on El-Arish, mismanaging the talks, chasing after fleeting moments of glory, and behaving dishonestly towards him. In short, he was not fit to lead the movement."[28]

Herzl was hurt, but even so, publicly declared that he had no doubt about Trietsch's talents and integrity.

Alfred Nossig

Alfred Nossig, a leading Galician Zionist with close ties to the Democratic Fraction, shared Trietsch's views.[29] He was a polymath – a gifted musician, playwright, poet, author and sculptor whose work was exhibited at a prestigious gallery in Paris on the Champs Elysees.[30] After the publication of *Der Judenstaat*, there was a rumor going around Lvov that Herzl was planning to visit. The Zionists of Galicia dispatched a letter to Nossig, who was in France at the time, asking what he thought about Herzl so they would know how to respond. Nossig wrote back about Herzl's "failures" in Constantinople, London and Paris, and openly stated that he was not an admirer of Dr. Herzl's scheme. Nonetheless, he was glad Herzl was coming to Lvov so the Zionists of the city could judge for themselves. Nossig also noted in the letter that back in 1886, he himself had put together a comprehensive plan for Jewish emigration for the purpose of settlement in Eretz Yisrael.[31]

So Nossig's objection was not to Herzl's initiative itself, since he was the author of a scheme that predated *Der Judenstaat* by a whole decade. His negativism focused on Herzl the man and leader. One of Herzl's most dangerous traits, he said, was that instead of persuasion and trying to win over his opponents, all he wanted was to fight with them.[32] It is not clear on what basis he made this claim, but saying so shook Herzl's credibility in the eyes of the Galician Zionist leaders. When they later consulted with him about cooperating with Herzl, Nos-

---

[28] Bein, *Biografia*, p. 370; *Encyclopedia ivrit*, vol. 18, p. 896; for more on Trietsch, see pp. 266, 288.
[29] Shmuel Almog, "Khayav umoto shel Alfred Nossig," in: *Yahadut Zmanenu*, 1985, vol. 2, p. 80.
[30] *Ibid.*, p. 77.
[31] Nathan Gelber, *Toldot hatnu'a hatzionit begalitzia*, p. 299.
[32] *Ibid.*

sig advised them to exercise caution in any dealings with him. Herzl was enthusiastic and ambitious, he conceded, but lacking in diplomatic and organizational skills.³³

Nossig attended the First Congress as a guest, not a full-fledged participant. His first time as a delegate was at the Sixth Congress, where he criticized Herzl during a lecture on the Sabbath, a day before the official opening on August 22, 1903. Nossig's tone was so vicious, his irate listeners would not let him finish.³⁴ Sammy Gronemann describes the incident:

> "Dr. Nossig was a multifaceted personality, a writer, poet and sculptor, who founded a new organization every other day. The session ended suddenly when the best word Dr. Nossig could find to define Nordau and Herzl was 'Jewish chutzpah.' A great outcry erupted, and the meeting broke up."³⁵

At the next session, on Tuesday, Nossig launched another personal tirade against Herzl, which put a damper on the mood of the Congress.³⁶ Davis Trietsch's negativity toward Herzl might be understandable in that he regarded Herzl as a usurper of his ideas, but why Nossig's antagonism? Historian Shmuel Almog suggests that Nossig's reasons were much like those of Nathan Birnbaum: He, too, was a forerunner of Herzl and felt he had been pushed to the sidelines.³⁷ It bears note that Herzl himself distinguished between the criticism of Trietsch and Nossig. He believed that Trietsch's remarks, unlike those of Nossig, were basically well-intended.

Homegrown Opposition

So now we have the gallery of opponents laid before us. However, to comprehend how opposition to Herzl evolved we also need to look at the dynamics in the World Zionist Organization, the Zionist congresses and the institutions of the Zionist Movement – the Greater Actions Committee (GAC), Smaller Actions Committee (SAC), Jewish Colonial Trust (JCT), Jewish National Fund (JNF) and others.

---

33 *Ibid.*, p. 303.
34 Bein, *Biografia*, p. 370.
35 Gronemann, *Zikhronot shel yekke*, p. 205.
36 Bein, *Biografia*, p. 370.
37 Almog, *Khayav umoto shel Nossig*, p. 76.

On the following pages, we will trace the emergence of anti-Herzl sentiment, which expressed itself in different forms and sprang from a variety of underlying motives. At the same time, we will look at the processes under way in the Zionist congresses and institutions which were affected by both world and Jewish affairs, and vice versa. When did Herzl's charisma help him through and when did it not? Why?

The institutionalization of the Zionist movement ushered in a new era. Dynamic communication opened up between Herzl and the masses of delegates and activists involved in the institutional frameworks of the Zionist Organization on the eve of the congresses, while they were in session, and from one congress to the next. However, budding opposition began to rear its head early on and steadily increased over time, reaching a peak at the Sixth Congress in Basel in 1903 and the Kharkov Conference in April 1904.

Chapter 8
The *'Kultura'* Debate

The institutionalization of the Zionist Congress changed the dynamics. As an organization in which rapid changes were being made by a leader as authoritative as Theodor Herzl, new challenges surfaced. As long as it was Herzl who shouldered the administrative and financial burdens, there was no competition. However, the moment there were elected officers and Herzl became president, other voices strove to make themselves heard, setting off a tug of war between competing forces and desires. It was the establishment of an organizational framework that enabled opposition.

Herzl was now the preeminent leader of the movement, the flagbearer of the distinctive message of political Zionism. He set organizational and financial policy and presided over the congresses with a firm but skillful hand. Yet charismatic as he was, it was only natural that there were those who resented his commanding leadership style or were dissatisfied with some decision he made. Furthermore, some Zionist movement activists had been around for a long time, going back to the days of Hibbat Zion, and were well-versed in the secrets of Zionism and Judaism. In their eyes, Herzl was a newcomer on the scene, a "Johnny-come-lately." While they accepted his authority on a grand scale, they did not hesitate to argue with him on the issues at hand.

Herzl's great achievement at the First Congress was in assembling Jews from Eastern and Western Europe, hailing from different social sectors and religious communities, under one roof. The key unifying factor was their enthusiasm for Herzl and his political Zionist program with its goal of founding a Jewish state. Over time, congresses opened and closed, bringing in their wake a string of disappointments and dashed hopes, first pinned on the Turks and then on the Germans. The eagerly awaited charter failed to materialize. Herzl clung to his belief that until such a charter was granted, settling in Palestine "like thieves in the night" or buying up tracts of land was out of the question. At the same time, a wellspring of opposition began to form among delegates who sought consolation in *Gegenwarstarbeit* ("present-day work") – immigration to Palestine, land purchase, the establishment of farm colonies and cultural activities. Adding fuel to the flames, fierce fighting erupted over three issues – *Kultura*, *Altneuland* and Uganda – that threatened to split the movement.

The Onset of the 'Kultura' Debate

The roots of the *Kultura* debate can be traced back to the days of Hibbat Zion. Ehud Luz sees a resemblance between the cultural polemic of that time and the polemic in Herzl's day. The fundamental question was one and the same: Which should take precedence – cultural-spiritual redemption or physical redemption? For Yehuda Leib Gordon, one of the great Hebrew poets of the Haskalah (Jewish enlightenment), culture came first, as it did for Ahad Ha'am in Herzl's time. Moshe Leib Lilienblum in the Hibbat Zion era took the opposing view, as did Herzl. Both felt that decisions on culture should wait until the Jews had achieved physical redemption. Lilienblum thought that the Jewish community needed to strengthen its foothold in Eretz Yisrael first, and Herzl urged waiting until after a Jewish state was in place. Both perceived this as the key to rallying all factions of the Jewish people, "in particular the Orthodox and the freethinkers, in order to realize the prime goal of Zionism: the end of the Exile."[1] While the debate over culture did not pose an existential threat to Hibbat Zion, in Herzl's day it endangered the unity of the Zionist movement and left Herzl weary and drained.

The question of culture already came up in Herzl's opening speech at the First Congress: "For Zionism is a return to Judaism even before there is a return to the Jewish land ... Hence the Congress will concern itself also with the spiritual means to be employed for reviving and fostering the national consciousness of the Jews. In this regard, too, we have misunderstandings to combat. We have no intention of yielding even one hand's-breadth of the culture we have acquired; on the contrary, we are aiming for a broadening of culture, such as any increase in knowledge brings."[2]

This approach was reinforced in the Basel Program, which cited among its goals the cultivation and strengthening of Jewish nationalism.[3] In practice, the Congress called for educational and outreach programs to enhance a sense of national pride and bring the message of Zionism to the masses, thereby boosting membership in the movement around the world. However, with all the good will in Herzl's opening remarks, he believed *kultura* should wait until after the establishment a Jewish state. He knew that the seeds of contention lay here: The Haredi Jews attending the Congress were leery of Hebrew culture that was not in the

---

[1] Luz, *Parallels Meet*, p. 140; *ibid*, footnote 5.
[2] *Zionist Writings*, vol. 1, pp. 133–134; see pp. 188–198, above.
[3] Haim Orlan (ed. and translator), Protokol hakongres hatzioni harishon, Reuben Mass, Jerusalem 1997, p. 97 (henceforth: Orlan, *Protokol hakongress*).

spirit of Torah and *mitzvot*, especially in light of their bitter encounter with the Haskalah movement and its assault on religion, and what they had seen of Hibbat Zion.

When these fears were raised at a rabbinic summit before the First Congress, Herzl reassured the rabbis that Zionism would not interfere in anyone's religious beliefs.[4] However, the Haredim saw signs that worried them. At the Congress, Dr. Jacob Bernstein-Kogan proposed the establishment of a committee to develop culture programs for academic and vocational schools. Dr. Mordecai Ehrenpreis submitted a similar proposal, emphasizing the importance of reviving the Hebrew language as the path to spiritual renaissance. Nathan Birnbaum's speech at the Congress posed a further challenge to traditional Judaism: "Let us build a homeland where the East European Jews will be representatives of modern liberalism, the West European Jews will be Jewish nationalists, and the two will come together to form a civilized Western nation with its own intrinsic culture ..."[5]

Birnbaum's words remained etched in the memory of the Congress attendees and were later quoted extensively by opponents of Zionism in the Haredi community.

As the First Congress was about to close its doors, Rabbi Asher Cohen, the chief rabbi of Basel, took the floor and asked about the commitment of the Congress to Jewish tradition. Herzl responded: "I can promise you that Zionism has no intention of doing anything to harm the religious convictions of any stream of thought within Judaism."[6]

Some Haredi rabbis were hesitant about attending the Congress. Yehoshua Heschel Farbstein, a leader of the religious Zionist community, felt that not inviting Rabbi Cohen to speak at the opening session was a mistake. In his view, if Cohen had voiced his concerns at that point rather than at the end, Herzl could have set Haredi fears to rest and the Haredim would have joined the Congress then and there. But Rabbi Cohen rose to speak just as the Congress was closing, and Herzl's answer was not clear enough. In Farbstein's opinion, Herzl should have pledged that Zionism would do nothing to violate Jewish religious law, and not just that it had no intention of hurting the religious sensibilities of any denomination. He believes that Herzl realized his mistake and

---

4 Eliyahu Akiva Rabinowitz, *Tzion bemishpat oh hashkafa rabanit al hatzionut*, Halter Press, Warsaw 1902, p. 32 (henceforth: Rabinowitz, *Tzion bemishpat*).
5 Yosef Salmon, "Tguvat hakharedim bemizrakh europa," in: *Hatzionut umitnagdeha ba'am hayehudi*, Jerusalem: Hasifria Hatzionit, 1990, p. 57 (henceforth: Salmon, "Tguvat hakharedim").
6 Orian, *Protokol hakongress*, pp. 71–80.

made his point more forcefully at the next Congresses, but by then, it was too late: The Haredim already had a solid pretext for opposition to Zionism.[7]

Herzl's assurances failed to restore the peace of mind of the Haredi participants. Within half a year, as the initial high of the Congress receded, they began to delve more deeply into how they should respond to the Zionist movement. They worried that the cultural proposals of the secular Zionists would be branded by the Haredi leadership as an extension of the Haskalah. They had learned from bitter experience that many of those who entered the "garden of enlightenment" stopped observing the *mitzvot*. A few had even converted to Christianity. Exacerbating the problem was the fact that "followers of the new movement were not traditional Jews joining an ad hoc organization to collect dues and spread a certain message but a young elite living a 'freewheeling' lifestyle."[8]

Indeed, many of the *Kultura* supporters at the Congress were young people who had turned their backs on religion. As Yisrael Klausner writes:

> "The students of the Democratic Fraction were both social and cultural rebels. Most Zionist students ended up at university after dropping out of *yeshiva* and becoming *maskilim* under the influence of their surroundings. In the towns of Russia, where religion was considered a remnant of the Middle Ages, many became opponents of religious ritual. Some even declared outright war on religion and the insistence on separating religion and nationalism became almost universal."[9]

This being the case, the Haredi minority supportive of Herzl and political Zionism worried that the demand for culture on the part of the *Kulturisten* would confirm the fears of the anti-Zionist Haredi leadership and prompt a mass boycott of the movement. These fears seem to have been associated as much with the character of the *Kulturisten* as with the cultural content they sought. Indeed, the lobby for *Kultura* was presumably colored by the ideology of the lobbyists, even if no one actually said so.

Geula Raphael dwells on the *Kultura* war in the early Zionist congresses:

> "The concept of '*Kultura*' burst into the world of early Zionism like a storm. It was defined and interpreted in all kinds of ways. Some broadened it and others narrowed it down. Only

---

[7] Farbstein, in: *Sefer hacongress* (1950), pp. 191–192.
[8] Yosef Salmon, "Tzionut ve'anti tzionut beyahadut hamesoratit bemizrakh europa," in: *Tzionut vedat*, Jerusalem, Mercaz Shazar, 1944, p. 58.
[9] Yisrael Klausner, *Opozitzia leherzl*, Jerusalem, Ahiever, 1964.

at the Fifth Zionist Congress was the term truly clarified ... But even before it was clearly delineated, any time it came up for discussion it generated a great uproar."¹⁰

Herzl tactfully navigated the crises that arose over the subject of *Kultura* at the congresses, steering away from final decisions that could create a rift between the parties in the Zionist movement. He employed both procedural measures and his personal charisma, all in order keep the Congress intact. For Herzl, the primary goal of the Zionist organization was the establishment of a Jewish state. He did everything he could to keep the movement focused on this shared goal and avoid any divisive decision. However, the pressure of the opposition escalated from congress to congress, and Herzl was forced to devote more and more of his energy and powers of persuasion to preserve the integrity of the movement. At the time, it seems he did not fully grasp the extent to which the *Kultura* debate would make his life miserable. He only foresaw that preoccupation with the topic was dangerous and tried to avoid it. But again, even when opposition was strongest, there was no intention of wresting the leadership from Herzl. No one could imagine the Zionist movement without him.

Kultura at the Second Congress

The writer Nahum Slouschz describes the atmosphere at the Second Zionist Congress. In his telling, the euphoria of the First Congress muffled the debate over *Kultura* at the Second Congress:

> "And the rabbis who came from all over...deliberated on how to respond to Zionism and decided that questions not adequately explored, such as *Kultura*, should be kept separate from Zionism, which needed to be above sectoral interests ... indeed the rabbis were the ones who insisted that political Zionism not stray from its designated path, and Herzl, upon hearing this, greatly rejoiced."¹¹

The Haredi fear of *Kultura* was unfounded at that time, Slouschz reasoned, because the goal was teaching Hebrew and Jewish history, neither of which conflicted with Haredi principles. However, the festive ambiance of the Second Congress, especially in its early days, seems to have misled him. Later the question

---

10 Geula Raphael, "She'elat hakultura bakongresim harishonim," in: *Sugiot betoldot hatzionu veyishuvt*, Am Oved and Tel Aviv University, Tel Aviv 1983, p. 39 (henceforth: Raphael, "She'elat hakultura").
11 Nahum Slouschz, *Knesset hagdola oh hakongres hasheni bebazel*, Tushia, Warsaw 1898, p. 11.

of *Kultura* aroused furious debate and a solid wall of opposition grew up around it. Disagreement continued and only grew stronger in the next congresses.

Before the opening of the Second Congress in August 1898, the Russian Zionists convened for the first time in Warsaw and *Kultura* was on the agenda. The Zionist Actions Committee was criticized for its lack of action on cultural matters, sparking worry among the Haredi rabbis that the conference would recommend talks on the subject at the Congress. They tried to head off such a motion but without success. A majority vote was passed in favor of cultural work and the formation of a culture committee. For the rabbis, this created a problem. Some began to wonder if joining the Zionist movement was still an option, especially after the death of Rabbi Shmuel Mohilever, the "strongman" upon whom they had depended to keep *Kultura* at bay.[12]

Two of these rabbis, Yehuda Leib Tsirelson of Priluki, who had been a stronger backer of Hovevei Zion, and Eliyahu Akiva Rabinowitz of Poltava, did not trust Herzl and sought further guarantees that the Congress would not discuss cultural matters. Rabbi Tsirelson made it clear that settling in Eretz Yisrael was a worthy goal and did not run counter to messianic aspirations. However, if he had to choose between the modern Western approach with its imitation of European nationalism as an answer to anti-Semitism, and the traditional approach rooted in Jewish law, which did not depend on transitory external factors, he preferred the Jewish approach. In an article published in *Hamelitz*, Tsirelson repeated his conviction that Zionism and Judaism could go hand in hand. However, Zionism had to be based on Torah, he wrote, so as not to become a vehicle for false messianism.[13] He proposed the establishment of a rabbinic committee that would work with the Zionist Actions Committee in Vienna to oversee the education of the younger generation. In his view, this would bring masses of Haredim into the Zionist movement. Tsirelson insisted that without such collaboration, it was better for religious Jews to "uphold our Torah in the lands of dispersion, however deficient, than move to the land of our forefathers which shuns us, the Haredim, and lusts after reformation."[14]

Rabbi Rabinowitz of Poltava, who was very much taken with Herzl, concurred with Herzl and Nordau's diagnosis of the socio-economic crisis facing the Jews and their predictions on the subject of anti-Semitism and emancipation. He was prepared to support modernization in the workplace and even in the

---

[12] Raphael, "She'elat hakultura," p. 40.
[13] *Hamelitz*, "Kotz shebaketz," no. 93–96, May 11–15, 1898.
[14] *Ibid.*; Salmon, "Tguvat hakharedim," pp. 59–60.

realm of culture. He could see the advantages of Zionism for the persecuted masses, and the potential of "core Zionism" as a cure delivering the Jews from their misery. Citing a Talmudic parable, he likened political Zionism and *Kultura* to a barrel of honey with a snake coiled around it. "Should we break the barrel and pour out the honey to kill the snake!?" he asked.[15] He did not object to culture in the framework of the Zionist movement, but felt there were priorities and *Kultura* could wait: "First Zionism should restore the nation materially and then breathe into it the soul of ancient life ... But if members of the Congress are pushing for cultural work, then this culture must be rooted in the bedrock of religion, because religion is the core of Jewish nationalism."[16]

As noted, the Russian Zionists at the convention in Warsaw rejected the proposal of the rabbis by a large majority and passed a resolution in favor of establishing a culture committee at the upcoming Second Congress. Infuriated, the rabbis walked out.[17] However, concerned that decisions on *Kultura* would be reached at the Congress without rabbinic oversight, they authorized Rabbi Rabinowitz to represent them there.[18] At a meeting with the rabbis and intellectuals convened by Herzl on the eve of the Congress, Rabbi Rabinowitz shared his colleagues' fears and pleaded with Herzl to drop the matter of *Kultura* from the agenda. However, he said, if the Zionist movement could not live without *Kultura*, then at least there should be a rabbinic authority to supervise it, which he would head. Herzl's response was that Zionism would not be challenging anyone's beliefs or religious convictions, hence the election of a cultural affairs committee would proceed as planned.[19]

Herzl's reply did not appease the rabbis, who held another meeting with Nahum Sokolow. Sokolow, a rabbinical scholar himself (Chaim Tchernowitz, who went by the pen name Rav Tza'ir, described him as a Talmudic prodigy worthy of being the rabbi of a big city),[20] spoke their language. He tried to set their minds at ease and assured them that Herzl's word should be enough to allay their fears.[21]

---

15 Rabinowitz, *Tzion bemishpat*, p. 21. See parable in *Gittin* 56b. Vespasian says to Rabbi Yochanan ben Zakai: "If you had a barrel of honey with a serpent coiled around it, would you not destroy the barrel for the sake of [getting rid] of the serpent?"
16 Raphael, "She'elat hakultura," p. 41.
17 Rabinowitz, *Tzion bemishpat*, pp. 65–69; Salmon, "Tguvat hakharedim," p. 62.
18 *Ibid.*, p. 42.
19 Klausner, *Opozitzia leherzl*, p. 31.
20 Rav Tza'ir, "Masekhet zikhronot: Partzufim veha'arakhot," in: *Kol Kitvei Rav Tza'ir*, Va'ad Hayovel Publishing, New York 1945, p. 197.
21 Klausner, *ibid.*

In the course of the Second Zionist Congress, a culture committee was elected which was chaired by the rabbi of the Sephardic congregation of London, Hakham Moses Gaster. The committee declared that cultural activities in the Zionist movement would be limited to nationalist content and therefore posed no problem for any stream of Judaism. The rabbis, however, were not satisfied. They insisted on submitting a draft proposal on the establishment of a rabbinic supervisory board. Gaster told Rabbi Rabinowitz that his committee would establish a panel of three rabbis – one from Russia, one from Galicia and one representing the rest of the Jewish world. Each rabbi would bring two colleagues and together they would constitute a "rabbinic executive committee" that would decide on religious matters. Meanwhile Gaster asked Rabinowitz to wait with the draft proposal, in the hope that his idea would suffice. After consulting with Aaron Marcus, a Chortkov hasid and Zionist activist, Rabinowitz gave his consent. But he waited in vain for the committee's response. Gaster did not keep his promise to assemble a rabbinic panel and never passed on Rabinowitz's proposal for a supervisory board. When Rabinowitz prodded him, Gaster came up with excuses. He claimed he was afraid of being turned down by a majority of the delegates and it was preferable for such matters to be inscribed directly in the protocols. Rabbi Rabinowitz was furious. He accused Gaster of duping both him and Zionism. Gaster countered that he was welcome to submit his proposal, but this left the rabbi even angrier, since it was too late to add proposals to the Congress agenda by that time.

In practice, the Second Congress passed a resolution that strayed from Herzl's tactical approach, venturing beyond economic and political renaissance into the realm of spiritual rebirth. A green light was given to *Kultura*, through the establishment of a Hebrew language society and other programs. The culture committee led by Gaster attempted to mollify the Haredi community, releasing a statement that nothing done by the Zionist movement would contravene religion.[22] However, harboring a fundamental mistrust of the pro-*Kultura* camp and further upset by Gaster's conduct, Tsirelson and Rabinowitz packed their bags and left.[23]

The problems of the Hibbat Zion era thus resurfaced in the days of political Zionism. The Haredim who had joined the Zionist movement in its early days found themselves in a dilemma. Should they stay and work from the inside or leave? The Haredim weighed two options: establishing a separate division or es-

---

[22] Raphael, "She'elat hakultura," pp. 42–43; Slouschz, *Knesset hagedola*, p. 97.
[23] Another reason for the pullout was Herzl's call for the "conquest of the Kehillot," as we shall see below.

tablishing a new Zionist organization that would vie with the existing movement. Yosef Salmon cites a lack of influential rabbis at this critical juncture, now that staunch supporters of Hibbat Zion were no longer alive, among them Naftali Zvi Yehuda Berlin of Volozhin (the Netziv), Rabbi Yitzhak Elchanan Spektor of Kovno, Rabbi Mordechai Eliasberg and Rabbi Shmuel Mohilever.[24] In the absence of such leadership, the dissenting rabbis became active anti-Zionists. Rabinowitz edited two anti-Zionist Haredi newspapers, *Hapeles* and *Hamodia*, and Tsirelson went on to become a prominent leader of Agudat Yisrael.[25]

Another reason for the rabbis' apprehension and plummeting trust in political Zionism was Herzl's call at the opening of the Second Congress for the "conquest of the Kehillot" (Jewish communities) which was seen as threatening Orthodox Judaism in East Europe and the primacy of the religious establishment. These fears, as we shall see, were not unfounded. It was an appeal that only aggravated the polarization. Some Zionist activists took Herzl's words seriously, wresting control of community institutions and organizing educational and cultural activities in the spirit of the Haskalah. In response, the rabbis began to close the doors of synagogues and *batei midrash* to Zionist preachers, equating them with the forces of evil. As Rabbi Rabinowitz put it: "All the Zionists want is for the Jews to abandon their religion."[26]

The anti-Zionist stance of the rabbis continued to gather force, as the Black Chamber in Kovno,[27] a semi-secret society which took its cue from the anti-Zionist ideology of Chabad, joined the fray.[28] The prevailing mood assumed tangible form in an anthology called "*Or layisharim*," compiled for the benefit of the entire anti-Zionist Haredi public – Hasidim and Lithuanians (non-Hasidim).[29] Essentially, it was an exposé of the true goal of Zionism, which was allegedly disseminating Haskalah ideology and secularization by coercion and deception masquerading as economic and political reform. Zionism was portrayed as a sect, like Karaite Judaism and Sabbateanism, which had once made inroads in the Jewish community. As such, there was no place for it in Judaism.

---

24 Salmon, "Tguvat hakharedim," p. 58.
25 *Ibid.*, pp. 59–60, 66–68.
26 *Ibid.*, pp. 59–66.
27 This was the name coined by the *maskilim* for the anti-Zionist endeavors of Yaakov Lifschitz of Kovno, Rabbi Yitzhak Elchanan Spektor's right-hand man.
28 On the grand rabbis of Chabad and their opposition to Zionism, see Aviezer Ravitzky, *Haketz hameguleh umedinat hayehudim*, Am Oved, Tel Aviv 1993, pp. 249–276 (henceforth: Ravitzky, *Haketz hameguleh*).
29 *Or layesharim* was published in Kovno in 1900. It was an anthology of letters by Haredi rabbis denouncing Zionism.

At the same time, there were nationalist Haredi rabbis who preferred to remain part of the movement and fight for their principles from within. One was Rabbi Shmuel Ya'akov Rabinowitz of Aleksot, who was among those who opposed *Kultura* but also recognized that it could have a positive side. His perspective on *Kultura* was intriguing: He believed that Zionism could bring back many lapsed Jews, interpreting Herzl's remark about Zionism first being a return to Judaism literally. Neither did he see anything wrong with the attempt to correct certain failings in Haredi Judaism: "The Haredim need *Kultura* to mend the human being inside and the 'enlightened' need *Kultura* to mend the Jew inside."[30]

Indeed, many *Kulturisten* who were put off by Orthodox Judaism, a symbol of backwardness in their mind, began celebrating the Jewish holidays again thanks to Zionism, with an emphasis on the national component. Nevertheless, the gulf remained very large and bridging the gap was not something that could be done overnight. For that reason, Rabinowitz believed that collaborative work on culture was not practical at this stage. He recommended that cultural matters be left up to the Zionist societies, which would work independently as best they could, without congressional funding.

After the Congress, Rabinowitz sent a letter to the administration in which he stated that the eagerness of the Zionists to put *Kultura* on the agenda was perceived by the Haredim as "a trumpet for the Haskalah camouflaged as nationalism and a tool for dimming religious feeling and planting new concepts in the heart of the nation." He repeated his recommendation "not to introduce controversial issues in a movement taking its first steps. Cultural work is a matter for the voluntary associations, each of which should act in keeping with its understanding and needs."[31]

Rabinowitz even went a step further, proposing a democratic solution to the *Kultura* problem. If masses of Haredim joined the Zionist movement, he said, they could exert their influence democratically.[32] Interestingly, he is not the only one to come up with such an idea. In his book *Tiferet Adam*, Pinhas Selig Glicksman tells the story of how his father, the *hasid* Avraham Hirsch Glicksman, visited Herzl at his home in Vienna and urged him to mobilize the

---

[30] Geula Raphael, *Ish hame'orot: Rabbi Yitzhak Ya'akov Reines*, Mossad Harav Kook, Jerusalem 1985, p. 95.
[31] Ibid., p. 98.
[32] Raphael, "She'elat hakultura," p. 43. Also see Rabinowitz's article "Hashkafa tova," published in *Hamelitz*, no. 153–173, July 23-August 15, 1899.

Haredi leaders for the Zionist cause because they had millions of Jews behind them:[33]

"If you gain the consent of the preeminent rabbis ... then all of the House of Jacob will be with you, and when we have millions of hands at the ready, then wait and see how this great enterprise will be executed with ease and the work done for us. So when you distinguished leaders and orators lift your voices on high at the Basel conference and begin by saying 'Assembled before us are the delegates of Jewish people,' you must know that this term 'Jewish people' is an exaggeration, because these delegates only represent a small group of young Jews, whereas you have almost none representing the elders of Israel.

Herzl: 'What you say is very true, and we, too, have spoken about the need to make a trip to the Russian capital.'

Glicksman: 'I doubt we will obtain a permit. After all, our exalted government says no to everyone ... and I cannot believe it will make an exception for the Jews.'

Herzl: 'I expect we will obtain one, and then I will come ... But there is nothing stopping the honorable rabbis from Russia from coming to Basel, like all the Zionist delegates from Russia. So what do they have against Zionist movement? Some of them oppose us and want to keep us from carrying out our mission... All we want is help those who are starving, and these Haredi rabbis are standing in our way? Does that make sense? And if you, sir, accuse us of sinning and not observing the commandment 'Go and gather,' we can argue that the rabbis... by standing in our way, are not observing the commandment 'Love thy neighbor as thyself,' and not 'If thy brother be waxen poor, and his means fail with thee.' By the same token, they are violating 'hide not thyself from thine own flesh,' and 'neither shalt thou stand idly by the blood of thy neighbor,' and I could go on and on. Does this not apply to you?...Ah, how wonderful are the ways of our rabbis.'

Glicksman: 'Forgive me, sir, if I may be so bold, but you alone are to blame for this, for mixing Zionism with culture ...'

Herzl: Sir, in Basel, before all those assembled there, we openly said that our movement has nothing at all to do with religious matters, and our only wish is to aid the poor, persecuted and misfortunate, to prepare for them a haven and a dignified livelihood in the land of our forefathers. Religion is not our business. We said this over and over. Why do not you believe us?... If, in spite of all our actions and promises, the Haredim in Russia have no faith in us, here is some advice for you, something very simple and easy: Let the Haredi rabbis come to Basel in their multitudes so that they will constitute an overwhelming majority, and then they can do as they please. They can erase *Kultura* completely from the assembly program or choose a *Kultura* committee with a Haredi majority and a *maskilim* minority. The Haredim could be the leaders of *Kultura* on their own and not allow the *maskilim* to have a say at all, or they could consult with them and devise a different arrangement. If the Haredim were in the majority, no one could dictate to them what to do.'"[34]

---

33 Pinhas Zelig Glicksman, *Tiferet adam: Te'urim biografi'im betzeruf mikhtavim me'et R. Avraham Hirsch Glicksman*, Lodz, Kultura, 1923 (henceforth: Glicksman, *Tiferet adam*); see p. 72 above.

34 *Hamelitz*, 1900, no. 66–87; Glicksman, *Tiferet adam*, pp. 13–16.

Another source, more acerbic in tone, is the anti-Zionist pamphlet *Kol hashem bekoakh* quoted in a sermon by Rabbi Moshe Sternbuch, court president of the Eda Haredit:

> "When Zionism was founded, the villain Herzl, may his name be blotted out, employed the tactic of community conquest and set out on an expedition to take over Jewish communities and impose Zionist rule. In the course of his travels, he reached Vilna, where, to our misfortune, he was treated with great respect, after which he headed for the city of Minsk and asked to meet with the city's Jewish leaders. Three *gaba'im* appeared before him: one was my grandfather, Rabbi Berl Pines z"tzl, another was Rabbi Berel Soldewitz z"tzl and the third was Rabbi Baruch Soldewitz z"tzl, who lived out his last years in Jerusalem. They met with Herzl, may his name be blotted out, and he appealed to them to support Zionism, because they had decided to establish an independent state in the Land of Israel and since the Haredi Jews were lovers of Zion, they ought to assist him in his mission. The *gaba'im* were astonished: 'What, we should help Zionism? You are Sabbath desecrators, you do not observe *shmitta* and you scoff at all that is sacred!' Herzl tried to persuade them: On the contrary, since the state will be democratic, if you join us, you will be the majority and can decide by majority vote that the Sabbath will be observed in the Land of Israel. Everything will be done democratically.' The three of them traveled to Brisk to consult with Rabbi Chaim of Brisk, who replied: 'Listen, if you wish to follow Herzl, do so. Tie your fate to him and reside forever in his heavenly palace. But if you wish to follow me, be in my heavenly palace. I will not sit together with Herzl, may his name be blotted out. You will have to choose between the two palaces.' Rabbi Chaim of Brisk's verdict was clear."[35]

All parties thus emerged frustrated from the Second Congress. All eyes were fixed on Herzl, and to anyone with discernment, the enormity of the threat to the Zionist movement should have been obvious. Some Haredim had already walked out and went on to become hostile anti-Zionists. But Herzl, who saw how the *Kultura* debate was undermining Zionist unity, dismissed the problem and did not look for a solution. Meanwhile, it continued to grow and sow discord.

Mounting Opposition on the Eve of the Third Congress

When the Second Congress ended, a group of fourteen Jewish students in Berlin got together and decided that the orientation of Leo Motzkin's Jewish Scientific

---

35 Moshe Sternbuch, in: *Kol hashem bekoakh*, no publisher cited, Jerusalem 1943, pp. 36–33. I was unable to find proof that Herzl visited Minsk, but the quoted argument certainly corresponds with the style of Rabinowitz and Herzl.

Society should be more Zionistic.[36] They renamed the society Kadimah,[37] electing Motzkin as chairman and Chaim Weizmann as secretary and office administrator. Kadimah was made up of lively, opinionated young people looking for a way to express themselves. They were faithful readers of the reports dispatched by Dr. Jacob Bernstein-Kogan, who ran the so-called Zionist "post office" (information center) and served as coordinator of the *murshim* (regional appointees of the Zionist movement in Russia). According to Yisrael Klausner, the main draw of these reports was their critical stance towards the Zionist Congress.[38] In appreciation of the work of Bernstein-Kogan, Kadimah drafted an opposition agenda and set itself up as the watchdog of democracy in the Zionist movement. The society meetings were devoted to general Zionist affairs, such as the rights of shareholders in the Jewish Colonial Trust and the importance of instituting congressional oversight. But there was nothing the members of Kadimah argued over more passionately than *Kultura*.[39] They knew that challenging Herzl on *Kultura* would resonate most of all, because it was a matter of ideology.

On careful scrutiny, however, there seems to have been more than ideology at work here. These were individuals who wanted to make their voices heard and sought to participate meaningfully in the running of the Congress, which was strictly monitored by Herzl. Along with their frustration over the deadlock on *Kultura*, they were dismayed to find Herzl deficient in both Zionist lore and Jewish learning. Supplying the tailwind for such grievances was their idol Ahad Ha'am, whose contempt for Herzl only stoked the fire. Herzl may have won them over to the cause of political Zionism but Ahad Ha'am was, and remained, their mentor and intellectual guide. When the *Kultura* storm erupted, it provided the perfect setting for a duel with Herzl while paying court to their teacher.[40] In this way, the tension continued to mount.

Third Zionist Congress: Kultura Woes

The agenda of the Third Congress held in Basel in the summer of 1899 was set by the Inner Actions Committee in Vienna without consulting the Greater Actions

---

36 It was originally established to aid immigrants from Eastern Europe.
37 Taking the name of the Jewish students' association founded in Vienna in 1882. See p. 166 above, note 32.
38 Klausner, *Opozitzia leherzl*, pp. 22–23.
39 Ibid., p. 23.
40 On the establishment of the Democratic Fraction and their correspondence with Ahad Ha'am, see pp. 206–207 below.

Committee, and *Kultura* was not on it.⁴¹ Many of the Russian delegates, including Herzl's great admirer Nahum Sokolow, were upset and demanded that the omission be rectified without delay. The *Kultura* camp was livid, accusing Herzl of not taking the issue seriously.

But *Kultura* was not the only challenge at the Third Congress. The Democratic Fraction, joining forces with a group of *murshim* from Russia, geared up to change the status quo. As the majority of delegates at this congress hailed from Eastern Europe, the Russian delegates were convinced they had the power to decide Zionist policy, "because the people are behind us."⁴² Based on this conviction, they took issue with:

(a) Herzl's management style, which they branded dictatorial. They accused him of not reporting on a regular basis to the Greater Actions Committee in Russia;
(b) Herzl's non-democratic leadership of the Jewish Colonial Trust;
(c) Herzl's optimistic declarations, which were deemed hasty and impulsive: Herzl talked about the establishment of a Jewish state but had no genuine results to show for it. At the opening of the Third Congress, when Herzl spoke of his meeting with the German Kaiser in Jerusalem, Motzkin lambasted him for "engaging in bombastic propaganda that fires up the masses and promises them things that cannot be achieved anytime soon." In particular, he lamented Herzl's remarks in London in early October 1898;⁴³
(d) Herzl's dismissal of *Kultura* as unimportant, not even taking the trouble to list it on the Congress agenda.

Neither did the Haredim sit idly by. They built up their strength at the Congress with an important addition: Rabbi Rabinowitz was joined this time by Rabbi Yaakov Reines, who was attending his first Zionist Congress. After giving the matter serious thought, Reines explains his decision to support the Zionist cause:

> "When the world began talking about the Zionist idea in 1987, the year of First Congress, a number of rabbis joined this movement ... but I did not. I kept my distance, since it is my custom never to do anything without personally studying and investigating every detail ... The same was true for my stance on the Zionist movement ... I made enquiries about the man behind this movement to see if he was worthy ... and began to follow him only when all my findings came back positive."⁴⁴

---

41 Luz, *Parallels Meet*, p. 149
42 Klausner, Opozitzia leherzl, pp. 35–36.
43 Vardi, *Malki betzion*, pp. 46–47. The speech was delivered after being invited to Palestine by the Kaiser, when Herzl was sure that a Jewish state would be established.
44 Raphael, *Ish hame'orot*, pp. 91–92.

Rabbi Reines's reputation as a Torah scholar and expert in Jewish law, combined with his skill as an orator, stood him in good stead: The moment he arrived at the Congress, he was crowned leader of the Haredi camp. Even though *Kultura* was not officially on the agenda, the *Kulturisten* had their way: The Congress proceeded to elect a *Kultura* committee, and Rabbi Reines became the Haredi representative. Many speakers addressed the committee, among them Joseph Klausner, Nahum Sokolow, Rabbi Reines and Hakham (Sephardi rabbi) Gaster. As passions ran high and the Congress was rocked by dissent, Reines was the only one who spoke out on behalf of Zionist unity, pleading for the exclusion of all controversial and contentious topics. Nahum Sokolow describes Reines's heartfelt plea:

> "Then Rabbi Reines spoke from the heart, calling for peace and unity, and beseeching those who had gathered there to eliminate from Zionism anything that separated and divided the parties. He quoted extensively from rabbinic lore and recited beautiful parables in a trembling voice, on the verge of tears. The sight of this man elicited reverence and good will ... Without expressing an opinion for or against *Kultura*, he begged the attendees to strengthen peace and harmony, to build rather than destroy. The appeal of this rabbi, so emotional and earnest, could not help but make an impression."[45]

The degree of apprehension over a *Kultura*-driven rupture comes across clearly in the comments of Dr. Leopold Cohen, a member of the Zionist Actions Committee, who spoke of *Kultura* as "*Das Schmerzenskind*" ("the pain child") of the Congress: "No other issue aroused such passion or disagreement as this, so much so that peace-seekers amongst us were all but unanimous in wishing it struck from the agenda."[46]

But the truth of the matter is that not everyone wanted the matter dropped. Yehiel Chlenov protested that a report on cultural activity had not been submitted, which he believed should have been done in keeping with the resolutions of the First Congress.[47] Herzl, annoyed that the issue had come up for debate without being on the agenda, replied that the Zionist movement would treat religion with respect, as was the norm among civilized people, and there was room in Zionism for all political and religious views. He reminded Chlenov that these were points he had already made at the First Congress. However, he went on: "My opinion, and I believe that of all members of the Actions Committee, is

---

45 *Sefer hashana: Me'asef sifruti*, ed. Nahum Sokolow, Warsaw 1900, p. 30; Raphael, *Ish hame'orot*, p. 109.
46 Raphael, *Ish hame'orot*, p. 107.
47 Klausner, Opozitzia leherzl, p. 36.

that for now and in the foreseeable future, we are omitting from the Congress all controversial issues that do not strengthen the movement."[48]

The victories of the opposition camp at the Third Congress revolved mainly around the running of the Jewish Colonial Trust. The matter of *Kultura* remained in limbo. A joint culture committee had been formed that included Haredi rabbis, most notably Rabbi Reines, as well as non-Haredi rabbis and intellectuals.[49] Rabbi Reines left the Congress with the feeling that the *Kultura* debate had been put on hold and in light of all the stormy debates, it was off the agenda. In response to an inquiry from Plonsk, he wrote: "*Kultura* has been canceled once and for all ..."[50] But the *Kulturisten* were not happy with the outcome, and the debate reared its head once more at the Fourth Congress.

Resurgence of the Kultura Debate: Fourth Zionist Congress

Haredi Achievements

At the Fourth Zionist Congress in the summer of 1900, the *Kultura* polemic resumed with even greater force. A culture committee composed of secular Zionists and rabbis of different denominations had been established, and both supporters and opponents of *Kultura* arrived in London prepared and ready for battle.

Although Rabbi Reines had gone home from the Third Congress feeling that fight was over, the hostility of the anti-Zionist Haredi front remained a worry. The rabbis were angry about a series of culture programs inaugurated by the Zionist movement (albeit on a local basis) and Reines feared that they would use their widespread influence to turn masses of Jews against Zionism. As a countermeasure, he assembled a delegation of fifteen pro-Zionist rabbis (including his son) to attend the Fourth Congress. At the Congress, Reines spoke in praise of unity and collaboration without mentioning *Kultura*. However, Rabbi Landau of Botosani, Romania, singled out *Kultura* as a "red flag" that was keeping Jews from joining the movement: "This Kultura business is intimidating. What goes by the name of culture in the West has inflicted grave injury on Judaism."[51] All the talk was sowing fear among the rabbis who held sway over the Jewish masses, he said. Sharp-tongued Leo Motzkin was quick to reply: The influence of the rabbis was not as

---

48 Raphael, "She'elat hakultura," p. 45.
49 Klausner, Opozitzia leherzl, p. 38.
50 Raphael, *Ish hame'orot*, p. 109, footnote 16.
51 Raphael, "She'elat hakultura," p. 47.

great as Rabbi Landau professed, he said, and *Shivat Tzion*, a rabbinic anthology on the return to Zion published in Warsaw in 1891, had not accomplished what Herzl's *Der Judenstaat* had. Moreover, by rights, religious Jews should be considerate of the feelings of secular people in the same way they were asking the secular to be considerate of theirs.[52] Chaim Weizmann bitterly attacked the rabbis, too, and said he was personally ashamed that a discussion of culture had to be declared outside congressional bounds.[53]

At that point, Rabbi Reines returned to the podium to say that the rabbis were not against culture but against cultural programming sponsored by the Zionist movement. Culture and Zionism were not synonymous, he argued, and those pushing for *Kultura* as part of the movement's operational program did not understand what Zionism was all about.[54]

The squabbling over *Kultura* rose to new heights at the Fourth Congress. The rabbis not only insisted on drawing a moratorium on culture but inundated the forum with proposals on religious issues.[55] This incensed the Russian delegates, and even Herzl said they were asking for too much.[56] Chaim Weizmann and Martin Buber wanted the Congress to officially declare that *Kultura* was a core subject and a mandatory one for those who called themselves Zionists.

Rather than putting this proposal to the vote Herzl did just the opposite: He submitted a counter-proposal that culture not be discussed at all. Once again, the force of his personality won out: Herzl's proposal was accepted by a majority, 125 versus 105. The young people accused Herzl of surrendering to the Haredim. As soon as the Fourth Congress was over, they began to organize under Chaim Weizmann to fight back.

In sum, neither camp left the Fourth Congress satisfied. The Haredim went home frustrated, and Rabbi Reines was unhappy about constantly being on the defensive and having to place his trust in Herzl.[57]

Ehud Luz writes that at the Fourth Congress, "the abyss that divided proponents and opponents of Hebrew culture gaped wide ... East European Orthodoxy was already at the crossroads with relation to Zionism. The intensity of cultural activities in Russia was pushing it farther and farther towards hostility ... At the Fourth Congress, the rabbis who remained inside the movement made one last and desperate effort to hold back the tide. Herzl's customary valedictory dec-

---

52 Nahum Slouschz, *Sefer haprotokolim shel hakongres harivi'i*, Warsaw, Tushia, 1905, p. 100.
53 Raphael, "She'elat hakultura," p. 49.
54 Raphael, *Ish hame'orot*, p. 120; *Hamelitz*, August 21, 1900, no. 177.
55 Luz, *Parallels Meet*, p. 150.
56 Ibid.
57 Raphael, "She'elat hakultura, p. 49.

laration that Zionism would do nothing against religion no longer satisfied them."[58]

The "young guard," as we have said, left the Congress downcast. They felt Herzl was strengthening the Haredi camp, and their opposition to him steadily mounted. Motzkin wrote that memories of the Congress gave him no rest for days on end. He was troubled by the way Zionism had been sullied by "foolish prattle" and the "forces of darkness." This seesaw between the young Zionists and the Haredim continued to impact on the unfolding of events. The fact that the Haredi rabbis had organized on the eve of the Fourth Congress to reinforce their ranks became an incentive for the young people to do the same. In the winter of 1901, they began to discuss the formation of a separate faction to advance their interests at the Fifth Congress.[59]

On the Eve of the Fifth Zionist Congress

Rise and Fall of the Democratic Fraction

At a gathering of Zionist youth in Munich in April 1901, Weizmann challenged Herzl and called for the establishment of a federation of young people "to revive the Zionist body which has frozen."[60] Pursuing political Zionist work as set out in the Basel program and waiting for a state to be founded was not enough, he declared. Until then, the Zionist movement could not turn a blind eye to the needs of the present and should be planning cultural activity "that is not limited to Jewish topics but embraces all the aspects of European culture."[61] Weizmann claimed that under Herzl, the Congress had become "reactionary." Asked to explain, he cited the vote on *Kultura* at the Fourth Congress. That is why personalities like Ahad Ha'am, Nathan Birnbaum and Yehoshua Buchmil kept their distance from the Congress, he said. He passionately argued in favor of a completely independent organization for young people.[62] In May 1901, Weizmann visited Ahad Ha'am in Paris. Ahad Ha'am supported the idea and advised him to keep the youth congress away from Basel and the main Zionist Congress. "I am looking forward to the outcome of this new endeavor to invest our movement

---

58 Luz, *Parallels Meet*, p. 150.
59 Klausner, *Opozitzia leherzl*, p. 45.
60 *Ibid.*, p. 53.
61 *Ibid.*
62 *Ibid.*

with genuine content. Will it succeed?" he wrote to Weizmann.[63] Hoping to please his mentor, Weizmann wrote back: "The main thing is to work on an organizational plan... There is already no doubt in my mind that full independence from the General Zionist Organization is a core principle, and there will be no compromise on this."[64]

In practice, Weizmann did not live up to his word. His ambitious plans to establish a Young People's Congress did not pass muster with Herzl. Herzl was concerned that a separate organization of youth would harm the Zionist Congress and objected to calling it a "congress." He sent a letter to Weizmann asking him to shelve the plan.[65] Weizmann did not balk at Herzl's request or even reply indignantly. On the contrary: He requested Herzl's permission to share the letter with his organizing committee. In the end, the young people's group led by Chaim Weizmann and Martin Buber retreated from its decision and reached an understanding with Herzl. They agreed that the organization would be an indivisible part of the political Zionist program and its convention would be held in Basel as one of the preparatory events for the Fifth Zionist Congress. Herzl was able to bridge the gap by having the young people's organization operate under the umbrella of the Congress and even promising help in organizing its convention. The event took place on December 18, 1901, a few days before the opening of the Zionist Congress on December 26. Herzl extended warm greetings and placed the staff of the Zionist Congress at its disposal.[66] Holding the convention under the aegis of the Congress, with the blessing and assistance of Herzl, blunted the sting.

The planned convention was denounced by Herzl's supporters, who saw it as a form of organized opposition and fought back. An article published in *Hamelitz* insinuated that the Zionist Actions Committee disapproved of the convention.[67] Weizmann, who had tried to be tough and establish himself as the leader of young people seeking independence from the Zionist movement, was revealed in all his weakness. He backed down in the face of criticism and requested that the Actions Committee publish a denial that it had any objection to the convention. Furthermore, he wanted a public affirmation of the group's loyalty. He even dictated the wording that should be used. Herzl brought the matter to the Actions Committee and with its consent, the denial was published almost word

---

63 Ahad Ha'am, *Igrot ahad ha'am*, vol. 2, Yavne Publishing, Jerusalem 1924, p. 236; Klausner, *Opozitzia leherzl*, p. 67.
64 Letter of Weizmann to Ahad Ha'am, June 9, 1901, in: Klausner, *Opozitzia leherzl*, p. 67.
65 Ibid., p. 87.
66 Ibid., p. 93.
67 A. Saltzman, "Leha'ir ozen," in: *Hamelitz*, no. 227, October 12, 1901.

for word in the newspaper of the Zionist movement[68] in the form of a notice from the Actions Committee.[69]

To grasp the ferocity of the dispute between the pro-*Kultura* Fraction members and the anti-*Kultura* Haredim, it is worth looking at the convention protocols and the attitudes voiced toward religion in general. At the convention, where Chaim Weizmann, Leo Motzkin and Jacob Bernstein-Kogan were voted into office, Yehoshua Buchmil demanded the separation of Zionism and religion. Orthodox Jews, he opined, were "the enemies of any intellectual movement for national independence."[70] A student by the name of Abramowitz proposed a "war" on religion. Motzkin replied that no war was necessary because religion was in the process of self-destructing through the influence of the Haskalah.[71] Sabbath observance was also an issue. Some participants wanted the convention to meet as usual on Saturday. In the end, it was decided to adjourn for the day, but making it clear that religious considerations were not the reason. Weizmann's argument that the Sabbath was a national day of rest, not necessarily a religious one, and all Jews rested on that day, was the only one that convinced Motzkin and all Saturday sessions were cancelled. At the convention, it was decided that cultural work would be pursued outside the framework of the Zionist movement. It was further agreed that extraneous elements such as religious opportunism should not be allowed to taint Zionism.

As noted earlier, Ahad Ha'am had advised Weizmann to stay away from Basel and any connection to the Zionist Congress. When his advice was not heeded, and he read about the fierce denunciation and censure of the Fraction by Zionist activists, he could not help gloating.[72] In a letter to Weizmann, he underscored that if Weizmann had listened to him and held the youth convention elsewhere, "many unpleasantries might have been avoided."[73] Ahad Ha'am was right, but Weizmann could not say no to Herzl.

---

68 *Die Welt*, November 8, 1901.
69 Klausner, *Opozitzia leherzl*, p. 94.
70 Ibid., p. 122.
71 Ibid., p. 126.
72 Ibid., p. 153.
73 Ahad Ha'am, *Igrot ahad ha'am*, vol. 3, p. 27; Klausner, *Opozitzia leherzl*, p. 153.

Fifth Zionist Congress

The Democratic Fraction Gains Strength

The establishment of the Democratic Fraction added a new source of contention. At the preparatory convention of Russian Zionists held on December 23, 1901, just before the opening of the Fifth Zionist Congress, a group of 35 delegates banded together under the leadership of Menachem Ussishkin to form an opposition to the Fraction. Dr. Philip (Feibush) Avinovitsky of Warsaw, a lawyer and one of the respected members of this opposition, explained that splinter groups like the Fraction only sowed confusion in the Zionist movement.[74]

The Fifth Congress convened in Basel on December 26, 1901 with 278 delegates. This congress was different from its predecessors. Ehud Luz writes that no trace remained of the old spirit of unity and signs of a split were in the air.[75] The festive atmosphere and novelty were gone, replaced by unrealized hopes for political progress, sparring between supporters and opponents of *Kultura*, and the relentless attempt of a variety of naysayers to tear Herzl down. It is worth remembering, however, that none of this marred the experience of first-time attendees. In their eyes, even the later congresses were extraordinary and moving, and they verbalize their awe in the same terms used to describe the first congresses.[76]

Once again, the *Kultura* debate loomed large. The Democratic Fraction, taking a lesson from the organizational efforts of the religious delegates on the eve of the Fourth Congress, arrived at the Fifth Congress with 37 delegates – almost half as many as the delegation from Russia, with a total of 80. In practice, their power was even greater because they had received mandates from several groups that joined the Zionist movement and paid enough dues to be entitled to a delegate of their own. Instead, they chose to grant this mandate to another delegate they felt was worthy. Klausner writes that at least nine organizations handed over their mandate to the Democratic Fraction: Chaim Weizmann won a mandate from Kharkov and Kishinev, Ephraim Moses Lilien from Kiev, Sonia Getzowa from Novogrudok, Ber Borochov from Ponevezh and so on. But while the turnout of rabbis at the Fourth Congress reached a peak with fifteen, this time there were only two Russian rabbis – Reines and Rabinowitz – leaving them a powerless minority.[77]

---

74 Klausner, *Opozitzia leherzl*, p. 134.
75 Luz, *Parallels Meet*, p. 150.
76 See p. 318.
77 Luz, *Parallels Meet*, p. 151.

Figure 2: Theodor Herzl, 1903, Courtesy of the Central Zionist Archives, Jerusalem.

Figure 3: Moses and Herzl: A cover of a book honoring Herzl, given to him by the Zionists movement of Argentina in the Fifth Zionist Congress, 1901, Courtesy of the Central Zionist Archives, Jerusalem.

Figure 4: The Second Zionist Congress, Basel, 1898, Courtesy of the Central Zionist Archives, Jerusalem.

Why did so few rabbis turn up this time? Presumably the national religious rabbis were no longer worried about the anti-Zionist rabbis publicly denouncing Zionism and winning people over to their view, since their all-out war on Zionism was already in full swing. In this respect, the confrontation was over. But another possibility is that the large rabbinic contingent at the Fourth Congress felt that the *Kultura* debate at the Congress had already run its course and Herzl had made up his mind and would not budge.

Five Democratic Fraction members were elected to the culture committee: Chaim Weizmann, Yosef Klausner, Berthold Feivel and Efraim Moses Lilien, with Martin Buber as chairman. Rabbi Reines was the sole Haredi representative. The Fraction members arrived feisty and battle-minded, and had no qualms about making it patently clear that they were in the opposition. This applied to matters of etiquette, such as refusing to applaud Francis Montefiore when he rose to speak, to protest against honoring members of the upper class, as well as issues of substance, such as how the Jewish Colonial Trust should be run, settlement in Palestine and the economic and physical hardships of the Jews.[78] The Fraction members were an organized, lively bunch who often brought up

---

[78] Yosef Klausner, in: *Hashiloah*, no. 9, p. 69; Israel Klausner, *Opozitzia leherzl*, p. 142.

Figure 5: The Cantor with the choir during Herzl's funeral in the cemetery in Vienna. Newspaper clipping from Hatzfira, 1904, Courtesy of the Central Zionist Archives, Jerusalem.

procedural issues, such as whether or not speakers should be given time limits. Their clear intention was to safeguard the democratic character of the Congress, but sometimes they went overboard, and Herzl had to remind Motzkin to watch his tone of voice.

Another contentious incident occurred when the Congress was in recess for the Sabbath and various factions met on their own. Herzl turned up at a meeting of the Russian delegation and asked to speak out of turn, citing the urgency of the matter and his heavy workload. He explained that he was a Russian delegate, too, since he had received a mandate from several organizations in Russia. In the course of his remarks, he urged his listeners not to stand by and let "a certain person" criticize the Congress and the Actions Committee. With that, he got up and left. "Who was Herzl talking about?" asks Klausner. "Weizmann or Motzkin? Motzkin was certain Herzl was referring to him."[79] By the same token, he might have been alluding to Bernstein-Kogen, who as head of the Zionist "post office" sent out information bulletins laden with criticism of Herzl.

As soon as Herzl was gone, Motzkin rushed to the podium to protest the fact that he had been permitted to address the meeting without waiting his turn. A

---

[79] Klausner, *Opozitzia leherzl*, p. 145.

great commotion broke out in the hall as Russian delegates not affiliated with the Fraction shouted at Motzkin and told him to get down from the podium. Members of the Fraction demanded that he be given the right to speak. Herzl, hearing the noise, returned to the hall and requested that Motzkin be given the floor. As tempers continued to flare, Herzl claimed that the room was needed by the Congress plenary and proposed an adjournment. The meeting ended in a huff, the atmosphere grim and volatile.[80]

When the Sabbath was over, the plenary reconvened. Buber wanted to begin with *Kultura* to avoid having the issue pushed off until the last day of the Congress and no resolution being passed for lack of time. His proposal was rejected, and the Fraction suspected the rejection was premeditated, following the same pattern as before. Lilien appealed to Herzl and Nordau requesting that *Kultura* be discussed and not dismissed automatically as in the past, and he was assured that it would be. The culture committee formulated a draft proposal that was worded in a way that everyone could accept, including the Haredim. The proposal emphasized the need for "national education," which in theory was not supposed to generate Haredi opposition. The Haredim were still resistant. Rabbi Rabinowitz said that the Haredim had lost their faith in *Kultura* initiatives, and Rabbi Reines called the entire endeavor a disaster that would drive masses of Russian Jews away from the Zionist movement. A storm erupted. Herzl called for the discussion to be postponed. Passing a resolution on such a complex issue, which had been debated at four congresses in a row, should not be done hastily, he said. He argued that elections for the Zionist institutions should be held first. Motzkin burst out laughing: He saw this as the same tactic Herzl had used at previous congresses. Buber demanded an immediate vote on all the proposals put forward by the culture committee. When his suggestion was voted down, the Fraction, claiming unfair intervention by Herzl, stalked out of the plenary and watched the rest of the proceedings from the balcony.[81]

After the elections, the *Kultura* debate resumed. So many delegates requested the floor that it was decided only four delegates would speak – two in favor and two against. Herzl repeated his argument from the First Congress that Zionism had no intention of interfering in anyone's religious beliefs, and then opened the vote. This time, the main proposal of the culture committee on the need for national education was accepted. By "*Kultura*," the Congress was referring to the national education of the Jewish people. National education was deemed a

---

80 *Ibid.*
81 This set a precedent for leaving the plenary in protest, which repeated itself during the Uganda debate.

major component of the Zionist program and all Zionists were bound by it. In response, the Fraction returned to the hall, apparently satisfied that its demands had been complied with.[82] Interestingly, Yosef Klausner, in his retelling of the episode, writes that "Herzl responded with steely discipline and mocked those who walked out and protested."[83] In contrast, Aharon Hermoni, an eye witness, does not recall any mockery:

> "I remember as if it were yesterday how the Democratic Fraction paraded out. I watched the leader, restrained, anger stifled inside. When the rebels returned to the hall after behind-the scene negotiations, Herzl scolded their ringleader, Dr. Bernstein-Kogan, who stood there like a schoolchild in the presence of his teacher, stammering an apology...
>
> Before I put these memories to paper, I thumbed through the stenographic report of that Congress, but this giant battle of wills comes across so faintly and weakly. For me, who heard and witnessed the spectacle, it has remained one of the most deeply etched experiences of that period of my life.
>
> Here, for example, is a brief excerpt from this report, from the argument between the returnees and the leader.
>
> Herzl wants to calm the storm and attributes it to a misunderstanding: 'The rejection of the Fraction's proposal should not be misconstrued as disdain for *Kultura*. On the contrary, the Congress sees this issue as exceedingly important and therefore does not want to reach impromptu decisions. This was the misunderstanding that led to the exit of the protestors. And if I said nothing, it was because I took into account the fact that we are all very tired, but I must vigorously protest Dr. Bernstein-Kogan's response to the plenary decision, saying that he is being forced to leave the hall ... Let us look into whether that is so ...'
>
> Dr. Bernstein-Kogan: 'When I have no freedom of speech ...'
>
> Dr. Herzl contends that as president he is making an effort to promote decisions that will not harm either side...But once a decision has been reached, it is your duty to comply even if you object ...
>
> Dr. Bernstein-Kogan: 'It seems to me that a Jewish Zionist Congress cannot oppose national education ... and I wanted to cleanse us of this disgraceful stain...'
>
> Dr. Herzl: 'To do that, you must formulate your proposals more clearly. You come up with a proposal that many of you regard as important and demand that everyone vote for it without argument. But every time this proposal has been brought to the Congress table, it has aroused utter chaos, which proves that it is not a neutral proposal! As for free speech, I do not believe that anyone here can claim I am not protecting freedom of speech. It seems to me that I have made it quite clear this incident was based on a misunderstanding. Believe me, there was nothing in the Congress vote that belittled any of the persons who felt they had to leave the hall. The Congress vetoed the proposal because it was not worded carefully enough, but now let us move on.'"[84]

---

82 Klausner, *Opozitzia leherzl*, pp. 144–148.
83 Ibid., p. 147.
84 Aharon Hermoni, *Be'ikvot habiluim*, Reuben Mass, 1952, pp. 215–217 (henceforth: Hermoni, *Be'ikvot habiluim*).

There is no question that this episode marked a victory for the Democratic Fraction. Its organizational skills, strategy and persistence produced results: The Congress accepted its main proposal on the promotion of national education.

The rabbis did not like this resolution, and Reines and Rabinowitz had their misgivings. At first, the outcome of the vote was seen as a resounding defeat and a blow to the Haredim.[85] On the face of it, the pro-*Kultura* camp had won. But appearances can be misleading. Ehud Luz points out the ironic twist here: "Both the Culturalists and the Orthodox went home happy. The Culturalists were pleased that for the first time a Zionist Congress had resolved that the promotion of national education was an obligation of all Zionists. The Orthodox saw the decision in a more realistic light: They were well aware that this decision, like those of previous Congresses relating to culture, was lacking teeth, since no funds had been allocated for its implementation."[86] In this spirit, Rabbi Rabinowitz published an analysis of the Fifth Congress and reassured his colleagues that the resolution was a compromise between support and opposition to cultural programming. Trying to calm the fears of the Haredi camp, he noted that just as the culture committee had done nothing in the past, it would do nothing now. "Everyone agrees that Zionism without culture is like a body without a soul," wrote Rabinowitz. "The difference between supporters and opponents is that supporters want the Congress to initiate, take responsibility and sponsor programs, while opponents argue that because of the ideological disagreements the Congress cannot and should not deal with this matter. It should be left in the hands of local organizations, each in accordance with its outlook."[87]

Nevertheless, Rabbi Reines was unhappy with way the young Democratic Fraction members were pressuring the Congress on the subject of *Kultura* and shared these feelings with Yehuda Leib Maimon. He lamented the fact that the religious delegates had to be constantly on the defensive against the secular delegates and were completely reliant on Herzl and his maneuvers to maintain the delicate balance. They reached the conclusion that there was no choice but to organize a solid counter group to offset the power of the Fraction.[88] In this way, the escalation came full circle: The pressure of the Haredim at the Fourth Congress led to the birth of the Democratic Fraction in the Fifth Congress, and

---

85 Raphael, *Ish hame'orot*, p. 125.
86 Luz, *Parallels Meet*, p. 152.
87 Raphael, *Ish hameorot*, pp. 125–126.
88 Ibid., pp. 122, 127.

the growing activism of the Fraction in the Fifth Congress led to a national Haredi convention in Vilna and the establishment of the Mizrahi movement.[89]

As stated, the balance of power at the Fifth Congress was tipped in favor of the Democratic Fraction and its support of *Kultura*. It arrived at the Congress as an organized group, full of vim and vigor, after a youth convention held on the eve of Congress. The Haredim, who turned out for the Fourth Congress in full strength, were a dwindling force at the Fifth Congress. In theory, the compromise reached on *Kultura* should have helped to tone down the battle in the Sixth Congress. But the Haredi Zionists, still frantic, founded the Mizrahi movement, and the issue loomed large once again at the convention of Russian Zionists in Minsk. A split in the Zionist movement seemed imminent until Ahad Ha'am came up with a compromise that saved the day, as we shall see below.

Minsk Conference and the Compromise of Ahad Ha'am

On August 22, 1902, the second national conference of Russian Zionists took place in Minsk. It was the first time a Zionist convention in Russia had been authorized by the government. Ahead of the conference, the Democratic Fraction and the rabbis geared up for battle on the subject of *Kultura*. The organizers were apprehensive over the anticipated showdown considering that the person invited to speak on the topic was none other than Ahad Ha'am. He had been asked to prepare a lecture on *Kultura* together with Jacob Bernstein-Kogan and author Yehoshua Hanna Ravnitzky. In effect, choosing this line-up reflected the organizers' interest in a lecture that would represent "the joint work of the culture committee elected by the Congress."[90]

Ahad Ha'am refused to lecture in the name of the culture committee. This was because his proposal to turn the Congress culture committee into an institution responsible for national education throughout the Jewish world was rejected by the Actions Committee, which limited the committee's job to preparing material for a lecture on *Kultura* at the next Congress. However, he agreed to

---

[89] *Ibid.*, p. 129. The Mizrahi movement of Haredi Zionists founded in Vilna in 1902 was distinct from the Mizrahi society (in this case Mizrahi was the Hebrew acronym for *mercaz ruhani* or spiritual center) established by Rabbi Shmuel Mohilever at the second Hovevei Zion convention in Druzgenik in 1887 to disseminate information on Zionist settlement to the wider Jewish community.

[90] Mordechai Nurok, *Ve'idat tzionei rusia beminsk*, trans. and introduction by Israel Klausner, Hasifria hatzionit, Jerusalem 1963, p. 23.

speak at the Minsk conference on behalf of the organizing committee, unconnected to the Zionist movement's culture committee.

The conference organizers worried there would be no time to discuss practical work as it was fairly certain that the presence of Ahad Ha'am would whip up a storm around *Kultura*. His view, after all, was that a self-standing Zionist organization should be established to deal with culture. The fact that the rabbis had bolstered their ranks and created the Mizrahi party made it likely that they would push for a decision against cultural work, which would be strongly opposed by the Fraction. The organizers feared that the conference would thus revolve solely around this matter and no other issues would be discussed. Their fears came true. *Kultura* monopolized the agenda and set off a fierce confrontation.[91]

Ahad Ha'am spoke about culture. True to his beliefs, he stressed that Eretz Yisrael could not solve the problem of the Jews politically or economically but only spiritually. Therefore, he repeated his call for a world organization to promote Jewish national culture. He also recommended the establishment of two education committees, one religious and one secular, which would enjoy equal rights. Indeed, a compromise proposal based on this idea was eventually approved after a bitter exchange with members of the religious camp.[92]

Ahad Ha'am's speech sparked a raucous debate, as Rabbi Reines warned yet again of the danger of pronouncements about *Kultura* that he claimed would only send Jews in the other direction. But while these arguments were raging in the plenary, representatives of the factions were sitting together on a draft resolution for two independent committees to address the issue of culture, one consisting of rabbis and the other of intellectuals like Ahad Ha'am, the Hebrew poet Chaim Nachman Bialik, and Dr. Yosef Klausner.[93] The resolution, inspired by Ahad Ha'am, achieved consensus, and the conference delegates, tensely awaiting the outcome of a bloody battle between the factions, were pleasantly surprised when the team pulled out a proposal agreed upon by all. Thunderous applause ensued, and Rabbi Reines and Weizmann shook hands. One of the rabbis came up on the podium and recited the verse: "'The Lord will give strength unto

---

[91] Shlomit Laskov, *Hayei ahad ha'am: Psifas metokh katavav vekatavim akherim*, Jerusalem, Institute for the Study of Zionism and Israel, Tel Aviv University and Hasifria hatzionit, 2006 p. 200.

[92] The speech was published as "Tkhiyat haru'akh" in *Hashiloah*, Heshvan 1903; Laskov, *Hayei ahad ha'am*, p. 202.

[93] Yosef Klausner (1874–1958), historian, literary critic and one of the founders of the Hebrew Language Academy.

His people and bless His people with peace." The rival factions had made peace.[94]

The fact that the compromise had come from Ahad Ha'am no doubt helped it win acceptance. But how did this man, he who had fought from the outside for an independent Zionist organization that concerned itself solely with matters of the spirit, suddenly become the peacemaker? In this case, he seems to have set aside his antagonism to Herzl because the issue was so important to him. Here was an opportunity to spur the Zionist movement into addressing *Kultura*, and his ability to resolve a nagging problem for which nobody else had yet found a solution was a profound source of satisfaction.

In short, it seems that the endless preoccupation with *Kultura* from one congress to next – prompting the students to establish the Democratic Fraction and the Haredim to assemble under the canopy of Hamizrahi – wore down the parties to the point where they were prepared for a compromise, all the more so when the driving spirit behind it was Ahad Ha'am, a champion of *Kultura* and the spiritual mentor of the *Kultura* camp.

Of course, it was still possible for the deal to fall through and *Kultura* to become a bone of contention once more at the Sixth Congress. However, certain developments took place before the congress that pushed *Kultura* into the shadows: Herzl published *Altneuland*, Ahad Ha'am published a mocking critique of the book, and Herzl, deviating from custom, asked Max Nordau to write a scathing reply. The level of animosity rose, dangerously rocking Herzl's boat. Of all the obstacles that loomed in his path, this one was surpassed only by Uganda. But death came soon after.

Herzl's policy on *Kultura* leaves one wondering whether it stemmed from a lack of understanding of Hebrew culture and failure to grasp its paramount importance. Luz believes the answer is yes: "Herzl was quite unfamiliar with the motives of his Russian colleagues. Since he knew of no 'Hebrew culture' other than religion, he could not understand the importance they assigned to the cultural question."[95] This is borne out by his remarks at the Third Congress, in response to Yehiel Chlenov's complaint that no situation report had been submitted on *Kultura*:

> "Speaking yesterday to Dr. Gaster ... I asked him: When I chair the Congress, the question of culture may come up. I should not like to seem as though I have no understanding of this matter. So please, tell me, what is it? What is this cultural question which, as I hear, is being so vehemently discussed in the corridors and committee rooms? As this was a private con-

---

94 Klausner, *Opozitzia leherzl*, p. 197.
95 Luz, *Parallels Meet*, p. 139.

versation, and anyway of a friendly and humorous kind, I shall not tell you his answer about whether the quarrel is over the Zionist approach to culture or the Congress's view of religion. All I can do is repeat…that Zionism is a movement that has undertaken to completely dissociate itself from matters of religion … We do not believe that allowing disputes over this issue to enter the discourse will contribute to the strength of our movement. We shall not weaken ourselves by our own hand … My view, and I believe also that of all members of the Actions Committee, is that the matter in its entirety should be kept out of the Congress today and in the foreseeable future [loud cheers and applause]."[96]

Sokolow recalls a conversation with Herzl on the subject: "You are hindering, not helping, with this *Kultura* slogan of yours,' he told me at the Langham hotel on July 21, 1900, during the Fourth Zionist Congress in London. 'What are you fighting about? First let the Jews come home, then they can choose whatever *Kultura* they want!"[97]

In Sokolow's view, Herzl was ignorant of Hebrew culture. As an honest man, however, he was reluctant to flaunt knowledge he did not have and that led him to ask the question he asked. But is it plausible that Herzl, the man of culture, would be clueless on this subject? Herzl knew he was dealing with two ideological groups, one Haredi and the other secular, and that the secular Jews wanted to pursue culture work. While they did not actually define the term, Herzl was aware that many in the pro-*Kultura* camp had foresworn religion and were now militantly anti-religious. Myriam Shach has this to say about the Democratic Fraction:

"Grouped together under this clever name which clearly attested to their opposition – long before they established a formal union – were a number of young intellectuals (of Russian, Polish and Galician origin) who left their mark on the Zionist movement.

They were for the most part very gifted, some with exceptional talents, the best and brightest of Europe … They were especially eager to divest themselves, once and for all, of the burden of tradition and the yoke of Torah and mitzvot. Like all young people, they knew better than their elders, and would judge them without mercy.

At first, there was no difference between them and Herzl's political camp, either in outlook or plans, but they bore hatred for the rightists of Hibbat Zion, i.e., those with roots in tradition. These young people, who had tasted the bitterness of the battle between fathers and sons, were fearful, consciously or not, of falling prey again to the 'dark' forces to whom the leader of the movement was granting 'numerous discounts,' and therefore they guarded their freedom with extra vigilance."[98]

---

96 *Bifnei am ve'olam*, vol. 2, pp. 13–14.
97 Sokolow, *Hatzofe levait yisrael*, p. 423.
98 Schach, *Asher itam*, pp. 35–36.

Herzl was presumably worried that the brand of culture they sought would be shaped by their negative attitude toward Torah Judaism and the rabbinic world, which would undoubtedly upset the Haredim. For the Haredim, who lived in fear of any form of culture that was not associated with religion, the specter of the Haskalah movement continued to loom. Moreover, the Haredi rabbis were afraid that secular culture would provide the non-Zionists rabbis with a pretext for condemning Zionism and distancing the Jewish masses. Thus, Herzl had no choice but to keep the issue off the agenda and look for unifying factors. If the Congress voted in favor of secular culture, the Haredim would see it as an affront to their religious beliefs.

Therefore, there appears little basis for the argument that Herzl was ignorant of Hebrew culture or assimilated and that had he understood more, he could have prevented the *kulturkampf* and found a way to bridge between the groups. In fact, Herzl had a Jewish upbringing and was part of the Jewish community as a child. Up to the age of 18, Jewish studies were part of his education. His grandfather, an observant Jew, died when Herzl was 19, and the family ties were close all those years. Furthermore, Herzl was a cultured man who made a living from culture: He was the literary editor of the *Neue Freie Presse*, an author and a playwright. So when he asked Gaster about culture, it was no doubt a rhetorical question. On top of that, the term itself had not even been defined by those warring over it. As Nahum Slouschz writes:

> "'The *Kultura* resolution of last year [still stands]' – so the Congress has declared. 'But it cannot be like last year!' cries one of our finest authors. With all due respect, esteemed author, if you had given more thought to your argument, maybe you would be speaking differently now. If you came to the Congress and offered positive suggestions, then we would have a better idea of what to do and what not to do. But if you simply declare 'we demand *Kultura*,' without defining what it is, then we know it is empty rhetoric of the kind that arouses resentment and hostility, and has already lost us so much good will."[99]

So why did Herzl agree to establish a culture committee at the Second Congress? After all, if he wanted the Congress to sidestep cultural issues, wouldn't instating such a committee only intensify the conflict he sought to avoid? Perhaps it had to do with the sense of harmony and euphoria he had managed to create at the First Congress. Maybe Herzl was so carried away by all this that he did not anticipate the seriousness of the problems that lay in store. He went ahead and established the committee on the assumption that committees were a way of stifling undesirable initiatives and gaining time until the birth of a Jewish state. He was wrong,

---

99 Slouschz, Sefer *haprotokolim shel hakongres harivi'i*, p. 62.

of course. He failed to stifle the debate, and the war over *Kultura* only resumed with greater force. The conflict at the Second Congress did not spur him into finding a solution, even though one was already available in the form of the proposal by Rabbi Rabinowitz of Aleksot, which would later be accepted by all the factions at the Russian Zionist conference in Minsk. By not addressing the issue, he paved the way for the Haredi rabbis to quit the Congress and become actively hostile toward political Zionism from then on.

When the pro-*Kultura* camp at the Third Zionist Congress protested that the topic was not on the agenda, Herzl was forced to compromise. The Congress ended with the election of a joint culture committee that was unable to find a viable solution. As a result, participants arrived at the Fourth Congress geared up for battle. Weizmann and Buber's proposal to officially declare the importance of cultural activity and make it the duty of every Zionist was dismissed by Herzl, who refused to bring it to a vote. He then submitted a counterproposal, which was approved, prompting the frustrated young people to organize politically and return to the Fifth Congress brimming with newfound confidence. When they felt that Herzl was putting them off again, they stalked out of the hall and returned only after the proposal was brought back to the table. In the end, the Congress passed a resolution defining *Kultura* as the national education of the Jewish people and a core component of the Zionist program to which Zionists everywhere were obligated. It was similar to the proposal of the Democratic Fraction which had been rejected at the Fourth Congress. However, this compromise did not solve the problem and the dispute resurfaced at the Minsk Conference. Peace was restored only in the wake of Ahad Ha'am's idea of appointing two culture committees, one religious and the other secular, with equal rights.

How could Herzl not have seen the growing magnitude of the problem? Why did he make no attempt to solve it right away? Again, it is hard to accept Ehud Luz's claim that Herzl did not comprehend the motives of his Russian colleagues due to his ignorance of Hebrew culture and failure to grasp its importance for these people.[100] There is no question that Herzl knew what their motives were and why the pro-*Kultura* camp felt cultural work was so critical. At the same time, he recognized the grim determination of the anti-*Kultura* camp and how disruptive the issue could be for the unity of the Congress. He was wrong only in his belief that he could win the Zionist movement over by the force of his personality and convince everyone to set *Kultura* aside until the establishment of a Jewish national home. Since Herzl had always had the majority behind him, he rightly thought he could beat out his opponents. Yet he failed to appreciate the

---

100 Luz, *Parallels Meet*, p. 139.

harm that a resolute opposition could do. Indeed, it succeeded in creating havoc, driving a wedge between the factions and pushing the Zionist movement to the breaking point.

Herzl erred in not seeking a compromise that would satisfy all parties. In the first congresses, he apparently lived with the hope that a Jewish state would soon be born and saw postponing the decision as preferable. He assumed that he could continue in this vein and put off the discussion. Herzl usually won a majority for almost anything he wanted. In this case, however, he did not take into consideration that the issues raised by the opposition were not always on topic. He erred further in underassessing the motivation of the young leaders of the Democratic Fraction. They knew that challenging Herzl ideologically was the only option, since criticism in every other sphere (his dictatorial leadership style, the charter of the Jewish Colonial Trust, etc.) led to a harsh outcry by nearly everyone at the Congress, including the Russian delegation. In theory, Herzl could have initiated a compromise with the aid of *Kultura* supporters who were loyal to him, such as Nahum Sokolow, thereby neutralizing the young people who, out of frustration, began tossing out ideas that undermined the Congress. Weizmann wanted to establish an autonomous party that would operate in parallel to the Congress. Bernstein-Kogan called for an independent Zionist organization that would concentrate on education (but unlike Weizmann's party, would be part of the Zionist movement). Motzkin was even bolder, proposing that the Fraction involve itself in diplomacy because such matters could not be left entirely to Herzl.[101]

Even so, Herzl did not come up with a creative solution on this question. Perhaps he thought that the message of political Zionism which the Congress had so warmly embraced was more important than cultural work, which threatened to split the Congress. Herzl was convinced that the overwhelming majority was behind him. In that, he was right. But this majority could not prevent the "pain child" of the Congress from yet again disrupting the political Zionist agenda.

At the start of the Zionist journey, Herzl was in top form. He patiently endured the challenges of the opposition and managed to steer the Zionist movement through the obstacle course set for him while maintaining his hegemony. However, there is no question that doing so demanded full attention and drew upon his reserves of energy, which were not infinite. It was an ordeal that left him drained and exhausted, later impacting on the *Altneuland* affair and reaching a peak with the Uganda crisis.

---

101 Klausner, *Opozitsia leherzl*, pp. 118–119.

Chapter 9
Altneuland

Herzl had barely caught his breath after the *Kultura* controversy when a great hue and cry erupted over his second book, *Altneuland*.

If Herzl's first book, *Der Judenstaat*, was a detailed plan for the establishment of a Jewish state, *Altneuland* was his vision for the spiritual and cultural fabric of that state. Herzl began to write *Altneuland* after his expedition to Palestine in 1898. In the book, published in October 1902, he describes a visit to the Land of Israel in the early twentieth century. The country lies barren and desolate. When the same visitors return twenty years later, they find an amazing transformation: a bustling Jewish state incorporating state-of-the-art technology that was nothing short of science fiction at the time. No less importantly, the Jewish state was being run as a model society, with a system of social justice as yet unparalleled anywhere else in the world.

Who was Herzl's target audience? Alex Bein believes that *Altneuland* was written for the non-Jews, to convince the world that a Jewish state was an attainable goal and would bring happiness to the Jews and the entire human race – not only due to its technological advancement, but because it offered a new form of human community that could become a model for resolving the world's social problems. Furthermore, mass emigration of the Jews would decrease the competitiveness between Jews and non-Jews in Europe, and thereby diminish anti-Semitism.[1]

In an article in *Hazman*, Zvi Prilotzky speculated that Herzl, witnessing the Great Powers' tug of war for control of the Holy Places, hoped that his depiction of Jewish tolerance in *Altneuland* would ease the minds of the non-Jews. According to Prilotzky, that is why Herzl sent copies of the book to the Turkish Sultan and many European leaders, among them Count von Goluchovsky, the Austrian foreign minister and Frederick I, the Grand Duke of Baden.[2]

Yossi Goldstein feels otherwise. In his view, Herzl's primary audience was the Russian Jewish community: "With the Zionists of Russia of critical importance for the Zionist movement, Herzl felt it was imperative to translate the book and distribute it there. He had hopes that tens of thousands of Russian Zionists would come to understand his ideas through the novel, as the realiza-

---

[1] Bein, *Theodore Herzl: A Biography*, pp. 399–404.
[2] Hazman, "On capriciousness," no. 19, March 26, 1903; no. 20, March 30, 1903; Shulamit Laskov, "The fight over *Altneuland*," in: *Hatzionut*, vol. 15, 1990, p. 45.

tion hit him that his strength was ebbing in this most important stronghold of Zionism."³

This hypothesis is backed up by the fact that a year and a half before the book was published, Herzl looked into the possibility of translating it into two widely spoken languages in the Russian Jewish community: Hebrew and Yiddish.⁴ The question of who he was writing for was important because Ahad Ha'am, Herzl's chief critic, was an idolized figure in the Jewish world, and if the book was intended for a Jewish audience, his poor opinion of it would have devastating implications for Herzl and his cause. The influence of the book on its readership, Jewish or non-Jewish, is not clear, but it certainly did not generate the same upsurge of interest as *Der Judenstaat* – at least not until Ahad Ha'am came along. For Ahad Ha'am, who never missed an opportunity to mock Herzl and belittle his work, the publication of *Altneuland* provided an excellent target for another round of biting sarcasm.⁵ It seems that Ahad Ha'am was still euphoric in the wake of the Minsk Conference,⁶ where he felt he had successfully defended the cause of *Kultura* in defiance of Herzl who sought its excision from the agenda. In *Altneuland* he found support for his claim that Herzl's cultural doctrine was empty of Jewish content, which provided yet another opportunity to cut Herzl down.⁷

Ahad Ha'am's review of *Altneuland* in *Hashiloah* was criticized for seeing "nothing of the positive side of Herzl's new work; he perceived neither the brilliant prophetic vision of the development of the country, nor the profound love for Eretz Yisrael, nor the faith in the land and the people; he felt nothing of its creative joy or of the earnest ethical impulse which informed every page."⁸

Ahad Ha'am goes on to scoff at the idea that building a model state and populating it with Jewish immigrants was possible within the span of twenty years. He then criticizes the absence of nationalist content in *Altneuland*, comparing the "Zionist idyll" of Elhanan Leib Lewinsky, whose Hebrew book about an imag-

---

3 Yossi Goldstein, *Ahad ha'am veherzl*, Mercaz Shazar, 2011, vol. 2, p. 45.
4 Later, we will see how angry and disappointed he was that Ahad Ha'am chose this community in particular as his chief sounding board.
5 Shulamit Laskov, "The fight over *Altneuland*," p. 35.
6 See above, pp. 217–218.
7 Ahad Ha'am must have resented the fact that Herzl, despite his sparse Jewish knowledge, had usurped his place on the throne. As a young man, Ahad Ha'am had been known as a Talmudic prodigy and Jewish scholar. It was not coincidental that he chose the pen name "Ahad Ha'am," based on Rashi's interpretation of the biblical phrase "one of the people" – "the special one of the people, the king" (*Genesis* 26:10).
8 *Hashiloah*, vol. 10, no. 60, Kislev 1903, file mem-bet; Bein, *Theodore Herzl: A Biography*, p. 405.

inary voyage to the Land of Israel "pulsates with a fresh national life,"⁹ with the limp efforts of the "Ashkenazi leader,"¹⁰ which were unoriginal and pandered to non-Jewish culture.¹¹ The state Herzl describes is not a Jewish state, declared Ahad Ha'am. On a personal level, he accuses Herzl of trying to curry favor with the *goyim*. He also accuses him of superficiality. All he did was "copy others, without showing even a spark of original talent."¹²

Ahad Ha'am pans the book on eight different counts, writes Shulamit Laskov.¹³ The bottom line: Herzl's was guilty of "mechanical aping," and his Altneuland revealed not a trace of independent national character. Rather, it exuded the odor of "indentured freedom" with "the scent of the western Galut wafting in every direction."¹⁴

The first to criticize Ahad Ha'am was Shmaryahu Levin, a devoted follower and former member of Ahad Ha'am's elitist society, Bnai Moshe. Levin published an open letter in *Hazman* reproaching his mentor and teacher:

> "Herzl builds up and you tear down; Herzl writes a novel of 342 pages and you write a 12-page essay that demolishes Herzl's edifice from top to bottom, leaving not one tile or one brick intact. That in itself does not attest to the superior power or talent of the destroyer… Herzl writes a novel which, like all novels, is a combination of truth and fabrication, and you come with your dry facts and figures searching for flaws…This time, you were so concerned that the non-Hebrew reading public receive its due that you took your whole pouch of bullets over to *Voskhod* [a Russian-language Jewish newspaper] even before *Hashiloah* went to print …"¹⁵

Levin goes on to list Ahad Ha'am's barbs and comment on them, one by one. He ends on this note:

> "Herzl recites the first verse of *Shir hama'alot* [Song of Ascents], 'When the Lord restores the fortunes of Zion, we shall be as dreamers,' but you skip that verse and start from the second: 'Then our mouths shall fill with laughter' … I am one of your greatest admirers and pride myself on your friendship. For that reason, I beg of you to stop tearing down and start building…"¹⁶

---

9 He is referring to a Hebrew novel by Elhanan Leib Lewinsky (1858–1910): *Masa le'eretz yisrael bishnat tat (Journey to Palestine in the Year 5800 (2040))*.
10 Herzl.
11 Goldstein, *Ahad ha'am veherzl*, p. 45.
12 Bein, *Theodore Herzl: A Biography*, p. 407.
13 Shulamit Laskov, "The fight over *Altneuland*," p. 35.
14 *Kol kitvey ahad ha'am*, p. 322; Bein, *Theodore Herzl: A Biography*, p. 408.
15 *Hazman*, March 2, 1903, no. 12; Goldstein, *Ahad ha'am veherzl*, pp. 70–74.
16 *Ibid.*

But Ahad Ha'am was not satisfied with publishing his review in Russian and Hebrew. He also wanted it to reach a German-speaking public. Towards that end, he submitted it to the editor of *Ost und West*, Yehuda Leib Wintz. Wintz sent the proofs to Herzl so he could prepare a rebuttal. Reading the review, Herzl was incensed and deeply offended. In his eyes it was a political attack masquerading as a literary critique, directed against political Zionism as a whole and himself personally. Reluctant to reply to Ahad Ha'am lest he be seen as someone who could not take criticism, he asked Nordau to respond. Nordau's sharply worded retort sneered at Ahad Ha'am and cast him as one of the worst enemies of political Zionism. He begins by challenging Ahad Ha'am's main arguments, "some of them foolish, and some petty and malicious," and accuses him of "viciously slandering Zionism and its ultimate goals." Ahad Ha'am's remarks are "so brazen that must drop the kid gloves and condemn him with all the force he deserves." At this point, Nordau turns increasingly ballistic: "Ahad Ha'am has a single point in his favor. He writes fluent, articulate Hebrew... Regretfully, he has nothing whatsoever to say in this eloquent Hebrew of his, absolutely nothing... His essays are... pure nonsense, pretentious and vacuous beyond definition ... Ahad Ha'am is among the foes of Zionism."[17] Nordau goes on to brand him a "secular protest rabbi," a "crude distorter of the ideas of political Zionism," and a "charlatan,"[18] and finally comments sarcastically on his East European origins: "Perhaps European culture is strange and foreign to Ahad Ha'am. If so, he ought to be grateful to us for showing him the light."[19]

Herzl read Nordau's article before it went to print in *Die Welt*, the organ of Zionist movement. Stung to the quick, he did not ask Nordau to tone down his remarks. He even urged him on, referring to Ahad Ha'am as "a hopelessly aging dimwit" and a "candidate for pope," while roundly applauding the article as a whole: "He deserves the divine rudeness you have meted out."[20]

To Ahad Ha'am's credit, he ignored the personal insults. On the contrary, In his response, entitled "Crime and punishment,"[21] he wrote that despite the "cannon fire," Nordau's greatness as a writer and orator remained undiminished.[22] Nevertheless, he resumed his attack on political Zionism and its leaders, portraying Nordau's remarks as a distortion of the truth and a failed attempt to derail

---

17 *Die Welt*, no. 11, 1903.
18 Goldstein, *Ahad ha'am veherzl*, pp. 75–83.
19 Nordau, *Katavim tzioni'im*, vol. 2, Hasifriya hatzionit, Jerusalem 1960, p. 113 (henceforth: Nordau, *Katavim*, vol. 2); Goldstein, *Ahad ha'am veherzl*, p. 78.
20 Laskov, p. 41; CZA HN iii, Herzl's letter to Nordau, March 6, 1903.
21 *Kol kitvay ahad ha'am*, pp. 320–322; Laskov, *ibid*.
22 *Hashiloah*, vol. 11, p. 394.

his ideological opponents. And so the battle began, with the first volleys fired at Nordau, while *Altneuland* and Herzl were relegated to the sidelines.

Herzl sought wider exposure for Nordau's article, but he was not entirely successful due to Ahad Ha'am's extraordinary repute as a spiritual and intellectual guide. Nordau's article appeared in full only in *Hamelitz* and *Hatzfira* in Russia, and the weekly *Jüdische Rundschau* in Germany. *Hamelitz* sided entirely with Herzl and Nordau, but apart from that, opinions were divided. Nachum Sokolow, who defended Herzl and Nordau in *Hatzfira*, was critical of Ahad Ha'am, but he also found fault with Nordau, for saying what he said and the way he said it. The same was true for *Jüdische Rundschau*. Other newspapers that backed Herzl and Nordau were the Russian-language Jewish weekly *Buducnost* and *Hakeshet*, published in Berlin.

An article in *Hakeshet* entitled "The truth from the Land of the Jews," a play on the name of Ahad Ha'am's column "The truth from the Land of Israel," by Rabbi Binyamin (the pen name of Joshua Redler-Feldman) observed that if Ahad Ha'am had not committed the sin of "maliciously seeking defects," he would have seen that Herzl had always promoted the *Altneuland* model and his idea was not utopian: "The mass return of the Jews to the land of our forefathers is no utopia in the days of the telegraph and the electron machine [electricity]."[23] On the other hand, the monthly *Ost und West* expressed full support for Ahad Ha'am. An editorial entitled "Jews Since Yesterday" was critical of both Herzl and Nordau.[24]

Ahad Ha'am also received a boost from Nathan Birnbaum, who published a pamphlet in German summarizing a lecture he delivered on the philosophy of Ahad Ha'am: "So that German speakers will be able to judge the man who has been called all sorts of derogatory names by Nordau, which are enumerated by Birnbaum one by one in this pamphlet ..."[25]

Hatzofeh published excerpts from Nordau's response interspersed with comparison quotes from Ahad Ha'am. The paper was critical of Ahad Ha'am, but it was Nordau who was the clear target. The editorial board of the paper emphasized that it had chosen this strategy in the wake of the enormous outcry over Nordau's statements, which *Hatzofeh* also condemned.[26]

---

[23] Joshua Redler, "Truth from the Land of the Jews," *Hakeshet*, Berlin, vol. 3, Adar 1903, p. 117.
[24] Bein, *Biografia*, p. 333.
[25] Mathias Acher, *Achad ha-am, ein Denker und Kämpfer der jüdischen Renaissance*, Jüdischer Verlag; Laskov, *ibid.*, p. 43, footnote 27.
[26] *Hatzofeh*, no. 56, March 19, 1903; Laskov, *ibid.*, p. 42.

Der Freund had harsh words for Ahad Ha'am but was horrified by Nordau's rebuttal. Even *Hashkafah*, the newspaper of Herzl loyalist Eliezer Ben-Yehuda, published a negative review of *Altneuland*.

The outpouring of opinion on the subject only inflamed the atmosphere. Most of the conflict revolved around Ahad Ha'am's reading of Herzl's book and Nordau's *ad hominem* attack on Ahad Ha'am. Tempers flared on both counts. However, two additional components fired up the debate: the perceived affront to the East European Zionists and freedom of expression.

The Affront to East European Jewry

The first cry of outrage came from Yehuda Leib Wintz, editor of *Ost und* West, who had sent Ahad Ha'am's book review to Herzl, requesting that he write a response to be printed alongside it. Wintz never heard back from Herzl even after contacting him a second time. Then he saw Nordau's article in *Die Welt*. To Wintz, Herzl's conduct was insulting and typical of the derisive attitude of the West European Jews towards the Ostjuden, the Jews of Eastern Europe. Nordau's belittling of Ahad Ha'am, who was idolized all over Eastern Europe, was more of the same. Indignant, Wintz published Ahad Ha'am's review together with an opinion piece of his own, "Jews Since Yesterday," in which he portrays Herzl and the Westjuden as embracing Judaism in response to anti-Semitism, with no past ties to religion or tradition. Their condescension was based on ignorance and animosity towards authentic Judaism and those who had "always been Jews," he writes. Armed with a sense of superiority over the downtrodden Ostjuden, they permitted themselves to dominate the ideological debate. It was an approach that could have dire consequences for the Zionist movement and had to be stopped, Wintz warns.[27]

There was some truth in Wintz's accusations, even without being aware that Herzl had written to Nordau on February 22, 1903 describing Ahad Ha'am as "one of those *shtetl* writers who would be completely ignored if we, whom they so sneeringly call 'European,' had not turned them into personages of note."[28] On the other hand, let us remember that this was Herzl's response to his being ridiculed by Ahad Ha'am as an Ashkenazi leader parroting the ideas of others. Still, Herzl read the draft of Nordau's article, with its attack on Ahad

---

27 *Ost und West*, vol. 4, April 1903, pp. 226–244; Laskov, *ibid.*, p. 46.
28 Letter of Herzl to Landau, in: Laskov, *ibid.*, p. 37, footnote 12.

Ha'am's Ostjuden provincialism and praise of Westjuden supremacy, without asking him to change a word.

Yosef Klausner, editor of *Hashiloah,* also writes about the East-West divide and sees Nordau's remarks as demeaning to East European Jewry.[29] *Der Freund* accuses Nordau of portraying Ahad Ha'am, the darling of the Russian Jews, as some anonymous Russian Jewboy or third-rate hack whom the German Jews acknowledged out of pity, "so as not to embarrass the Russian Zionists, who are – horror of horrors – half-Asian."[30]

Thus Herzl, who waved the banner of national unity, found himself drawn into a polemic that accentuated the age-old clash between Ostjuden and Westjuden. It was an issue that he would have been wise to avoid, and in the end, it came back to haunt him.[31]

Freedom of Expression

Die Welt's role as an incubator of Zionist unity also suffered in the wake of the *Altneuland* affair. As noted earlier, the paper's editorial board refused to accept articles supportive of Ahad Ha'am. It was a policy that drew the ire of *Hatzofeh:* "Is criticism of the Zionist leadership against the law? Is party discipline tantamount to an order to surrender?"[32] At the third assembly of Vienna Zionists in June 1903, one of the delegates proposed that *Die Welt* be exhorted "to embark on the path of democracy and desist from tyranny." The proposal was rejected, but the debate surrounding it invariably left its mark.[33]

As the uproar over *Altneuland* escalated, so did the level of hostility between the parties, and the Democratic Fraction was much to blame.

The Democratic Fraction and Altneuland

The Democratic Fraction's stance on *Altneuland* is worthy of special mention. After the Minsk conference, the Fraction, which had been the main opposition bloc to Herzl, was left without a solid pretext for opposing him in light of the compromise reached there on *Kultura.* Nordau's callous attack on Ahad Ha'am

---

[29] *Hatzfirah*, no. 75, April 10, 1903; no. 77, April 15, 1903; Laskov, *ibid.*, p. 46.
[30] I.L. Peretz, "Thunder and Lightning," *Hatzofeh*, no. 56, March 19, 1903; Laskov, *ibid.*, p. 47.
[31] On Herzl's blunders, see pp. 233, 243, 250, 338–344.
[32] *Hatzofeh*, no. 60, March 24, 1903.
[33] *Hashiloah*, vol. 15, no. 66 in: Hashkafa ivrit," *Hamashkif*, p. 548; Laskov, *ibid.*, p. 47.

infused the group with newfound energy. Furious over the affront to their revered spiritual leader, they sent an open letter of denunciation to *Hazman* signed by sixteen Jewish thinkers and intellectuals.[34] Even Shmaryahu Levin, who had been the first to speak out against Ahad Ha'am, agreed that Nordau's article had crossed the line: "In my opinion, Ahad Ha'am deserves to be strongly condemned by the Zionist leadership, but not in such a crude way," he wrote to Yosef Luria.[35]

Herzl mistakenly assumed that the Fraction had read Ahad Ha'am's critique ahead of time and done nothing to keep it from being published. He was hurt that these young people could pass over Ahad Ha'am's diatribe in silence yet find Nordau's rebuttal so unconscionable. He took their response not only as a personal slight but as a challenge to the movement as a whole and called upon them to return to the Zionist fold. They dismissed these accusations. What they objected to was Nordau's coarse style, they said. As for Herzl's claim that they had advance knowledge of Ahad Ha'am's article, Buber clarified that the editor of *Ost und West* had sent them a copy on April 3 but published it the very next day, leaving no time to respond: "As you can see, and as is clear to me now, Mr. Wintz sent me the proofs a day before publication merely so he could say that I knew about the article before it came out."[36]

Buber also denied not responding to this: At a meeting in Vienna after the incident, he informed Herzl, he had publicly castigated Wintz as a spineless scoundrel. Finally, he wrote, "returning to the Zionist fold" was unnecessary because he and his friends had never left it. At the same time, he rejected the idea of Herzl as the arbiter on Zionist matters: "With all my respect for you, I cannot allow you to be the sole decisionmaker."[37]

Towards this end, Buber wrote to Ahad Ha'am announcing his plan to publish a monthly journal, *Der Jude*, much of which would be devoted to the ideas of Ahad Ha'am. Berthold Feiwel and Nathan Birnbaum would also contribute content and "address the recent scandal that has affected us so deeply, fully restoring your honor."[38] In the end, the journal never came out.

By this point, the Democratic Fraction was struggling to stay afloat. It had failed to increase its membership or achieve the goals it had set for itself, and in many respects suffered from the same organizational ineffectiveness that

---

[34] Klausner, *Opozitzia leherzl*, p. 213.
[35] CZA A23/2/6; Goldstein, *Ahad ha'am veherzl*, p. 89.
[36] Letter of Buber to Herzl, May 26, 1903, in: Martin Buber, *Khilufay igrot*, vol. 1, Mossad Bialik, Jerusalem 1982, p. 161 (henceforth: Buber, *Khilufay igrot*).
[37] Klausner, *Opozitzia leherzl*, p. 215.
[38] *Ibid.*, p. 215, footnote 8.

plagued the Hovevei Zion. The Fraction's plans for *Der Jude* fell through because it could not raise the required funding, in the same way that Nathan Birnbaum's plan to send out invitations to a Zionist conference in 1893 went up in smoke because he had no money for postage stamps.[39]

The *Altneuland* affair briefly restored the Fraction to life but could not keep it going for long. After the Kishinev program in April 1903, Weizmann came up with another revival plan. Aware of the gravity of the situation in Russia, he envisioned the Fraction as a tool for bettering the lot of the Jews there. On May 6, 1903, he and Berthold Feiwel wrote to Herzl reproaching him for the failures of the Zionist leadership over the past seven years but proposing a plan of action: "Who can awaken the Zionist movement from its stagnation? The Democratic Fraction." Weizmann ended with the hope that the Congress would be more accommodating toward the young people, but also expressed the thinly veiled threat that if not, they would rebel.[40]

Weizmann, however, knew that the Fraction was too weak to carry out such a threat. In a letter to Herzl on June 27, 1903, he complained that the Fraction was under attack:

> "It's terrible! Everyone is name-calling and spreading lies in the name of Zionism! I am so upset at the way I am being forced to fight against the other side, I thought of coming to Vienna to talk to you about everything that is going on, and I mean everything! At the moment, you may feel very bitter towards the Fraction, and perhaps furious with it. But I know you would oppose this kind of war on the Fraction with every fiber of your being because you are not one who would tolerate dishonesty in the Zionist movement."[41]

The Democratic Fraction was in such organizational disarray that its members refused to convene before the Sixth Congress "to discuss strategies for putting its cultural principles, etc. into practice … because they did not want to hear speeches about how nothing was being done."[42] Revitalizing the Fraction was attempted once more in response to the Uganda controversy. Weizmann tried to take advantage of the opposition to Herzl but failed to turn matters around and the Fraction basically came to the end of its road.[43]

The loud opposition of the Fraction was not acceptable to most members of the Zionist movement, who felt it threatened the unity of the organization and

---

[39] See p. 109, above.
[40] Jehuda Reinharz, *Chaim Weizmann: Baderekh el hamanhigut*, Hasifriya Hatzionit, Jerusalem 1987, pp. 172–173 (henceforth: Reinharz, *Chaim Weizmann*).
[41] Klausner, *Opozitzia leherzl*, p. 223.
[42] Ibid., p. 224.
[43] See pp. 273–275, below.

showed unnecessary disrespect towards its founder. There is no question that the Fraction pushed negativity toward Herzl to new heights and steadily poisoned the atmosphere.

At this stage, Herzl's supporters began to retaliate. Eliezer Ben-Yehuda accused Ahad Ha'am of "coiling around Herzl like a snake with his queries and questions, obsessing over petty details and pouncing on him for the absence of Hebrew in [*Altneuland*] ... Since when does Ahad Ha'am care about colloquial Hebrew, when he himself is dismissive of it?...Ahad Ha'am is the Great Destroyer."[44]

Leon Rabinowitz, editor of *Hamelitz*, called Ahad Ha'am "a mourner among the bridegrooms"[45] for "belittling everything and having the gall to accuse those who yearn for salvation of being rash and hasty." From Ahad Ha'am's critique, "one might think the book was written by some peddler in the marketplace, not one of the most indefatigable men of action the Jewish world has seen for generations."[46] Dr. Y. Margolin retorted that Herzl, however little he knew about Judaism, "has done much more for the Jews than the scribblers who are only good with words ... Herzl has aroused the Jewish people from its deep slumber, and even Ahad Ha'am cannot deny that we would not be having this debate if Herzl had not come along to shake up the Jewish masses."[47] The whole philosophy of a spiritual center was worthless if Ahad Ha'am could not explain how this center would arise without an "ingathering" of the Jews. It is worth noting that the pro-Ahad Ha'am camp spent its time attacking Nordau, not Herzl, while the pro-Herzl camp directly addressed the claims of Ahad Ha'am.

Looking at the timeline of opposition to Herzl, it seems clear that Herzl's fatal error began with his policy on *Kultura*. If he had confronted the issue early on and reached a compromise that satisfied both the Democratic Fraction and the Haredim, the Fraction would have had no ideological basis for challenging him with such ferocity. If the young people had channeled their rebelliousness into less dramatic matters, such as democratization or the management of the Jewish Colonial Trust, where standing up to Herzl would have been more difficult, perhaps Ahad Ha'am would not have stalked him on *Kultura* and the tempest over *Altneuland* would not have occurred. Even if Ahad Ha'am had been critical and written what he wrote, Herzl might have taken it less to heart, accepted

---

44 *Hashkafa (Yerushalayim)*, no. 36, April 10, 1903; Laskov, *ibid.*, p. 215.
45 In Ahad Ha'am's report on the First Zionist Congress, he described himself as a "mourner at a wedding party."
46 *Hamelitz*, no. 80, April 22, 1903; Laskov, *ibid.*, p. 48.
47 Dr. Y. Margolin, "Ahad Ha'am and Altneuland," *Buducnost*, no. 13, April 10, 1903; Laskov, *ibid.*, p. 38.

the barbs with stoicism or dashed off a sharp rebuttal himself. That way he would have arrived at the Sixth Congress less stressed and more in command.

But that was not to be. The cumulative effect of the pressure building up over years of battling for the Zionist cause, compounded by the wall of opposition on *Kultura*, took their toll. In this case, the extensive press coverage given to both sides was not helpful.[48] In contrast to those occasions when retaliation for attacks on Herzl yielded positive results and contributed to the public visibility that Herzl so strongly wished for, here the battle revolved around Ahad Ha'am and Nordau. The mutual mudslinging and hostile atmosphere ended up sapping Herzl strength and opened the door to unbridled personal attacks such as those that marred the Sixth Congress. Herzl, as we have said, made the mistake of not confronting the issue of culture head on, despite all the signs that ignoring it was not the solution. When Ahad Ha'am unleashed his attack on *Altneuland*, Herzl was already worn down, so much so that he could not let the matter go or move on, let alone fight back on his own. He erred again in not responding to Wintz, which seems to have been more a product of dwindling energy than anything of greater substance.[49]

A further misstep was not asking Nordau to tone down his scornful remarks about the Ostjuden before the article went to print. Nordau's castigation of Ahad Ha'am hit hard and went far beyond a literary rebuttal. Likewise, it was a poor decision on Herzl's part not to allow *Die Welt* to publish articles that were critical of him. These errors of judgment accelerated the destructive process that would reach a peak in the Uganda affair.

"The furious discussion in the Zionist press accentuated the differences between the two tendencies in the movement," writes Alex Bein. "They strengthened the opposition to Herzl and prepared the way for the developments of the Sixth Congress which cannot, in fact, be understood without reference to this accentuation of the controversy."[50]

From *Altneuland* to Kishinev and Uganda

The events that followed the Kishinev pogrom completely changed the agenda of the opposition camp.[51] Herzl, who had long been seeking an audience with the

---

48 For more on this matter, see p. 76.
49 Herzl's letter to Nordau, see p. 341, footnote 118. Also see p. 227.
50 Bein, *Theodore Herzl: A Biography*, p. 410.
51 The Kishinev pogrom began on April 6, 1903 (Julian calendar), as the Christians of Kishinev left church on Easter Sunday. During the 3-day rampage, 49 Jews were killed, 92 gravely injured

Russian authorities, submitted another request and was received by the Russian minister of the interior, Vyacheslav von Plehve, the man whom many held responsible for the pogrom (sparking the ire of the Russian Zionists who were furious at Herzl for agreeing to meet him). The plan for settling Jews in El Arish had fallen through just then, and the British Colonial Secretary repeated his offer of East Africa (mistakenly referred to as Uganda). When Herzl brought this proposal before the Sixth Congress, all hell broke loose. From here on, he found himself facing his greatest opposition yet, at the Congress and then the Kharkov Conference, as his exit from the stage of history drew near.

---

and 500 lightly injured. More than 700 homes and businesses were looted and destroyed. Neither the police nor the army took any measures to stop the violence, which was seen as proof that the pogrom had been carried out under government aegis.

Chapter 10
Uganda and the Sixth Congress

"I am thinking of giving the movement a closer territorial goal, preserving Zion as the final goal."[1]

The East Africa affair – better known as the Uganda affair – took the protests of the opposition to new heights and gravely challenged Herzl's standing as leader of the Zionist movement. It is important to note that at no time was he without a congressional majority behind him: Even the delegates from Eastern Europe who fought bitterly against him ended up siding with him when they cast their ballots. Still, Herzl's authority suffered a blow and his leadership was put to a critical test. His trademark charisma continued to stand him in good stead, but not at the same level as the previous congresses.

In the spring of 1903, while the Jews were celebrating Passover, the Kishinev pogrom erupted. Over a period of several days, Russian mobs attacked their Jewish neighbors under the aegis of the authorities.[2] The world on the cusp of the 20th century, an era that placed great store in liberalism and humanism, reeled in shock. Herzl knew that something must be done immediately to address the plight of the Jews and sought a temporary shelter for them until the ideal solution, a Jewish state in Eretz Yisrael, could be established. The idea of finding an alternative location to tide the Jews over in times of trouble was not new for Herzl. It was a concept he borrowed from Izzet Bey, one of the most powerful figures in the court of Turkish Sultan Abdul Hamid. His advice to the Jews: "Purchase another territory and then offer it, together with an additional sum of money, for Palestine."[3] The Kishinev pogrom was the third tangible instance of "Jewish misfortune" since the start of Herzl's Zionist journey.

First came the pogroms in Galicia in the summer of 1898. Herzl already mulled the possibility of finding a temporary refuge for the Jews of Galicia outside of Palestine back then. As he wrote in his diary:

"I am thinking of giving the movement a closer territorial goal, preserving Zion as the final goal. The poor masses need immediate help, and Turkey is not yet so desperate as to accede to our wishes … Thus we must organize ourselves for a goal attainable soon, under the Zion

---

1 *Complete Diaries of Theodor Herzl*, vol. 2, p. 644.
2 For more on the Kishinev pogrom, see p. 234, footnote 51.
3 Vital, *Hamahapekha hatzionit*, vol. 1, p. 225.

flag and maintaining all of our historic claims. Perhaps we can demand Cyprus from England, and even keep an eye on South Africa or America – until Turkey is dissolved."[4]

However, thoughts about a temporary haven were pushed aside when the German Kaiser invited Herzl and his entourage to Jerusalem where he planned to announce the granting of a charter in Palestine. It was an expedition that ended in disappointment, as we know. Nevertheless, Herzl persisted in his diplomatic efforts, convinced that Turkey's economic distress would lead to a change of heart and it would hand over the charter if was offered enough money.

The next incident took place in the spring of 1900. The "misery of the Jewish masses" resurged as Jewish migration from Romania moved in a "bloody trail" across Europe.[5] Herzl again considered temporary alternatives, recording his thoughts on Cyprus as a "station on the road to Palestine."[6] The Cyprus option was never more than an idea, as talks with Turkey began in 1901. They continued into the following year, but without success. "I have reached an iron wall and cannot penetrate it," Herzl exclaimed in frustration.[7]

Then came the Kishinev pogrom. In response to this pogrom and the fact that the creation of a Jewish state in Palestine did not seem realistic in the foreseeable future, Herzl explored other temporary options for Jewish resettlement. One idea was to approach the cash-strapped government of Portugal and purchase the colony of Mozambique which would be traded for a place closer to Palestine:

> "I started out from Chamberlain's Uganda suggestion – and hit upon Mozambique. I will try to get this inactive land for a Chartered Company from the Portuguese government, which needs money ... I want to acquire Mozambique only as an object of barter in order to get for it from the English government the entire Sinai Peninsula with Nile water summer and winter, and possibly Cyprus as well – and for nothing!"[8]

Towards this end, Herzl requested and received a recommendation from the Austrian prime minister, Ernest von Koerber, which was submitted to the Portuguese

---

4 *Complete Diaries of Theodor Herzl*, vol. 2, p. 644.
5 Bein, *Theodor Herzl: A Biography*, p. 412.
6 *Ibid.*, p. 414.
7 *Ost und West*, vol. 3, no. 11, 1903, col. 724; Michael Heymann, "Herzl vetzionei rusia: makhloket vehaskama," in: *Hatzionut*, vol. 3, Tel Aviv 1973, p. 59 (henceforth: Heymann, "Herzl vetzionei rusia").
8 Joseph Chamberlain (1836–1914), British colonial secretary, offered territory in East Africa for Jewish settlement (a proposal that became popularly – but erroneously – known as the "Uganda Scheme"); *Complete Diaries of Theodor Herzl*, vol. 4, p. 1487.

ambassador in Vienna, Count Miguel de Paraty, who promised to look into the matter.[9] The El Arish project also came up for consideration at this time (after the Fifth Congress).[10] Herzl hoped that finally he could bring the Zionist movement news of a genuine achievement but in May 1903, after the plan was studied, he was sadly forced to admit defeat. "My whole Sinai plan has broken down,"[11] as he put it.

Three times Herzl had been certain that his efforts to establish a Jewish state were on the verge of success, and three times his hopes were dashed. Each of these disappointments weighed heavily upon him. In October 1898, when he was invited by the German Kaiser to Jerusalem, he believed the charter for Jewish settlement in Palestine was a given, but he was wrong. The second time around, in 1901 and 1902, he was sure the talks with Turkey would succeed, but again he was disappointed. Finally, the plan for El Arish in Sinai fell through. On May 16, 1903, he wrote in his diary: "I thought the Sinai plan was such a sure thing that I no longer wanted to buy a family vault in the Döbling cemetery, where my father is provisionally laid to rest. Now I consider the affair so wrecked that I have already been to the district court and am acquiring vault No. 28."[12]

Alex Bein tells a story that sheds light on Herzl's mood: "When his father's body was being exhumed and transferred to his new resting place, Herzl attended in the company of A.H. Reich, the secretary of the Zionist office. Toward the end of the ceremony Herzl pointed to the family vault and said to Reich: 'Soon, soon I too shall be lying down there.'"[13]

Thus Herzl, at the age of 43, found himself worn down by endless work, constantly struggling on several fronts at once, with a long history of disappointments. The Sixth Congress was about to open with no political progress to report. Convinced that he had to reach the Congress with a breakthrough, he embarked on an obstacle course that led him to his final hurdle, possibly the most problematic of his career, which almost ended in the split of the Zionist movement: the Uganda controversy.

Herzl found himself accused of territorial opportunism and betraying Zion. "Herzl, stripped naked, is nothing but a Territorialist masquerading as a Zionist," charged Menachem Ussishkin.[14] The heads of the opposition threatened

---

[9] Bein, *Theodor Herzl: A Biography*, p. 446.
[10] The El Arish project was a plan proposed by Herzl in 1903 after failing to obtain a charter for Palestine.
[11] Letter to Lord Rothschild, May 30, 1903, *Complete Diaries of Theodor Herzl*, vol. 4, p. 1501.
[12] *Complete Diaries of Theodor Herzl*, vol. 4, p. 1491; Bein, *Theodor Herzl: A Biography*, p. 437.
[13] Bein, *Theodor Herzl: A Biography*, p. 437.
[14] Heymann, "Herzl vetzionei rusia": in *Hatzionut*, vol. 3, pp. 66–67.

to depose him as head of the Zionist movement or force him to step down, posing a humiliating ultimatum.

Were these accusations justified? How could it be that with all Herzl's efforts to establish a state in the Land of Israel, there were still people who suspected that Eretz Yisrael was not a top priority for him and questioned his belief that the Jewish state had to be there and nowhere else? Was Herzl a Territorialist at heart? How important was it to Herzl that the Zionist state be founded in Zion?

The answers to these questions are not simple. Herzl's attitude toward Eretz Yisrael is a matter of dispute. Ehud Luz is in the camp that believes Herzl's political vision was not linked exclusively to Zion: "Herzl sought a charter for Jewish settlement in Palestine only because he had to take into account the sentiments of the East European masses. He had no special attachment to that land; as his rivals suspected, he was always a covert Territorialist."[15]

The Zionist historian and researcher Isaiah Friedman is a representative of the opposite camp: He maintains that Herzl was an unwavering supporter of Eretz Yisrael.[16]

On closer inspection, it appears that prior to the publication of *Der Judenstaat*, Herzl saw Palestine as the natural and ideal location for a Jewish state. In his appeal to the Rothschilds in June 1895, he notes: "I am taking up once again the torn thread of the tradition of our people, I am leading it to the Promised Land."[17] While it is true that in the book he writes about a state in either Palestine or Argentina,[18] Michael Berkowicz, his Hebrew secretary and translator, published an explanatory letter in *Hamaggid* a few months later at Herzl's request:

> "On the matter of where to settle, [Herzl] reneged on what he had written in the chapter 'Palestine or Argentina?' after recognizing that our national aspirations are bound solely to the land of our forefathers and our fervent love for that land. This is evident from his speech to the Maccabean Society in London in the summer of 1896, where he no longer mentions Argentina and speaks only of settling in Eretz Yisrael."[19]

Herzl asked Berkowicz to omit this material, but he explains: "... for the literary truth I chose to present the book with its original content and format."[20] Isaiah

---

15 Luz, *Parallels Meet*, p. 257.
16 Friedman *Germania, turkia vehatzionut*, pp. 177–188.
17 *Complete Diaries of Theodor Herzl*, vol. 1, p. 16.
18 *Medinat hayehudim*, Smilansky Publishing, Tel Aviv 1939, p. 29.
19 *Hamaggid*, no. 23, June 11, 1896, and the translator's remarks in the second edition of *Der Judenstaat*, appended to the introduction of the first edition, Smilansky Press, Tel Aviv 1939.
20 *Ibid.*, translator's remarks.

Friedman is convinced that Herzl did not consider Argentina a real alternative, and only cited it "for the sake of comparison, because without so much as a pause he goes on to portray the 'ever-memorable historic home' of the Jews as preferable to Argentina ... If Herzl tried his luck negotiating over Cyprus, El Arish and Mozambique, he did so mainly to reinforce his bargaining position vis a vis the Grande Porte ... and to put the Jewish Question on the international agenda."[21]

This hypothesis is strengthened by Erwin Rosenberger, who describes Herzl's first meeting with the Zionist students of Vienna on February 8, 1896, a few days before the appearance of *Der Judenstaat*. Rosenberger recounts the conversation between Herzl and Rabbi Lowy, who was also at the meeting:

> "Herzl went on: 'A territory for the Jewish state? We will ask the Sultan of Turkey to give us Palestine; in return, we will put his finances in order. The Jews will undoubtedly be able to provide the money and also the necessary *sechel*.'
> Rabbi Lowy broke in once again. 'We need the month of *Kislev*,' he said mysteriously. 'The month of Kislev?' Herzl did not understand, nor did the rest of us.
> '*Kis* means 'pocket' in Hebrew; *lev* is 'heart,' explained the old man.
> Herzl acknowledged the pun with a smile and took up the thread of his discourse once again: 'In my pamphlet, I suggest Argentina in addition to Palestine as a state territory. Why? We are among ourselves here, and I can tell you the reason: It's so the people in Constantinople won't think that we have our hearts set exclusively on a piece of Turkish territory and that they can name any price they want for it.'"[22]

Georges Yitshak Weisz also believes that Herzl's seeming hesitation in *Der Judenstaat* regarding the location of the Promised Land was merely rhetorical and ultimately a bargaining chip to encourage the Turks to grant a charter to the Jews in Palestine. In his book, he cites many sources testifying to the fact that Herzl fully comprehended the attraction of the Jewish people to Eretz Yisrael.[23] This would seem to leave us with two possibilities: (a) that Herzl saw Argentina as a realistic option for a Jewish state and (b) that he saw it as a bargaining chip. But there is also a third possibility, rarely considered, which is that Argentina represented the building of Zion "in stages." In other words, Herzl understood that the real goal was Eretz Yisrael, but that did not conflict with the notion of attaining Zion step by step. He had faith in his ability to make the dream of Zion come true, even if the Jews had to accept a charter in Cyprus or Uganda along the way. In his mind, these were simply political cards on the road to a

---

21 Friedman, *Germania*, turkia vehatzionut, p. 106.
22 Rosenberger, *Herzl as I Remember Him*, p. 16.
23 Weisz, "The Promised Land of Our Fathers, or The Uganda Myth," in *Theodor Herzl: A New Reading*, pp. 165–177; *ibid.*, "Palestine or Argentina?", p. 187–189.

Jewish state in Eretz Yisrael. What seemed possible to Herzl was perceived by his opponents as contradictory, and by some, a betrayal of Zion.

This was how the story unfolded: England, perceived as a safe haven by the Jews of Eastern Europe, would soon be asked to take in an influx of refugees from Kishinev, as it had done in the past. This proved to the British Colonial Secretary, Joseph Chamberlain, how right Herzl had been in demanding an orderly migration from Eastern Europe. Chamberlain was prepared to extend aid, but the question was where the refugees should be sent.

On May 20, 1903, Leopold Greenberg, Herzl's emissary to the British government and the future editor of the *Jewish Chronicle*, met Chamberlain and presented him with a series of requests from Herzl. Most importantly, Herzl wanted Britain to convene an international conference to find a solution to the Jewish Question. The goal was obtaining Palestine for the Jews. Chamberlain turned him down, saying that the time was not yet ripe and the Great Powers could not reach an agreement on any issue, much less this one.[24] At that point, Greenberg put forward Herzl's second request – an alternative region. The argument was that since Palestine under the Turks was not within reach at this time, Herzl was prepared to consider Cyprus or the El Arish valley (a smaller territory which was presumed at the time not to be reliant on the waters of the Nile). Chamberlain replied that Cyprus was not suitable for Jewish colonization, and as for El Arish, Lord Cromer, the British High Commissioner in Egypt, would not agree.[25"] Chamberlain, basically well-intentioned, told Greenberg that he had not wanted to pressure Herzl on the subject of East Africa "because he sympathized with his longing for Palestine and thoroughly understood the significance of the El Arish plan in that connection," but if nothing came of it, he hoped that Herzl would take his suggestion seriously.[26]

The idea of offering Uganda occurred to Chamberlain after his first meeting with Herzl on October 22, 1902. Chamberlain had visited East Africa and come away with the impression that Jewish settlement could succeed there. At the time, he wrote himself a note: "If Dr. Herzl were at all inclined to transfer his efforts to East Africa there would be no difficulty in finding suitable land for Jewish settlers, but I assume that this country is too far removed from Palestine to have any attractions for him."[27]

---

24 Friedman, *Germania, turkia vehatzionut*, p. 108.
25 Bein, *Theodore Herzl: A Biography*, p. 439–440.
26 Friedman, *Germania, turkia vehatzionut*, p. 108.
27 *Ibid.*, p. 107.

At their next meeting on April 24, 1903, Chamberlain told Herzl: "I have seen a land for you on my travels, and that's Uganda ... And I thought to myself, that would be a land for Dr. Herzl. But of course he wants to go only to Palestine or its vicinity." To which Herzl replied: 'Yes, I have to. Our base must be in or near Palestine.'"[28]

However, following the failure of the El Arish plan and the atrocities in Kishinev, Chamberlain brought up Uganda again. After their meeting on May 20, Greenberg immediately reported this to Herzl, emphasizing Chamberlain's support for the Zionist enterprise and his willingness to assist in establishing a secure home for the refugees of the Kishinev pogrom (which Chamberlain described as horrifying). Greenberg told Herzl that even if he did not agree with Chamberlain and was dismissive of the East Africa proposal, he should not reject the colonial secretary's overtures out of hand. The main issue, Greenberg said, was whether the plan would bring them closer to Palestine or push them away, "but it seems to me no small gain from the political point of view to be able to say that the British government has offered us a refuge territory, and I believe it could be used as a drill ground for our national forces."[29]

Herzl was won over. In his reply to Greenberg on May 23, he wrote that since the El Arish plan was no longer relevant, the Uganda proposition should be taken into serious consideration, but only if it was shown to be genuinely advantageous. He asked Greenberg to find out more details from Chamberlain.[30]

On June 7, 1903, Greenberg sent the following reply to Herzl:

"It seems to me that intrinsically there is no great value in East Africa. It will not form a great attraction to our people for it has no moral or historical claim. But the value of the proposal of Chamberlain is politically immense if we use it to its full. An essential of this is, I submit, that the Agreement we get from the British Government should be as well a definite declaration of its desire to assist our people ... That will be of infinite value to you, both within our Movement and outside ... It matters not if East Africa is afterwards refused by us – we shall have obtained from the British Government a recognition that it cannot ever go back on and which no other British Government will ever be able to upset ... If it is found that East Africa is no good they will have to make a further suggestion and this, it is possible, will gradually and surely lead us to Palestine."[31]

---

[28] *Complete Diaries of Theodor Herzl*, vol.4, p. 1473.
[29] Bein, *Theodore Herzl: A Biography*, p. 440.
[30] *Complete Diaries of Theodor Herzl*, vol. 4, p. 1498.
[31] Friedman, *Germania, turkia vehatzionut*, pp. 104–105.

Four days later, on June 11, Herzl wrote back to say that he agreed entirely and the main object was to get the British to recognize the Jews as a nation.[32] Turning down the proposal of a loyal friend like Chamberlain was impossible, he argued, and beyond that, once the British acknowledged that the Jews were a nation, they would have a firmer basis for demanding a state, since only nations were entitled to a state of their own.[33]

On July 20, 1903, Greenberg learned from Herzl that there were objections to the plan. It was Max Nordau who was opposed: "He went wild, bitterly denouncing the plan and calling it foolish and dangerous. The Jews will not follow Herzl to Uganda ... If not to Palestine, they will go to England and America ... He concluded with the warning that the plan would lead to a schism in the movement and begged Herzl not to even think of raising it at the Congress."[34]

Herzl did not heed Nordau's warnings. That was his first mistake in the Uganda affair. If he had taken Nordau's advice, perhaps the outcome would have been different. One possible explanation is the tremendous load he was juggling: Along with so many other pursuits, Herzl was trying to arrange an interview with the Russian authorities to alleviate the deplorable situation of the country's Jews and advance the Zionist cause.

On July 23, three days after writing to Greenberg, he noted in his diary: "Mme. von Korvin has procured an audience for me with Plehve."[35] Finally, after much exertion, he managed to obtain a formal invitation to meet with the Russian interior minister, following numerous failed attempts to gain access to the Tsar.

In April 1896, Herzl described the many fronts on which he was active and the array of sensitive issues and challenges he dealt with as an "egg-dance."[36] The load had not lightened, and Herzl continued to work simultaneously in different realms. In addition to his diplomatic activity on the Turkish and British fronts, Herzl tried to gain a foothold in Russia, but without success. From the earliest days of his Zionist journey, he sought an audience with the Tsar. In his diary, he records a conversation in April 1896 with the Grand Duke of Baden, the uncle of the German Kaiser: "I said: Does Your Royal Highness consider it possible that I shall be received by the Tsar?"[37]

---

32 *Ibid.*, p. 180, footnote 22.
33 *Ibid.*, p. 181.
34 Bein, *Biografia*, p. 358.
35 *Complete Diaries of Theodor Herzl*, vol. 4, p. 1514.
36 *Ibid.*, vol. 2, p. 578.
37 *Ibid.*, vol. 1, p. 339.

In July 1896, Philipp Michael Newlinsky[38] introduced Herzl to Ferdinand, the crown prince of Bulgaria. Herzl shared with him his vision for a Jewish state, hoping to win Ferdinand's assistance. Their conversation as recorded by Herzl went like this:

> "Ferdinand: It is a magnificent idea. No one has ever talked to me about the Jewish Question this way ... Your idea has my full sympathy – but what can I do for it?
> Herzl: I should like to ask Your Royal Highness to prepare the Tsar for my plan and, if possible, to obtain an audience for me."[39]

Nothing came of it. In June 1899, Herzl traveled to the Hague where the international peace conference was in session (May 18-July 29). There he hoped to make the acquaintance of the Russian delegates and through them perhaps win an audience with the Tsar. He wanted to present a plan for Jewish emigration from Russia which he believed would interest the Russians and generate support for his campaign to obtain a charter from the Turks (along the same lines as the plan presented to Wilhelm II).[40] He also had another reason for seeking an interview with the Tsar: He felt it would help to calm the fears of the Russian Jewish community. Again, these efforts came to naught.

Five years went by. In 1903, Herzl renewed his efforts to establish contact with the Russian authorities. The primary goal was to aid the persecuted Jews of Kishinev, but there was another motive: In June of that year, he learned that von Plehve, the interior minister, had sent out a confidential circular calling for the suppression of the Zionist movement. Herzl hoped to dissuade him and at the same time promote the idea of Palestine as a refuge for the Jews of Russia.

Herzl thus embarked on another bid to convene with someone of influence in the Russian government, this time not Tsar Nicholas, but Plehve and other ministers.[41] His chances were greater now because the violence in Kishinev, the first photographed pogrom of the twentieth century, had been covered in the world press and had left readers enraged. The Russians, who were reliant on international loans, were afraid of Jewish influence on the big banks. Plevhe, it should be pointed out, was among those blamed for the pogrom in the media. Herzl enlisted the Polish writer Pauline von Korvin Piatrowska, a friend of Plehve's, to advocate on his behalf. She reported back to Herzl that Plehve

---

[38] Philipp Michael Newlinsky was Herzl's diplomatic agent in Constantinople and the Balkan countries.
[39] *Complete Diaries of Theodor Herzl*, vol. 2, p. 436.
[40] Bein, *Theodore Herzl: A Biography*, pp. 319–321.
[41] Maor, *Hatnu'a hatzionit berusia*, p. 223.

was "looking forward to making the acquaintance of so interesting a personality as Dr. H. and will *de tout son coeur* support emigration without the right of reentry."[42] The world peace activist Berta von Suttner also sent a recommendation. The joint efforts of these women did the trick.[43] Herzl traveled to Russia and met Plehve twice. At their first meeting on August 8, Herzl requested (a) diplomatic pressure on the Turks to grant a charter to Jews in Palestine; (b) financial assistance for Jewish emigration drawing on the taxes paid by the Jewish community; and (c) freedom of association for the Zionists of Russia, which was then illegal. At their second meeting on August 13, Plehve informed Herzl that the Tsar had personally approved all three requests. Before he left, Herzl was given a letter confirming this.

Yitzhak Maor maintains that this letter was ultimately an imperial writ since Plehve assured Herzl it had passed through the Tsar, who had given it his blessing.[44] In an ironic twist of fate, Tsarist Russia, the enemy of the Jews, thus became the first country to issue an official letter of support for the Jewish state.

During his visit to Russia, Herzl met with the finance minister, Sergei Witte, who promised to cancel the prohibition on the sale of Jewish Colonial Trust shares. He also met with Nicholas Hartwig, director of the Asiatic department of the Russian Foreign Office, who said he would encourage the Turks to cooperate with the Zionist movement. Herzl came away with the feeling that his visit had been a tremendous success. The fact that he had been received by high-ranking figures like Plehve, Witte and Hartwig was an achievement in itself. However, most important in his eyes was the letter accepting his three conditions which the Tsar had approved for publication and the verbal promises that went with it. The Zionist movement had won Russian recognition.

However, Herzl was not yet aware of the barrage of criticism that would be heaped upon him by the Russian Zionists. What Herzl hailed as a historic accomplishment was condemned in the loudest terms by the Jews of Russia, who were beside themselves with anger. Herzl's visit with the tyrant they saw as responsible for the Kishinev pogrom aroused fury and resentment. To many, meeting with such a person was an affront to the dignity of the Jewish people and the Zionist movement. They scoffed at the promises of Plehve and his associates, calling them worthless and untrustworthy. "Didn't Moses go to Pharaoh, king of Egypt?" asked Herzl, responding to their outrage.[45] Yitzhak Maor believes

---

42 *Complete Diaries of Theodor Herzl*, vol. 4, p. 1514.
43 Berta von Suttner won the Nobel Prize for Peace in 1905.
44 Maor, *Hatnu'a hatzionit berusia*, p. 227.
45 Ibid., p. 223.

the criticism was shortsighted: "As a Jewish statesman, Herzl was ahead of his times, as a result of which he was widely misunderstood and criticized."[46]

There was another aspect of Herzl's trip which would impact greatly on the chronicle of events. Until then, the Zionists Herzl met were the representatives of the Jewish intelligentsia who attended his congresses. In Russia, Herzl encountered the Jewish masses for the first time, and was deeply moved by their distress. He wrote in his diary: "Things are so bad with them that a poor devil like myself seems to them to be a liberator."[47] These feelings reached a peak in Vilna, where thousands of Jews turned out to greet him. Despite the ban imposed by the authorities and the brutality of the mounted police and Cossacks, the Russian Jews were not deterred, and thronged the streets to see "the greatest son of the Jewish people."[48] While the opposition denounced him, for the Jews of Vilna and its rabbis and dignitaries, Herzl remained the same charismatic figure. After watching crowds of Jews rushing to see him even as the police beat them back, he reflected: "In the numerous addresses I was enormously overpraised, but the unhappiness of these sorely oppressed people was genuine."[49] The hardship he witnessed in Vilna shocked him to the core and contributed to his decision to unveil the Uganda plan at the Sixth Congress although Max Nordau and Yehiel Chlenov had warned him against it.

On the Eve of the Congress

Herzl returned from his grueling trip to Russia with an overload of experiences to process. He left the capital, St. Petersburg, on an emotional high, sensing that history was being made and the Jewish state was now closer. On the other hand, he was horrified by the scenes of Jewish misery and felt a pressing need to help. All this emotional turmoil and his heavy schedule in the summer of 1903 may explain in part why Herzl was not at his best when the Congress opened. This further aggravated the Uganda crisis.

Herzl departed for Russia on August 5 and reached St. Petersburg two days later. There he met with the ministers of the interior and treasury, as well as other persons of rank. On August 12, he met with the local Zionists, and on August 16 he reached Vilna. After Vilna, he spent one day at the baths at Bad Aussee and then set out to Basel, for the Sixth Congress.

---

46 *Ibid.*
47 Bein, *Theodore Herzl: A Biography*, p. 450.
48 *Ibid.*, p. 451.
49 *Complete Diaries of Theodor Herzl*, vol. 4, p. 1543.

On Friday, August 21, 1903, Herzl was already in Basel. That same day, he reported to the Greater Action Committee on his trip to Russia, the meetings he had held and Phleve's letter, endorsed by the Tsar. The letter, as noted, was a promise to exert pressure on the Turks and provide imperial encouragement and support for the resettlement of Russian Jewry in the Jewish state.

To his chagrin, the response of the Russian delegates was the opposite of what he had expected. Herzl had worked so hard to secure an audience as the statesman of the Jewish people, and to his mind, it was an enormous accomplishment. But instead of gratitude, he faced a storm of protest. As the Congress listened to his report on the meeting with Plehve, the atmosphere turned volatile. The accounts of what transpired next differ. Herzl's biographer Ernst Pawel writes that while the delegates were still digesting this news, Herzl surprised them again:

> "And while they were still in a state of shock, he dropped the other 'bomb' – the British charter for East Africa. It was late Friday afternoon, and before they had a chance to react, he adjourned the session in time for the Sabbath services."[50]

Michael Heymann's narrative is similar: "The Uganda proposal came as a complete surprise to the congressional delegates, including the Action Committee members from Russia who had heard about it two days before the Congress."[51]

Others, however, say the scheme was already known and challenged at an earlier stage: In his memoirs, Yosef Eliash (1874–1955) writes:

> "Before the elections for the Sixth Congress, I happened to be in Vilna. As usual, I tried to meet Zionist activists and from them learned that the Zionist societies in Vilna and environs were meeting to discuss the new project of our leader Herzl. I managed to get invited to the meeting. There they read a bulletin sent out by the national center or Bernstein-Kogan announcing that after the El Arish plan had fallen through, Joseph Chamberlain, secretary of the British Colonial Office, was offering Herzl a vast tract of land in East Africa … for which the British government was prepared to grant a charter for settlement… and the establishment of a Jewish state based on Herzl's program. The bulletin further stated that in view of the deplorable plight of the East European Jews in Romania, Galicia and Russia, Herzl was willing in principle to negotiate with the British."[52]

---

50 Ernst Pawel, *The Labyrinth of Exile*, p. 506.
51 Heymann, Herzl vetzionei rusia, in: *Hatzionut* 3, p. 66, footnote 33.
52 Eliash, *Zikhronot tzioni merusia*, p. 126.

Eliash describes what happened next:

> "This letter came down like a sledgehammer on the heads of all those in the room. The speeches began right away, against the proposal for being non-Zionist, and especially against Herzl. Some said they knew from the start that Herzl would never bring us to the Land of Israel and what a pity it was that we did not heed the warnings of Ahad Ha'am ... Others showered Herzl with curses. 'Herzl is a traitor,' they shouted. 'Herzl is a charlatan,' 'Herzl is a dreamer,' 'Herzl is gambling at the expense of the Jewish people ...' All kinds of suggestions came up. If he dares to raise the issue of East Africa at the Congress or refuses to strike it from the agenda, we will not hold elections for the Congress institutions, and so on ..."[53]

Eliash relates that when he returned from Vilna, the Zionist office in Minsk, his hometown, received a communiqué from the national office strongly denouncing Herzl for straying from the Zionist path. He was now prepared to substitute another country for Eretz Yisrael and planned to put East Africa on the agenda of the Sixth Congress. All Zionists were thus urged to be vigilant in electing delegates to the Congress and choose only those whose belief in Zionism was impeccable and had the strength to oppose schemes that ran counter to the Zionist ideal.

Bein's version of the story differs entirely. In his telling, the Congress delegates responded to the Uganda proposal at that Friday session, but this initial reaction was positive. Even Jacob Bernstein-Kogen of Kishinev, whom we remember as a frequent critic of Herzl and one of the leaders of the opposition camp, did not reject the idea at first, and believed that "in their present circumstances, the Jews of Russia would be prepared to emigrate anywhere, even to hell." Israel Jasinowski of Warsaw agreed with him. Among the Russian delegates, only Chlenov expressed doubt, and not very forcefully.

The delegates from Western Europe, among them Max Bodenheimer and Alexander Marmorek, who were friends and admirers of Herzl, were the opponents in this instance. They decried the Uganda plan as "a change in the Basel program, which confined itself exclusively to Palestine."[54]

So we are looking at a kind of topsy-turvy moment in Zionist history: The East Europeans delegates stood in awe of Herzl's achievement while the West Europeans protested that he was deviating from the principles of Basel. Perhaps the explanation is that the East Europeans had personally experienced the tyranny of the Russian regime and the Uganda scheme offered the specter of relief, whereas the West Europeans, who had not gone through the same torment, saw

---

53 *Ibid.*
54 Bein, *Theodore Herzl: A Biography*, p. 453.

it as a departure from the path of Zionism. However, even the admiration of the East Europeans was short-lived. Soon they also turned against the scheme, branding it a betrayal of the Zionist idea.

Action Committee member Oscar Marmorek proposed postponing the vote on whether the Uganda plan should be presented to the Congress until the next meeting and his suggestion was accepted. This interval between meetings allowed time to think. In his memoirs, Chlenov recalls that the Russian members were not comfortable with this decision: "We came to the clear conclusion that we, as Zionists, had no interest in Africa...We were sure ...that our proposal [to refrain from raising the subject at the Congress] would not arouse any serious opposition from Dr. Herzl... but as it transpired, we were wrong."[55]

The following morning, Saturday, August 22, 1903, Chlenov and another Russian delegate sat down with Herzl and tried to convince him not to go public with the Uganda plan. He would not listen. Bein writes that Chlenov and his colleague felt it was enough to acknowledge the political importance of the British offer. Herzl was unable to grasp or accept this advice. Having personally witnessed the distress of the Jews on his visit to Russia, he regarded Uganda as a temporary solution but a vital one for the Jewish masses whose time was running out. In fact, he did not see it as conflicting with the ultimate goal of a Jewish state in Eretz Yisrael. Another possibility that cannot be discounted is that Herzl badly needed a tangible achievement after so many years of thankless hard labor fraught with disappointment.

If we reconstruct the talks on that Sabbath day, we see that the mood fluctuated and Herzl might have easily concluded that everyone would agree in the end that the scheme was a beneficial one. In the afternoon, Herzl invited a small group of leaders to meet with him. At this gathering, Leopold Greenberg pulled out the official document confirming Great Britain's willingness to grant a charter in East Africa. The room buzzed with excitement. Even Chlenov, who that morning had tried to get Herzl to abandon the plan, rose and recited the *Shehekheyanu* prayer, giving thanks for the recognition of the Jewish people for the first time since the destruction of the Temple. However, despite the historic nature of the document and the positive feedback, a heated four-hour debate ensued between those who supported the presentation of the plan at the Congress and those who objected.

Herzl, not wanting his presence to impede free speech, left the room for the duration of the debate. When he returned, he was told that opinions were divid-

---

55 Yehiel Chlenov, *Pirkei khayav upeulato*, Eretz Yisrael Press, Tel Aviv, 1937, pp. 183–184 (henceforth: *Sefer Chlenov*).

ed and many were opposed, but the plan would be added to the agenda nonetheless. While we have no protocols from the second meeting of the Greater Action Committee, we know that the main subject was not Uganda but the dissatisfaction of several Russian Zionist *murshim* with Herzl's visit to Plehve.

It was a tragic moment from Herzl's perspective. For years he had been working to bring home results, and now that he was on the verge of what he believed was an important historic breakthrough, instead of basking in the warm glow of praise, he was bombarded with criticism and lack of appreciation by a handful of Russian emissaries.

With the response to the Uganda plan not entirely straightforward, Herzl might have misinterpreted the true intentions of the Action Committee. The East European delegates, as we have said, were initially enthusiastic. Particularly notable in this regard was the remark of opposition member Bernstein-Kogan, that under the circumstances the Jews would happily move even to Uganda. Herzl could certainly have left the meeting with a sense that the Congress attendees would feel the same way. Isaiah Friedmann concludes that Herzl was under the impression – justifiably so – that he had a majority behind him.[56] Bein, too, notes Herzl's claim, "frequently reasserted," that he had been empowered by the Greater Action Committee to bring the Uganda proposal to the Congress.[57]

Herzl, who, as we have said, did not see Uganda as deviating from the Basel program, misread those who opposed the plan out of allegiance to the Land of Israel. He was wrong to think he could convince them that Zion was attainable in stages. He did not heed the pleas of Nordau and Chlenov and did not foresee the great rift on the horizon.

The Congress Opens

The Sixth Congress opened in Basel on Sunday, August 23, 1903, and closed on Friday, August 23 with a record attendance of 592 delegates. It was a week full of unexpected twists and turns. Herzl's charisma had weakened, but even in the darkest hours, his leadership endured. He still had the power to influence the crowd, although it came at a price. Herzlian charisma was, and remained, as a force to be reckoned with.

Herzl, still in the grip of his visit to Russia, where he had personally witnessed the suffering of the Jews and the hopes pinned on him, ignored Chlenov's

---

56 Friedmann, *Germania, turkia vehatzionut*, p. 112, footnote 34.
57 Bein, *Theodore Herzl: A Biography*, p. 454.

advice to stress the political benefit of the Uganda proposal. In his opening speech, he spoke about the necessity of finding a practical solution for the growing wretchedness of the Jews:

> "Truly, the situation of the Jews all over the world is no more favorable today than it was in the years of the earlier Congresses ... Here and there a change has taken place, but not a change for the better. Many of us thought that things could not get any worse, but they have gotten worse. Misery has swept over Jewry like a tidal wave ... For the bloody days in that Bessarabian city must not cause us to forget that there are many other Kishinevs, and not only in Russia. Kishinev exists wherever Jews are tortured physically or spiritually ... because they are Jews. Let us save those who can still be saved! It is high time. Whoever is not totally blind to visible signs must perceive that there has been a downright disastrous change for the worse in the situation."
>
> Herzl goes on to emphasize the urgency of the situation: "... Jewish communities regarded emigration as a panacea [but] emigration could continue only until the countries of immigration began to take measures against this influx of a desperate proletariat ... The countries of immigration have begun to fight back ... Our solution ... seeks to provide the Jewish people with a homeland."[58]

He describes his tireless efforts to obtain a charter for Palestine, which had yet to bear fruit, and then shares the news of Great Britain's offer of settlement in East Africa. He insists, however, that the final goal is Eretz Yisrael: "Zion this is certainly not, and can never become," he declares, assuring his listeners that he had made this abundantly clear to the British government. At the same time, he is certain the Congress will recognize the political benefits of the offer and find a way to make use of it to alleviate the hardship of the Jewish people "without our abandoning any of the great principles on which our movement is founded."[59]

It was a speech that left the majority of the delegates transfixed. Herzl's words were met with enthusiasm and thunderous applause. Nowhere in the hall was there any sign of protest.[60] On a final note, Herzl proposed the establishment of a special commission to explore the British offer. A handful Russian delegates decided to form their own exploratory committee. All in all, Herzl felt that he had made the right decision to open up the debate. The newspaper *Ost und West*, which covered the event, thought so, too: "The storm of applause

---

58 "Opening Address at the Sixth Zionist Congress," *Zionist Writings*, Herzl Press, New York, 1975, vol. 2, p. 221–230.
59 Ibid., p. 228.
60 Bein, *Theodor Herzl: A Biography*, p. 454.

would not have been greater if Herzl ... had announced to the Congress: Palestine is ours and the masses can set out.'"[61]

Chaim Weizmann also commented on the impact of Herzl's speech, describing the delegates as "electrified" by his disclosure: "It was the first time in the history of the Jews in exile that a world power had negotiated with representatives of the Jewish people, thereby re-establishing it as a national and judicial entity. The achievement was enormous."[62]

Shmaryahu Levin, who watched the proceedings from the dais, came away with a somewhat different impression. His account dwells less on applause and more on the lack of enthusiasm he discerned in people's faces:

> "I was on the Congress dais since I was one of the secretaries, so I was able to closely study the faces of all the delegates. Everyone listened to the opening speech intently, concentrating with all their might, and I saw surprise on those faces, but no sign of protest or rebellion ... The magnitude of the offer by the world's greatest power eclipsed any other thoughts, considerations or doubt. On the other hand, there was no overwhelming sense of exhilaration as one might have anticipated. Only at the Landsmanshaft meetings [meetings of delegates from the same geographical region] did the delegates grasp that we were approaching a grave crisis."[63]

So there seems to be some contradiction here. People apparently saw what they wanted to see: Shmaryahu Levin, who opposed the scheme, did not discern enthusiasm, whereas Herzl interpreted the applause as a sign that he was on the right track and would succeed in pushing the scheme through by a large majority. But Herzl was wrong. He did not detect the storm on the horizon and took no measures to prevent it.

The initial excitement in the plenary turned to doubt. Rumblings of discontent began to surface at the Landsmanshaft meetings. The great debate over Uganda took place on August 25, the third day of the Congress. The atmosphere was charged and emotional, and the audience raucous and outspoken. What caused this crisis? Could it have been averted? Isaiah Friedman believes that those who voted no at the Congress were victims of a mistake and had completely misread Herzl's intentions.[64] He maintains that the whole affair was based on a fundamental misunderstanding. The choice was not between Zion and Uganda, but whether to send an expedition to Uganda to scout out the territory

---

[61] *Ibid.*, pp. 454–455.
[62] Weizmann, *Masa u-ma'as*, pp. 89–90.
[63] Shmaryahu Levin, Bama'arakha, p. 225; Bein, *Theodore Herzl: A Biography*, p. 455.
[64] Friedman, *Germania, turkia vehatzionut*, p. 145.

and report back to the Greater Action Committee, which would bring the findings to the next Congress.

The source of this misunderstanding is not clear. After all, Nordau had explained that Herzl was talking about an expeditionary commission that would submit a report to the Seventh Congress, and any further action would necessitate a decision of the Congress. So what were they afraid of? Perhaps the volatile atmosphere clouded their perception of what the vote was really about and led them to think that anything they said yes to with respect to Uganda was a betrayal of Zion. Another possibility is that they saw even an exploratory visit to a place outside Zion as unthinkable.

In such an atmosphere, Herzl found it hard to keep the Congress running smoothly. If he had managed to maintain an aura of order and decorum, he might have been able to shift the weight of the argument to the political benefits of the proposal and convince the plenum that approving an expedition was not a crime. However, the debate over Uganda took a hostile, combative turn that was more than the exhausted Herzl could handle. The truth of the matter is that the Sixth Congress started off in a contentious mood due to the fierce disapproval of Herzl's visit to St. Petersburg on the part of the Russian delegates. The Uganda proposal only accelerated the buildup of ill feeling and opposition to Herzl, which steadily mounted and sought an outlet for release. All that was needed was a "fuse," which was duly supplied by Davis Trietsch and Alfred Nossig.[65]

Trietsch and Nossig added to the toxic atmosphere not so much in what they said about Herzl but how they said it. Nossig, who was attending as a congressional delegate for the first time, attacked Herzl from the very start, at a gathering on Saturday morning. His remarks were so savage and personally insulting that the audience would not let him finish. His ally, Trietsch, also had plenty to say. Continuing in the same personal vein, he accused Herzl of belittling the El Arish plan, of poorly managing the negotiations, of chasing after fleeting success and not being honest with him. In short, Herzl was not worthy or fit to lead the movement. "Just grant me and my friends a small portion of the powers that have currently been squandered with no success to speak of, and I will find something better than East Africa, closer to the Land of Israel," he said in conclusion.[66]

Trietsch and Nossig's tirades ultimately backfired. Bein writes that their attacks only reinforced support for Herzl at the Zionist Congress. Most of the participants refused to tolerate this kind of mudslinging and cheered Herzl on. Thus

---

65 For more on Trietsch and Nossig, see pp. 185–187, 273.
66 Bein, *Biografia*, p. 370.

even if some of Trietsch and Nossig's criticism was legitimate, it was not accepted and did not achieve its objective.[67]

However, the opposition camp adopted a shrill, confrontational style to amplify its message which kept Herzl from presiding over the Congress, chairing its sessions and passing resolutions with the calmness and festivity of the previous congresses. The mood was volatile. In an attempt to ease the tension, Herzl suggested that a special committee be formed to study the Uganda question, but the Russian delegates would not hear of it. They were adamant that the scheme was a bid to replace Zion. The ensuing debate was emotionally fraught, but Herzl did not intervene. Friedman believes he sat on the sidelines so as not to sway opinion in his favor,[68] but there may have been another factor: Herzl's health. In his memoirs, Jacob Bernstein-Kogan, a medical doctor, states that in the course of this Congress he was called in to treat Herzl for two heart attacks.[69]

The plenary debate was tumultuous. Passions ran high as people rose to share their views on the subject, which veered from side to side. The last to speak was Leopold Greenberg, Herzl's representative in London. Greenberg reported on the talks with England and reminded the audience that when the Uganda offer first came up in October 1902, Herzl turned it down because there was still hope of obtaining a charter closer to Palestine, in El Arish. Even at this stage, however, Herzl believed that the Uganda proposal could make it through: Despite the crisis and despondent atmosphere, when Greenberg read out Sir Clement Hill's letter with its formal proposal from the British government, the whole Congress rose to its feet and cheered. Rabbi Pines announced a fundraising campaign to inscribe the British government in the Golden Book of the Jewish National Fund.[70] Herzl then declared a short break and convened the Greater Action Committee to formulate a draft resolution.

The resolution called for: (a) A nine-member steering committee to collaborate with the Action Committee until the dispatch of an exploratory mission for Uganda; (b) No funding for the expedition from the Congress, Jewish Colonial Trust or Jewish National Fund; (c) The final decision on Uganda to be delivered at a special Congress convened for this purpose; (d) The submission of a bloc vote by the Action Committee for the purpose of reaching a unanimous decision. Anyone who voted against the resolution would be disqualified from sitting on the committee.

---

67 Ibid.
68 Friedman, *Germania, turkia vehatzionut*, p. 114.
69 *Sefer Bernstein-Kogan*, p. 140.
70 Friedman, *Germania, turkia vehatzionut*, p. 115. Rabbi Yechiel Michal Pines (1842–1912) was a religious Zionist leader who was involved in land purchase and settlement.

The first three clauses were designed to make it easier for those in the opposition to change their minds and vote in favor of the proposal but turned out to have little effect. The fourth clause became a minefield, as Herzl himself confessed later on.

Looking back, Sammy Gronemann laments his great squandered opportunity to save the day:

> "Here I feel obligated to recount an episode that I cannot speak of without shame. Had I been able at the time to rise above my fears and apprehensions, I could have averted a great disaster. On page 21 of the Congress protocol, the following comment appears: The meeting adjourned at 4:10 p.m. and resumed at 4:15 p.m. In the span of these five minutes, this is what happened: All of a sudden, I had an insight about how to rephrase the proposal which would enable it to be unanimously accepted and would allay all the fears of those planning to vote against it. My suggestion, which was never brought to the plenum, went something like this: First, an emphatic statement that the Land of Israel was an inalienable goal, then a declaration that in view of the magnanimous offer of the British government and the possibility that an alternative might be found by another Jewish association which in principle the Zionist Organization could not implement due to being outside its purview, the proper course of action would be to appoint an exploratory commission. The moment this revelation came to me, I rushed onto the podium to Shmaryahu Levin and excitedly set forth my proposal. He grabbed my hand and I could clearly see what was going on in his mind. Instinctively, he turned toward the door behind which the Action Committee had disappeared, strode toward it as if about to enter, then he hesitated. A few steps away stood Dr. Franz Oppenheimer ... I called out to him: 'Dr. Oppenheimer, please help me!' Oppenheimer came over slowly with a smile on his face – but at that very moment, the door opened, and Herzl burst out with the Action Committee behind him. 'Too late!' cried Shmaryahu Levin. I was mortified but did not have the courage to approach Herzl, who looked overwrought and not in the mood to listen to anyone ... Disaster was on its way."[71]

At that point, a vote was held on whether or not to approve an exploratory mission to Uganda. 292 delegates voted yes, 176 voted no, and 143 abstained. When the results were announced, Yehiel Chlenov picked himself up and walked out, with the rest of the *"Neinsagers"* (the German term for those who voted no) on his heels.

The walk-Out of the "Neinsagers"

What was the reason for the dramatic walk-out of Chlenov and his fellow naysayers? It seems there are several answers to this question. Chlenov offers one in his

---

71 Gronemann, *Zikhronot shel yekke*, pp. 210–211.

memoirs: "Where was I going and why? At that moment I did not know. I only felt one thing: that I could no longer stay in that hall ... I left but had no idea if anyone else would follow. We had not discussed it with each other, but apparently one spark was enough."[72]

In fact, the reason for his exit is completely clear: The fourth clause of the resolution stated that any member of the Action Committee voting against the resolution could not remain a member of that body. Chlenov understood from this that he had forfeited his committee membership. The moment the ballot ended, he went up to the dais, handed Herzl a declaration that the *Neinsagers* had voted against the resolution and headed for the door. It was Herzl's own party discipline that was to blame. Herzl himself admitted that he had erred.[73]

At the time, neither Herzl nor Chlenov grasped the seriousness of this act, and Herzl made no move to hold him back.[74] If Herzl had approached Chlenov, the whole Uganda showdown might have been avoided, as Chlenov had great respect for Herzl and would certainly have stayed at his request. But there were other accounts and interpretations of the incident. According to Yosef Eliash, the Mogilev delegate, attorney Dov Gissin, called out: "We have no part in Herzl and no parcel in Uganda. To your tents, O Israel!" According to Eliash, this was a signal to the *Neinsagers* to get up and leave.[75] Isaiah Friedman believes those who left the room were still laboring under the misconception that the resolution passed by the Congress was a formal decision to renounce Zion and Eretz Yisrael.[76] Historian David Vital cites a *Jewish Chronicle* report based on the testimony of Dr. Avigdor Jacobson that Chlenov was not planning to leave, but after the vote he turned to Jacobson, who was sitting next to him, and said: "What's the point? Let's have lunch." When they rose from their seats, their colleagues thought it was a protest and filed out after them. The only trouble with this story, writes Vital, is that the vote was held at 7:00 p.m.[77] The exodus of the group impacted on the whole Congress, delegates and guests alike. Avraham Yaakov Slutzky offers a glimpse of the drama: "As they retired to the side hall, some of them burst into tears, their cries audible from afar."[78] Amos Elon says that Leon Trotsky, who was sitting in the gallery as a journalist predicted the imminent demise of the Zionist movement[79].

---

72 *Sefer Chlenov*, p. 203.
73 *Complete Diaries of Theodor Herzl*, vol. 4, p. 1549.
74 In his memoirs, Chlenov voices regret (see *Sefer Chlenov*, ibid.).
75 Eliash, Zikhronot tzioni merusia,' p. 128.
76 Friedman, *Germania, turkia vehatzionut*, p. 116.
77 *Jewish Chronicle*, September 4, 1903, p. 12; Vital, *Hamahapekha hatzionit*, 1, p. 224.
78 Slutzky, in: *Hamelitz*, 186, August 17, 1903; *Ish hame'orot*, p. 214, footnote 41.

And what happened in the hall where the *Neinsagers* gathered? Nachman Syrkin describes the scene:

> "Entering the hall filled me with dread and fear. It was like going into a synagogue on Yom Kippur. People were everywhere, each in their own corner, crying their eyes out over their life's dream that had come to a tragic end, their world destroyed."[80] The more aggressive among them cursed and shouted. Yehoshua Buchmil, one of Herzl's earliest supporters, branded him a traitor.[81] Passions rose to the point where Chlenov had to climb up on a chair and plead with them to refrain from attacks on Herzl, which he said would only harm the Zionist enterprise.

Herzl and the Dissidents in the Small Hall

This was the second time Herzl had to deal with opponents who walked out in protest. At the Fifth Congress, members of the Democratic Fraction left the hall when Herzl postponed the debate on culture. Angry that their concerns were being brushed aside, they went to sit in the visitors' gallery. Only when the topic was brought to the floor did they return to their seats.[82]

Perhaps Herzl thought this was a repeat of the same scenario. At any rate, he failed to understand how deep the rift was, and did not see in his actions any deviation from the principles of the Basel program. After a short while, though, he realized that the walk-out was not a political statement but an expression of genuine sorrow. Although he had already gone back to his hotel, he set pride aside, retraced his steps and went to see the dissenters in the hopes of reassuring them. He tried to enter the hall where they were gathered but was stopped by Avraham Moshe Shapira (whose nickname was "Zionist and a half" because of his height) and Asher Ehrlich, who were the "gatekeepers." Ehrlich went in to inquire whether Herzl should be admitted. The response of the chairman was that the meeting was only for Russian delegates. Herzl returned to the hotel and came back with a certificate showing he was a Russian delegate (the "shekel-payers" in Kishinev had elected him as their official representative to the Congress). Again, the gatekeepers asked the chairman if they could let

---

79 Leon Trotsky (1879–1940), Communist revolutionary, founder of the Red Army, became a supporter of Zionism in his old age. See Elon, *Herzl*, p. 426.
80 *Hatzefirah*, 186, August 24, 1903.
81 Bein, *Theodore Herzl: A Biography*, p. 461.
82 See p. 214; Klausner, *Opozitzia leherzl*, p. 147.

Herzl in. At that point, the chairman himself came out and told Herzl that "his very presence could sway the delegates whichever way he wanted."[83]

Thus, even now when the crisis was at its peak, there was no ignoring Herzl. Even at this most difficult hour, when the finger of blame was on Herzl, they could not say no to him and allowed him into the hall. Herzl turned to the dissidents and reiterated his commitment to the Basel program. The Uganda offer did not break with Basel in any way, he insisted, and Eretz Yisrael remained the true goal of the Zionist movement. Jabotinsky, who was present at this nighttime meeting, took notes, which were later published.[84]

At the urging of Yehiel Chlenov, the dissidents returned to the plenary:

> "All of us fully recognized that it was our duty to do everything we could to prevent a schism in the Zionist organization, and that we must not retreat from the ideological battlefield and let the majority take it over. We believed in our ability and saw it as our sacred duty to keep the Land of Israel for the Zionist Organization and the Zionist Organization for the Land of Israel ... By breaking away, we would be pushing our opponents into extremism ... We all thought that secession was not only pointless, but criminal. We had not given up on Zionism or on those who had voted yes ... Our decision was clear: We must go back to the assembly hall!... We returned to the hall in order to wage our battle with more success..."[85]

Chlenov stresses that Herzl's speech did not placate the *Neinsagers*. He writes that he was surprised to read in the newspapers of the "colossal impression" it had made when in fact his colleagues were still racked by doubt.[86]

The next morning, at a meeting with the minority camp, it was confirmed that an expedition would be sent to East Africa but not at the expense of the Zionist movement. This expedition would report to the Greater Action Committee before the next Congress, as stipulated in the resolution. At that point, a Uganda committee was elected, and Chaim Weizmann, who had now become a fierce opponent of the scheme, agreed to be on it. The Congress then went back to its affairs, but only outwardly. Analyzing Chlenov's account, it is clear that this Congress was a game-changer:

> "I will say no more about what went on that night and the following morning before our return to the hall. Pathetic attempts were made to 'balance the score' [electing a committee

---

83 Eliash, *Zikhronot tzioni merusia*, p. 128.
84 *Die Welt*, 27, July 3, 1914, p. 671.
85 *Sefer Chlenov*, pp. 284–285.
86 *Ibid.*

and Herzl's concessions in favor of *Gegenswartarbeit*].[87] It was all petty and insignificant compared to the events of the day ... but as far as we were concerned, only these two issues really mattered, because we were heading back to the movement to fight and influence from within ..."[88]

Herzl brought the Sixth Congress to a close on this note:

> "When I thought all hope must be abandoned for the foreseeable future ... I proposed a stopgap, and having learned meanwhile to know your hearts, I will offer you some ancient words of consolation, and at the same time a pledge on my part, in the language of our forefathers: *Im eshkakekh yerushalayim tishkakh yemini*. If I forget thee, O Jerusalem, may my right hand forget her cunning.'"[89]

Most of the delegates were profoundly moved by these closing remarks. Herzl succeeded in heading off a crisis that seemed insurmountable and was able to convince the *Neinsagers* to return to the Congress. But from their perspective, the beginning of their fight against the Uganda plan had just begun.

Aftermath of the Sixth Congress

When the audience applauded at the close of the Sixth Congress, it seems the applause was meant more for Herzl than the Uganda plan. The *Neinsagers* had not changed their minds and the tension continued to mount, reaching a boiling point at the Kharkov conference in November 1903. It was a crisis that continued to rage until the meeting of the Action Committee in April 1904, which became known as the Reconciliation Conference.

Chlenov was a vehement opponent of settlement in Uganda, but he greatly admired Herzl, deeply cared about the Zionist movement and had no wish to see Herzl gone. Therefore, if he had been the opposition leader, the battle would presumably have been waged without harming Herzl, who would have ended up convincing him and his colleagues with the same arguments that succeeded in April 1904. The problem was Ussishkin and his leadership ambitions. The Uganda crisis provided him with an opportunity to spar with Herzl and perhaps fed

---

87 Proponents of *Gegenswartsarbeit* (present-day work) challenged Herzl in that they called for educational and cultural activity, land redemption and strengthening the Yishuv before the establishment of a Jewish state.
88 *Sefer Chlenov*, p. 286.
89 Pawel, *Labyrinth*, p. 511. The Congress responded to this speech with a storm of applause. Friedman, *Germania, turkia vehatzionut*, p. 189, footnote 61.

his hopes of climbing to the top. Chaim Weizmann, another failed competitor, also did everything in his power to fan the flames. And then, of course, there was Ahad Ha'am, their revered teacher and mentor, who pumped up the fire with his invective.

Ahad Ha'am refused to attend the Sixth Congress. To his associates, he explained that the outrage over the *Altneuland* controversy had not yet subsided "and I do not want to give these people an opportunity to saddle me with the blame, as if my presence were the trigger."[90]

Even so, Ahad Ha'am continued to stir the political Zionist pot. In an article entitled "The Weepers," he stated that he had no bone to pick with those who voted for Uganda because Eretz Yisrael was not important to them and in their eyes, the Jewish state could be anywhere. The ones he was angry with were "the weepers" who had returned to Congress, surrendered to Herzl and let the resolution pass. It was their actions that effectively "granted a divorce from Zion," and ensured that "Zion will remain only in the prayer book."[91] In a private letter to A.L. Bautenberg, an early member of Bnai Moshe, Ahad Ha'am wrote: "Looking at it calmly and rationally, what you did in Basel was equivalent to apostasy. You followed Herzl like – forgive me – a mindless herd of sheep... Look at this matter of the bank ... The herd cried 'Hurrah' and returned to its slumber. In vain I shouted until my throat was hoarse ... This Herzl is the man who destroyed your faith and aspirations."[92]

In this article, penned in August but published in *Hashiloah* only in November, Ahad Ha'am concludes almost gleefully: "[Herzlian] Zionism born in Basel on the first of the month of Elul 1887 died in Basel on the first of the month of Elul 1903."[93] The spirit of Ahad Ha'am hovering over his followers, especially Ussishkin and Weizmann, was thus easy to discern.

Herzl and Ussishkin

Of special prominence among Herzl's opponents in the Uganda affair was former Hibbat Zion activist Menachem Mendel Ussishkin, a born leader who had willingly subordinated himself to Herzl from the earliest days of the political Zionist

---

[90] Letter of Ahad Ha'am to Buber, June 25, 1903; Buber, *Khilufay igrot*, 1, p. 166; Goldstein, *Ahad Ha'am: Biografia*, p. 307.
[91] Ahad Ha'am, *Al parashat drakhim*, vol. 3, pp. 200–209.
[92] August 31, 1903, *Igrot Ahad Ha'am*, vol. 3, p. 136.
[93] Ahad Ha'am, "The weepers," in: *Kol kitvay Ahad Ha'am*, Dvir Publishing, Tel Aviv 1947, p. 341.

enterprise.⁹⁴ Why would he, of all people, adopt such a personal and passionate stance against Herzl? Ernst Pawel concludes that at this point, the real issue was no longer Uganda but the leadership of the movement.⁹⁵ If this was so, then the clash between Ussishkin and Herzl was not just an ideological argument but a struggle for the crown. Ussishkin, who stoked the fire, sowed dissent and pushed the Zionist movement to the brink on Uganda, was tough and uncompromising, a man of action who cared nothing for politeness and diplomatic mannerisms. His friend, Chaim Weizmann, described him as "an energetic but obstinate man, big and sensible with a solid mind, perhaps too solid at times. There was something autocratic about him, and he had no patience for young people."⁹⁶ Chaim Nachman Bialik's portrayal is more nuanced:

> "He is not as solid and hard as people say. Those who knew him well find in him a good measure of emotion and sentimentality. There is a little bit of fantasy in him, too. His eyes tend to fill with tears. His supposed hardness stems more from stubbornness and inflexibility. His thoughts move as heavily as a bear and when he is set on an idea he cannot easily move away from it or turn right or left in the slightest degree: He is by nature and in spirit limited; he is straight. And very conservative ... He recognizes no colors or shadings ... In sum: a man who is not very complicated – but nevertheless a man whose greatness is in his simplicity, his primitivity, and in all his impulses, small as well as big."⁹⁷

Isaiah Friedman contends that Ussishkin harbored ambitions of leadership that he never denied.⁹⁸ Louis Lipsky, describing the road traveled by Ussishkin from Hibbat Zion to political Zionism, agrees: "This man of granite seemed made to rule. That was what he thought, too. He had the nature of a czar whose opinions issued in the form of edicts. He was dead sure that he was always right and no one else could be as right as he. But he found no kingdom at hand to rule."⁹⁹

Lipsky explains that Ussishkin, who had been an active Zionist since the early days of Hibbat Zion, envisaged himself as the successor of Leon Pinsker, but never achieved this standing. When Herzl appeared on the scene, Ussishkin and his Hibbat Zion and Bnai Moshe colleagues attended the Zionist Congress with a certain resentment in their hearts: How could a man so foreign to the Jewish way of life become the leader of the return to Zion?¹⁰⁰

---

94 *Sefer Ussishkin*, pp. 352–354.
95 Pawel, *Labyrinth*, p. 514.
96 Friedman, *Germania, turkia vehatzionut*, pp. 121–122; Weizmann, *Masa u-ma'as*, p. 64.
97 Pawel, *Labyrinth*, p. 515; Vital, *Hamahapekha hatzionit*, 1, p. 143.
98 Friedman, *Germania, turkia vehatzionut*, p. 122.
99 Lipsky, *A Gallery of Zionist Profiles*, p. 75.
100 *Ibid.*

From these accounts it is obvious that Ussishkin was a frustrated man with untapped leadership potential. Despite his intensive and successful Zionist activism (the region he coordinated ranked highest in Zionist fundraising and other parameters), he suffered from character flaws that stood in the way of his drive to lead. It was a drive that could not be satisfied in the framework of the Zionist movement as long as Herzl reigned supreme. The issue, then, was not so much Uganda as lust for leadership. Ussishkin "lowered his horns and went for the kill," writes Pawel.[101]

What motivated Ussishkin and set him on the warpath was the breakdown of his faith in Herzl. He had believed Herzl was more capable of leading the Zionist revolution than himself, but time was passing, and Herzl had not made good on his promises of obtaining a charter for Palestine. At the same time, he continued to oppose immigration and settlement until such a charter was in their hands. Ussishkin, exasperated, began to feel certain that he could do a better job. The Uganda affair was an opportune moment: It supplied him at long last with the ideological pretext for going after the crown. When Moshe Levin of Jaffa met Ussishkin in Palestine,[102] Ussishkin told him: "We can go on without [him]."[103] So while the goal of the other Uganda opponents was to convince Herzl to drop the scheme and remain at the helm, Ussishkin had his heart set on replacing Herzl, which intensified the conflict.

Ussishkin was in Palestine while the Sixth Congress was in session and could not attend. What would have happened if he had? He might have gone to even greater extremes, making an organizational split even more likely. On the other hand, under the moderating influence of Chlenov and Goldberg, together with Herzl's charisma, he might have followed in the footsteps of the other *Neinsagers* both during the Congress and afterwards. But Ussishkin did not experience what his colleagues did, and the Uganda affair provided him with what he believed was a justified reason for challenging Herzl and inciting the *Neinsagers* to declare all-out war. Without Ussishkin, in fact, the battle might not have flared up to the extent that it did, and the Tzionei Tzion faction led by Chlenov would have made peace with Herzl, as the opposition camp did at the Reconciliation Conference in Vienna in April 1904.[104]

---

101 Pawel, *Labyrinth*, p. 515.
102 Ussishkin was in Palestine to purchase land for the Geula settlement society and preside over a convention in Zikhron Ya'akov where he established the Teachers Association of the Land of Israel.
103 *The Jewish World*, January 8, 1904; Heymann, "Herzl and the Russian Zionists," in: *Hatzionut*, vol. 3, p. 69, footnote 39.
104 See pp. 259, 171–172.

Ussishkin learned of the Uganda scheme from a telegram sent by Bernstein-Kogan calling him to action. Upon his return from Europe, Ussishkin discovered that the Congress had made him a member of the Greater Action Committee. Without speaking to Herzl, he fired off a series of blistering letters to the newspapers in which he stated that sending a commission to Uganda was a betrayal of the Zionist idea. Despite being a member of the Action Committee, he did not feel bound by the decision of the Congress and swore to do all he could to block it. Until then, Ussishkin had opposed the splintering of the Zionist movement into parties, including the establishment of the Democratic Fraction, but he now joined forces with the Fraction to fight the *Jasagers*. He sent Herzl an ultimatum demanding that he cancel the decision on Uganda, accusing him of recklessness and calling him a "Territorialist in Zionist clothing."

Herzl did not pass over this provocation in silence. His response to Ussishkin was two-pronged: From an organizational standpoint, he informed Ussishkin that if he could not, or would not, accept the policy agreed upon by the movement, he would have to resign. It was impossible to continue serving on the Action Committee while criticizing it. At the same time, he defended the embrace of diplomacy to advance the Zionist cause. He rejected Ussishkin's strategy of "practical work" and the purchase of land before a state was founded. The acquisition of land did not confer sovereignty, Herzl argued. If Ussishkin, by way of analogy, bought up all the lands in Yekatrinoslav, they would still be part of Russia. On the subject of Uganda, Herzl let it be understood that negotiating with Britain was a tactic to strengthen his bargaining power with Turkey, but this was not for public consumption lest it jeopardize relations with Britain.[105] Ussishkin remained unconvinced. As Isaiah Friedman observes: "Herzl put his opponent in place, but Ussishkin was not one to accept authority or admit error."[106] He continued his attacks on Herzl, arguing that his leadership was endangering the Zionist movement. As far as he was concerned Herzl had two choices: To renounce the Uganda initiative or resign.

Kharkov Conference

Ussishkin took the battle to the next rung. He summoned an emergency conference that brought together Zionist *murshim* (regional promoters of Zionism) from across Russia. The gathering took place in Kharkov on November 11–14, 1903 at

---

[105] Friedman, *Germania, turkia vehatzionut*, p. 122, footnote 84.
[106] *Ibid.*, p. 122.

the home of Dr. Jacob Bernstein-Kogen, who was then serving as the town's government-appointed rabbi. The stated aim of the conference was to consolidate a policy on Uganda.

Max Emmanuel Mandelstamm, a devotee of Herzl, opened the proceedings with a question: "Is it right for us to be discussing a motion to overturn a resolution passed by a majority at the Zionist Congress? Ussishkin replied that in his opinion the majority was entitled to decide on procedural matters – not on matters of ideology. In his view, challenging the resolution was imperative. Most of the *murshim* sided with Ussishkin. They felt that Herzl and the Congress had deviated from the Basel program and it was their right, and even their duty, to fight what they saw as an illegitimate decision. Mandelstamm stomped out in anger, leaving only a single Herzl supporter: the Zionist coordinator of the Warsaw district, attorney Isidore (Israel) Jasinowski. Jasinowski stayed until the end and he was presumably the one who reported back to Herzl, although the decisions of this conference were meant to be confidential.

So what were the dynamics of this conference? How did Ussishkin convince even moderates and admirers of Herzl like Yehiel Chlenov, Isaac Leib Goldberg and others, to adopt an aggressive line? It seems that apart from Ussishkin's impassioned rhetoric, a report submitted by Professor Zvi Belkovsky helped to tip the scales. Belkovsky had been sent to Herzl in early November to clarify his position. During their four-hour meeting, Herzl went to extraordinary lengths to convince him that the goal was Eretz Yisrael. He even pulled out a letter he had written to Plehve as proof that his diplomatic efforts on behalf of a Jewish state in Palestine were ongoing. Belkovsky, however, concluded that Herzl was being disingenuous. While Palestine was indeed Herzl's first choice, Belkovsky felt that he would not object to a Jewish home elsewhere if a charter for Palestine could not be obtained in the near future.[107] On this basis, the Kharkov Conference resolved:

(a) To embark on a large-scale campaign to convince the masses of the justice of their cause and explain where Herzl had erred;
(b) To finance this campaign with the money collected from Zionist shekel dues.

Herzl was also presented with an ultimatum:
(a) Herzl would submit a written pledge that no territorial projects outside of Palestine would be brought before the Congress;

---

107 *Ibid.*

(b) Herzl would cease his autocratic decision-making and the Congress would discuss only issues on which the Greater Action Committee would have the final say.[108]

The conference closed on November 14 with a decision to dispatch a 4-man delegation to Vienna: Zvi Belkovsky, Vladimir (Ze'ev) Tiomkin, Simon (Shimshon) Rosenbaum and Yehiel Chlenov. The conference resolutions were to be kept strictly confidential until their departure on January 4, 1904, for fear of an outraged reaction from Herzl's followers.

Ussishkin thus succeeded in reversing the decision reached by the *Neinsagers* at the Sixth Congress where Chlenov had persuaded them to pursue their struggle within the movement without trampling Herzl's dignity or endangering Zionist unity. At Kharkov, Chlenov and the moderates had tried to do the same, but Ussishkin pushed for a head-on battle and won.

Michael Heymann divides the *murshim* at Kharkov into two groups based on their attitude toward Herzl. The moderate group headed by Chlenov, which included Zvi Brock, Hillel Zlatopolsky and Isaac Leib Goldberg, did not wish to jeopardize the organizational integrity of the Zionist movement. "They could not imagine the Zionist movement without Herzl. They hoped he could be brought back to pure Zionism and all would be well again."[109] Then there were the radicals led by Ussishkin: Jacob Bernstein-Kogan, Victor (Avigdor) Jacobson, Zvi Belkovsky, Vladimir Tiomkin and Simon Rosenbaum, who were "prepared, at least mentally, for a split from the current Zionist organization, after reaching the conclusion that Herzl had come to the end of his Zionist mission and become an impediment."[110] David Vital describes Rosenbaum as the most brazen of the lot: "He made remarks in public that even Weizmann, whose views were similar, saved for private consumption."[111] It was Rosenbaum who was responsible for the comment "*Der Mohr hat seine Arbeit getan, der Mohr kann gehen*" ("The Moor has done his work, the Moor can go"), which set off a massive outcry in December 1903.[112]

The Kharkov conference also voted in favor of organizational reforms that posed a challenge to Herzl. Max Mandelstamm, a Herzl supporter, was removed

---

108 Bein points out the "long history of discord "on this matter: "For years the Russian members of the Action Committee had objected to what they called Herzl's dictatorial direction of political action." See Bein, *Theodore Herzl: A Biography*, p. 479.
109 Heymann, "Herzl and the Russian Zionists," in: *Hatzionut*, vol. 3, p. 68.
110 *Ibid.*, pp. 68–69.
111 Vital, *Hamahapekha hatzionit*, vol. 2, p. 244.
112 Gronemann, *Zikhronot shel yekke*, pp. 68–69. See pp. 270.

from his position as treasurer and replaced by Isaac Leib Goldberg, *murshe* of the Vilna district, thereby reshuffling the whole structure of the Russian Zionist leadership. At Ussishkin's initiative, a new national committee was formed to lead the Russian Zionist movement from Odessa. The committee was to be chaired by Ussishkin himself, along with three of Herzl's fiercest opponents: Bernstein-Kogan, Tiomkin and Jacobson.

Ussishkin's triumph at Kharkov emboldened him. Upon his return to Yekatrinoslav, he proclaimed himself head of the Central Committee of Russian Zionists and authorized to determine its policies. In parallel, he notified the Action Committee in Vienna of his new status and took pleasure in informing Herzl that "henceforth you must apprise me of any issues related to our general organization, be it propaganda or finance."[113] Many of the Zionist activists in Russia were not happy about this. Isidore Jasinowski, a Herzl supporter, let it be known that he did not recognize Ussishkin's new committee.

On December 4, Herzl noted in his diary: "The Russian members of the A.C., particularly Ussishkin, Jacobson, etc. are in open rebellion. They want to give me an ultimatum: I must drop the idea of East Africa (although, or because, at Edlach[114] I showed Belkowsky the letter I wrote to Plehve on September 5th)."[115]

From the behavior of the Kharkov rebels, Herzl understood that they were not interested in dialogue. From his perspective, it was pure and simple mutiny. Herzl challenged the authority of the Kharkov conference and launched a counter-offensive. First, he did all he could to mobilize the Russian Zionists against them and encourage them to organize protest meetings. Herzl feared, and not without reason, that Ussishkin's actions were directed not only against him personally, but against Zionism in its current form. So he also sought to block the group on an organizational level, calling for its expulsion from the Zionist movement. He was convinced that Ussishkin's motives were impure, and his true aim was to strengthen himself politically and take over the helm.[116]

Herzl's efforts bore fruit. On December 6, 1903, Isidore Jasinowski organized a conference in Warsaw at which he and 12 pro-Herzl Zionist leaders declared war on Ussishkin and his supporters.[117] They embarked on a passionate media campaign to make it clear that Ussishkin did not represent all the Zionists in Russia. The group, which became known as the "Zionist Organization defenders," published the protocols of the Kharkov conference to prove that the pri-

---

113 Goldstein, *Ussishkin*, vol. 2, p. 170.
114 A resort town in Austria where the Herzls often stayed. Herzl died there.
115 *Complete Diaries of Theodor Herzl*, vol. 4, pp. 1571–1572.
116 Goldstein, *Ussishkin*, vol. 2, p. 170.
117 Letter of Jasinowski to Herzl, December 9, 1903, *ibid.*, p. 172.

mary intention of Ussishkin and his colleagues was to oust Herzl, against the wishes of the majority of the *Neinsagers*. The battle grew more and more heated. Some of the *murshim* at Kharkov balked at Ussishkin's aggressive tactics, which sowed disunity in the Zionist movement and above all, were damaging to Herzl. Even though *Hatzfira* editor Nahum Sokolow opposed the Uganda plan, he published a scathing attack on Ussishkin in his paper. Rabbi Samuel Jacob Rabinowitz, who had also sided with *Neinsagers*, switched camps for fear that Herzl would quit, and without him "the whole movement will come crashing down."[118] Likeminded committees were established in England and other countries to protest "the conspirators and destroyers of unity."[119]

In consequence, a growing number of *Neinsagers* began to have second thoughts about Ussishkin and his chosen path. Chlenov and his followers sent Herzl conciliatory messages and Ussishkin's protests notwithstanding, restored the financial portfolio to Mandelstamm.

Original Uganda Proposal Rescinded

Meanwhile, a plot twist occurred with the potential to resolve the feud in the Zionist movement. Herzl's envoy Leopold Greenberg, who had continued the give and take with Great Britain, discovered that the East African territory proposed by Chamberlain, which was large enough for 1.5 million people, was under colonization by other white settlers. The British offered the province of Tanaland as an alternative, but Herzl made inquiries and found that the climate was unsuited to European settlement. On December 5, 1903, when Greenberg delivered the news that the British had backtracked on the Uganda proposal, Herzl was glad that the episode was over without harm to the Zionist movement. "Herzl shed no tears," writes Friedman. "He could not have hoped for a better outcome. It aligned with the strategy he and Greenberg had agreed upon in June, which was to gradually get the British to acknowledge that Palestine was the only answer to the Jewish question."[120]

This chance that came along to withdraw from the Uganda plan and restore peace in the Zionist movement mattered less to Herzl than the advancement of the Zionist cause. Herzl initially thought that the British had canceled their offer due to the dissent of the *Neinsagers* and worried that the window of oppor-

---

118 Letter of Rabbi Rabinowitz to Ussishkin, December 16, 1903, *ibid.*, p. 176.
119 Friedman, *Germania, turkia vehatzionut*, p. 123.
120 *Ibid., p. 125.*

tunity had now closed. However, the fact that the British proposed an alternative clarified that the goodwill was still there. Herzl thus instructed Greenberg to renew negotiations and request El Arish as compensation: Only if this failed, was Greenberg to ask for the allocation of another territory.

Greenberg, aware of Herzl's desperate situation and the grave threat that hovered over the Zionist movement, counseled him to let the matter lie, at least until public opinion had been won over. Yet Herzl refused to be discouraged and continued to display faith in his own convictions. He did not allow the existence of an opposition at the Congress to deter him. To his opponents he declared: "I shall carry on an agitation against you, and I promise you will be defeated ... We have a tremendous majority on our side."[121]

Alongside his negotiations with the British, Herzl appealed again to Russia, hoping that it would prod Turkey into granting a charter for Zionist settlement. He also tried to drum up support from the Austrian foreign minister.

All the while, the battle raged on between the Ussishkin loyalists (Tzionei Tzion) and supporters of Herzl (Committee for the Defense of the Zionist Organization). Looking for a way out of the rut, Greenberg proposed that Herzl publish a public renunciation of the East Africa project in the form of a letter to Sir Francis Montefiore (Sir Moses Montefiore's nephew). In the letter, Herzl would explain why Uganda had been struck from the agenda, which would ultimately pull the rug out from beneath his opponents' feet.

On December 14, 1903, Greenberg sent Herzl a draft of the letter to Sir Francis. It was mainly an attempt to refute the accusations that Herzl's goal was to divert Zionist settlement from Eretz Yisrael:

> "I am a sworn Zionist convinced that the settlement of our people's question can only be effected in that country, Palestine, with which are indelibly associated the historic and sentimental bias of its national existence. No place on earth could therefore, in my mind, supplant or take the place which Palestine holds as the object for which we are striving ... To my mind [certain] elements were necessary, perhaps governing all – the enthusiasm of our own people in respect to the offer had to be of such a nature as to overcome all the obvious difficulties which even under the most favorable conditions would be bound to arise in the creation of the settlement ... It must be quite clear ... that [this] condition has been, to some extent, absent."[122]

The letter went on to explain that Herzl was not surprised or sorry about this. On the contrary, he was conscious of the deep and abiding love of the Jewish people

---

121 Bein, *Theodore Herzl: A Biography*, pp. 494, 497.
122 Published in *The Jewish World* and the *Jewish Chronicle* on December 25, 1903. See "What Herzl Thought of East Africa," Theodor Herzl, A Memorial, p. 185.

for Eretz Yisrael. He noted with "no small satisfaction" that the strongest opposition to the scheme came precisely from those people who had experienced the horrors and were in dire need of a land of refuge. For these reasons, as well as objections which had surfaced in East Africa, the plan was declared unimplementable. The letter ended with words of thanks to the British government.[123]

Herzl was in no rush to approve the publication of this letter. While caving in to opposition pressure was distasteful to him, he was even more troubled by the idea of publicly waiving a commitment by the British government: "He remained firm in his view that the Foreign Office had either to withdraw the offer or make a satisfactory substitute offer."[124] He would not allow dissent to frighten him, he declared, whether it came from Rabbi Gaster or Ussishkin.

As long as there was a chance, however slight, that Uganda could serve as a bargaining chip, Herzl would not back down. Moreover, signals from Russia, England and Italy indicated that Palestine was still an option.[125] Herzl intended to continue the fight, but then something happened that changed his mind.

On December 19, 1903, a mentally deranged student, Chaim Zelig Louban, attempted to assassinate Max Nordau at a Zionist party in Paris. He fired two shots at Nordau, crying "Death to Nordau the East African!" He missed, injuring a bystander, but Herzl, shocked by the incident, decided to call off the battle. He asked Greenberg to read out the Montefiore letter at a meeting at the home of Rabbi Gaster. On December 25, he published it in *Die Welt* as "Greenberg's speech in London" calling for a retreat from the Uganda project.

Two days later, on December 27, Herzl sent a confidential circular to members of the Greater Action Committee announcing withdrawal from the British-sponsored scheme.

Once Uganda was off the agenda, Ussishkin and his colleagues had no reason to keep up the fight against Herzl, but they refused to let go. Herzl's hopes that the tempest would subside and the "ultimatum delegation" would cancel its departure for Vienna were in vain. Johan Kremenezky cabled Ussishkin to say that Herzl would not receive the party, but to no avail.[126] The delegation arrived in town on January 4, 1904, but was pared down to two committee members: Rosenbaum and Belkovsky.

Sammy Gronemann describes Rosenbaum's visit to Berlin en route to Vienna:

---

123 Friedman, *Germania, turkia vehatzionut*, pp. 125–126; "What Herzl Thought of East Africa," Theodor Herzl, A Memorial, p. 185.
124 Bein, *Theodore Herzl: A Biography*, p. 485.
125 Ibid.
126 Vital, *Hamahapekha hatzionit*, vol. 2, p. 244.

> "Everyone knows the story of the ultimatum and how it was to be delivered by a delegation sent to Vienna. One of the envoys, attorney Simon Rosenbaum of Minsk, later a minister in Lithuania, a dear friend of mine, stopped off in Berlin on his way to Vienna with the intention of explaining the decisions of the Kharkov conference to the local Zionists. When [Arthur] Hantke and others praised Herzl's great merits, Rosenbaum blurted out: *'Der Mohr hat seine Arbeit getan, der Mohr kann gehen'* (the Moor has done his work, the Moor may go). A storm of protest erupted, and Mr. Rosenbaum left the meeting in something of a huff over the way his lecture was received."[127]

When the pair got to Vienna, Herzl refused to recognize them as a delegation. He agreed to receive them as private guests and invited them to a meeting of the Viennese Action Committee on the express condition that they did not present themselves as envoys. Belkovsky and Rosenbaum accepted Herzl's terms and showed up at the meeting on January 6 after promising to say nothing more about an ultimatum. At the meeting, Herzl repeated his allegation that the rebels of Kharkov were undermining the tenets of democracy and went on to reprimand the two of them as they sat there like defendants in the dock. *Hatzfira* later published a comic strip showing the "ultimatum delegation" leaving Kharkov with great pomp and circumstance, only to return with its tail between its legs.[128]

Herzl's attempts to revive the El Arish option failed. When Leopold Greenberg visited the British Foreign Office on January 5, 1904, he was informed that it was impossible to go forward with the project because the Egyptian authorities were against it.[129]

After the El Arish plan fell through, there were no other options. On January 27, however, the tables turned yet again. Herzl received a telegram from Greenberg with another offer from the British government, this time a territory in the Nandi region (today part of western Kenya) that could accommodate mass settlement. Greenberg advised accepting the offer and dispatching an expedition to examine feasibility, but Herzl was hesitant. He had already asked Greenberg to try to restart talks on El Arish and Sinai, hoping that Uganda could serve as a lever for diplomacy with the British or for prodding the Turks into action. This meant that Herzl was faced once again with Uganda as a realistic option, which would only create more discord in the Zionist movement. Indeed, the clash between Tzionei Tzion and the Committee for the Defense of the Zionist Organization was on the verge of splitting the movement. Worried, Herzl

---

[127] Gronemann, *ZIkhronot shel yekke*, p. 222.
[128] *Hatzfira*, no. 41, pp. 162–164.
[129] CZA, HVIII/294, Greenberg to Herzl, January 7, 1904; Friedman, *Germania, turkia vehatzionut*, p. 126, footnote 104.

called together the members of the Greater Action Committee for a conference to calm the storm.

The Reconciliation Conference, as it became known, was held in Vienna on April 11–15, 1904, with the goal of restoring peace and good relations. All the participants, with the exception of Ussishkin and his friends, were in favor of reconciliation. They had no desire to harm Herzl or tear the movement apart. At this forum, Herzl repeated his commitment to Zion and explained that the Uganda proposal had no operative significance at that time, since only the Seventh Congress would decide whether or not to implement it. Meanwhile, however, it was important not to ruin the relationship with England.

The Russian *murshim* were appeased. They believed Herzl. They were convinced that his intentions were pure, and it was unlikely that the Uganda plan would be acted on anytime soon. Only Ussishkin, Jacobson and Bernstein-Kogan continued to be negative and employ hostile language. Ussishkin was adamant that Herzl's plan was "a betrayal of the goals of Zionism."[130] Herzl was prepared to act for the sake of Uganda, he said, but for the sake of Eretz Yisrael, all he did was talk.[131] Ussishkin tried to persuade the Action Committee that Herzl's arguments were not serious. It was not until Chlenov warned Ussishkin to tone down his rhetoric, otherwise he and the other *Neinsagers* would be forced to dissociate themselves from him, that he realized the battle was lost. The Greater Action Committee unanimously adopted Herzl's resolution and reaffirmed its unconditional faith in his leadership. It declared itself convinced by Herzl's words and prepared to resume work with renewed energy and confidence. It also approved an expedition to East Africa. Everyone understood that it was impossible to treat the British proposal dismissively.[132] Inside, Ussishkin realized that his bid for leadership had failed but his retreat was tactical at best. He was not one to admit defeat. The gathering may have gone down in Zionist history as a "reconciliation conference," but Heymann feels this is an overstatement: The moment the conference closed its doors, Ussishkin announced that neither peace nor unity had been achieved. Still, the sides understood each other better, so there was more chance of the East African project being buried at the next congress and peaceable relations being achieved. According to Heymann, this was a more realistic conclusion.[133]

---

130 Goldstein, Ussishkin, vol. 2, pp. 194–195; Bein, *Theodore Herzl: A Biography*, p. 498.
131 Vital, *Hamahapekha hatzionit*, vol. 2, p. 251.
132 Friedman, *Germania, turkia vehatzionut*, p. 128.
133 Heymann, "Herzl and the Russian Zionists": in *Hatzionut*, vol. 3, p. 70; *Hamahapekha hatzionit*, vol. 2, p. 255.

Looking at the outcome of the conference, the biggest loser in the Uganda crisis was Ussishkin. He had not come for the purpose of reconciliation: While Chlenov and his colleagues yearned to make amends with Herzl, Ussishkin was headed in a different direction. In a letter to Yehoshua Barzilai-Eisenstadt a week before the conference, he wrote: "So what lies in store? A raging open battle until one of the sides wins. If Herzl is victorious, the *murshim* and Tzionei Tzion will walk out, Territorialism will be the winner and Eretz Yisrael will be lost – and if we are the victors, Herzl goes."[134]

Was full confidence in Herzl restored in the wake of this conference? It is hard to know given that Herzl died that summer. However, one can certainly say that despite his illness and exhaustion, Herzl did win this last battle: He managed to keep the Zionist movement together, and the organization continued to fulfill its mission as the administrative and political pillar of Zionism even after he was gone.

Views on Uganda

Reactions to the Uganda plan fell into three categories:
(a) "*Jasagers*" (Yea-sayers): There were two types of *Jasagers* – the Territorialists, such as Israel Zangwill and Nachman Sirkin; and those who may have thought otherwise but voted yes because they were not willing to oppose Herzl, such as Nahum Sokolow, Joseph Chazanovitch and many members of Hamizrahi, as we shall see below.
(b) Ideological "*Neinsagers*" (Nay-sayers): Yehiel Chlenov, Y.L. Goldberg and others who despite their admiration for Herzl could not abide by the thought of the Jewish people settling anywhere but Eretz Yisrael, even temporarily. The idea of "Zion in stages" was not acceptable to them. They held that after the establishment of a state in Uganda, the Jews would never win a charter for Palestine because the world would say they already had a state. In their minds, the one solution to the Jewish problem was a Jewish homeland in the Land of Israel. Members of this group fought the Uganda plan but were reluctant to harm Herzl, whom they revered as the founder of political Zionism, or the unity of the Zionist movement. They feared that any blow to Herzl would hurt the Zionist Congress. Hence they battled Herzl only until he convinced them of his loyalty to Zion, and were happy to reconcile with him and keep the movement intact.

---

134 Heymann, *ibid.*, p. 70, footnote 42.

(c) Militant *Neinsagers:* This group fought Herzl out of personal antagonism, because of who he was or his standing in the Zionist movement. Notable members were Davis Trietsch, Alfred Nossig and Chaim Weizmann (who was angling for a top spot in the group). Some were incited by frustrated leaders pushing an agenda of their own who pretended that Zionist ideology was their key concern but used Uganda as a cover for driving Herzl out and usurping his place. Menachem Mendel Ussishkin was one of these. In the end, his followers Belkovsky and Rosenbaum voted for Herzl at the Reconciliation Conference, like everyone else.

If Herzl had been at his prime, if he had not suffered from a weak heart or been worn out by an impossible schedule, chances are he might have dealt with the Uganda affair differently and headed off the crisis. However, he was not in good health. He knew he was living on borrowed time and his physical end was around the corner. To his friends, he often spoke about his impending death.[135] At the same time, he felt that a solution to the Jewish question was not yet guaranteed and the lives of Jews in Europe were in jeopardy. His conduct in the Uganda crisis was guided by a sense of urgency. The hourglass was running out, for Herzl personally and for the Jews as a nation, and this colored his ability to cope with opposition and manage the battle effectively.

The End of the Democratic Fraction

> "On one side you have politicians and disciples of Herzl, and on the other, masses who could be steered either way but who revere Herzl without the slightest criticism. Between these two blocs lies the Fraction, whose role is to comment, shake up and get the movement rolling in the right direction."[136]

The Uganda affair marked the beginning of the end of the Democratic Fraction, the first organized opposition group in the political Zionist movement. The Fraction harbored numerous grievances against Herzl, both procedural (management of the Jewish Colonial Trust) and ideological (support of present-day work in Eretz Yisrael and *kultura*). However, *kultura,* one of the primary reasons for the establishment of the group, was no longer on the agenda. "After the agreement

---

135 Before leaving for Edlach in a final attempt to seek a health cure, he left a note on his desk that said: "In the midst of life there is death." See Pinhas Blumenthal, *Ein zo agada,* p. 290.
136 Martin Buber, in: Klausner, *Opozitzia leherzl,* p. 241.

at the Minsk conference,[137] which removed the sting of the culture controversy, the Fraction was left with no special message that would justify it as a separate faction,"[138] writes Klausner.

With *kultura* gone, the arguments of the Fraction rang hollow. Most of the delegates at the Congress backed Herzl even without wholly agreeing with him, setting the stage for the Fraction's downward slide. Over the course of 1903, Weizmann's organizational and administrative duties passed into the hands of his rival, Leo Motzkin; activity dwindled; bonds between the old-time members weakened; and the group ceased to attract new blood.[139] About a month before the Sixth Congress, Weizmann wrote:

> "I cannot accept the Fraction as it is now. As one of the 'chief instigators and troublemakers,' as someone who founded the Fraction and build it up, I will be the first to say that it cannot go on this way. Why? Because the Fraction has not achieved a single one of its objectives ... Because most of its activists have been sleeping when they ought to have been out in the field ... The Fraction exists only in the defamatory speeches against us..."[140]

The leadership began to wonder whether to attend the Sixth Congress as a faction at all. In the end, a handful of delegates was sent out, but their performance was lackluster. The group was disorganized and remained in the shadows: "The Fraction sensed its organizational weakness at the Congress and ultimately found itself at this great historical moment without a satisfactory answer."[141]

Initially some of the Fraction members vacillated on Uganda but in the end, they joined the *Neinsagers*. Weizmann himself was in favor of the plan at first. After Herzl's speech at the opening of the Sixth Congress, when the Russian Zionists decided to establish a committee of their own to explore the matter, Weizmann sided with Herzl. As Jehuda Reinharz observes: "In the beginning, Weizmann ... was a moderate supporter of Herzl's East Africa proposal...as reflected in his speech on August 24, the second day of Congress ... That afternoon, at a meeting chaired by Max Bodenheimer, Weizmann touched briefly on the East Africa offer, openly declaring his 'favorable view' of the program ... Without a second thought, he proposed the following draft resolution: 'The Congress does not view settlement in Africa as the final goal of the Jews but believes

---

137 See pp. 217–218.
138 Klausner, *Opozitzia leherzl*, p. 224.
139 Ehud Luz, *Makbilim nifgashim*, p. 337.
140 Klausner, *Opozitzia leherzl*, pp. 225–226.
141 *Ibid.*, p. 231.

that organized emigration is necessary, thereby obligating the Zionists ... to convene a conference where the matter of East Africa will be decided."¹⁴²

Two days later, on August 26, Weizmann switched sides. This see-sawing did not endear him to the Russian Zionist leadership. Reinharz argues that deep inside Weizmann recognized the immediate benefits of the Uganda proposal: providing refuge for the persecuted Jews, making the most of Britain's political support and giving Herzlian diplomacy a chance. But there was another reason for his support: Weizmann was looking for a route to power. With Yehiel Chlenov, the *Neinsager* leader, wavering on Uganda, Weizmann took a gamble and came up with a proposal that aligned with Chlenov's position. But then Chlenov turned around and became a fierce opponent. Weizmann, in danger of political isolation, chose political survival over his real feelings: "Earlier in the week he had backed the leader of the movement on East Africa and demonstrated understanding for his motives, and now he had moved entirely into the uncompromising rival camp ... In less than a week, he had become a keen and passionate *Neinsager* ... With his shrewd political instincts, he knew that in his first public statement after the Congress, he must find a way to join forces with them. Adopting a hardline position would help erase his blunder."¹⁴³

At the last session of the Congress, new officeholders were elected and Weizmann became a member of the Uganda advisory committee. Isaiah Friedman wonders how he saw nothing wrong with being on the congressional steering committee of such an expedition.¹⁴⁴ Reinharz speculates that the *Neinsagers* may have sent him to keep a watchful eye on things.¹⁴⁵

True to the new line he had adopted, Weizmann attended a *Neinsager* meeting in Basel less than 48 hours after the Congress closed its doors. At this gathering, chaired by Chlenov, Weizmann had some very harsh words for Herzl, which were published in *Hatzofeh* in early September:

> "Herzl's influence over the nation is so powerful that even the *Neinsagers* cannot resist ... The truth of the matter is that Herzl is not a nationalist but a project developer. He took Hibbat Zion's idea and entered into a contract for a specific period of time. When the time was up and the idea had not succeeded, he bowed out. He only cares about what is on the outside, whereas our source of power is the psychology of the nation and its innermost aspirations. We know that we cannot obtain Palestine any time soon, so

---

142 Reinharz, *Chaim Weizmann*, p. 187.
143 *Ibid.*, p. 193.
144 Friedman, *Germania, turkia vehatzionut*, p. 176.
145 Reinharz, *Chaim Weizmann*, p. 192.

we are not disheartened when one attempt or another other fails. We must heighten the people's awareness that cultural work comes first."[146]

For Weizmann, Uganda was like a shot in the arm, supplying a pretext for reorganization. On October 26, 1903, he sent a circular to the Fraction in which he linked the group's position on Uganda to its policy on culture. It was no coincidence, he wrote, that those who were vehemently opposed to Zionist cultural programing were now passionate supporters of the Uganda proposal. For these people, Zionism was something mechanical and hollow, devoid of Jewish content and characterized mainly by philanthropic diplomacy. The Fraction, by contrast, perceived Zionism as a map for national life on the road to liberty. In another circular sent from Geneva, he stated that the Zionist movement's change of direction came as no surprise to the Fraction, which had warned against dependence upon one man. Now, as predicted, the leader had decided on his own to go a different way.[147]

But Weizmann's campaign was hopeless without an organization behind him. When Ussishkin resumed his fight against Herzl, the Fraction under Weizmann was prepared to bend to his demands. Invited by Weizmann to speak at the Democratic Fraction's upcoming conference,[148] Ussishkin agreed to participate on condition that the Fraction bill itself a "work group."[149] From Weizmann's response, one can see that he was now the uncontested leader: The Democratic Fraction was not an entity with defined parameters, he said, and would not be able to exist in the same format.[150] To show that he was as good as his word, Weizmann quickly wrote to two of the leading Russian *murshim*, Chlenov and Bernstein-Kogan, to say that henceforth the Fraction would operate as a work group affiliated with the *Neinsagers*. Weizmann's efforts succeeded: Ussishkin agreed to cooperate with the Fraction in its fight against the *Jasagers* and even allocated a budget of 1,200 rubles.[151]

Meanwhile, the Kharkov conference convened (November 11–14, 1903) and voted to keep its decisions confidential until the return of the ultimatum delegation. Weizmann, to his chagrin, received no reports on the proceedings: The de-

---

146 *Hatzofeh*, September 3, 1903; *Hatmahapekha hatzionit*, vol. 2, p. 225; Reinharz, *Chaim Weizmann*, p. 193, footnote 53.
147 Klausner, *Opozitzia leherzl*, p. 234.
148 Ussishkin opposed the establishment of the Democratic Fraction because he was against any breakdown into parties in the Zionist movement.
149 Klausner, *Opozitzia leherzl*, p. 137.
150 *Ibid.*, p. 236.
151 *Ibid.*, p. 238.

cisions were kept secret even from him. So despite his hopes of active participation and hosting the Fraction at a conference attended by Ussishkin, he was forced to sit by with his hands folded.

In early January 1904, a month and a half after the Kharkov conference, the ultimatum delegates set out for Vienna. Rosenbaum advised Weizmann to postpone the joint conference and wait until they were back from Vienna. The consultation they scheduled for January 6 in Berlin never took place: The pair returned red-faced straight to St. Petersburg to report to Ussishkin on the fiasco. Weizmann, Feiwel, and Buber – the Fraction members awaiting them in Berlin – sent Ussishkin a frantic cable: "To leave us in the lurch is unpardonable. If you do not arrive immediately, our future work together is at stake." A letter Weizmann wrote that day goes into further detail: "We are in a terrible state. We know nothing. Work is at a standstill. Behavior of this sort on the part of our comrades is infuriating, especially in these difficult times. Please inform us if someone will be coming or not, otherwise there is nothing for us to do..."[152]

The Fraction had great, but apparently groundless, pretensions. Neither the telegram nor the letter had any effect. The Fraction conference that was supposed to take place in Berlin at the end of December in cooperation with Ussishkin was postponed because the Kharkov resolutions were unknown, and it was held in mid-January 1904 with only a partial turnout.[153]

Weizmann believed that even though the Russian *Neinsagers* had been a source of disappointment, cooperating with them offered the only chance for success. They were at war, he said, and no positive work could be done unless Herzl's approach was shot down. As he wrote to Victor Jacobson: "Herzl is a fast worker, and this 'great leader' can easily turn decent people away from the movement using battle tactics that others would never permit themselves to think of."

Despite his efforts, Weizmann failed to gain a spot for himself in the rebel leadership. Meanwhile, the Greater Action Committee met in Vienna for the so-called Reconciliation Conference, which ended with a unanimous vote of confidence in Herzl. Weizmann, who was in Pinsk at the time, was surprised by the results. According to Klausner, he could not understand how the Russian *murshim* had agreed to this. He set out for Minsk to meet Rosenbaum, the great opposition leader, to hear his explanation, but even afterwards, was sure that peace

---

152 *Ibid.*, p. 239.
153 *Ibid.*

was an illusion and Herzl was preparing a takeover: "All [Herzl] has done is pacify the Russian Zionists but in the interim he is organizing the Uganda-ists."[154]

Reinharz analyzes the stages of Weizmann's relationship towards Herzl. At first, he was full of admiration and awe for Herzl, with only minor criticisms from time to time.[155] From 1901, he grew increasingly critical, due to a combination of disagreement on core subjects, personal rivalry and political ambitions. It was after the establishment of the Democratic Fraction, whose very establishment posed a direct challenge to Herzl, that Weizmann's disillusionment with Herzl began. To his friends, he would complain about Herzl's superficial understanding of Zionism and Judaism. More and more, Weizmann began to compare himself to Herzl, subtly and then more openly. Aside from disagreement on fundamental Zionist and Jewish issues, fierce jealousy burned within him. Herzl was blessed with all the qualities that Weizmann had yet to acquire: personal charisma, fame, leadership, money and diplomatic skill.[156]

It should be noted that with all his negative feelings Weizmann had never sought to polarize the Zionist movement. He could not envisage the future of the organization without Herzl. As someone who had tried to lead Democratic Faction, he fully appreciated Herzl's abilities. Concerned that Herzl was irreplaceable at the helm, he wrote to Ussishkin: "Now, more than ever, you and some of our colleagues in Russia need to assert yourselves at the head of the enterprise, but for now without smashing the idols we have created."[157] After the Reconciliation Conference, however, when his leadership hopes were dashed, he wrote in despair: "If the Uganda affair is not defeated, schism is inevitable..."[158]

In conclusion, the Democratic Fraction under Weizmann was at its peak at the Fifth Congress when it stood up to the Haredim on the subject of *kultura*. After the Minsk conference, the power of the Fraction waned. Handing over the reins to Motzkin brought no improvement and the demise of the party neared. Due to the unpleasant dynamics of his relationship with Herzl, Weizmann was not welcomed into the cadre of West European leadership. Reinharz explains:

> "As time passed and Weizmann's approach to Zionism matured, he became increasingly critical of Herzl. This can be seen clearly in the bluntly worded memorandum he sent to

---

154 *Ibid.*
155 The Second Congress in 1898 was Weizmann's first time at a Zionist congress.
156 Reinharz, *Chaim Weizmann*, pp. 213–214.
157 *Ibid.*, p. 214, footnote 182.
158 *Ibid.*, p. 215, footnote 187.

Herzl on May 6, 1903. Weizmann criticizes his over-reliance on the Mizrahi movement and insensitivity to the emotional and intellectual despair of the Jewish intelligentsia in Russia and tries to offer Herzl a solution for the various troubles plaguing the Zionist movement in both the East and the West. But to no avail. There was no change in Herzl's attitude toward the Mizrahi movement, nor did a new chapter open in his relations with the Democratic Fraction. On a personal level, it spelled the end of Weizmann's relationship with Herzl. Henceforth, Weizmann became a *persona non grata* in [Herzl's] circle of associates in Vienna. Rumors spread that Herzl had taken a dislike to him. Weizmann's scorn and contempt for Herzl grew fiercer and more offensive, compounded by irony and condescension."[159]

Weizmann, hungry for leadership, jumped on the Uganda bandwagon using the Fraction as a springboard. He agreed to alter the classification of the group, calling it a "work group."[160] But the East European leadership led by Ussishkin still refused to open the door to him, and he felt mortified: "Weizmann was convinced he had reached a dead end in his Zionist and professional career. All his endeavors had failed... In Western Europe he was tagged as an opponent of Herzl, and in Eastern Europe, Ussishkin continued to block his entry into the inner sanctum of Russian Zionism. Not only that, but his European colleagues were often dismissive and jeering."[161]

When Weizmann left Geneva for England in July 1904, his career as a scientist and a Zionist leader took off. As the inventor of synthetic acetone, which was vital for Britain's victory in World War I, and a prominent figure in the Zionist movement, he moved in social and political circles where his input helped to push through the Balfour Declaration, the 1917 policy statement that set the stage for the UN partition plan and recognition of a Jewish state in Palestine.

The Mizrahi Movement

The Mizrahi movement attended the Sixth Congress as an organized body of 200 delegates – the largest faction in the Congress. The real surprise in the Uganda affair was the support of this group. One would have thought that as a religious movement, Mizrahi would have been a major foe. As Chlenov put it: "From the Mizrahi camp, whose members were people of tradition and faith who prayed every day for the return to Zion, we never expected any agreement at all on Uganda."[162]

---

159 *Ibid.*, p. 213.
160 Letter of Weizmann to Bernstein-Kogan; *ibid.*, pp. 199–200.
161 *Ibid.*, p. 225, footnote 252.
162 *Sefer Chlenov*, p. 290.

In practice, the majority of the delegates voted in favor, with the exception of a handful of *Neinsagers*, among them Rabbi Rabinowitz. The founder of the movement, Rabbi Yitzhak Yaacov Reines, was originally against sending an expedition to Uganda and in favor of electing a congressional investigation committee. However, when he found out about the ultimatum of the *murshim* in Kharkov, he made haste to write to Ussishkin to say that he could not agree to such a thing and had therefore changed his mind:

> "Even the most straightforward and honest of men may be forced to become fickle and retract today something agreed upon yesterday... I have now changed my mind and contest this ultimatum. I am afraid it could lead to a split between us and Herzl, and we could, God forbid, lose everything we believe in by our own doing. With all Herzl's errors and transgressions, even his opponents will agree that we have a very great need for him, and without him the whole movement could fall apart. Therefore I protest with all my might against this ultimatum strategy, and request that my name be added to the list of opponents, along with our colleagues Mandelstamm and Jasinowski, even though I do not agree with them on everything ... The delegation that travels to Herzl should negotiate with him, not threaten a breakaway."[163]

The Mizrahi movement chose to support Uganda because of Herzl, as is clear from Rabbi Reines' outpouring of love and admiration. Rabbi Reines saw the Ussishkin-led mutiny as illegitimate because it ran in the face of resolutions passed by the Congress, and felt that pressure on Herzl to go against these resolutions was wrong. The secretary of Mizrahi expressed similar sentiments: "If we respect the Congress we must see to it that its decisions are implemented in full. Otherwise, the Congress will lose its value and become the butt of ridicule."[164] He also justified Herzl on the grounds that "his view is always more political and pragmatic."[165]

On December 6, 1903, Rabbi Reines wrote a letter to Herzl that opens with lavish praise for the man and his enterprise:

> "To the warrior sacrificing his life for his nation, to the man toward whom all eyes turn, to the creator and commander of Zionism, to the man chosen by the people ... Disturbing rumors have been coming our way that the *murshim* in Russia led by Ussishkin have reached a decision to dissuade you from pursuit of the African proposal, come what may ... Our hearts ache to hear these sad tidings. The Russian authorities are growing less tolerant of Zionism ... and the whole organization is on the verge of collapse, but the *murshim* care only about war on Uganda as a way of satisfying their caprice and emerging as victors

---

163 Raphael, *Ish hame'orot*, p. 220.
164 *Ibid.*, p. 221.
165 *Ibid.*

in this fight. Their concern is not for the nation ... We must realize that that welfare of our people is dearer to us than the Land of Israel. For that reason, we must have a safe haven somewhere, while assuring that Zion is not forgotten and the Zionist movement and its leader continue to devote their energies to its upbuilding and release from captivity ... Those who oppose Uganda are not only sealing the fate of the nation but murdering the soul of Zionism and must be seen as enemies of Israel."[166]

Rabbi Reines saw acceptance of the British offer as evidence of the pragmatism of Zionism and claimed that many people who had been suspicious of the movement had become more amenable to it in the wake of the Uganda plan. The letter goes on to sing Herzl's praises and offer encouragement: "Know that our people are with you, and those who support you outnumber the others many times over ... Be strong and courageous, and the nation will do all that you command."[167]

Rabbi Reines had become an admirer of Herzl at the Third Zionist Congress, the first he attended, and was consistently effusive in his praise.[168] His support of Herzl during the Uganda crisis brought the two even closer together. S.L. Citron writes that according to the journalists covering the Sixth Congress, Herzl was seen frequently consulting with him. After the Kharkov conference, Rabbi Reines wrote to the *murshim* to say that its decisions as publicized "undermine the institutions of Zionism, strip it of all Jewish national substance and nullify the views and wishes of the majority." It was hard for him to believe that these were indeed the conference decisions, and he hoped there had been a mistake. He then offered the Russian *murshim* three options:

(a) To publish a notice within three weeks saying that these decisions did not reflect their opinion and it was all a mistake;
(b) If it was not a mistake, to retract these decisions, declare regret for reaching them and affirm their faith in all the strategies adopted by the Zionist movement heretofore, as well as loyalty in its exalted leader;
(c) In the event that neither of the first two options was pursued, and the *murshim* had indeed made the publicized decisions, "we shall be the first to defend the Zionist movement."[169]

Rabbi Reines's letter contained a veiled threat that ties with the *murshim* would be cut, all further dealings would be with the Viennese Action Committee and

---

[166] Ibid.
[167] Ibid., p. 222.
[168] Yitzhak Yaacov Reines, *Or khadash al tzion*, New York, Posy-Shoulson Press, 1946, chapter 10, pp. 278 ff; Raphael, *Ish hame'orot*, p. 110.
[169] Raphael, *Ish hame'orot*, pp. 226–227.

shekel dues would be sent directly to Vienna. He hoped the rebels would change their minds and peace would be restored. But when he heard that the ultimatum delegation was on its way, he wrote another letter to Herzl urging him not to make amends until they complied with his list of demands: "It is the least one could ask, considering that they have insulted not only the leader but all Zionists and the Zionist movement as a whole."[170]

Reines' comments show that Herzl's prestige was at a low point. He had been charting a veritable obstacle course since the Second Congress. From where did he derive the emotional strength to risk everything he had and continue shouldering the burden of Zionist leadership? That is the question we shall explore in the third part of the book.

---

170 *Ibid.*, p. 229.

Figure 6: An obituary poster on Herzl's death, text by Naftali Herz Imber author of "Hatikvah", Vilna 1904. Author's Collection.

Part 3: **Legend and Reality**

Chapter 11
The Moses and Messiah Syndrome

How can I alone bear the trouble of you, and the burden, and the bickering?
(Deuteronomy 1:12)

"The radical conversion of a man before the eyes of the world is always an overwhelming phenomenon. It is to be found at the beginning of every great religious foundation, as witness Moses, Paul, Buddha, Mohammed. It was as an improbable and legendary figure that Herzl dawned upon the eastern masses of Jewry ... Herzl had called his 'Society of the Jews' the new Moses. The masses, however, saw the new Moses in him ..."[1]

Herzl embarked on his Zionist odyssey at the pinnacle of his professional career. At the end of 1895, he returned in triumph from Paris, where he had been sent by the *Neue Freie Presse*. As chief editor of the newspaper's culture section, he was highly respected and handsomely paid. When he embraced Zionism, however, he became the butt of scorn and ridicule, later followed by bitter, sometimes unfair opposition. He lived in constant fear of being fired by his paper, which did not take kindly to his Zionist activity. His finances also took a turn for the worse when he began to pay for the Zionist enterprise out of his own pocket: His trip to Constantinople accompanied by Baron Philipp Michael Newlinsky,[2] the First Zionist Congress,[3] and the establishment of the Zionist movement newspaper, *Die Welt*, which he bankrolled from June 1897 to May 31, 1900. At that point, he was so low on money that he was forced to turn over the financing of *Die Welt* to several wealthy individuals in the Action Committee of the Zionist movement in Vienna.[4]

When his friends, who were worried about his health, offered to pay him an annuity so he could give up his job at the *Neue Freie Presse*, he turned them down in genuine fury. To Wolffsohn, he wrote: "You are a good fellow, but what sort of person do you think I am?...Well, what about my self-respect?

---

1 Bein, *Theodore Herzl: A Biography*, p. 184.
2 Newlinsky, who had contacts in the Turkish court, went to Constantinople at Herzl's expense. Herzl paid his travel costs, room and board and *baksheesh* to all the intermediaries at the Sultan's palace. This was in addition to a monthly allowance of 200 gulden (see Herzl's diary, December 18, 1897). However, Newlinsky had another consideration in mind: Suffering from heart trouble, he was hoping that the Zionists would support his survivors in the event of his death, and in fact Herzl paid the family 500 gulden out of his own pocket when that day came (see Elon, *Herzl*, p. 342); Pawel, pp. 402–403.
3 On the lease of the municipal concert hall, see above p. 117.
4 E. Rosenberger, *Herzl as I Remember Him*, Herzl Press, New York 1959, pp. 216–217.

Why would I accept money from you? Because I act according to my convictions?"[5] To Zangwill, who assured him of total discretion, he replied: "You say no one will know. One person would know. I would know."[6] In a letter to Joseph Cowen on December 31, 1903, he wrote: "That I should ever let myself be supported by our movement, in any way whatever, is the most ridiculous idea. In the first place, I don't have the character required for this. In the second place, even if I had the character, may God graciously protect and preserve me from it."[7]

Herzl's investment in the Jewish Colonial Trust further depleted his financial resources, including the dowry of his wife, Julie. When an opportunity arose to further the Zionist cause, he did not hesitate to dip deeply into his own pocket. An example of this was sending Baroness Bertha von Suttner to the Peace Conference in Hague as a correspondent for *Die Welt*. Covering her expenses amounted to a quarter of his annual income.[8]

Herzl and his family were accustomed to a high standard of living. However, the funding of the Zionist movement quickly drained Herzl's savings and became a constant source of concern. At the same time, he was subject to a host of other pressures that weighed on him and sapped his strength. Among them was the fear of losing his job at the *Neue Freie Presse*, which constituted his primary source of income and social prestige, and the battles he fought over *kultura*, *Altneuland* and Uganda. The cumulative effect of working at such an intensive pace took an inevitable toll: Herzl packed what might have been accomplished in decades of work into nine years. It wore him down to the point where he could no longer accept the opposition with equanimity and made grievous errors that had implications for his otherwise charismatic leadership.

There were two factors, it seems, that enabled Herzl to persevere despite the difficulties that came his way: the sense of urgency that informed his work and his sense of calling. Herzl was convinced that the "wretchedness of the Jews" would only worsen and there was no future for them in Europe. As Rabbi Binyamin (pseudonym of Yehoshua Radler-Feldman) wrote:

---

[5] Pawel, p. 517.
[6] *Ibid.*
[7] *Complete Diaries of Theodor Herzl*, vol. 4, p. 1587.
[8] See above, p. 79.

"The terrifying truth is that Herzl was the only Zionist leader who knew that the ground was burning under our feet.[9] He was not among the complacent ones. [He was] the only one who predicted catastrophe, a holocaust. He had a sixth sense in this regard. He saw that the 'grace period allotted to hunted animals' was coming to an end. He was the sole individual who discerned the underlying cry, back in the days of relative calm: 'Hang on, the day will come when hunting Jews will be allowed!'"[10]

In view of the impending horror, Herzl felt it was incumbent upon the Jews to leave Europe. Only a Jewish state could save them, and time was of the essence. They had to make haste so that the worst would not befall them before a Zionist solution was in place. That was his reason for working himself to the bone.

To pursue what he felt was a calling, Herzl set his own needs aside and dedicated himself to the common good. On June 16, 1895, he wrote in his diary: "I believe that for me life has ended and world history has begun." That same day he added another sentence: "The Jewish State is a world necessity."[11]

These two parameters, urgency and sense of purpose, led to parallels between Herzl, the biblical figure of Moses and the Messiah. His admirers made this association, but he himself was aware of it and drew inspiration from it. Being compared to Moses and the Messiah was a source of strength: It fortified him and helped him through tough times on his Zionist journey. But it began to fade in later years, as opposition grew.

The comparison between Herzl and Moses can be divided into three categories:
(a) Herzl's self-image as Moses, to which he refers in his own writing;
(b) Comparisons to Moses by his associates and inner circle which reached Herzl's ears and presumably affected him, emotionally and psychologically;
(c) Comparisons by contemporaries during his lifetime, though not necessarily to his face, or after his death, as a way of understanding his success and influence.

---

9 Benzion Netanyahu maintains that Herzl's views on antisemitism influenced Jabotinsky: Soon after Hitler's rise to power, Jabotinsky warned of an impending Holocaust. See *Khameshet Avot*, pp. 278–279.
10 Rabbi Binyamin, "Herzl," in: *Shivat tzion: Sefer shana lekheker hatzionut vetkumat yisrael*, vol. 1, Hasifriya Hatzionit, Jerusalem, 1949, p. 352 (henceforth: *Shivat tzion*, vol. 1).
11 *Complete Diaries of Theodor Herzl*, vol. 1, pp. 105–106.

Herzl as Moses: Self-Image

From the very start of the Zionist endeavor, Herzl has visions of himself that drew inspiration from the biblical figure of Moses, the first redeemer of the Jewish people. His earliest thoughts about the exodus, Moses and the Messiah came to him in a dream at the age of twelve. Reuben Brainin writes:

> "Once I managed to extract from Herzl an important detail about his inner life as a child, which I will relay here as it was told to me:
> "When I was a boy, the story of the exodus from Egypt made a very profound impression on me ... This impression quickly faded from heart and mind, but when I was about twelve years old, I chanced upon a German book – I can no longer remember the name – where I read about the Messiah, King of Israel, whose arrival, as a poor man riding on a donkey, many Jews even in our generation await every day ...
> These fragments of messianic legend stirred my imagination. My heart filled with sorrow but also with vague longing. At first, I did not know the cause of my sadness and whom I longed for. And then one night, as I lay in bed, I remembered the story of the exodus from Egypt. The historic tale of the exodus and the legend of future redemption by the Messiah King ran together in my mind. Past and present – it was all a beautiful and magical story, a kind of uplifting and glorious poem. The idea came to me of writing a poem about the Messiah King. It was an idea that kept me awake for nights. I was too embarrassed to share my thoughts about the Messiah King with anyone. I knew they would only mock me and shout 'Here comes the dreamer.'
> Then came examination time at school, diverting my mind from the birth-pangs of the Messiah. But in the depths of my soul, the legend continued to unfold, albeit unconsciously. One night, I dreamt a marvelous dream: The Messiah King arrived, a noble and majestic old man, who took me in his arms and glided with me on the wings of the wind. On one of the shimmering clouds we encountered the figure of Moses Rabbenu (his face carved in marble by Michelangelo – a sculpture I had loved to look at since boyhood). The Messiah called out to Moses: 'It is for this boy that I have prayed!' And to me, he said: 'Go tell the Jews that I shall soon be coming and will perform great wonders and deeds for my people and the entire world!' I woke up and realized it was a dream – a dream that I kept in my heart and never confided to a soul."[12]

Assuming that Herzl really had this dream and it was not some childhood memory embellished at a later date,[13] this is a wonderful example of the revelation that many great leaders in history claim to have experienced which gave them their mission in life. Herzl's story attests to his recognition of Moses' importance for the Jews as well as his own self-perception. The Messiah tells Moses that 'this

---

[12] Reuben Brainin, *Khayei Herzl*, vol. 1, Assaf Publishing, New York, 1919, pp. 16–18 (henceforth: Brainin, *Khayei Herzl*, vol. 1).
[13] Bein, *Theodor Herzl: A Biography*, p. 11; Brainin, *Khayei Herzl*, vol. 1, p. 18.

boy,' i.e., Herzl, is the one he has prayed for and has chosen to bring tidings to the people of Israel.

Meeting Baron Hirsch in 1895, Herzl told him: "... It will be a long time before we arrive in the Promised Land. It took Moses forty years. We may require twenty or thirty ..." Later, he writes: "I know all the things [the plan] involves: Money, money, and more money; means of transportation; the provisioning of great multitudes (which does not mean just food and drink, as in the simple days of Moses) ..."[14]

Drawing up notes in preparation for his next meeting with Hirsch, he continues in this vein: "But if the Jews want to be a people within a short time, in ten or twenty years, or forty as in the days of Moses, then they must emigrate. From all over the world ..."[15] That month, we find several references to Moses in his diary, as well as a comparison to the Israelite exodus from Egypt: "The Exodus under Moses bears the same relation to this project as a Shrovetide Play by Hans Sachs does to a Wagner opera."[16] Employing yet another biblical analogy, he writes: "I am prepared for anything: lamenting for the flesh-pots of Egypt, the dance around the Golden Calf – also the ingratitude of those who are most indebted to us ..."[17] Once we are over there, the dancers around the Golden Calf will be furious at my barring them from the Stock Exchange."[18]

Herzl was aware of being compared to Moses and spoke about the Jews of Europe on several occasions in much the same tone that Moses spoke about the children of Israel. In a biographical sketch for the *Jewish Chronicle* prior to the publication of *Der Judenstaat*,[19] Herzl writes freely about the "new exodus from Egypt."[20]

Georges Yitshak Weisz notes that Herzl's use of the Hebrew word *Mitzraim* (Egypt) was far from accidental and reappears in his writings like a refrain.[21] Moreover, the Bible tells us that Joseph's bones were carried to the Promised Land, and Herzl makes a similar commitment: "We shall also take our dead along with us."[22]

---

14 *Complete Diaries of Theodor Herzl*, vol. 1, pp. 20, 27 (June 1895).
15 Bein, *Im herzl ube'ikvotav: Ma'amarim vete'udot*, Tel Aviv: Masada, 1953, p. 62.
16 *Complete Diaries of Theodor Herzl*, vol. 1, p. 38 (June 7, 1895).
17 Ibid.
18 Ibid., p. 54 (June 9, 1895).
19 See pp. 5–7.
20 Weisz, *A New Reading*, p. 103.
21 Ibid., p. 104.
22 Weisz, *A New Reading*, p. 110.

A troubling incident that comes up in Herzl's writing further explains the equivalence in his mind between the deliverance of the Israelites in ancient times and their deliverance in his own day. In his diary, he reconstructs from memory the anti-Semitic graffiti he saw on a bathhouse locker:

> "Lord almighty, let Moses arrive
> Off to the Promised Land with all his tribe
> When the Jews are all there
> In the heart of the sea,
> Slam the lid shut
> And let Christians be."[23]

In June 1895, making notes in his diary that were expanded upon in *Der Judenstaat*, Herzl writes: "We shall have to go through bitter struggles: with a reluctant Pharaoh, with enemies, and especially with ourselves. The Golden Calf!"[24] Six months later, he met with the Zionist youth of Vienna. Erwin Rosenberger remembers the clear biblical associations that arose in the course of this meeting:

> "Herzl told us that his pamphlet, *The Jewish State*, would appear shortly.
> 'A regular state?' he was asked, 'a real state on its own territory, with its own laws, inhabited, governed and administered by Jews?'
> 'Yes,' Herzl said. 'Our Jewish state will be just such a state. An independent state like Austria, France and England. Jews from all countries will found it and settle it ...'
> His eyes searched our faces. These young people – would they smile in disbelief or amusement, would they raise objections?
> Nothing of the sort happened. There were, to be sure skeptical and irreverent souls among us, but this man, who spoke so matter-of-factly of a Jewish state, inspired a deep trust in us...
> 'And where will you find the Moses who will lead the Jews there?' cried a voice from the rear, over the heads of those in the front. It was not the voice of one of us students. The question had been asked by Rabbi Lowy, a man in his seventies with a gentle smile, who often attended our affairs as a guest.
> Courteously, Herzl went over to the old gentleman. They introduced themselves, and the ranks closed around them. 'A Moses?' asked Herzl. 'If he is not to be found, we will create him.'
> Dr. Jacob Kohn, obviously aroused by the reference to Moses, interjected: 'Moses led the Jews about in the desert for forty years before he could bring them into the Promised Land.'
> 'With modern transportation facilities, it will take forty hours,' replied Herzl."[25]

---

[23] *Complete Diaries of Theodor Herzl*, July 29, 1896, vol. 1, p. 220.
[24] Ibid., June 6, 1895, vol. 1, p. 33.
[25] Rosenberger, *Herzl as I Remember Him*, pp. 14–15.

On March 26, 1898, Herzl writes about how a friend's childhood memories of studying Moses' victory song became a source of inspiration:

> "Kellner, my dearest, best friend ... reminisced the other day about schoolboy days in the *heder*. He was daydreaming in a class when they got to the place in the Bible where Moses sings: Exodus, 15. I immediately looked up the passage, and it moved me. Suddenly the idea popped into my mind to write a Biblical drama, *Moses*.
>
> The conditions in Egypt, the internal and external struggles, the exodus, the desert, Moses' death. I imagine him as a tall, vital, superior man with a sense of humor. The drama: how he is shaken inwardly and yet holds himself upright by his will. He is the leader, because he has no personal desire. He does not care about the goal, but about the migration. Education through migration.
>
> Act I. Moses' Return to Egypt. Conditions, wretchedness of the Israelites; Moses, embittered, shakes them up.
>
> Act II. Korah.
>
> Act III. The Golden Calf.
>
> Act IV. Miriam.
>
> Act V. Moses' Death.
>
> Pageantry in the desert: the Ark of the Covenant, then Joseph's bones at the head of the procession of slaves. He is exhausted by all this, and yet he has to lure them onward with ever renewed vigor.
>
> It is the tragedy of the leader, of any leader of men who is not a misleader."[26]

According to Rabbi David Golinkin, Herzl was already under great strain at this time and these parallels to Moses in every parameter of the play were an emotional outlet. In the end, however, the script of this biblical drama was never written.[27]

Summing up his meeting with the German secretary of state, Bernhard von Bülow, before leaving for Palestine, Herzl writes about how the conversation turned to socialism and Moses as an individualist:

> "I mentioned something that I had recently read: Pre-Mosaic Egypt was a Socialist state. Through the Decalogue Moses created an individualistic form of society. And the Jews, I said, are and will remain individualists."[28]

---

26 *Complete Diaries of Theodor Herzl*, vol. 2, pp. 623–624.

27 David Golinkin, *Insight Israel: The View from Schechter*, Schechter Institute, Jerusalem 2006, pp. 166–167.

28 *Complete Diaries of Theodor Herzl*, vol. 2, p. 667.

During his visit to Egypt in 1903, when discussing the quantities of water that would need to be diverted to the parched homeland of the Jews, he notes: "... I looked out the cabin window at the brown river, which flows along as it did in the days of Moses, our teacher."[29]

"Did Moses not go to Pharaoh?" retorted Herzl when the Russian Zionists censured him for meeting with von Plehve, the Russian interior minister perceived as the architect of the Kishinev pogrom.[30]

From all these testimonies it seems clear that the role of Moses and his place in the history of the Jewish people were known to Herzl even before he set out on his Zionist journey. This awareness of the parallels between them accompanied him every step of the way, becoming an inseparable part of his persona.

Moses Analogy Heard from Others

Herzl's image of himself was no doubt strengthened by being openly likened to Moses by others. On August 17, 1895, after a long exchange of letters and telegrams, Herzl met Rabbi Gudemann, the chief rabbi of Vienna, in Munich. Upon listening to Herzl's plan,[31] Gudemann exclaims: "You remind me of Moses." Later, he adds: "Remain as you are. Perhaps you are the one called of God."[32]

The following year, Herzl writes about the mass meeting in London's East End: "Succeeding speakers eulogized me. One of them, Ish-Kishor, compared me to Moses, Columbus, etc."[33]

When times grew rough, David Wolffsohn implored him: "Hold your hands high, Herr Doctor ... When Moses raised his hands, Israel triumphed over Amalek."[34]

Avraham Zvi Gliksman, the Polish *hasid* who came to see Herzl in Vienna, also uses the Moses analogy:

---

29 Ibid., vol. 4, pp. 1452–1453. When the Viennese author Richard Beer-Hoffman conceived of building a magnificent water fountain in the Jewish State, Herzl's immediate association was Moses striking the rock and drawing water from it. See Weisz, *A New Reading*, p. 110.
30 Maor, *Hatnu'a hatzionit berusia*, p. 223.
31 Herzl read out his letter to the Rothschilds, which went on to become *Der Judenstaat*.
32 *Complete Diaries of Theodor Herzl*, vol. 1, p. 233.
33 Ibid., p. 418–419.
34 Vital, *Hamahapekha hatzionit*, vol. 1, p. 250; Wolffsohn to Herzl, August 10, 1896, CZA H VIII 940/5.

"When the Lord sent Moses to the children of Israel in Egypt, He said: 'Go and gather the elders of Israel.' You are sitting at the highest place in the city, in the Casino in Basel, and from those lofty heights, you must call upon the Jews to join you! You are obligated to go to the elders of Israel. And since the overwhelming majority of Jews live in Russia, it is incumbent upon you, Sir, to first go there ... and speak to the elders."[35]

Following the success of the First Congress, the *New York Times* reported on Herzl's newfound prestige and called him the "new Moses" from then on.[36] All the newspapers and weeklies that covered the Fourth Congress in London were filled with photographs of Zionist leaders and Congress as a whole, but the one who captured the hearts of Jews and non-Jews alike with his splendor and impeccable taste was Dr. Herzl, who began to be called the "new Moses" by a number of leading publications.[37]

Moses Analogy as an Explanation for Success

Herzl's associates and admirers frequently compared him to Moses. Most of the comparisons did not go beyond the kind of enthusiastic praise that fans heap upon their idols. However, some showed deeper insight and greatly enhanced the desire to come to the aid of the Zionist enterprise. Many members of Herzl's close circle pinned the reason for his success on his likeness to Moses. George Clemenceau, for example, claimed that Herzl and Moses were cut from the same cloth. Therefore, Herzl could not be judged or measured by the same criteria as ordinary human beings: "I am not going to analyze Herzl's philosophy ... But the spirit of God rested upon Herzl the man. He saw the Burning Bush ... He was a man of genius, which should not be confused with talent."[38]

Sammy Gronemann discerns yet another point of similarity between Herzl and Moses: "The fact that the two leaders came from the outside, not from within the community, helped them both in their leadership challenge." Herzl formed a picture of Jewish life while observing the differences and alienation between the Jews of Eastern and Western Europe:

---

35 Avraham Zvi Gliksman, *Tiferet adam*, p. 63 (see p. 28 above).
36 Mordechai Naor, *Meherzl ve'ad ben gurion*, Tel Aviv, Ministry of Defense, 1996, p. 38.
37 Nahum Slouschz, *Hacongress hatzioni harivi'ee*, Tushia Publishing, Warsaw, 1900, p. 11 (henceforth: Slouschz, *Hacongress*).
38 "Herzl in my eyes," from an interview with Pierre Van Paassen, May 1929; *Herzl bekhazon hador*, Uma umoledet Publishing, Tel Aviv, 1946, p. 39 (henceforth: *Herzl bekhazon hador*).

> "He was a product of assimilation, which would seem to be a drawback. But it was just the opposite. All these deficiencies were an advantage for someone like Theodor. He could never have acquired such authority without being from the outside. As strange as this sounds, there is national psychology behind it. The redeemer of the Jews has always come from afar: Moses was raised in Pharaoh's palace; Ezra and Nehemiah hailed from the courts of Babylon, and Herzl's milieu was also remote from the center of Jewish life."[39]

Gronemann even applies the argument to Herzl's successor, David Wolffsohn. He says Wolffsohn would never have faced such opposition from the community if he had not been a part of it. This is consistent with the approach of the medieval biblical commentator Rabbi Abraham Ibn Ezra: "Perhaps God had Moses raised in the royal palace so that he would not imbibe the customs of people in bondage ... Moreover, had he grown up among his brethren, they would not have obeyed him or stood in awe of him because they would have known him all their lives."[40]

Mordecai Ehrenpreis makes the same point, from a more personal angle, in connection with Herzl foreignness to spiritual Zionism:

> "We saw his shortcomings clearly: We knew that he came to us from a foreign world and was not rooted in the Jewish past as we were, that he stood outside the doorstep of Jewish religious and spiritual life. The fact that he was alien to our spiritual Zionism hovered like a shadow over the radiance of his personality. But these flaws did not discourage us. We felt that he was a new type of person, the embodiment of qualities that we had been lacking until now. We clung to his leadership, come what may."[41]

Alongside other such comments,[42] a broad analogy was drawn between Moses and Herzl when the Zionist societies met in Vilna on the eve of the Sixth Congress. At the meeting, a letter from Bernstein-Kogan was read out announcing that in the wake of the failure of the El Arish plan,[43] Chamberlain was offering Uganda. Chaos erupted in the hall, and name-calling began. Herzl was called a traitor and a charlatan. Yosef Eliash took the floor and said he was not happy with Herzl's proposal. However:

---

39 Gronemann, *Zikhronot shel yekke*, pp. 186–187.
40 Rabbi Abraham Ibn Ezra, commentary on *Exodus* 3: 2.
41 Ehrenpreis, *Bein mizrakh lama'arav: Autobiografia*, Am Oved, 1953, p. 70.
42 Shmuel Pevzner's description of Herzl at the First Congress: "Standing before us was not a prophet bringing tidings of redemption or the messiah we hoped for, but a leader calling for war – a new Moses," *Sefer hacongress* (1923).
43 The El Arish plan, proposed by Herzl in January 1903, was to settle the Jews in a British-mandated territory near Palestine after the Ottomans refused to grant a charter for Palestine.

"I propose that we not be hasty or make any decision until Herzl's true intentions become clear. As for the personality of our great leader, I think we should point out what the Torah tells us: 'And it came to pass, when Pharaoh had let the people go, that God led them not by the way of the land of the Philistines, although that was near ...' The journey should have taken only a few days, but instead of leading the people northward, Moses led them eastward ... The real reason why Moses did not take the short route is unknown. How did the people behave during these forty years of wandering? Constant rebellion. The Israelites complained about Moses and Aaron. They remembered the pot of meat they ate in Egypt. They journeyed through the wilderness of Zin and camped in Refidim. There they were thirsty for water and complained to Moses. Then came the rebellion of Korah and his men, and the decision to return to Egypt. If you had delved deeper into the history of our people, my friends, we would not be hearing Herzl called a traitor and a charlatan and a swindler tonight ... I am certain that even Moshe Rabbeinu was called such names. But we know that Moses responded with great patience out of his desire to achieve one goal: to take the Children of Israel to Eretz Yisrael. I am sure that East Africa is not the last stop on our way to Eretz Yisrael, and I am equally sure that our illustrious leader Dr. Herzl, like Moshe Rabbeinu in his time, has a single goal in mind, to steer the Jewish people from one station until the next to Eretz Yisrael."[44]

Eliash went on to say how surprised he was at all those who were so quick to accuse Herzl without taking any responsibility or blame on themselves. If Herzl had been granted the two million Turkish pounds he sought from the outset, "it would have been possible to purchase the entire Land of Israel," he wrote, "so there would have been no need to continuously 'journey and pitch their tents,' as in the days of Moses."[45]

Rabbi Zvi Perez Chajes, Gudemann's successor as chief rabbi of Vienna, cites two reasons why Moses was chosen to bring redemption: (a) So that his prodigious gifts would not be lost "to himself, his people and the world"; (b) because he had not tasted slavery he was in a position to fully understand the meaning of freedom. Therefore, although Eastern Europe had produced great spiritual leaders, it was Herzl who was the right man for the mission for the same reasons: "Thus Herzl, of all people, like Moses in his time, was the one destined to carry out this historic liberation enterprise, which was of importance not only for our people but all of humanity."[46] Rabbi Chajes eulogized Herzl on numerous occasions and frequently employed this comparison to Moses.[47]

---

44 Eliash, *Zikronot tzioni merusia*, pp. 124–126.
45 Ibid.
46 Zvi Perez Chajes, *Besod ami*, Hasifria hatzionit, Jerusalem 1962, pp. 208–209.
47 Ibid., pp. 157, 223, 402.

German-Jewish philosopher Franz Rosenzweig finds in Herzl decisive proof of the historicity of Moses: "With Herzl alone one feels Jewish Antiquity ... Herzl is 'Moses and the Prophets.'"[48]

Herzl as Moses in Jewish Sermons

After reviewing the analogies to Moses in Herzl's day and after his death, let us look at a series of comparisons between the two that are homiletic in nature and a kind of commentary on both Scripture and Herzl's actions.[49] Obviously, we are not equating Herzl, who was avowedly secular, with the "prophet of the prophets," the supreme representative of the Jewish religion. However, for scholars well-versed in Judaic lore, these associations invariably sprang to mind when they encountered Herzl or heard about his character and deeds.

Age

According to the Midrash, Moses was forty years old when he went out to his brothers.[50] Herzl was thirty-five at the start of his Zionist journey, which began with his letter to Baron Hirsch in May 1895.

Education and Identity

> "And the child grew, and she brought him unto Pharaoh's daughter, and he became her son. And she called his name Moses and said: 'Because I drew him out of the water.' And it came to pass in those days, when Moses was grown up, that he went out unto his brethren, and looked on their burdens ..."[51]

Herzl attended a Jewish elementary school in Pest. At the age of eight, he joined the Hevra Kadisha burial society, which served at the time as the coordinator of local Jewish affairs, and at thirteen, he celebrated his bar mitzva in keeping with Jewish tradition. Later, however, under his mother's influence, he developed a

---

[48] Weisz, *A New Reading*, p. 112.
[49] Many of these comparisons have been noted by Golinkin, pp. 151–165, and Weisz, pp. 112–120.
[50] *Sifrei Dvarim*, chapter 357; *Exodus Raba* 1:27.
[51] *Exodus* 2:10–11.

love for German culture which grew even stronger when he moved to Vienna and became a student there.[52]

Humility

"Now the man Moses was very humble, above all the men upon the face of the earth."[53]

Herzl's humility is described by Max Nordau:

"Once, at lunch, in the company of Alexander Marmorek, I said to Herzl: 'If I were a religious man, a believer, and spoke in mystic terms, I would say that your appearance just as the Jews were experiencing the worst crisis in their history, is a sign of divine providence ... At this terrifying time, we needed someone, and then you arrived to bring hope to the desperate ... Herzl, whose modesty was so sincere and so natural, blushed and replied almost angrily: 'I beg of you, as someone who knows the value of language, do not speak like that! There is nothing at all special about my case, nothing out of the ordinary. If I were gone, there would be a hundred thousand others to choose from who could take my place, and they would continue in a straight line from the point where I left off'... What I did not want to envisage as possible at the time actually came to pass. Herzl died ... and there is not one person, let alone a hundred or a thousand, worthy of replacing him. He was unique."[54]

Mordechai Ben Hillel Hacohen relates that during the First Congress, while he was walking toward the Congress hall, a carriage caught up with him:

"Inside sat Herzl and Wolffsohn ... and Dr. Herzl invited me to join them in the carriage. With a show of outstanding courtesy, Dr. Herzl vacated his seat for me and he went to sit behind the driver. Naturally I protested and refused to sit there. 'But you are older than me,' said Dr. Herzl.

'First of all,' I replied, 'you are the chairman, and secondly, regarding the age difference I am not so certain.'

'But you are older than me in the art of loving Zion. You visited Eretz Yisrael twice,' said Dr. Herzl. Only after I insisted that today he was our king did he return to his seat, quietly protesting and sighing over the heavy burden of the royal crown."[55]

---

52 Bein, *A Biography*, p. 10.
53 *Numbers* 12:3.
54 Nordau, *Katavim tzioni'im*, vol. 2, pp. 174–175.
55 Mordechai Ben Hillel Hacohen, in: *Sefer hacongress* (1950), pp. 111–112.

Motivation

Given how the two leaders were raised, there was no logical reason for Moses and Herzl to devote themselves to the affairs of the Jewish people. However, both were clearly motivated by their sense of conscience: Neither could stand idly by in the face of injustice.

Moses could have continued to live comfortably in Pharaoh's palace, but his heart would not let him remain indifferent to the misery of the Israelites. The Midrash says: "He would see their anguish and weep, saying: 'I feel for your suffering. Would that I might die in your stead.' There was no harder labor than preparing mortar for bricks. He would pitch in and help each and every one of them."[56]

Golinkin draws our attention to seven verses in the Book of Exodus where Moses intervenes in fights in which he had no personal stake:[57] First, when he sees an Egyptian man striking a Hebrew, next when he sees two Hebrews fighting, and finally, when he rescues the daughters of Jethro from the Midianite shepherds.

Herzl, too, could have easily pursued his brilliant career at the *Neue Freie Presse* where he was celebrated as a cultural icon. What propelled him into action was his inability to sit on the sidelines when the Jews around him were in distress, even if he himself was not affected.

In a letter to his friend Arthur Schnitzler, he writes about his transformation, attributing it to the "terrible suffering of the people." "I have often wept over the misfortunes of my people," he wrote in his diary at the time.[58] "I confess to you that I have tears in my eyes as I write this," he confides to Rabbi Gudemann.[59]

Ahad Ha'am writes about two traits that distinguish the prophet from the rest of humanity: "First he is a man of truth ... and secondly, [he] is an extremist. From these two fundamental characteristics there results a third, which is a combination of the other two: namely supremacy of absolute righteousness in the Prophet's soul, in his every word and action."[60]

Moses sprang into action at the sight of an Egyptian striking a Hebrew and two Hebrews quarreling. Herzl, too, could not bear to see the humiliation of Jewish existence in Western Europe. In his play *The New Ghetto*, he puts his cry of pain in the mouth of the Jewish hero, who with his last breath reveals his will

---

56 *Exodus Rabbah* 1:27.
57 *Exodus* 2:11–17.
58 *Complete Diaries of Theodor Herzl*, vol. 1, p. 104
59 *Ibid.*, vol. 1, p. 111 (June 16, 1895).
60 Golinkin, pp. 158–159.

and testament: "Those who are not willing to fight for their honor will not be allowed to live in honor." It was this insight that set Herzl on his Zionist path.

Physical Appearance

To Jethro's daughters, Moses looked like an Egyptian (*Exodus* 2:19). Herzl, too, did not fit the stereotype of a Jew.[61]

The Plan

Moses tells Pharaoh: "Let my people go." His plan was to lead them out of bondage and transform them into a free people in their own land, Eretz Yisrael.[62] Visiting Baron Hirsch in June 1895, Herzl unveils a similar plan: "To the Kaiser I shall say: Let our people go! We are strangers here; we are not permitted to assimilate with the people ..."[63] In his diary, he writes: "I am leading [our people] to the Promised Land."[64]

The People's Response – Rebellion and Skepticism

The response of the Israelites in Egypt was colored by their slave mentality. They saw Moses as responsible for Pharaoh's decision to increase their work load,[65] and refused to believe his promise of divine redemption.[66] Right from the start, they began to complain: "Was it for want of graves in Egypt that you brought us to die in the wilderness? What have you done to us, taking us out of Egypt?" (*Exodus* 14:11).

The Jews of Europe reacted similarly to Herzl's ideas, with mockery in the best of cases and fierce opposition in others. Herzl's friend Friedrich Schiff was con-

---

[61] Michael Berkowitz, "Art in Zionism: Popular culture and Jewish national self-consciousness 1897–1914," in Ezra Mendelsohn (ed.), *Art and Its Uses*, New York: Oxford, 1990, p. 10.
[62] *Exodus* 5:1
[63] *Complete Diaries of Theodor Herzl*, vol. 1, p. 23.
[64] *Ibid.*, p. 64.
[65] *Exodus*, 5:21.
[66] *Exodus*, 6:9.

vinced Herzl had lost his mind.[67] The Viennese Jews ridiculed him,[68] and worried that Herzl was providing fodder for the European anti-Semites.

The skepticism of the Jewish community was also reflected in the response of Rabbi Gudemann, who initially supported Herzl but then changed his tune in the wake of pressure from the local leadership and published a pamphlet against political Zionism.[69]

In both cases, the Jews feared that they would suffer even more due to the actions of their leader and resisted. When Moses went to Pharaoh, the Egyptian monarch imposed an even greater burden on the Israelites, eliciting a wave of protest: "May the Lord look upon you and punish you for making us objectionable to Pharaoh and his courtiers – putting a sword in their hands to slay us."[70]

Herzl was accused of aggravating Turkish antagonism to Jewish settlement and prompting them to restrict immigration to Palestine.

Insurrection against Moses began from the earliest days of the exodus. Bowed by the hardships of the journey, some of the Israelites clamored to return to Egypt. Later, Korah and his followers led an uprising against Moses. While they were yet in Egypt, Moses asks God: "O Lord, why did You bring harm upon this people? Why did You send me? Ever since I can to Pharaoh to speak in Your name, it has gone worse with this people; yet You have not delivered Your people at all" (*Exodus* 5: 22–23)… "The Israelites would not listen to me; how then should Pharaoh heed me, a man of impeded speech!" (*Exodus* 6:12).

In the case of Herzl, the picture was not much different: In the early days, most of the community was not prepared to hear him out. Initially, the response of the Viennese community was very negative.[71] Even after Herzl's death, there were those who cast doubt on the purity of his motives and his sincerity.[72]

---

67 See pp. 160–161, 167, above.
68 See p. 165, above.
69 See pp. 162–164, above.
70 *Exodus*, 5:21
71 See remarks of Stefan Zweig, p. 167, above.
72 See, for example, Brainin's comments on Herzl's dream about Moses and the Messiah. Brainin wonders whether this was an actual childhood dream or Herzl had come up with it as they spoke. Observing the signs of premature aging on Herzl's face, he speculates that Herzl may have been feeling unwell and perhaps the story was an attempt, conscious or unconscious, to revive innocent childhood memories as death drew near. Brainin suggests this as a psychological explanation for Herzl's decision to write about scenes from his childhood in later years (see Brainin, *Hayei herzl*). Georges Yitshak Weisz finds Brainin's doubts about the authenticity of the dream hard to understand. He also sees Pawel's reading as tendentious and "quite absurd." According to Pawel, "Herzl gave a somewhat different account of the incident, according to which

The Plight of the Jews

Both Moses and Herzl recognized the necessity of swift action to address the plight of the Jews and this became the source of their strength. The Israelites in Egypt were immersed in "49 levels of impurity" (the 50th level is the lowest), as the rabbis put it: They were on a very low rung morally and spiritually, with almost no way out. It was imperative for Moses to save them before they became fully assimilated in Egypt.[73]

Herzl foresaw the impending doom of the Jews of Europe, and it was this sense of urgency and the need to act before it was too late that propelled him.

Unrelenting Pressure

Moses and Herzl both faced heavy pressure from the people and were advised to lighten their burden.

In the case of Moses:

> "... Moses sat as a magistrate among the people, while the people stood about Moses from morning until evening. But when Moses' father-in-law saw how much he had to do for the people, he said, 'What is this thing that you have undertaken for the people? Why do you act alone, while all the people stand about you from morning until evening?'... But Moses' father-in-law said to him, 'The thing you are doing is not right; you will surely wear yourself out, you as well as this people. For the task is too heavy for you; you cannot do it alone. Now listen to me. I will give you counsel ... You shall also seek out from among all the people capable men who fear God, trustworthy men who spurn ill-gotten gain; and set these over them as chiefs of thousands, hundreds, fifties, and tens. Let them bring every major dispute to you, but decide every minor dispute themselves. Make it easier for yourself and let them share the burden with you" (*Exodus* 18:13–22).

Herzl testifies to this phenomenon at the First Zionist Congress:

> "Everybody came to me for information about everything, important and indifferent. Four or five people were always talking to me at the same time. An enormous mental strain,

---

he had simply been led to believe that the teacher had made up the whole fantastic story of the flight from Egypt" (*Labyrinth of Exile*, pp. 12–13). Weisz also points out that Pawel "severed the link between Herzl's messianic dream and its relationship to the Exodus." Finally, he takes Pawel to task for associating between the dream and Herzl's unrequited love for Madeleine Kurz, as if the dream were some kind of compensation (Weisz, *A New Reading*, p. 109).

73 According to the Talmud, *Tractate Megillah* 9a, the period of servitude in Egypt was meant to last 400 years but was reduced to 210 because if the Israelites had stayed longer, Moses would no longer have been able to save them.

since everybody had to be given a definite decision. I felt as though I had to play thirty-two games of chess simultaneously."[74]

Seeing this, Herzl's friends Zangwill, Wolffsohn and Cowen proposed paying him a salary so he could leave his newspaper job and devote himself to the Zionist cause.[75]

Family Life

The family lives of Moses and Herzl were not strewn with roses. Moses eventually separated from his wife, and Herzl considered divorce early on in his marriage, even before the start of his Zionist quest. Neither circumcised their sons. When Eliezer, Moses' second son was born, the Midrash says that Moses did not circumcise him, which almost led to tragedy (*Exodus* 4:24–26). Herzl did not circumcise his son Hans. The offspring of these men did not continue in their fathers' footsteps, and the fate of their wives remains obscure. The Bible does not mention Moses' sons when counting the Israelites, and one of his grandchildren is implicated in a troubling case of idol worship.[76] The fate of Moses' wife Zipporah is also unknown.

Herzl's wife died three years after him. Paulina, his oldest daughter, died in a French sanitorium after a tormented life. Herzl's son Hans converted to various denominations of Christianity before returning to Judaism and committed suicide upon learning of the death of his sister. Herzl's youngest daughter Trude, who suffered from mental illness, perished in the Holocaust after being deported to Theresienstadt with her husband. Their son, Stephen (Neumann) Norman, the last scion of the house of Herzl, was found dead under the Massachusetts Avenue bridge in Washington D.C. a few days after receiving a letter that his parents had perished in Theresienstadt.

---

74 *Complete Diaries of Theodor Herzl*, vol. 2, p. 586.
75 Pawel, p. 517.
76 "The Danites set up the sculpted image for themselves; and Jonathan son of Gershom son of Manasseh, and his descendants, served the priests of the Danite tribe until the land went into exile" (*Judges* 18: 30). According to *Avot D'Rabbi Natan* 34:4, he was not the son of Manasseh but the son of Moses. However, because his deeds were unlike those of Moses, he was associated with Manasseh.

Personal Integrity

When it came to personal integrity, the people had more faith in Herzl than they did in Moses. The Midrash tells us that the Israelites spoke ill of Moses: "They would look at him from behind and one would say to the other: Behold his neck! Behold his thighs! He eats and drinks on our account. And his friend would answer: Fool! How could you expect the man responsible for building the Mishkan, in charge of bars of silver and gold, with no one looking over his shoulder to weigh or count, not be rich?" (Midrash Tanhuma, Pekudei, *Yalkut Shimoni, Exodus* 38: 415).

Moses was forced to defend himself: "I have not taken the ass of any one of them, nor have I wronged any one of them" (*Numbers* 16:15). Rashi, attuned to Moses' pain, explains: "I have not taken an ass from any one of them. Even when I went from Midian to Egypt with my wife and son, and could have taken one of their donkeys, I took only my own." In Rashi's reading, Moses is a man who refuses to take a penny from the public. Herzl says something similar: "True, I was fought and vilified from many quarters, but since even my worst enemies were never able to say of me that I sought or found material benefits for myself in this movement, I was able to bear these attacks with equanimity."[77] Elsewhere, he writes: "I ... have been pure of heart and utterly selfless in the Zionist cause."[78]

Beauty

Moses' physical beauty is mentioned in a number of sources. The Midrash states that Moses was so beautiful people could not take their eyes off him.[79] Philo of Alexandria describes him as a child of extraordinary beauty.[80] Josephus Flavius is even more effusive: "When he was three years old ... no one could be indifferent to his looks."[81] In *Antiquities of the Jews*, Josephus writes that "people who happened to meet him as he was borne along the road turned back at the

---

77 Weisz, *A New Reading*, p. 120, footnote 83.
78 *Complete Diaries of Theodor Herzl*, 3, January 24, 1903, p. 1202; in this context, it is worth recalling Herzl's indignant response when his friends offered to help cover expenses for his public activities.
79 *Exodus Rabbah*, 1:26.
80 Golinkin, p. 164, footnote 38.
81 *Ibid.*, footnote 39.

sight of the child ... For the vast and undiluted childish charm that enveloped him captivated those who saw him."[82]

We have already dealt at length with Herzl's beauty.[83]

Fate

> "You may view the land from a distance, but you shall not enter it" (*Deuteronomy* 32:52), God told Moses.

Herzl did not witness the Balfour Declaration, the 1947 UN vote or international recognition of the Jewish state, which he foresaw as the key to a better future for the Jewish people. He did not live to see the establishment of the State of Israel.[84] Yet his remains were reinterred in Israel and a national and military cemetery grew up around his gravesite in its capital city.

The frequent analogies between Moses and Herzl, made both by Herzl himself and those around him, back the contention that he found the comparison inspirational. It served him as a source of strength and fortified him against the difficulties that cropped up along the way, while cementing his status as a leader.

The Herzl-Messiah Analogy

Another figure that shaped Herzl's chosen path and influenced the way many Jews felt about him, for better or for worse, was the Messiah.

Messianism was a problematic issue for Zionism.[85] Herzlian Zionism was a Jewish national liberation movement whose goal was to redeem the Jews and take them to the Land of Israel. Messianic associations inevitably arose that triggered opposition in many parts of the Jewish world. The ultra-Orthodox rejected salvation in any earthly form, believing only in miraculous redemption by the

---

82 Josephus Flavius, *Antiquities II*, pp. 197–198 (English translation: L.H. Feldman, Judean Antiquities, 1–4 (Flavius Josephus, translation and commentary, 3, Leiden: Brill 2000). Although none of these testimonies were from people who lived in Moses' day, his admirers evidently considered it important to portray him as a handsome man since good looks were deemed vital for a leader.
83 See pp. 21–29 above.
84 Golinkin, p. 166.
85 Shmuel Almog, *Tzionut vehistoria*, Magnes Press, Jerusalem 1982, p. 42.

Messiah. Any human action to bring the Jews out of exile on a national scale was seen as a rebellion against God's decree and the oaths by which the Jewish people were bound.[86] On top of this were memories of Sabbatai Zvi and other false messiahs, deeply etched in the Jewish psyche, which made the Jews skeptical of any talk of messianic deliverance and redemption.

This collective trauma was not the preserve of the ultra-Orthodox. As early as 1881, Hibbat Zion leader Peretz Smolenskin warned Eliezer Ben-Yehuda against linking messianism and Zionism: "If you say that you are paving the road to the Messiah by your actions, both the faithful and the enlightened will rise up against you."[87] In 1896, we already have Yehoshua (Josias) Thon claiming that "from a historical standpoint, political Zionism is a continuation of messianism."[88]

The rise of Herzl and political Zionism in 1897 only sharpened the tension. Herzl's political Zionism was meant to solve the Jewish question in one fell swoop and on a large, public scale. This constituted all the hallmarks of a classic messianic movement, "both in its presumption of hastening the messianic era by human hands and disrupting the essential perfection of the vision of redemption."[89]

To his admirers, Herzl was an epic hero, the King of the Jews and Mashiach ben David.[90] His detractors used the same terms, but mockingly. Bernstein-Kogen, one of the ringleaders of opposition to Herzl, wrote sarcastically about the rabbis "demonstratively kissing the hand of the new Messiah."[91] Eulogizing Herzl, Rabbi Avraham Yitzhak Kook compared him to Mashiach ben Yosef, the first Messiah.[92]

The risks of linking messianism and political Zionism were clear to all, given the nation's bitter experience with false messiahs. Ahad Ha'am decried the messianic pretensions of the movement and accused Herzl of spreading dangerous illusions. He felt sure that Zionism could never meet the expectations being created. Ahad Ha'am also found Herzl's charisma troubling, and detected signs of

---

[86] Aviezer Ravitzky, *Haketz hameguleh umedinat hayehudim*, Am Oved, Tel Aviv, 1993, p. 33 (henceforth: Ravitzky, *Haketz hameguleh*).
[87] Almog, *Tzionut vehistoria*, p. 42, footnote 44.
[88] *Ibid.*, p. 43.
[89] Ravitzky, *Haketz hameguleh*, p. 29.
[90] Almog, *Tzionut vehistoria*, p. 43.
[91] *Sefer Bernstein-Kogen*, p. 22; *Tzionut vehistoria*, p. 46.
[92] In rabbinic sources, Mashiach ben Yosef appears in the final battle that will usher in the messianic age. He embodies the inevitability of crisis and defeat. He heralds the footsteps of the Messiah but is doomed to die in battle, paving the way for Mashiach ben David, who will bring the final salvation. See Ravitzky, *Haketz hameguleh*, p. 136.

messianism in the way he was adored by the masses. Almog points out the similarity between the concerns of Ahad Ha'am, a secular Jew, and the concerns of the ultra-Orthodox. Both were apprehensive about *dekhikat haketz* (attempting to hasten salvation) and creating illusions likely to end in despair. Nordau, cognizant of the danger, stressed that the leaders of the movement made no pretense that they could perform miracles and harbored no blasphemous thoughts in their hearts about being messianic or even "messiahs in miniature." "None of us profess to be the Messiah or the Messiah's helpmate," he insisted.[93]

Looking at the Herzl-Messiah analogy, it is worth considering what Herzl knew about the Messiah or heard from others on the subject. From the childhood dream discussed earlier, it is clear he was aware of the role of the Messiah in Jewish thinking. He recognized the folly of identifying the Zionist movement as messianic and himself as the Messiah, although he often encountered people who saw in him traits of the Messiah.

When Herzl visited Palestine at the end of 1898, the analogy came up several times. Moshe Smilansky describes how a group of Sephardi Jews received him in Rehovot: "Two of them, elderly men, approached Herzl, got down on their knees, bowed their heads and blessed him, kissing his footprints in the sand. Herzl unnerved, backed away. 'This is how one greets Mashiach ben Yosef,' one of the men explained."[94]

But there were those who detected in him the hallmarks of a Sabbatai Zvi. On March 29, 1896, Herzl recounts how he sat at a Passover seder next to a man "who reminded me of Sabbatai Zvi, who enchanted all people, and winked in a way that seemed to say that I ought to become such a Sabbatai. Or did he mean that I already was one?"[95] Reflecting on the possible parallels between him and Sabbatai Zvi, he wrote:

> "The difference between myself and Sabbatai Zvi (the way I imagine him), apart from the difference in the technical means inherent in the times, is that Sabbatai made himself great so as to be the equal of the great of the earth. I, however, find the great small, as small as myself."[96]

Herzl worried about being branded a false messiah. He wrote about this after meeting with the King of Italy, "... Then, all at once, we found ourselves talking about Sabbatai Zvi, whose story he knew well...Next he spoke of messiahs (with

---

93 Almog, *Tzionut vehistoria*, p. 44.
94 *Malki betzion*, p. 114.
95 *Complete Diaries of Theodor Herzl*, vol. 1, p. 317 (March 29, 1896)
96 *Complete Diaries of Theodor Herzl*, vol. 3, p. 960 (June 11, 1900}

understandable roguishness), and asked if there were still Jews who expected a Messiah ... And to his amusement I also told him how in Palestine I had avoided mounting a white donkey or a white horse, so no one would embarrass me by thinking I was the Messiah. He laughed."[97]

Herzl knew of the danger from Bernstein-Kogan, who cautioned him: "Your name is on everyone's lips as if you were a saint. They are all waiting for you to perform wonderous deeds."[98]

On the other hand, we have a series of testimonies from people outside Herzl's immediate circle who were in awe of him and his messianic grandeur.[99] Itamar Ben-Avi, for example, describes the impression he made on Jerusalem residents who saw him walking around the city: "Herzl strolling [through the streets] was a sight to behold ... It was like a messianic spectacle unfolding before our eyes."[100]

Alongside the Zionist enthusiasts who equated Herzl with the Messiah, there were others who shied away from such comparisons, which they viewed as exaggerated and likely to end in disillusionment. Those who pushed the messianic image of Herzl most of all were the Zionist lecturers and preachers. The low level of religiosity of these local and itinerant preachers worried the Zionist leadership, lest they detract from the prestige of the movement. As Ehud Luz tells us: "The preachers had a great deal to do with fostering the messianic aura that surrounded Herzl... There were *mattifim* who went so far as to say that 'Herzl and Nordau are our true messiahs.'"[101]

H.D. Horowitz also dwells on this: "Zionist preaching is a way of raising our hopes and increasing faith in our leaders ... It overstates the greatness of the leaders and portrays them as veritable giants and angels. Herzl is almost the Messiah in miniature."[102]

Of course, this idea also had opponents outside the movement, among the Haredi rabbis, for a start. Associating between Herzl and the Messiah was a threat to the Haredi view of exile and redemption, so it was an analogy that

---

97 *Complete Diaries of Theodor Herzl*, vol. 4, pp. 1598–1599.
98 Y. Klausner, "Hatnu'a hatzionit bebesarabia," in: *Yahadut Bessarabia*, eds. Y. Koren and B. Michali, Khevrat entziklopediya shel galuyot, Jerusalem, 1971, p. 540.
99 Avraham Solomiak (1863–1943), a Bilu member and head of the Russian post office in Jerusalem, reminisces about his conversation with Herzl in Jerusalem: "From here to there, the conversation turned to the Old Yishuv. I told him about Safed, the birthplace of Kabbalah, and about Tiberias... I mentioned there were some in the Yishuv who regarded him as Mashiach ben Yosef...Herzl listened very intently," *Malki betzion*, p. 175.
100 Itamar Ben Avi, in: *Malki betzion*, p. 153.
101 Ehud Luz, *Parallels Meet*, p. 121, p. 316, note 50.
102 Dr. Hayim Dov Horowitz in: *Luah Ahiasaf*, 1903, pp. 118–119.

they invariably rejected. Paradoxically, it came as a relief to rabbis that Herzl did not fit the image of a utopian Messiah due to his not being a practicing Jew. David Yeshayahu Silberbusch tells the story of a Hungarian rabbi, a disciple of the Hatam Sofer and an anti-Zionist, who was visiting his son in Frankfurt and was convinced by him to join him at the Third Zionist Congress in Basel:

> "On the day after their return from Basel, [the Hungarian rabbi] was visited by Dr. Mordechai Halevi Horowitz, rabbi of the Orthodox community in Frankfurt, who had studied at Pressberg Yeshiva with him. Dr. Horowitz rebuked his friend for allowing himself to be persuaded to attend this 'assembly of Jewish criminals.' Dr. Horowitz heaped scorn and ridicule on Max Nordau, evoking his sin of taking a gentile wife, while the Hungarian rabbi listened in stony silence, not batting an eyelash. But the moment he began to insult Herzl for his laxness in religious observance, the elderly man, tall, broad-shouldered and elegant despite his years, leapt to his feet as if bitten by a scorpion, drawing himself up to his full height, lifting his right hand and roaring like a cascading waterfall: 'By the holy sparks of my beard I vow to praise the Lord of Israel seven times a day that Herzl does not observe Torah and mitzvot. For if, heaven forbid, he did, I would be roaming the streets and shouting from the rooftops that he and no other is the Messiah.' And what was it that he said? Did you really hear such things from him? It was not that I heard such things, replied the aged rabbi in a quavering voice, as if scared by his own words. It was what I saw in him myself."[103]

Reuben Brainin brings a similar anecdote from the First Congress:

> "A group of rabbis went to see Herzl to find out more about the man. They came out overjoyed. Asked to explain, the rabbis replied that Herzl had said he did not intend to observe the mitzvot. So why rejoice? 'Well, if Herzl says he will not observe the mitzvot, it means he does not wish to be seen as the Messiah, but only the leader of a political movement.' For the rabbis, this was a great relief."[104]

After his death, many touched on the analogy between Herzl's life and work and the Messiah. At a memorial for Herzl in June 1927, Zvi Perez Chajes observed:

> "The Danish poet Geijerstam wrote in one of his books that Moses was able to view the whole of the Land of Israel only because he had convinced God to act on his dream of settling the Israelites in the Land of Israel. If Moses had not succeeded in bringing the Israelites to this land, he would have had to return them to the desert, and then perhaps they would have become a nation of bandits. Woe to us, if Herzl's idea does not come to fruition. The Jews have sensed the reality of Herzl's dream. Woe to us, I repeat, if Herzl's dream

---

103 Silberbusch, *Mepinkas zikhronotai*, Tel Aviv, Hapoel Hatz'air, 1936, pp. 247–249.
104 Shmuel Almog, "The secular attitude toward religion and pious Jews in the early Zionist era," *Sugiot betoldot hatzionut vehayishuv*, p. 37.

should go up in smoke and leave the same emptiness as that of Sabbatai Zvi in his time ..."[105]

In conclusion, as we saw in his comparison to Moses, it was likely that Herzl recognized the resemblance between his role and the role of a messianic redeemer. It was an awareness that came to him early on, in a childhood dream. At the same time, he understood the dangers of being perceived as a messiah, especially a false one, and took pains to avoid this kind of negative association. Nevertheless, the similarity of his mission and identification with the role of the Messiah no doubt strengthened him and made it possible for him to withstand the difficulties that came his way.

Herzl as a Biblical Figure: An Iconographic Comparison

In the first chapters of this book, we dealt at length with Herzl's appearance, also touching on iconography.[106] Below we will focus on comparative iconography, looking at the portrayals of Herzl as opposed to Moses and other biblical heroes.

Herzl was painted, photographed and drawn by numerous artists in many different styles. Hermann Struck and Boris Schatz chose to present him gazing into the distance, projecting farsightedness, vision and willpower. Herzl comes across in their renderings as larger than life, a kind of figurehead for the national goals of Zionism. Ephraim Moses Lilien, whose multidimensional personality came through in his art, depicted Herzl in a more complex manner. He photographed and drew Herzl so many times, there were those who saw him as the "official illustrator" of the Zionist movement. Lilien was a member of the Democratic Fraction and disagreed with Herzl in the debates over culture and Uganda. However, like many others, this opposition did not diminish his admiration of Herzl as a leader. He publicly applauded Herzl's diplomatic achievements, such his meetings with the Turkish Sultan and the German emperor, and was proud of Herzl's good looks.[107]

---

[105] Zvi Perez Chajes, *Speeches and Lectures*, Rabbinical Assembly, Boston 1953, p. 169.
[106] See pp. 58–61 above.
[107] Milly Heyd, 'Lilien: Between Herzl and Ahasver,' in: R. Wistrich and G. Shimoni (eds), *Theodor Herzl: Visionary of the Jewish State*, Hebrew University, Magnes Press, Jerusalem, 1999, p. 272. Lilien had a privileged relationship with Herzl, to the point where some say Herzl even let him photograph him in the nude. See: Gideon Ofrat, *Al ha'aretz: Ha'omanut ha'eretz yisraelit*, vol. 1, Yaron Golan, Tel Aviv, 1933, p. 166.

The famous portrait of Herzl on the balcony in Basel was taken by Lilien. It conveys his attitude toward Herzl and his view of Herzl as an embodiment of the "new Jew," similar to the works of Struck and Schatz. However, aside from this photograph, he created many works in which Herzl looks like a character out of the ancient Orient.[108] In 1902, Lilien drew "The Creation of Man" using Herzl's features for Adam. In 1908, he was commissioned to illustrate the Bible and the New Testament. Herzl appears three times as an angel, once as Jacob and twice as Aaron the priest. He also turns up as Joshua, King David (or Solomon) and King Hezekiah, and as Moses kneeling before the Burning Bush, smashing the Tablets of Law, and hovering between heaven and earth holding the Ten Commandments.

In his illustrations for *Songs from the Ghetto* by Morris Rosenfeld,[109] Lilien uses Herzl for his portrayal of Adam in the Garden of Eden and the angel who appears before Balaam and his ass. In his stained-glass windows for the B'nai Brith hall in Hamburg, he depicts Moses with the face of Herzl.[110]

Conclusion

Even before he published *Der Judenstaat* Herzl recognized the importance of Moses and his role in collective Jewish memory. From the start of his Zionist journey, people around him compared him to Moses, which seems to have cemented the association in his mind and led him to cast himself in this role to some extent.[111]

Herzl presumably saw the analogy as a source of inspiration and commitment. It enabled him to tolerate the suffering and fierce criticism that came his way in the knowledge that this was the way the people of Israel were, and this was how they treated their leaders. Like Moses, he was willing to pay a personal price for his leadership.

There were two dimensions to the analogy between Moses and Herzl:
(1) the capacity of the leader to assess the situation from an outside perspective and take action;

---

[108] Heyd, p. 265; Golinkin, p. 152.
[109] Songs from the Ghetto, Morris Rosenfeld, illustrations by E.M. Lilien, in: Heyd, illustration 4.
[110] Golinkin, p. 152; Heyd, p. 293.
[111] Rosenberger, p. 15.

(2) the capacity of the people to see him as their leader and bow to his authority. Both dimensions were applicable to Moses and Herzl. Moses did not grow up as a slave and having the mentality of a free man helped him in his stand-off with Pharaoh. Herzl was largely unfamiliar with Jewish experience in East Europe and how the Jews of the East differed from those of the West. In fact, this worked to his advantage when he turned to world leaders in the name of the entire Jewish people.[112] In both cases, the majority accepted the authority of the leader, despite resistance and insurrection, and in the end, paid everlasting tribute to him.

The rabbinic lore and sermons cited above attest that the schemes of Moses and Herzl, which did not seem possible or realistic at the time, succeeded in the long run, but required self-sacrifice. It was an outcome that would seem to back up those who believe in the power of the lone individual to change the face of history.

---

[112] Ussishkin noted this after their first meeting, and said it was fortunate that Herzl knew nothing about the "wars of the Jews," otherwise he might have despaired from the start. See *Sefer Ussishkin*, p. 353.

Chapter 12
"Akhrei Mot Kedoshim Emor" ("Speak Well of the Dead")

> "Few men may truly be said to be epochal. Within our millenary of Jewish history not more than four men may so be styled – Maimonides, Spinoza, Mendelssohn, Herzl."[1]

Was Herzl a Legend in His Lifetime?

We have dwelled at length on Herzl's character and the personality traits that enabled him to change the course of Jewish history in the span of less than nine years. Some of the testimonies to Herzl's greatness were published during his lifetime and others posthumously. This leads us to new questions.

Question 1: Who was the real Herzl? With so much adulation, which of these accounts tell the truth about Herzl and solidify his reputation as a legend in his own time, and which constitute hagiography? Which follow the dictum of "*akhrei mot kedoshim emor*,"[2] the custom of speaking well of the dead, to the point of over-glorification or meting out higher praise than is warranted which is liable to have the opposite effect.

Question 2: Was Herzl's untimely death a great loss for the Jewish people or had he already reached the pinnacle of his leadership ability and done all that he could do, so that death only saved him heartache?

Question 3: How is historic memory created? When is it faithful to reality and when is it not? To answer this, we will look at observations about people who have gone down in history as giants and consider why they are remembered this way.

And finally, Herzl's life was strewn with errors of judgment. We will look at them more closely and assess how they affected his strength as a leader.

So, to begin, was Herzl a legend in his lifetime?

From the testimony below, it seems clear that the answer is yes. Avraham Ludwipol,[3] who covered the First Zionist Congress as a journalist and confessed that he was not a blind follower of Herzl, attempted to explain the man's mystique:

---

[1] Dr. Stephen S. Wise, in: *Ha'olam*, no. 31, July 30, 1929.
[2] An aphorism stringing together the names of three consecutive *parashot* in the Book of Leviticus but used to mean "Speak only praise of those who have died."
[3] See p. 37, above.

"Although I was not overly enthusiastic about the man himself, it was impossible for me to ignore the secret power he wields over the masses. The very fact that he has attracted hundreds and thousands of admirers aroused in me a sense of awe and respect. I searched his face again and again, looking for the source of this great power. There was no question we were beholding a unique historical spectacle. The delegates of one of the most stiff-necked peoples in the universe, emissaries of a nationality least likely to surrender to authority, stood in the presence of a mighty force imbued with an iron will, perhaps without even realizing or understanding that they were captivated and all but enthralled by this power."[4]

This is all the more striking when one considers that Ludwipol's boss at *Hashiloah* was Herzl's adversary Ahad Ha'am, who did not stop him from publishing this paean of praise and portraying the Congress as a "unique historical spectacle."

Then we have Dr. Hillel Yaffe's letter to Ahad Ha'am on November 16, 1898, immediately after Herzl's visit to Palestine:

"On a hot summer's day, we all assembled in the great hall at Mikveh Yisrael – administration, teachers and students. Herzl's entourage arrived, followed by Herzl, towering and majestic, his measured but mighty words leaving the audience enchanted. You cannot imagine the excitement. He won everyone over. After that we drove to Rishon Lezion. The administrator in Rishon, an executive of the Alliance Israelite Universelle, a short fellow contemptuous of Zionism and Herzl, was taken by surprise and had not managed to escape before Herzl and his party walked in. Within minutes, he too was converted, swept up in the general enthusiasm. All of Rishon was roiling. Cries and cheers pierced the air. Old and young squeezed together to get nearer and see Herzl ... The Kaiser shook his hand. At that moment, it mattered little what they said, but the crowd was seized by excitement, pride and fulfilment. Herzl had grown in their eyes."[5]

It seems safe to assume that Hillel Yaffe knew what Ahad Ha'am thought of the First Congress and Herzl in particular.[6] So the fact that he wrote to Ahad Ha'am about Herzl's success in captivating and impressing his audiences would also seem to back up the contention that Herzl was a living legend.

Dr. Y. Sapir collected testimonies praising Herzl as the founder of the Zionist Congress and published them in a book that came out in Herzl's lifetime. He quotes Mordecai Ben-Ami:

---

4 Avraham Ludwipol, "Memories from the First Congress," in: *Luah Akhiasaf*, 1903, p. 56.
5 Hillel Yaffe, *Dor hama'apilim: Zikhronot, yomanim, mikhtavim*, Ministry of Defense, Tel Aviv, 1983, pp. 36–37.
6 For Ahad Ha'am on the First Zionist Congress, see p. 125 above.

"Herzlian political Zionism also created the Congress, of which there had never been the like in majesty and scale in the 1,800 years of our dispersion, and whose future importance one cannot even begin to imagine."[7]

Sapir also brings this observation from Israel Zangwill:

"The vision of the Prophet Ezekiel has come true in our day. The dry bones, consumed by rot, have joined together from all the places where they were scattered ... breath has entered them, making them live again and stand upon their feet ... Our people are no longer the wandering dead. [The poet Heinrich] Heine portrayed the Jew as accursed, living in the body of a dog and returning each week to his beloved Sabbath Queen. The magic of the Congress has even outdone the magic of the Queen. It has shown the whole world the gloriousness of the Jew."[8]

Sapir then goes on to add thoughts of his own:

"Until now, everyone thought of Hebrew congresses as a fantasy and an impossible dream, but now they have become a reality.[9] A few words here about the celebrated man of many deeds whose name invariably comes to our lips whenever the subject is political Zionism – Dr. Herzl, of course. We can rightly say that our movement exists thanks to this exceptional human being, the personification of power and grace. Like a sea captain dedicated to skillfully steering his ship to safety, Dr. Herzl is known by one and all as the greatest and most acclaimed leader of the Zionist movement...Dr. Herzl is the man who has accomplished a historic feat that will be remembered in generations to come for bringing the idea of national resurrection, contemplated for thousands of years in the misty upper realms, down into the real world ... His unstoppable pace, his fearlessness and courage in the face of all the obstacles on the way to his goal, his feisty defense of his views and opinions, entrenched like an iron wall, and then, recently, his decision to back down and accept the will of the majority for the time being – all these qualities make Herzl, the leader of the Hebrew national movement, a character unique beyond compare ... If our people, in these times of distress, is capable of producing individuals like Herzl, then we have no reason to despair. Our future is assured."[10]

We also have testimony from contemporaries of Herzl who were active in the Zionist Organization and wrote about him after his death.

Ussishkin, who was known for his bluntness, delivered a eulogy for Herzl in praise of his accomplishments despite their bitter feud over Uganda. Thanks to Herzl, he said, the Jews had a flag, a national parliament in the form of a congress, a bank and the Jewish National Fund. He did not stop there:

---

7 Y. Sapir, *Hatzionut*, Vilna, Shraga Feivel Garber, 1903.
8 *Ibid.*, p. 135.
9 *Ibid.*, p. 134.
10 *Ibid.*, pp. 139–140.

"[Herzl is our] national political hero. Over the generations, our nation has been rich in heroes, but these heroes in the Diaspora have always been heroes of the spirit, great in piety, in ethics, in art and science. We did not have national heroes ... And then Herzl's light shone upon us. We have not had a political hero so dynamic and venerated by the people since the days of Nehemiah. He became a beloved symbol in our days of renaissance, the hero without which no nation could paint its political masterpiece."[11]

The same was true for Herzl's veteran opponent, Dr. Jacob Bernstein-Kogan,[12] who minces no words about Herzl's shortcomings in his memoirs but then goes on to sing his praises:

"I saw in him a superhuman, a powerhouse who could turn the wheels of Jewish history. So I indulged him, I watched over him, I took note of his every move, guarding against any reckless deviation that could adversely affect the future of the Jewish people. Even though I openly fought against him, I am certain that if he were alive we would have worked together until today, shoulder to shoulder but still quarreling from time to time. Herzl's glory is sealed in my heart forever. His character, courage and beauty remain alive in my memory, exuding sublime radiance."[13]

In his recollections of the Sixth Congress, Littman-Rosenthal of Bialystok describes how Dr. Joseph Chazanovitz, who assembled the core collection of the Jewish National Library, fell under Herzl's spell. In a chapter entitled "Farewell to Herzl," he writes:

"I remember that after the vote, when we were all miserable and depressed, I could not find the late Dr. Chazanovitz, who had been at my side throughout the entire Congress ... I was feeling anxious and went to look for him in his room. There I found the young-old fighter-dreamer lying in bed, a cold compress on his head and two hot water bottles at his feet, feverish, his face pale as death.
    I asked him: 'Dr, what is wrong?' and he replied: 'Littman, I am sick!' As I presume you know, I went to see Herzl some time ago. He asked me to come a number of times, but I refused. You know I cannot bear to be in his midst. When he looks at me, a kind of electric current runs through my whole body. The third time he sent me a note and invited me to come see him – here it is (at which point the speaker took the note, brought it to his lips and kissed it) – I felt compelled to go. As I approached the Congress hall, Herzl was already waiting for me. He came towards me, grabbed me with two hands and said in that enchanting voice of his: 'Dr. Chazanovitz, you, the veteran Palestinian who has devoted his whole life for the past decades to the ideal of Eretz Yisrael, how could you have voted yes?...' Under his gaze my heart ripped to shreds. I could barely stand on my feet and stood there mute. At that moment Herzl embraced me in his delightful, supple arms as if he were

---

11 *Sefer hacongress* (1923), p. 24.
12 Jacob Bernstein-Kogan (1859–1929), see p. 201, above.
13 *Sefer Bernstein-Kogan*, p. 123.

a mother speaking to her child: 'Tell me darling' ... I voted for your proposal because my faith in you is infinite. Even if you are wrong, which I do not believe because you are our leader ... you will lead us with God's help to victory. That is why I voted yes ..."[14]

In her memoirs, Myriam Schach[15] describes the aura of the early Congresses in which she herself took an active part:

"But the special atmosphere that prevailed in the hall, can anyone bring it back? Can anyone restore to life that wonderful audience, so passionate and wracked by pain? Those who have never experienced in the flesh the hushed silence that fell in the hall which had buzzed like a beehive, those who have never seen with their own eyes an audience of three or four thousand holding its breath in awe and anticipation, can they ever understand ...[16]

The speech with which Herzl inaugurated this 'national theater' was so new for us, so exciting, that we felt we were living in some wonderful dream. We were afraid of falling back into the real world when we woke up. But even outside, in the non-Jewish world, the impact was profound... It was like the unanticipated ring of a bell with a powerful new sound."[17]

Nordau applies the principle of "inverse perspective" to Herzl:

"In the case of an ordinary person, the laws of sight apply: The further one moves away in time and space, the smaller the image of the person and hazier his contours. However, the dimensions of a genius only expand: The more time that passes, the greater and more brilliant he appears, and the more pronounced his features. This is the wonderous phenomenon we see in Herzl. Is there anyone who still doubts that he was a genius of the kind that Jewish history produces only once in hundreds of years?"[18]

Rabbi Meir Bar Ilan and Rabbi Binyamin (Yehoshua Radler-Feldmann), both born in 1880, were young men in Herzl's day. Hence their observations offer insights about how he was perceived during his lifetime.

Rabbi Bar Ilan maintains that Herzl was the stuff of legend even before he died. He defines the criteria for true greatness and shows that Herzl fit the bill:

"True personal greatness is often discernable in figures who are perceived as legends in their own time. While they are in the company of people who see in them virtues and shortcomings like any human being, they are still treated as extraordinary – not as a human being but as a chapter in history. This was so for Herzl. He was already enveloped by legend

---

14 *Ha'olam*, no. 31, July 30, 1929, pp. 602–604.
15 Myriam Schach (1867–1956).
16 Schach, *Et asher itam halakhti*, p. 23.
17 *Ibid.*, p. 32.
18 Rabbi Meir Bar Ilan, "A legend in his lifetime," in: *Mevolozhin ad yerushalayim*, Committee for the Publication of the Writings of Rabbi Meir Bar Ilan, Tel Aviv, 1971, pp. 337–349.

when he was young, healthy and strong. At least he was thought to be healthy and strong. When it was revealed that Herzl was ill, no one believed it. It was hard to believe that this man, who was not only the source of life but resurrection, could be ailing! In the mind of the people, Herzl was walking history, not an ordinary person. How could he be sick, let alone critically ill? Had they not just seen and heard that Herzl had made a whirlwind visit to a number of Jewish towns and gone all the way to St. Petersburg, with people talking, or whispering, to be more precise, about what an extraordinary expedition it had been? Everything that Herzl did and wherever he went, be it Constantinople or Jerusalem, Rome or London, was interpreted as *Pardes (pshat, remez, drash, sod)*. It was well known that his trip to Plehve in St. Petersburg was physically and emotionally trying, but he had withstood all the hardship, so how could he be unwell?...That was Herzl's strength – in life and in death it was felt that he had the power to save the Jewish people like no one else. All the time he spent in talks with the sultan and the pope, with Wilhelm and Plehve, no one asked about the expediency of his endeavors or from whence he drew the courage and strength to approach these leaders on matters that nobody before him had ever succeeded in raising.

This created a sense that with Herzl we had something to look forward to. Without Herzl we were all helpless. For the great mass of Jews who believed in Zionism, the feeling in their hearts about Herzl was not of his being a great leader, superior to others. It was what little children feel for their fathers. He could do what no one could do, and when Herzl died, we were left orphans."[19]

Rabbi Binyamin says something similar.[20] In a column published to mark the arrival of Herzl's remains in Israel in 1949, he writes that the "miracle of Herzl," which included his retreat from assimilation, his activism on behalf of political Zionism and his devotion to the cause, created a "star that would forever shine in the heavenly constellation of the Jewish people."[21] It was Herzl the man who launched the process in which Zionism burst from its narrow confines and ended in the founding of the State of Israel … All these things were apparent while Herzl was still alive."[22]

So it is evident from the above testimonies, both those written in Herzl's day and those written posthumously, that he was a legendary figure in his lifetime, which answers our first question. Now let us turn to the second question: Was Herzl's premature death a loss to the Jewish people, or had he already maximized his potential before he died and was thereby saved future grief?

Examining a large body of writings and eulogies, we discerned three different approaches:

---

19 *Ibid.*
20 Rabbi Binyamin (1880–1957).
21 Rabbi Binyamin, *Shivat zion*, vol. 1, p. 352.
22 *Ibid.*, p. 347.

a) Outpourings of grief by friends and admirers, among them Stefan Zweig, Mordecai Ben-Hillel Hacohen and Yeshayahu Zlotnick, which express shock and sorrow, and portray Herzl's demise as a profound loss;
b) Responses that mourn Herzl's loss because of what the Jewish people might have gained had he lived longer, as in the responses of Rabbi Binyamin and Moshe Glickson;
c) Tributes or eulogies in which Herzl's death is hailed as the pinnacle of his life, a theme which also runs through the writing of contemporaries who were not active in the Zionist movement, such as Shaul Tchernichovsky, David Frishman and Ahad Ha'am. Subscribers to this approach include admirers who were awed by Herzl's accomplishments but felt his job was over (such as Martin Buber), and those who thought he had reached the end of his road and living longer would have been tragic, both for Herzl personally and the Zionist movement (such as his trusted friend Max Nordau).[23]

Approach A:

After Herzl's death, Rabbi Reines declared: "May heaven be my witness, the death of our leader has left me depressed and may send me to my own deathbed."[24] In a bulletin he put out, he wrote: "The Zionists weep, as do all people with a heart and all knowledgeable people the world over."[25]

In his memoirs, Rabbi Meir Bar Ilan writes in the same spirit: "In Herzl's case the saying 'speak no ill of the deceased' was not relevant because even in his lifetime he was judged favorably at a time when others would be severely criticized. One would have to be deserving indeed for everyone to speak of him so highly."[26]

The writer Stefan Zweig, who was not a member of the Zionist camp, describes a chance encounter with Herzl a few months before his death.[27] Herzl invited him to visit him at his home:

---

[23] Nordau, *Katavim tzioni'im*, vol. 3, pp. 101–105.
[24] Reines, *Ish hame'orot*, p. 239, footnote 45.
[25] Ibid.
[26] Bar Ilan, *Mevolozhin ad yerushalayim*, p. 310.
[27] On the one hand it was hard for Zweig not to join the Zionist camp, if only because Herzl had been the first to support him as a writer, but the fanaticism and ill-will with which Herzl was treated by members of the Zionist movement and the lack of obedience put him off. See Zweig, *The World of Yesterday*, p. 106–107.

"I promised him, firmly determined not to keep that promise, for the more I love someone, the more I respect his time.

But I did go see him after all, only a few months later ... and now I could accompany him only to the cemetery. It was a strange day, a day in July, and no one who was there will ever forget it. For suddenly people arrived at all the Viennese railway stations, coming with every train by day and night, from all lands and countries; Western, Eastern, Russian, Turkish Jews – from all the provinces and small towns they suddenly stormed in, the shock of the news of his death still showing on their faces. You never felt more clearly what their quarrels and talking had veiled over – the leader of a great movement was being carried to his grave. It was an endless procession. Suddenly Vienna realized that it was not only a writer, an author of modern importance, who had died, but one of those original thinkers who rise victorious in a country and among its people only at rare intervals. There was uproar in the cemetery itself; too many mourners suddenly poured like a torrent up to his coffin, weeping, howling and screaming in a wild explosion of despair. There was an almost raging turmoil; all order failed in the face of a kind of elementary, ecstatic grief. I have never seen anything like it at a funeral before or since. And I could tell for the first time from all this pain, rising in sudden great outbursts from the hearts of a crowd a million strong, how much passion and hope this one lonely man had brought into the world by the force of his ideas."[28]

Mordechai Ben-Hillel Hacohen describes the general mood following Herzl's death:

"Many families named their newborn sons after the great leader, using his first or last name, all desirous of commemorating the House of Herzl ... Attending the Eighth Congress, I searched in vain for traces of the Divine Presence that had hovered over the First Congress. It had departed, and I never again had the desire to participate in these congresses. That much I knew: Herzl was gone ... the heart aches even now, decades later."[29]

Rabbi Yeshayahu Zlotnick (1892–1943) writes about his feelings and the response of those around him when Herzl died:

"My boyish heart was so small it could hardly contain the sorrow, but upon reaching the *beit midrash*, I was inundated with questions about news of the war. These were the days of the war between Russia and Japan, and I was the only subscriber to *Hatzfira* in our town. Gloomy and depressed, I stood and listened to their questions: Are the Russians still in retreat?...I replied in a weak voice: Brothers! I have no news for you today. But you should be aware that a great calamity has befallen us: Dr. Herzl, president of the Zionists, has died! I raised my head slightly and tears filled my eyes ... How angry I was to see not a trace of sadness clouding their faces. In my fury I made some angry remarks and rushed out of the *beit midrash*, loudly slamming the door behind me... I wept profusely ... The one Zionist in town, an old medic with whom I would discuss these issues, came to

---

28 Zweig, *The World of Yesterday*, pp. 108–109.
29 Mordechai Ben-Hillel Hacohen, *Olami*, vol. 3, Eretz Yisrael Publishing, Jerusalem, 1927, p. 199.

mind: Moshe Ya'akov, a short fellow with a big belly and broad shoulders famous all over the Galilee for his 'medical expertise.' Entering his house, I found him cutting the hair of an old farmer. He had already done half his head. Upon hearing the terrible news about Herzl's death, he threw up his hands and cried loudly *'barukh dayan ha'emet'* ['Blessed be the true judge']. Then he sat with me on the sofa, groaning and moaning. Meanwhile, the old farmer recovered from the shock of this puzzling scene and demanded that the 'doctor' finish his haircut because he had to get back to work. But Reb Moshe Yaakov did not move, gently appealing to him in a pleading voice: 'I can't, my friend. A terrible tragedy has befallen us.' The farmer, who thought the doctor had gone crazy, began to holler, scratching his pate and protesting that he would be a laughingstock if he went out with his head half shorn. But all his threats and pleas were useless. Reb Moshe Ya'akov refused to comply and the farmer was forced to leave the house in despair, huffing and cursing."[30]

Zlotnick writes about traveling to a small town to deliver a eulogy to members of the local Zionist society. As the audience gathered at the *beit midrash* and he began his talk, a group of Hasidim suddenly burst in:

"They began to heckle me because in their opinion my talk violated the sanctity of the place. Heading the group was the old town rabbi, an honest and upright man, whose participation in this protest had not been easy for the Hasidim to secure. Leaning one hand on the *bima* in the center of the *beit midrash* where I was standing, he asked me gently, without the least sign of anger in his face: 'My young friend, the Sages teach that "there is nothing that is not alluded to in the Torah." If so, is Herzl in the Torah? Where does it hint in the Torah that the Zionist movement is permissible, and most importantly, where does it imply that Herzl will appear and become head of the Zionists?' Armed as I was with all the evidence and allusions in rabbinic lore that could grant Zionism legitimacy, I answered in a voice full of confidence: 'Yes, Rabbi, there is a clear allusion to Herzl in the words of our sages (*Bava Batra* 17a): Four died only because of the snake [due to Adam's sin]: Benjamin son of Jacob, Amram, father of Moses, etc … What virtue did our sages find in Benjamin son of Jacob that he is singled out as one of those who died without sin? In my opinion this is a reference to Benjamin son of Jacob Herzl, the leader who gave his life for the people of Israel … Look at his labors and sacred work, now terminated on the altar of love for the Jewish people. That is why the legend says he only died because of the snake!' When I finished speaking, I looked up at the rabbi … Zionism was awarded a kosher stamp and from then on, no one tried to interfere" (*ibid.*).

Approach B

Then there were those who saw Herzl's untimely death as a loss and believed that he would have accomplished great things for the Jewish people if he had lived. Rabbi Binyamin subscribed to this approach:

---

30 *Ha'olam*, no. 29, 1935, p. 459.

"There is room for listing all the achievements of the Herzl miracle in the nine years [of his Zionist journey] and its significance, but it is also legitimate to explore latent possibilities that might have unfolded if had he lived a normal lifespan, let's say another thirty years."[31]

Rabbi David Neumark, who initially opposed Herzl and then changed his mind, wrote:

"While Herzl was alive, I did not fully appreciate the historic significance of the man, but upon hearing the news of his sudden death, I sensed the magnitude of the loss to us all. At the same time, I felt that his death signified the end of a great enterprise ... [He was endowed with] an outsize historic personality, towering above his generation, projecting splendor, luminescence and glory ... I was an eyewitness to a new historical creation, one of global stature and historic grandeur of the highest degree."[32]

In 1917, when the Balfour Declaration changed the course of events, Moshe Zvi Glickson lamented Herzl's absence:

"A special feeling, a sense of pain, fills our hearts this year on the 20th of Tammuz, the day on which the founder and head of the Political Zionist Organization, Dr. Theodor Herzl, left our ranks.

The opportune moment that Herzl so yearned for has arrived ... What seemed like a fairy tale to him and to all of us is now nearing reality. Global events have made the Zionist question timely and the doors on which Herzl knocked to no avail are now opening as if by themselves.

The first thought that comes to mind on this day of remembrance is this: Oh, if only Herzl were among us ... In these times we sorely need the skills of the first Jewish diplomat who showed us how to conduct Hebrew politics to promote the welfare of the Hebrew nation and its historic homeland."[33]

Approach C:

The responses and eulogies implying that Herzl's death came at the right time can be sorted into a number of sub-categories:
- Ahad Ha'am was critical of Herzl during his lifetime but foresaw that he would become a legend after death and hence a blessing for the Jewish people.

---

31 Rabbi Binyamin, *Shivat tzion*, vol. 1, pp. 347–353.
32 On David Neumark, see pp. 124–125; *Sefer hacongress* (1950), pp. 174–175.
33 Moshe Zvi Glickson, *Kitvey M. Glickson*, vol. 1: "Zionist personalities," Hava'ad lehotza'at kitvey glickson, Dvir, Tel Aviv, 1939, p. 35.

- David Frishman and Shaul Tchernichovsky praised Herzl's lifetime endeavors but regarded his death in mid-life as a blessing in the belief that a longer life would have ended in failure.
- Buber and Nordau were involved in the Zionist enterprise and also thought the timing of Herzl's death was fortuitous. Buber felt that Herzl had reached his peak, while Nordau feared harm to the Zionist movement if it continued on its path without Herzl while he was still living.

Ahad Ha'am did not pretend to mourn. He mocked the "'crocodile tears' shed in an orgy of sanctimonious grief by people for whom Herzl had been an obstacle in the path of self-promotion."[34] Kadish Yehuda Silman[35] remembers Ahad Ha'am's response to the news in real time:

> "Unfortunately, I was the one who had to inform Ahad Ha'am of our leader's death (he was staying for the summer at the residence of Mordechai Ben-Hillel Hacohen, not far from my town). Ahad Ha'am was taken aback for a moment and then remarked: 'Good timing. Now he will be crowned a legend.'"[36]

A few days after Herzl's death, Ahad Ha'am wrote to Ben-Hillel Hacohen:

> "Herzl is dead! Who would have thought that a man so full of life and energy would die so soon? Happy was the man in life, and also in death. For truly he reached the limit. He did all he could – and died 'at the right time.' The life and deeds of this man over the past seven years were the stuff of fiction. If some great writer had written a story like this, he too would have 'killed off' the hero after the Sixth Congress [the Uganda Congress – M.F.]."[37]

In the introduction to the third volume of his book *Al parshat drakhim* ("At the Crossroads"), an anthology of all the articles he wrote for *Hashiloah*,[38] Ahad Ha'am shares his view that the Zionist movement had shrunk since Herzl's death:

> "because no matter who comes to take his place, his place can never be filled. Personal conviction is not inherited, and it is not acquired by majority vote. Without the hypnotic

---

34 Pawel, *The Labyrinth of Exile*: p. 530.
35 Kadish Yehuda-Leib Silman (1880–1937) a Lithuanian-born linguist, was one of the founders of Tel Aviv and the Beit Hakerem neighborhood of Jerusalem.
36 K.Y. Silman, in: *Ha'olam*, no. 31, July 30, 1929, p. 609.
37 Ahad Ha'am, *Iggrot ahad ha'am*, vol. 3, Yavne and Moriah Publishing, Jerusalem and Berlin, 1904, p. 186.
38 Introduction to "Al parashat drakhim," vol. 3, in: *Kol kitvey ahad ha'am*, pp. 249–251.

influence of the sole individual who could exert it, the eyes of the masses will open to see things as they are."³⁹

To Ahad Ha'am political Zionism was an illusion nourished by Herzl that would not survive without him. He accused those lamenting Herzl's death of competing with each other over who could wail louder and sail farther in flights of fantasy.⁴⁰

As for himself, he says: "I have no intention of adding my tears to the same sea. Lord knows how much of it is just a wave of 'cold water' noisily sweeping through the Diaspora."⁴¹ But even Ahad Ha'am could not ignore Herzl's singularity: "Even without the fairy tales, our 'dearly departed' has plenty left to commend him as an extraordinary man."⁴² He stands in awe of what Herzl was able to achieve:

> "To launch such a large movement, no matter how superficial or high-pitched, within such a short time, could only be accomplished by a man with the spark of those one-of-a-kind miracle workers who surface on rare occasions and forcefully forge a new path. For those who oppose the ideas and deeds of the departed leader, like myself, the miracle is so much the greater: Because this one man has been able to entrench in the heart of the masses a powerful belief in that which is beyond nature and logic, and persuade a stiff-necked, long-suffering people to follow him to wherever the spirit takes him, with closed eyes, even when an abyss separates between what he sees and they see ... History has known such men, who are endowed with all the virtues and flaws needed to control the minds of the masses and are capable of turning worlds upside down with their personal power, winning over the crowd without our being able to say how."⁴³

However, Ahad Ha'am is careful to temper his praise, and was thus among those who disparaged Herzl even in the midst of tribute. Ahad Ha'am portrays Herzl's power as hypnotic, and the phenomenon of people flocking after him as pseudo-messianic, alluding to Shabbetai Zvi. Herzl's accomplishments could only have been achieved by one of those rare individuals endowed with a special spark of genius who arise in every nation, he wrote. That being so, the hypnotic spell would dissipate once Herzl was gone because his power was personal, not "passed down." Now people would be able see the truth. Following this line of thought, a dead Herzl was thus more beneficial to the Jews than a live Herzl:

---

39 *Ibid.*, pp. 250–251.
40 *Ibid.*, p. 249.
41 *Ibid.*
42 *Ibid.*
43 *Ibid.*, p. 250.

> "The departed leader will become a great driving force, perhaps more so than when he was alive. People of this kind have two faces…: As living beings they are only powerful for the short length of a human lifetime … However their true power and historical significance lies not in themselves and their actual deeds but in the ideal they come to represent in the imagination of the people, who see in their heroes what their heart desires … Herzl the living man – one could have had many misgivings about what he said and did. Those who refused to close their eyes to the truth were forced to strongly oppose him at times and protest the strategies he employed. But Herzl the portrait of perfection now being created before our eyes – how splendid he will be, and how great his power to influence the people once more … As days go by and the ideal face of the 'national hero' receives its finishing touches, perhaps [Herzl] will be for the Jews of our generation what the ancient heroes of the nation were for our forefathers in times of yore."[44]

In the introduction of *Al parashat drakhim*, Ahad Ha'am contemplates Herzl's contribution:

> "We do not know yet if Herzl's deeds – bringing us the Congress, the [Zionist] Organization, the bank, the 'Jewish National Fund' – are of value. It all depends on whether they endure … But Herzl gave us something unconsciously that may be of greater importance than what he gave us consciously: He gave us himself as the theme of a 'hymn of resurrection' … in which he is transformed into a Hebrew national hero embodying our national aspirations in their truest form."[45]

Some time later, in a letter to Joseph Klausner dated October 16, 1905, he writes:

> "I will not conceal from you that I am watching how matters develop in the Zionist Organization without sentimentality. You know from my introduction to the third volume of *At the Crossroads* that I do not believe in 'messianism.' Now that the 'messiah' is dead, Zionism is gradually liberating itself from its messianic delusions."[46]

Frishman and Tchernichovsky were also in the "praise and damn" group. They deliver emotional eulogies for Herzl but at the same time disparage him. Frishman's brief lament is a kind of prose poem in which the poet cites Herzl's prodigious gifts but also counts his death as a blessing:

> "Even his death, however sad, was a gift to the man and his people. Why? It was not so much spoken as felt … After nine years of activity, Herzl had reached a peak. If he had lived longer, he could not have climbed higher and descent was inevitable. Death came

---

44 *Ibid.*, p. 251.
45 *Ibid.*
46 *Iggrot ahad ha'am*, vol. 3, pp. 210–211.

and saved him, sparing both him and us from this difficult sight. So Herzl's death in his prime was ultimately a beautiful gift from the Divine to the chosen one and his people."[47]

"*Le-ven ha'agada*" ("To the man of the legend"), a poem by Shaul Tchernichovsky, touches on a similar theme:

> "You were our song, a thousand years intoned Sung by the people, a festive prayer enthroned Who would have thought it, wonder of wonders In our dark airless attic, foreseeing only thunder!... In death, too, that came fortuitously in life's prime You walked before the tribes, ahead of your time. At an hour wholly yours, in a dream-cloud enshrined ..."[48]

The adulation of Herzl by the poets seems to have been related more to their recognition of Herzl as a phenomenon than to personal sentiment. However, there were some Herzl allies who felt that Herzl had gone as far as he could, and the time had come for him to take a bow and leave the stage. In this sense, his death had come at the right hour. Buber and Nordau belonged to this category.[49]

Martin Buber shares his thoughts on the death of Herzl in a letter to his wife, Paula:

> "... You have certainly heard of Herzl's death; the funeral is tomorrow. It came so terribly unexpectedly and incomprehensibly. Yet for him it was the finest time to die – before all the inevitable disappointments and descents, still at the summit. What shape the movement will take from now on cannot yet be foreseen. But it is hard even to think about that, so deep is the shock from a human perspective."[50]

In 1910, Max Nordau decries the misfortune of the Jews at having lost the man who could deliver them from their misery. Summing up Herzl's accomplishments from the age of 36 (the start of his Zionist journey), he writes: "From this point on, the plot moves forward in giant steps, from one spectacular scene to the next, from one surprise to another, until a sudden drop of the curtain brings all the glorious action to a halt."[51]

Nordau goes on to list Herzl's achievements one by one, and concludes:

---

[47] Rabbi Binyamin, *Shivat tzion*, vol. 1, p. 348.
[48] *Ha'olam*, July 30, 1929, no. 31, p. 606.
[49] Nordau, *Katavim tzioni'im*, vol. 3, pp. 101–105.
[50] *The Letters of Martin Buber*, ed. Nahum Glatzer and Paul Mendes-Flohr, Knopf Doubleday Publishing, 2013, letter no. 57, July 6, 1904. Soon afterwards, Buber quit the Zionist movement on the grounds that "With Herzl, the *grand seigneur*, it was possible to come to an understanding.; it is impossible to deal with these pompous nonentities" (Pawel, *The Labyrinth of Exile*, p. 530).
[51] Nordau, *Katavim tzioni'im*, vol. 3, pp. 101–105.

"With his mental power and skill, he quashes the insurrection in his camp, heals the rift caused by the offer of Uganda, or Nairobi to be more exact, and readies himself for a new battle, but then, all of a sudden, the thread of his life snaps, ending the historic drama."[52]

In the next breath, however, Nordau observes that after all the accomplishments, the time had come for the Zionist Organization to settle into a routine, and Herzl, had he lived, would have had to do so, too. Herzl himself doubted that the coming days could ever top what had gone before:

"He had the feeling that the grand deeds were winding down and after all the thunder and lightning ... a quiet period of routine work was approaching ... Fear crept into his heart over the implications of a change of pace in the Zionist movement, knowing as he did that the Jews were a restless people, eager for excitement and thrills ... Sometimes, when his mood was low, due in part to his health, but mostly because of the thoughts alluded to above, he began to despair of his mission altogether and felt his leadership role was over."[53]

Guided by these sentiments, Herzl showed a small circle of close friends the outline of a speech he intended to deliver at the Seventh Congress, announcing his resignation. Nordau writes about their response:

"We managed to prove to him that what he was dreaming of was impossible. Herzl still alive and not the head of the Zionist movement? Herzl exclusively a journalist and a playwright, far from the Zionist movement goes on its way without him, far from the congresses that proceed in his absence? Such a scenario was unthinkable. But if such a thing did come to pass? Here an anguished cry erupts from my breast: How fortunate are we that death prevented a breakdown in Herzl's relationship with Zionism."[54]

After reviewing the thinking of these different groups, let us try to understand where they were coming from.

According to Shulamit Laskov, Ahad Ha'am's response to Herzl's death was consistent with his attitude towards him throughout his lifetime. Ahad Ha'am was a ruthless critic of Herzl both in public and private, lambasting the movement he founded and the leadership model he adopted. He was convinced that Herzl's path would destroy Zionist aspirations.[55]

Alex Bein also detects a personal slant in Ahad Ha'am's remarks, a carryover of his feelings from when his nemesis was alive. To Bein, Ahad Ha'am's response

---

52 *Ibid.*
53 *Ibid.*
54 *Ibid.*, p. 103.
55 Laskov, *Hayei ahad ha'am*, p. 234.

reflected a sense of triumph over the dead and satisfaction over "the lion's downfall."[56] He holds that Herzl's death came as a relief to Ahad Ha'am and those of his camp who joined in the mockery of Herzl opponents who posthumously sang his praise. "God knows how much of their tears are nothing but cold water," he wrote.[57]

Bein is convinced that Herzl's death freed quite a few individuals from the shackles of personal rivalry and dominion that kept them from developing views and aspirations of their own. Every force has an opposing force, he explained, and if one of those forces is an extraordinarily powerful one, it will necessarily repress many of the weaker forces – i.e., people whose views did not align with those of Herzl. With Herzl's death, they were able to carve out a path for themselves.[58]

Rabbi Binyamin describes Ahad Ha'am as a "bitter rival and harsh critic" of Herzl who saw political Zionism as the deluded ideology of a false messiah and worried that disaster lay in store if the masses followed him.[59] Commenting on the "tributes" of Frishman and Tchernichovsky, Rabbi Binyamin asserts that they were never pro-Herzlian but merely "high and mighty literati" watching from the sidelines. Therefore, their eulogizing of Herzl and depiction of his early death as a blessing was just a way of fishing for something good to say about him.[60] While neither were active proponents of political Zionist movement or personally influenced by Herzl, they were admirers of Ahad Ha'am and his teachings. Nordau's reason for calling Herzl's premature death a blessing was that it had prevented a schism in the Zionist movement.

Finally, we need to understand why those who shared in the euphoria of the Zionist Congresses and admired Herzl even when they disagreed with him might nevertheless consider his death timely. Bein's explanation is that Herzl could not have gone on as he had since 1897, with his authority badly eroded by the Uganda affair and facing a widening circle of criticism that could be expected to grow.[61]

Like Nordau, Bein estimates that political Zionism still had a long wait ahead: In 1904, the Ottoman Empire was crumbling but nobody could put a time estimate on it.[62] If opposition to Herzl increased, as Bein supposed, Herzl

---

56 Bein, *Biografia*, p. 411.
57 Al parshat hadrakhim, *Kol kitvey*, p. 249.
58 Bein, *Biografia*, p. 411.
59 For more on Ahad Ha'am and Herzl, see pp. 184–185, 206–208, 217–218, 224–230, 259–260.
60 Rabbi Binyamin, *Shivat tzion*, vol. 1, p. 345.
61 Bein, *Biografia*, p. 412.
62 Ibid.

would have had to change course and settle for practical work in Eretz Yisrael, just as he had agreed to early land acquisition efforts and the opening of a branch of the Jewish Colonial Trust in Jaffa.[63]

This contention is puzzling. Where did the idea come from that Herzl thought Zionism had entered a routine and humdrum stage from which he might as well retire? Herzl's diplomatic overtures continued even after the Uganda Congress, almost up to the day he died. From his relentless endeavors in this sphere it seems clear that he believed in his chosen path, and had he lived longer, there is a good chance his efforts would have borne fruit.

Herzl's flurry of activity towards the end of his life would seem to back this up. On September 11, 1903, a few days after the Congress, Herzl wrote to the German ambassador to Vienna, Philipp von Eulenberg, explaining that he had meant to write for the past two weeks but had not done so due to heart trouble. In the letter, he requests von Eulenberg's assistance in gaining Germany's support for a charter in Eretz Yisrael.[64] In reference to England's promise of territory in British East Africa, he writes: "Yet we stubborn Jews are more attached to the sand and chalk of Palestine ..."[65]

On September 13, he sent Ernest von Koerber[66] a copy of his letter to Plehve requesting Austrian support for the political endeavors of the Zionist movement.[67]

On December 11, 1903, Herzl sought an audience with the Austrian foreign minister and replied to the letter he had received from Plehve on December 6 informing him that the Russian ambassador in Constantinople had received orders to take diplomatic action in favor of Zionism in Russia and Constantinople. Herzl wrote to say that in his opinion, only the public intervention of the Tsar would be effective. He also submitted a request to open a branch of the Jewish Colonial Trust in Russia.

Around the same time, Herzl wrote again to Izzat Bey[68] asking him to look into the matter of a charter for Palestine. Upon the signing of the charter, Herzl promised to pay him 10,000 pounds. On January 17, 1904, he set out for Italy to meet with the king, Victor Emanuel III, who was considered a supporter of Zionism and interested in making his acquaintance. However, a chance en-

---

63 Ibid.
64 *Complete Diaries of Theodor Herzl*, vol. 4, pp. 1557–1558.
65 Ibid.
66 Ernest Koerber (1850–1919), prime minister of the Austrian portion of the Austro-Hungarian empire, was a friend and supporter of Herzl.
67 *Complete Diaries of Theodor Herzl*, vol. 4, pp. 1561–1562.
68 Second secretary of the Sultan, Abdul Hamid.

counter in Venice with Berthold Dominik Lippay, an Austrian portrait painter, opened the door to an even more exciting possibility: an audience with the Pope. On January 22, 1904, Herzl met Cardinal Rafael Merry del Val, Secretary of State of the Vatican, and three days later he was received by the Pope.

In the interim, Herzl met with the King of Italy. At all these meetings he asked his hosts to use their influence in Russia and Constantinople to help him secure a charter for Jewish settlement in Palestine. During this period, Herzl maintained a correspondence with Dr. Yitzhak Levy from which we learn that Herzl embarked on a "a gargantuan effort on behalf of Eretz Yisrael" from November 1903 to March 1904. The letters make mention of Herzl's bitter dispute with the Hovevei Zion, who favored practical work, and his dealings with the Democratic Fraction, which criticized his political program on a daily basis. The fiercest battle of all arose over Herzl's Uganda proposal at the Sixth Congress. There is no doubt in Levy's mind that the vitriol published in the Zionist press for and against Herzl shortened the illustrious leader's life:

> "I am now publishing letters written by Herzl which prove that he was being attacked from all sides over the impracticality of his vision for Eretz Yisrael, yet even when he proposed Uganda as a *Nachtasyl* [an emergency shelter] for the oppressed Jews, his heart never strayed from Eretz Yisrael ..."[69]

Levy offers a detailed description of his correspondence with Herzl, which ended on March 14, 1904. All the endeavors he enumerates attest to the fact that Herzl never ceased his diplomatic activity or lost faith in his ability to carry out his plan.

The argument has been put forward that no one could predict when the Ottoman Empire would fall so that Herzl had no horizon of expectations. Yet Herzl already foresaw the collapse of the Ottoman Empire in 1897, before the First Congress, and recognized the need to prepare for the day when the Jews could lawfully establish a Jewish state in Palestine. Littman-Rosenthal recounts a conversation in Basel in the days before the Congress, where he had come to interview Herzl at Rabbi Samuel Mohilever's behest. Herzl was open about his plans:

---

[69] Yitzhak Levy, "What nobody knows about Herzl," in: *Hed Hamizrah*, 15, January 14, 1944. Levy is certain these letters were never published because Herzl had become wary after his assistants and friends failed to protect his privacy and made a point of writing confidential letters by hand. None of Herzl's biographers, including Bein, de Haas and Adolf Friedman, knew about this exchange of letters in 1903–1904, shortly before Herzl's death, on the subject of large-scale settlement in Eretz Yisrael which Levy compares to "a second edition of *Altneuland*."

"'Our object is to enter into contacts with the Turkish government ... We will explain that the Hebrew nation has more to offer the Turks than the Turks have to offer us ... If Turkey is not interested or does not understand us, our work will not cease. We shall seek other paths. The question of the East is now looming. Sooner or later, it will end in a quarrel. A European war in the near future is inevitable.'

I began to smile. Herzl studied me with his mesmerizing eyes. 'An ironic smile, sir?' he said. 'You do not have much faith in what I say, but a great European war will erupt, of that I am sure ... With my watch in hand, I await that calamitous moment! After the great war in Europe, a global peace conference will convene. We, the representatives of the Jewish people, must be prepared. The countries of the world will have to admit us to the Great Council of Nations ... We shall prove that the question of the Jewish people is not a matter of this or that country. It is a global problem which only a global solution can resolve, and the solution is to restore the Land of Israel to the Jewish people. Once that is done, the Jewish question will leave the stage."[70]

As the state of the Ottoman Empire did not seem to be improving since that conversation, Herzl presumably thought his political solution would soon be relevant. His policy was never to allow obstacles to stand in his way. If one door closed, Herzl would search and find another. He never gave up, methodically moving ahead a step at a time. He worked tirelessly for two years to build up a relationship with the Grand Duke which finally landed him an audience with the German Kaiser in Palestine. He also spent years paving the way for an invitation to Russia. Herzl worked around the clock, oblivious to his health. He knew he was endangering himself, but nothing stopped him.[71] He foresaw the horrifying future that lay in store for European Jewry[72] and a sense of calling[73] drove him to do all he could to save his people.

It has been argued that Herzl reached the end of his career in the wake of the Uganda affair, which seriously eroded his authority. There is no question that Herzl lost some of his cachet at the Uganda Congress: He was maligned by radicals who spoke out in a way that no one would have dared at preceding congresses.[74] However, the argument that Herzl's days were over is far from correct. In the vote on whether to send an expedition to Uganda, 292 delegates voted in

---

[70] *Sefer hacongress* (1950), p. 193.
[71] See article of G. Sil-Vara in which he recounts a conversation with Herzl. "You must not work so hard – you will kill yourself," Sil-Vara warned him, to which he replied: "I *will* work, until I kill myself." "At Herzl's Grave: The Burial of the Leader – and Other Memories," *Theodor Herzl – A Memorial*, ed. Meir Weisgal, New York 1929.
[72] He predicted the Holocaust. See *Shivat tzion*, vol. 1, p. 350.
[73] See comparison to Moses, pp. 290–294.
[74] On Trietsch and Nossig, see pp. 185–187; also see the accusations of treason by Yehoshua Buchmil, p. 257.

favor (among them many who were against the Uganda proposal and hence their vote constituted a vote of confidence in Herzl).[75] Together with the 143 delegates who abstained (largely to avoid challenging Herzl), they constituted an absolute majority. A total of 176 delegates voted no. The results of the vote were thus a faithful reflection of the thinking in the Zionist movement, and Herzl's prestige was not harmed to the point where he could no longer continue his work.

Even the bitter post-Congress fight between *Tzionei tzion* (Ussishkin supporters) and the defenders of the Histadrut (Herzl supporters) was not specifically attributed to the disintegration of Herzl's authority. Bein describes the establishment of "Committees for the Defense of the Congress, or of the Organization," with the "larger half opposed to the Kharkov group."[76] Among the Kharkov rebels themselves there were quite a few who opposed Uganda but not Herzl himself, such as Chlenov and Goldberg, who were anxious to end the dispute while preserving the unity of the Congress under Herzl. The fact is that Herzl succeeded in convincing the mutineers[77] and restoring their belief that Eretz Yisrael was, and remained, his foremost concern. So why should we doubt that had Herzl been healthy he would have continued his diplomatic efforts?

From here, let us move on to those who saw Herzl's premature death as a loss:

According to Rabbi Binyamin, the idea that Zionism would have taken on a different shape and form if Herzl had lived goes back to Herzl's sense that the ground was burning under the feet of the Jews of Europe: "Amid all the nonchalant members of the Zionist movement, he was the only one who predicted the Holocaust!"[78]

Indeed, two of Herzl's prophecies came true: the war between the European powers and the Ottoman Empire (World War I) and his conviction that the State of Israel would come into being when it ended.

Rabbi Binyamin felt that in view of these two prophecies, it was perfectly legitimate to reflect on what Herzl might have done. In hindsight he is probably right. Herzl, who foresaw a great calamity in store for the Jews, would likely have acted differently from the other Zionist leaders, "who did not see the Holocaust coming and almost refused to believe it when it did."[79] Rabbi Binyamin speculates that Herzl would have used all his skills and contacts to head off the disaster and find a refuge for millions of Jews. For all we know, he might

---

75 Dr. Chazanovitz, see p. 317.
76 Bein, *Theodor Herzl: A Biography*, p. 488.
77 With the exception of Ussishkin. See pp. 238, 259, 271–272.
78 Rabbi Binyamin, *Shivat tzion*, vol. 1, p. 350.
79 Ibid.

have succeeded. Wouldn't it have been possible for Herzl to achieve even more than the Balfour Declaration owing to his ties with the British government? Is it far-fetched to think that he might have phrased the British Mandate to ensure that the greater part of Eretz Yisrael would become the Jewish national home, or that he could have kept the British from watering down their great promise to the Jews, especially since they were the ones who approached Herzl on the subject of Uganda?

One presumes that Herzl would have been successful in convincing the world at large, and England in particular, of the urgency of finding a solution to the Jewish problem. After all, he foresaw the threat to the Jews of Europe. If he had been alive in the 1930s and 1940s, it seems likely he would have used his clout with the British government to keep the gates of Palestine from being closed to European Jews seeking refuge.

We will conclude with the third question: Who was the real Herzl? How is historic memory created? When is it true or not true to life, and why?

The difficulty of assessing Herzl's true character is noted by Daniel Gutwein in his study of the re-construction of Herzl's image in Israeli collective memory.[80] Gutwein does not discuss Herzl's positive or negative qualities but rather how he has been remembered over time and the reasons behind it. He talks about "collective memory" and explores the distinction between "historic truth and archaeological truth." His claim is that collective memory obscures the authentic Herzl and idealizes him. He attributes this to a process in which the ideals of a nation change over time and create a new collective memory of its heroes.[81]

The implication is that the Herzl of "collective memory" is not necessarily Herzl as he was in real life. Gutwein divides the evolution of Herzl's image into three stages: up until the 1970s; from the 1970s to the 1990s; and from the 1990s into the 21st century.

Before the 1970s, there were two perceptions: one, the official Zionist narrative, which enjoyed national consensus, and two, the narrative of other ideologies which appropriated Herzl's doctrine as if it were an authentic component of their thinking.[82]

This appropriation by other ideological streams ultimately led to a distorted picture. Throughout his life, Herzl sensed that he was being misrepresented and misquoted.[83] In his book, Berl Katznelson decried this misreading of the Herzl

---

[80] Daniel Gutwein, "The reconstruction of Herzl's image in Israeli collective memory: From formative radicalism to adaptive fringe," in: *Iyunim betkumat yisrael*, vol. 12, 2002, p. 3.
[81] *Ibid.*
[82] *Ibid.*
[83] See p. 336.

story,[84] and Herzl himself wrote, in connection to Uganda, that "the wildest statements have been freely indulged in ... Nothing could be further from the truth."[85]

Nahum Sokolow protests this perversion of Herzl's image after his death:

> "It is painful to watch the Herzl legend being turned into a doormat... for that is the tragic outcome of the distorted image that has stuck like a 'skin' ... Is there no one left who knew our first leader? Has the time already come to neuter Herzl's life and character?"[86]

Benzion Netanyahu complains about ideological opponents of Herzl, like the socialists, who spoke day and night about following in his footsteps when Herzl flatly rejected socialism and often said so publicly.[87]

Weisz discusses this phenomenon, alleging that it was part of an effort to tear Herzl down and defame him.[88] By way of example, he cites Katznelson's lament that Herzl's image was being manipulated "by malice or by ignorance."[89] He sees the argument over Herzl's height as part of the same trend.[90] According to Weisz and others, many have tried to hitch Herzl to their ideological bandwagon even when this is clearly unjustified.[91]

1970s – 1990s

In the 1970s, perceptions of Herzl began to change in the wake of Amos Elon's bestselling biography of the Zionist leader.[92] Gutwein claims that this biography reflected modern currents in the historical study of Herzl, but also precipitated a new era in which the spotlight began to shine on Herzl as a person. "The broad reception of this new image of Herzl was mainly a product of changing values in Israeli society in the 1970s and 1980s," he writes.[93]

---

84 Katznelson, *Bekhevlei adam*, p. 68.
85 Weisz, *A New Reading*, p. 206.
86 Sokolow, *Hatzofeh levait yisrael*, p. 411; also see the disagreement over Herzl's height, pp. 32–35.
87 Netanyahu, *Khameshet avot hatzionut*, pp. 866–867.
88 Weisz, *A New Reading*, pp. 6–17.
89 Weisz, *A New Reading*, p. 23.
90 See pp. 32–33.
91 See p. 336.
92 See p. 32, footnote 48, Getzel Kressel's review of Elon's biography.
93 Gutwein, *ibid*.

1990s Onwards

The 1990s were marked by the decline of official narratives, growing sectoral gaps and privatization. Collective memory also underwent certain changes. On the 100th anniversary of the publication of *Der Judenstaat* and the First Zionist Congress, post-Zionists on both sides of the political spectrum hailed Herzl as their ideological father.[94] As Gutwein observes, historic figures are sometimes assessed differently over time, but these assessments tend to align more with the ideology of the assessor than the figure in question.[95] While he warns against ideological opportunism, i.e., appropriating a historic figure for the purpose of glorifying an ideology that is essentially foreign to that person, he offers no objective criteria for determining how authentic the portrayal is, thereby leaving the door open for creating a persona that serves an ideological purpose.

Rabbi Meir Bar Ilan does specify objective criteria: True greatness, he says, is found in those who are already perceived as legendary in their own day. In this respect, Herzl fit the bill.[96] I Historian Ben-Zion Dinur (1884–1973) bases his study of greatness in what he terms "historic personalities" on two components: how the historic personality is evaluated by coming generations and how the historic personality and his generation fit into the sweep of Jewish history. For Dinur, it is important to compare the legend to reality, examine the actions of the person in the context of his own era, and identify the different strands of the legend.[97] He believes that scrutiny of two illustrious figures in the modern Jewish world – the Ba'al Shem Tov and Herzl – can offer important insights in this regard: "The legend of the Ba'al Shem Tov is the only historical reality we know, whereas the historical reality of Herzl has become the legend."[98]

For Dinur, a historical personality is (a) someone whose actions and influence go beyond the norm and become his claim to fame; (b) someone whose impact is perceptible outside his immediate surroundings; (c) someone who is personally involved in fomenting a change; (d) someone who is famous among his contemporaries and whose name continues to be cited in future generations.

Herzl appears to answer all four criteria. So how can we tell if what we know about these figures is true? How does one separate fact from fiction? Dinur claims that the legend surrounding a historic personality is an integral part of that personality. One is reflected in the other. With the passage of time, facts

---

[94] Gutwein, *ibid*.
[95] Gutwein, p. 62.
[96] Rabbi Meir Bar-Ilan, in: *Mevolozhin ad yerushalayim*, pp. 306–308.
[97] Ben-Zion Dinur, *Binyamin ze'ev herzl: Al ha'ish, darko udmuto, khazono upo'alo*, Masada, Ramat Gan, 1968, p. 12 (henceforth: Dinur, *Herzl*).
[98] *Ibid*., pp. 9–13.

that do not serve the legend become hazy, so that the blanks and missing links are filled in with the help of imagination. In this way, legend sometimes creates the reality, and the hero's life becomes a projection and rounded out version of the legend. Applying these established criteria to Herzl, we see that if the historical truths about Herzl's personality gleaned from his actions are combined with testimony about his life and work, the outcome is a realistic picture of him.

That Herzl was truly great is also borne out by Dinur's comparison between the historical giants of Israel and the rest of the world. He argues that the Jewish people was the product of a national religious ideology and emanated from the idea that the individual belongs in a collective. Abraham, in fulfilling the divine commandment to "get thee out of thy country, and from thy kindred, and from thy father's house," leaves his natural habitat and joins up with others who willingly come together to form a new people. It is not frameworks and organizations that steer the ideology but persons of stature. Since then, figures of this kind have been highly influential in Judaism.

Dinur points out that organizational ideology played a crucial role in Jewish history of Israel, and its historical giants throughout the generations have been intellectuals and thinkers.[99] At the same time, not all Jewish leaders have exerted a long-term influence. In looking for those whose impact has spanned generations, Dinur finds only three: Rabbi Saadia Gaon, Maimonides and Herzl. One senses that all three were of "their generation," but they also left an indelible personal stamp on the Jewish world of their day, and their actions have continued to have influence on future generations. There is no denying that they were extraordinary and exceptional.[100]

On the 25th anniversary of Herzl's passing, Dr. Stephen S. Wise told a mass assembly of Jews in London:

> "Few men may truly be said to be epochal. Within our millenary of Jewish history not more than four men may be so styled – Maimonides, Spinoza, Mendelssohn, Herzl ... Theodor Herzl was epochal because he had dared to bid the Jew to be what, for nearly two millennia, he had not dared to be – a Jew .... In pre-Herzlian days, the Jewish questions were asked by others – by non-Jews ... The Jews listened and obeyed. Herzl asked ' What will we do?' and provided the Jewish answer with a capital J."[101]

---

99 *Ibid.*, p. 13.
100 *Ibid.*
101 *Ha'olam*, no. 31, July 30, 1929, p. 603.

Herzl's triumphs were both conceptual and political.[102] The political track initiated by Herzl led to the Balfour Declaration and then the UN vote and the establishment of the State of Israel.[103] The criteria established by Dinur and Bar Ilan seem apt in the case of Herzl. He was an historic personality whose influence on his generation and generations to come is clear.

Conclusions

> *"The founders of religions and states, inventors and reformers, famous conquerors and celebrated intellectuals ... all paid a heavy price for the great adventure of their extraordinary lives."*[104]

In the introduction to this book we set ourselves the goal of reexamining Herzl's life and work in light of his abilities, his personality and the powerful charisma that affected those around him, near and far. We have followed him descending onto the stage of history like a meteor, leaving his stamp and then being swept to heaven in a whirlwind. But as we have seen, the trajectory of his life was riddled by mistakes. As we reach the end of this essay, it is worth reviewing these mistakes and considering whether they were the root cause of the emergence of adversaries who embittered his life, undermined his leadership and ruined his health, which only led to more mistakes.

Let us go back to these mistakes and look at how responsible they were for the heavy price he paid for his Zionist journey. It exacted a bloody price tag in the most literal sense – compromising his health, disastrous for his finances, wiping out his family fortune and precipitating a horrific end for his loved ones.[105] Could some of this misfortune have been prevented? Earlier, we listed

---

102 Herzl explains this in his diary. See *Complete Diaries of Theodor Herzl*, vol. 2, September 3, 1897, pp. 580–581.
103 In 1902, David Lloyd George, then a member of the British Parliament and an acting solicitor, was hired to draft a charter for the Uganda plan. Balfour was Prime Minister at the time. When the Balfour Declaration was issued in 1917, Balfour was Foreign Secretary and Lloyd George was Prime Minister.
104 Myriam Schach, *Et asher itam hithalakhti*, p. 151.
105 His wife died three years later from heart disease; his daughter Paulina died in 1930 in Bordeaux, sick and childless; his son Hans committed suicide upon hearing of his sister's death; Trude, his youngest daughter, spent years hospitalized due to mental illness and perished with her husband in Theresienstadt; and their son Stephen killed himself after World War II.

three cardinal issues where Herzl went wrong: *kultura*, *Altneuland* and Uganda. But there were additional mistakes, as we shall see below.[106]

The Kultura Controversy

The *kultura* controversy provided the young Zionists with a prime motive for clashing with Herzl from the very first congresses, and Herzl erred in not going out of his way to placate them. The opposition refused to back down, raising the issue time and again. The escalating protests of the pro-*kultura* camp, one can assume, became a springboard for rage over Herzl's response to criticism of *Altneuland*. A compromise on the issue of *kultura*, first proposed by Rabbi Samuel Jacob Rabinowitz of Aleksot at the Second Congress and rejected,[107] was brought up again by Ahad Ha'am at the Minsk Conference and accepted by all parties.[108] If Herzl had managed to bring the sides together in the early days of the Zionist movement, when he was at the height of his power, perhaps the opposition would not have been so aggressive at the Fifth Congress. Perhaps the Democratic Fraction would not have rushed out of the hall in anger when its demands were rejected,[109] and its response to *Altneuland* would have been more subdued as well. Perhaps Herzl's greatest folly was assuming that the road to a Jewish state was short, and therefore reaching a decision for or against cultural programming and upsetting one camp or another was unnecessary. In his view, the question of culture would be resolved once a state was in place. It was not a wise move to allow the opposition to organize and grow stronger. In this way, his opponents reached *Altneuland* all fired up and ready to fight, using the strongest language they could muster.

The Altneuland Affair

Herzl's power and the forcefulness of his leadership lay, among other things, in his ability to accept what came his way with equanimity. Early on, he explains this in his diary: "People are irritated at one another because they use different

---

106 On *kultura*, see Chapter 8, pp. 189–204; *Altneuland*, see Chapter 9, pp. 224–235; Uganda, Chapter 10, pp. 236–241.
107 See pp. 197–198, above.
108 The Minsk compromise proposed by Ahad Ha'am was accepted by both the young Zionists and the ultra-Orthodox. See Chapter 8, pp. 217–218.
109 See pp. 214–215, above.

words for the same thing ... But I want to be understood, now and in the future, and I make my greatest concession in the terms that I use. I don't fight over words. I have no time for that."[110]

Herzl's stoicism became a distinguishing feature of his leadership. We have seen the restraint and forbearance with which he responded to the raucous attacks of the Democratic Fraction. He held himself in check, able to appreciate their talents and abilities even when they castigated him and behaved badly. Once, after he was criticized for being overly tolerant, he replied: "Our movement cannot depend only on two eyes or on one generation."[111]

Another reason for this stoic acceptance, which he also demonstrated in the battle over *kultura*, was his recognition of the need for unity in the Zionist ranks. It was very important to him to win the confidence of all the Congress delegates because unity enabled him to speak on behalf of the Zionist movement and represent it in dealings with the outside world. In her account of the fourth and fifth congresses, Myriam Schach writes: "The opposition was so fierce and ruthless, one had to wonder: Why don't these angry 'pretenders to the throne' overthrow the 'government' they so dislike? Parliamentary law gave them the means and the right to do so. Within a short while, Herzl had taught his friends to think in 'parliamentary terms'... They could have simply abstained in the 'confidence vote.' It was true they were only a minority, but Herzl needed them for negotiating with the outside world, so as to have the authority of a united congress behind him."[112]

If Herzl had continued in this vein and passed over Ahad Ha'am's criticism in silence, if he had gone back to business and said nothing, the head-on battle between the defenders of Herzl and the defenders of Ahad Ha'am might have been avoided. What led Herzl to act as he did? Yossi Goldstein says it was Herzl's shaky political standing: "As long as he felt he was politically secure, he did not bother to respond to Ahad Ha'am's attacks. With his keen instincts, he knew that anything he said would only serve his opponent. But now, with his political strength on the wane and concerned that Ahad Ha'am's article would harm him, he declared open war. It was also an opportunity to get back at the man who had been belittling him without letup for six years."[113]

In all likelihood, Herzl's response was triggered by the nature of Ahad Ha'am's criticism: "If Ahad Ha'am had made do with a literary critique of *Altneu-*

---

110 *Complete Diaries of Theodor Herzl*, vol. 1, p. 122.
111 Schach, *Et asher itam hithalakhti*, p. 39.
112 *Ibid.*, p. 42.
113 Goldstein, *Ahad Ha'am: A Biography*, Keter, Jerusalem, 1992, p. 301.

land, even of the most biting kind, one can assume that Herzl would have seen it as his legitimate right as a literary critic and not taken personal offense. However, Ahad Ha'am was challenging him as president of the Zionist Organization, which left his pride deeply wounded."[114]

If Herzl had picked up his pen and replied to Ahad Ha'am himself, in the same way that he responded to the criticism of Rabbi Gudemann[115] and the protest rabbis[116], he probably would have done better and avoided stirring up a tempest. As Yossi Goldstein puts is, "Herzl had been severely criticized in the past, and he was good at restraint. It was a successful tactic, as even his adversaries admitted ... After his book *Altneuland* was panned by Ahad Ha'am, he could not hold back any longer. However, instead of answering Ahad Ha'am directly, he asked Nordau to reply in his stead ..."[117]

What led Herzl to react this way? It may have been a combination of physical and mental exhaustion, a release of pent up anger at Ahad Ha'am, who was constantly attacking him. In a fit of exasperation, he turned to Nordau, who wrote a sarcastic reply that only infuriated the opposition more, as one can see from their actions at the Sixth Congress.

But Herzl's mistake was worse than that. He read Nordau's reply before publication and let it be published as is. If at least he had asked Nordau to tone it down or edit out the insulting personal remarks, the Democratic Faction would not have had to defend Ahad Ha'am and the ground would not have been set for their incivility at the Congress, where Herzl was taunted and called names. Shmaryahu Levin, who had initially come out in Herzl's defense, joined the pro-Ahad Ha'am camp after Nordau's attack.[118] Other members of the Fraction might have done the same.[119] An exchange of letters between Herzl and Martin Buber shows the inappropriateness of Herzl 's response:

> "I regret that you have responded so heatedly to my factual and loyal comments, and as before, you completely misunderstand the whole issue," Buber writes. "On the other hand, I must make it perfectly clear that finding our way back to the movement is not necessary, because we stand proud and tall within the movement like everyone else, and with all due respect, I do not believe you have the right to decide on this matter."[120]

---

114 *Hatnu'a hatzionit berusia*, p. 206.
115 See pp. 162–163, above.
116 On the protest rabbis, see pp. 169, 190–191, 196–202, 214–216.
117 Ussishkin, *Biografia*, p. 171.
118 Nordau showed Herzl the draft. Herzl made a few edits but praises him in a letter for his "divine coarseness" (*Gottliche Grobheit*). Laskov, *Hayei ahad ha'am*, p. 212.
119 See Chapter 9, pp. 230–231.
120 Buber, *Khilufei igrot*, vol. 1, p. 163.

Looking closer at the chronicle of events shows that Herzl jumped to conclusions and accused the Democratic Faction falsely.[121] It was the conduct of someone who was overburdened, worn out and tense. This again leads to speculation: If Herzl had been healthy and in a calmer state of mind, perhaps he might never have reached this point.

The Uganda crisis

In the Uganda crisis Herzl committed one misstep after another, escalating the tension between the camps. Taking a cue from the *Dayenu* song sung at the Passover seder, one could come up with a whole "if only" list:
- If only Herzl had listened to Nordau and refrained from bringing the Uganda proposal to the Congress;
- If only he had convened a meeting of the Greater Action Committee as promised,[122] and gained approval for the text of his plenary speech as was the norm for other issues, if necessary changing the wording;
- If only he had listened to Chlenov and accentuated the political expediency of the plan more than the need for a temporary shelter outside Eretz Yisrael;

And once the Uganda proposal was on the agenda:
- If only he had allowed members of the Action Committee to voice opposition if they so desired, which would have headed off their resignation;
- If only he had allowed the Action Committee members to vote according to their conscience and not implied that any other vote was tantamount to resignation. If so, the group would not have walked out and the Zionist Movement would have been spared a " weeping fest";

If Herzl had done any of these things, "it would have sufficed," to quote the Haggadah – and how much more so if he had done all of them.

Herzl himself admitted to blunders in the Uganda affair. As he sat on the train on September 1, 1903, returning home from the Sixth Congress, he summed them up in his diary:

> "My two mistakes at the Sixth Congress were peculiar. At a session of the Greater A.C., prior to the East Africa vote, I told the popularity hounds Chlenov, Bernstein-Kohan and company that anyone who voted against it could not stay on the A.C. any longer. As a result, they

---

121 See Chapter 9, pp. 233–234.
122 *Sefer Chlenov*, pp. 182–205.

no longer cared what might happen afterwards, and they left the Congress hall, which in turn led to the big scene.

The second mistake was to give the floor to Montefiore instead of to an interesting speaker who would have held them in the hall. Thus the people who fled from good Sir Francis gave the impression that they were joining the self-exiled opposition, which was actually not the case."[123]

But was that all? Another miscalculation was his assumption that he would continue to lead political initiatives after the Sixth Congress just as he had before. It shows that the enormity of the outrage over Uganda was lost on him.[124] In addition, he was wrong about Chlenov, whom he characterized as one of the "popularity hounds."[125] Throughout the crisis, Chlenov was adamant about loyalty to Zion but equally passionate about respect for Herzl.[126]

An interesting perspective is added by Myriam Schach. She believes the failure of Herzl's expedition to Palestine boils down to a single factor: His blindness to the change in world politics. Government ministers were now the "true lords of the hour," she writes, not the kings. Wilhelm II, the emperor of Germany, had made Herzl a promise, and Herzl could and should have gone to Palestine, but he underestimated the hostility of von Bülow, who was antagonistic to his project. In Schach's view, this was the real reason Herzl returned from Palestine without a charter in hand.[127] As noted above,[128] von Bülow, who had German interests at heart, was wary of entering into unnecessary competition with the other European powers.[129] Another factor may have been Herzl's answering questions that should have been answered by von Bülow at the meeting with Chancellor Hohenlohe.[130]

Likewise, Schach offers a different take on Herzl's conduct in the Uganda affair:

"I, and doubtless many others, have spent long hours trying to find where Herzl's fatal error lay, although I myself have found only mistakes stemming from what were no doubt fine

---

123 *Complete Diaries of Theodor Herzl*, vol. 4, pp. 1549–1550.
124 Even if Herzl was not totally mistaken and his assumptions in this regard were not unfounded – there were *Neinsagers* among the West European Jews just as there were *Jasagers* among the East European Jews – he failed to predict the powerfulness of the emotions unleashed by the Uganda proposition and the threat to congressional unity.
125 *Complete Diaries of Theodor Herzl*, vol. 4, pp. 1549–1550.
126 *Sefer Chlenov*, pp. 201–202.
127 Schach, *Asher itam hithalakhti*, p. 158.
128 See p. 139 above.
129 *Germania, turkia vehatzionut*, pp. 75–77.
130 See p. 136 above.

intentions. For as all those who truly knew Herzl can unanimously attest, he was incapable of vice, duplicity or tyranny, in thought or deed. Never in his life would he use a poison-tipped arrow ... Before the Zionist era, Herzl had not a single personal enemy, and later his mistakes were considered 'grievous' only within our own ranks."[131]

Schach sees Herzl's decision on Uganda as the most disastrous of his career, not because he accepted Chamberlain's offer and recommended it to the Congress, for "what else could he have done? A tremendous responsibility lay on his shoulders ... Herzl's mistake was more psychological than political: He never imagined that the proposal would be viewed as a sacrilege, and that he himself, the founding father of the movement, would be branded a traitor – when in effect he had sacrificed everything for the cause!"[132]

Schach goes on to say that even if Herzl had foreseen the outcome, he would have been right to bring the proposal to the Congress, except that he should have gone about it differently, so as not to split the ranks and spare himself needless anguish.

At the beginning of this book, we spoke about the Herzl conundrum. We wondered how he accomplished such impressive feats within a few short years while battling stubborn opposition from every side. We pondered the source of his strength. We asked how he succeeded in launching the political Zionist enterprise and reshaping the political and international map in ways that remain in force until today.

At this point it seems clear that the secret lies in Herzl's character.

> "The more we know about the breadth of Herzl's enterprise, the deeper the enigma surrounding his personality," writes Dov Sadan.[133] "How did the architect create such a spectacle from bricks that were largely fragile and crumbling, and embed these bricks in the souls of men as dispersed and scattered as the Jews?...How could he erect a permanent building without knowing the fate of the exiled nation? This is a matter for scholarly research and even more so artistic research. For people like us, outside observers, it is an enigma and remains an enigma."[134]

However, even if we never fully solve the puzzle, there are clues in his will and testament.

---

[131] Schach, *Asher itam hithalakhti*, pp. 157–160.
[132] Ibid.
[133] Dov Sadan, "From solving a riddle to creating one," in: *Shivat Tzion – Sefer hashana lekheker hatzionut utkumat yisrael*, Hasifria hatzionit, p. 354.
[134] Ibid., p. 359.

Herzl died on July 3, 1904, the 20th of the Hebrew month of Tammuz. His request to be buried in a coffin draped in the white flag that had flown from the roof of the hall where the First Zionist Congress was held testified to his profound faith in political Zionism. He was laid to rest beside his father in the hope that his remains and those of his family would someday be taken by representatives of the Jewish people for reburial in the Jewish state.

Thirteen years after Herzl's death, on November 2, 1917, the British foreign secretary, Lord Balfour, handed the letter known as the Balfour Declaration to Lord Rothschild. Balfour was the representative of Britain, whose government had discussed with Herzl the possibility of allocating land for a Jewish home in Uganda and El Arish. An attorney by the name of Lloyd George was the man who drafted the charter for the Uganda plan. Now, thirteen years later, Lloyd George was the prime minister of Great Britain.

Another thirty years passed from the Balfour Declaration until the United Nations resolution in November 1947. The establishment of the State of Israel was declared on May 14, 1948, "secured by public law," as Herzl desired.

The State of Israel did not forget its great visionary. In 1949, Theodor Herzl's remains were reinterred in the Jewish state.

Years have gone by, but carrying out Herzl's last wish remains our solemn duty:

> "I once called Zionism an unending ideal. And I truly believe that Zionism will not cease to be an ideal even after we will have attained our land of Palestine. For inherent in Zionism, as I understand it, is not only the striving for a legally secured homeland for our unfortunate people, but also the striving for moral and intellectual perfection."[135]

---

135 *Zionist Writings*, "A blessing on the journey," vol. 2, p. 240.

Bibliography

Books (Hebrew)

Ahad Ha'am. *Igrot Ahad Ha'am*, vol. 2. (Letters). (Hebrew). Jerusalem: Yavne Publishing, 1924.
Ahad Ha'am. *Iggrot Ahad Ha'am*, vol. 3. (Letters). (Hebrew). Jerusalem and Berlin: Yavne and Moriah Publishing, 1924.
Ahad Ha'am. *Kol Kitvei Ahad Ha'am*, (*Ahad Haam's Writings*). (Hebrew). Tel Aviv: Dvir, 1947.
Alfes, Ben-Zion and Nissan Ben Moshe Rabin. *Ma'aseh Alfes, Toldot Vezikhronot*, (Memories). (Hebrew). Jerusalem: Diskin Orphanage, 1941.
Almog, Shmuel. *Tzionut Vehistoria*, (*Zionism and History*). (Hebrew). Jerusalem: Magnes Press, 1982.
Appel, Judah. *Reisheet Hat'hiya: Zikhronot Vekatavim Miyamei 'Hovevei Zion' berusiya*, (*Memories and Writings from the Days of 'Hovevei Zion' in Russia*). (Hebrew). Tel Aviv: Gutenberg, 1936.
Avineri, Shlomo. *Varieties of Zionist Thought*. (Hebrew). Tel Aviv: Am Oved, 1980.
Bar Ilan, Meir. *Mevolozhin Ad Yerushalayim*, (*From Valozhyn to Jerusalem*). (Hebrew). Tel Aviv: Committee for the Publication of the Writings of Rabbi Meir Bar Ilan, 1971.
Barzilai, Yehoshua. *Kitvei Yehoshua Barzilai Eisenstad*, (*Yehoshua Barzilai Eisenstad's Writings*). (Hebrew). Jaffa: Etin Press, 1913.
Bein, Alexander. (ed.). *Iggrot Herzl*, vol. 1. (*Herzl's Letters*). (Hebrew). Tel Aviv: Neuman, 1945.
Bein, Alexander. (ed.). *Iggrot Herzl*, vol. 2. (*Herzl's Letters*). (Hebrew). Tel Aviv: Neuman, 1958.
Bein, Alexander. (ed.). *Iggrot Herzl*, vol. 3. (*Herzl's Letters*). (Hebrew). Jerusalem: Neuman and Hasifriya Hatzionit, 1958.
Bein, Alexander. *Im Herzl Ube'ikvotav: Ma'amarim Vete'udot*, (*In Herzl's Footsteps*). (Hebrew). Tel Aviv: Masada, 1953.
Bein, Alexander. *Theodor Herzl: A Biography*. (Hebrew). Jerusalem: Hasifriya Haziyonit, 1977.
Bein, Alexander. (ed). *Sefer Motzkin*, (*The Motzkin Book*). (Hebrew). Jerusalem: Zionist Executive Publishing, 1939.
Ben Amotz, Dahn. *What's New*. (Hebrew). Jerusalem: Ahiasaf, 1965.
Ben Hillel, Mordechai. *Olami*, (*My World*). (Hebrew). Jerusalem: Hapo'alim, 1929.
Ben-Avi, Itamar. *Im Shahar Atzmautenu: Memoirs of the First Hebrew Child*. (Hebrew). Jerusalem: Public Committee for the Publication of the Writings of Itamar Ben-Avi, 1961.
Chlenov, Yehiel. *Pirkei Khayav Upeulato*, (*Chapters of His Life and Work*). (Hebrew). Tel Aviv: Eretz Yisrael Press, 1937.
Citron, Shmuel Leib. (ed.). *Herzl: Khayav Upe'ulotav*, (*His Life and Activities*). (Hebrew). Vilna: Shreberk, 1921.
Citron, Shmuel Leib. *Lexicon Tzioni*, (*Zionist Lexicon*). (Hebrew). Vilna: S. Shreberk, 1924.
Dinur, Ben-Zion. *Binyamin Ze'ev Herzl*. (Hebrew). Ramat Gan: Masada, 1968.
Ehrenpreis, Mordecai. *Bein Mizrakh Lama'arav*, (*Between East and West*). (Hebrew). Tel Aviv: Am Oved, 1953.
Ellerin Hermann. (ed.). *Herzl, Hechler, Hadukas Hagadol Mebaden Vekaisar Germania 1896–1904*, (*Herzl, Hechler, Grand Duke of Baden and the German Kaiser 1896–1904*). (Hebrew). Tel Aviv: Bank Elran Publishing, 1961.
Elon, Amos. *Herzl*. (Hebrew). Tel Aviv: Am Oved, 1977.

Glicksman, Avraham Zvi. *Tiferet Adam: Biographical Sketches and Letters of Pinhas Selig Glicksman*, (*The Human Glory*). (Hebrew). Lodz: Kultura, 1923.

Glickson, Moshe Zvi. *Kitvey M. Glickson, vol. 1: "Zionist Personalities"*, (*M. Glickson's Writings*). (Hebrew). Tel Aviv: Hava'ad Lehotza'at Kitvey Glickson, Dvir, 1939.

Goldstein, Yossi. *Ahad Ha-Am and Herzl: The Struggle for Political and Cultural Nature of Zionism In the Shade of Altneuland Affair.* (Hebrew). Jerusalem: Dinur Center Press, Zalman Shazar Center, 2011.

Goldstein, Yossi. *Ahad Ha-Am: A Biography.* (Hebrew). Jerusalem: Keter Publishers, 1992.

Goldstein, Yossi. *Ussishkin's Biography.* (Hebrew). Jerusalem: Magnes Press, 2001.

Gonen, Itzik and Eliav Zakai. (eds.). *Leadership and Leadership Development.* (Hebrew). Tel Aviv: Ministry of Defense, 1999.

Gronemann, Sammy. *Zikhronot Shel Yekke*, (*Memories of a Yekke*). (Hebrew). Tel Aviv: Am Oved, 1946.

Heftman, Joseph. *Herzl Bechazon Hador*, (*Herzl in the Vision of the Generation*). (Hebrew). Tel Aviv: Uma Umoledet Ltd., 1946.

Hermoni, Aharon. *Be'ikvot Habiluim*, (*In the Footsteps of the Bilu'im*). (Hebrew). Jerusalem: Reuben Mass, 1952.

Herzl, Theodor. *Hacongress Habazila'I*, (*The Congress in Basel*). (Hebrew). Warsaw: Ahiasaf, 1897.

Herzl, Theodor. *The Jewish Cause – Diaries, Volume One: 1895–1898.* (Hebrew). Jerusalem: Bialik Institute and Hasifriya Hatzionit, 1997.

Herzl, Theodor. *The Jewish Cause – Diaries, Volume Two: 1898–1902.* (Hebrew). Jerusalem: Bialik Institute and Hasifriya Hatzionit, 1999.

Herzl, Theodor. *The Jewish Cause – Diaries, Volume Three: 1902–1904.* (Hebrew). Jerusalem: Bialik Institute and Hasifriya Hatzionit, 2001.

Jabotinsky, Ze'ev. *Ktavim: Autobiografia, Vol. 1.* (*Writings: Autobiography*). (Hebrew). Jerusalem: Eri Jabotinsky, 1947.

Jaffe, Leib. (ed.). *Sefer Hacongress: 25th Anniversary of the First Zionist Congress,* (*The Congress Book*). (Hebrew). Jerusalem; Tel Aviv: A. Eitan and S. Shoshani Press, 1923.

Jaffe, Leib. (ed.). *Sefer Hacongress: 50th Anniversary of the First Zionist Congress.* (*The Congress Book*). (Hebrew). Jerusalem: Jewish Agency, 1950.

Katz, Shmuel. *Jabo – A Biography.* (Hebrew). Tel Aviv: Dvir, 1993.

Katzir: Kovetz Letoldot Hatnu'a Hatzionit Berusia, (*History of the Zionist Movement in Russia*). (Hebrew). Tel Aviv: Masada, 1964.

Katznelson, Berl. *Bekhavlei Adam: Al morim vehaverim*, (*Revolution and Roots: Selected Writings and Letters*). (Hebrew). Tel Aviv: Am Oved, 1964.

Klausner, Israel. "Scholem Aleichem Hatzioni," (Zionis Scholem Aleichem). In *Scholem Aleichem, Why Do the Jews Need a Land of Their Own.* (Hebrew). Tel Aviv: Dvir and Beit Scholem Aleichem, 1981.

Klausner, Israel. *Opozitzia leherzl*, (*Opposition to Herzl*). (Hebrew). Jerusalem: Ahiever, 1964.

Kouts, Gideon. *News and History: Studies in History of the Hebrew and Jewish Press and Communication.* (Hebrew). Jerusalem: Mossad Bialik, 2013.

Kressel, Getzel. *Reisheet Tza'aday Herzl Be'aspaklaria Shel Ha'itonut Ha'ivrit Bagolah*, (*Herzls First Steps in the Hebrew Press in the Diaspora*). Jerusalem: Reuben Mass, 1943.

Lang, Yoseph. *Speak Hebrew! The Life of Eliezer Ben Yehuda.* (Hebrew). Jerusalem: Yad Ben Zvi, 2008.

Laskov, Shlomit. *The Life of Ahad Haam*. (Hebrew). Jerusalem: Institute for Zionist Research, Tel Aviv University and Hasifriya Hatzionit, 2006.
Levin, Shmaryahu. *Mizikhronot Khayai, vol. 3, (Memories from My Life), Bama'arakha*. (Hebrew). Tel Aviv: Dvir, 1939.
Maimon, Yehuda Leib. *Sarei hame'ah: Reshumot al gedolei yisrael, vol. 6*. (Hebrew). Jerusalem: Mossad Harav Kook, 1999.
Mann, Yitzhak. *Hermann Struck: Ha'adam veha'oman, (The Man and the Artist)*. (Hebrew). Tel Aviv: Dvir, 1954.
Maor, Yitzhak. *The Zionist Mouvment in Russia*. (Hebrew). Jerusalem: Hasifriya Hatzionit and Magnes Press, 1986.
Margalit, Michael. *The Prophet and the Emperor, History of the Correspondence: Herzl and Wilhelm II, 1896–1904*. (Hebrew) Tel Aviv: Beit El-Ram Foundation, Department of the History of the Jewish People, Tel Aviv University, 2007.
Masliansky, Zvi Hirsch. *Kitvei Masliansky: Neumim, Zikhronot Umasa'ot, vol. 3. (Masliansky's Writings: Speeches, Memories and Journeys)*. (Hebrew). New York: Hebrew Publishing Company, 1929.
Mayorek, Yoram. *With Herzl to Jerusalem*. (Hebrew). Jerusalem: karta, 1998.
Naor, Mordechai. *From Herzl to Ben-Gurion*. (Hebrew). Tel Aviv: Ministry of Defense, 1996.
Netanyahu, Benzion. *"Introduction". In Max Nordau to his People: A Summons and a Challenge*. (Hebrew). Tel Aviv: Hozaah Medinit, 1946.
Netanyahu, Benzion. *The Founding Fathers of Zionism*. (Hebrew). Tel Aviv: Yedioth Ahronoth, 2003.
Nissenbaum, Yitzhak. *Alay kheldi, (My World), 1869–1899*. (Hebrew). Jerusalem: Reuben Mass, 1968.
Nordau, Max. *Katavim Tzioni'im, vol. 2. (Zionist Writings)*. (Hebrew). Jerusalem: Hasifriya hatzionit, 1960.
Nordau, Max. *Katavim Tzioni'im, vol. 3. (Zionist Writings)*. (Hebrew). Jerusalem: Hasifriya hatzionit, 1960.
Ofrat, Gideon. *Al ha'aretz: Ha'omanut ha'eretz yisraelit, vol. 1. (The Art in Israel)*. (Hebrew). Tel Aviv: Yaron Golan, 1993.
Orlan, Haim (ed. and translator). *The First Zionist-Congres in Basel – Protocol*. (Hebrew). Jerusalem: Reuben Mass, 1997.
Pinsker, Y.L.. "Autoemancipatzia: Kol Koreh El Bnei Amo," In *Sefer Pinsker*. ("Autoemancipation" In *The Pinsker Book*). (Hebrew). Tel Aviv: Dvir, 1949.
Rabinowitz, Eliyahu Akiva. *Tzion Bemishpat Oh Hashkafa Rabanit Al Hatzionut, (The Rabinical Perspective on Zionism)*. (Hebrew). Warsaw: Halter Press, 1902.
Rav Tzair, *Book of Memoirs: Portraits and Appraisals*. (Hebrew). New York: Jubilee Committee, 1945.
Ravitzky, Aviezer. *Messianism, Zionism and Jewish Religious Radicalism*. (Hebrew). Tel Aviv: Am Oved, 1993.
Reines, Isaac Yaacov. *Or Chodosh Al Zion, (A New Lighte Upon Zion)*. New York: Possy Shoulson Press, 1946.
Reinharz, Jehuda. *Chaim Weizmann: Baderekh El Hamanhigut, (On the Way to the Leadership)*. (Hebrew). Jerusalem: Hasifriya Hatzionit, 1987.
Salom Aleichem. *Why Do Jews Need a Land of Their Own?* (Hebrew). Tel Aviv: Dvir, 1950.

Schach, Myriam. *Asher Itam Hit'halakhti*, (*Those with Whom I Walked*). (Hebrew). Tel Aviv: Dvir, 1951.
Schwartz, Shalom. *Herzl Besifrei Yamav*, (*Herzl in His Books*). (Hebrew). Jerusalem: Hasolel Press, 1931.
Salmon, Yosef. *Do Not Provoke Providence: Orthodoxy in the Grip of Nationalism.* (Hebrew). Jerusalem: The Zalman Shazar Center for Jewish History, 2006.
Shazar, Zalman: "Berthold Feiwel" In *Berthold Feiwel Ha'ish Upoalo*, (*Berthold Feiwel The Man and His Work*). (Hebrew). Jerusalem: Hasifriya hatzionit, 1960.
Shub, Moshe David. *Zikhronot Levait David: Sheevim Shnot Avoda Besadeh Hat'hiya Vehayishuv*, (*Memories of the House of David*). (Hebrew). Jerusalem: Reuben Mass, 1973.
Silberbusch, David Isaiah. *Mipinkas Zikhronotai*, (*Memories from My Notebook*). (Hebrew). Tel Aviv: Hapoel Hatza'ir Press, 1936.
Slouschz, Nahum. *Knesset Hagdola Oh Hakongres Hasheni Bebazel*, (*Protocols of the 2nd Congress*). (Hebrew). Warsaw: Tushia, 1898.
Slouschz, Nahum. *Sefer Haprotokolim Shel Hakongres Harivi'I*, (*Protocols of the 4th Congress*). (Hebrew). Warsaw: Tushia, 1905.
Sofer, Oren. *Ein Lefalpel! Iton Hatzfira Vehamodernizatzia Shel Hasiakh Hakhevrati Politi*, (*Hasfira Magazin and the Modernization of the Political and Social Environment*). (Hebrew). Jerusalem: Mosad Bialik, 2008.
Sokolow, Nahum. *Hatzofeh Leveit Yisrael*, (*Selected Works*). (Hebrew). Jerusalem: Hasifria Hatzionit, 1961.
Tartakover, David. *Herzl in Profile: Herzl's Image in the Applaide Arts.* (Hebrew and English). Tel Aviv: Tel Aviv Museum, 1979.
Vardi, Aharon. *Malki Betzion*, (*My King in Zion*). (Hebrew). Tel Aviv: Hapoel Hatza'ir, 1931.
Vital, David. *The Origin of Zionism.* (Hebrew). Tel Aviv: Am Oved 1978.
Wistrich, Robert and David Ohana. (eds.). *Myth, Memory: Transfigurations of Israeli Consciousness.* (Hebrew). Tel Aviv: Van Leer Institute and Hakibbutz Hameuchad, 1996.
Yaffe, Hillel. *Dor Hama'apilim: Zikhronot, Yomanim, Mikhtavim*, (*The Generation of the Ma'apilim: Memories, Diaries and Letters*). (Hebrew). Tel Aviv: Ministry of Defense, 1983.
Zangwill, Israel. *Haderech La'atzmaut*, (*The Way to Independence*). (Hebrew). Tel Aviv: Hozaah Medinit, 1938.

Books (English)

Ben-Gurion, David. *Recollections.* Tel Aviv: Bitan, 1970.
Golinkin, David. *Insight Israel: The View from Schechter.* Jerusalem: Schechter Institute, 2006.
Herzl, Theodor. *The Jewish State.* New York: American Zionist Emergency Council, 1946.
Heyd, Milly. "Lilien: Between Herzl and Ahasver". In *Theodor Herzl: Visionary of the Jewish State.* Edited by R. Wistrich and G. Shimoni. Jerusalem: Magnes Press and Herzl Press, 1999.
Louis, Lipsky. *Gallery of Zionist Profiles.* New York: Farrar, Straus and Cudahy, 1956.
Luz, Ehud. *Parallels Meet: Religion and Nationalism in Early Zionist Movement (1882–1904).* Philadelphia: Jewish Publication Society, 1988.
Mendelsohn, Ezra (ed.). *Art and Its Uses: The Visual Image and Modern Jewish Society.* New York: Oxford, 1990.

Nordau, Anna and Maxa. *Max Nordau: A Biography.* New York: The Nordau Committee, 1943.
Rosenberger, Erwin. *Herzl as I Remember Him.* New York: Herzl Press, 1959.
Pawel, Ernst. *The Labyrinth of Exile: A Life of Theodor Herzl.* New York: Farrar, Straus & Giroux, 1989.
Weber, Max. *On Charisma and Institution Building.* Chicago: University of Chicago Press, 1947.
Weisgal, Meyer. *Theodor Herzl, A Memorial.* New York: 1929.
Weisz, Yitshak. *Theodor Herzl: A New Reading.* Jerusalem: Gefen, 2013.
Weizmann, Chaim. *Trial and Error: The Autobiography of Chaim Weizmann.* New York: Harper & Brothers, 1949.
Wistrich, R. and Shimoni, G. (eds.). *Theodor Herzl: Visionary of the Jewish State.* Jerusalem: Magnes Press and Herzl Press, 1999.
Zweig, Stefan. *The World of Yesterday: An Autobiography.* Lincoln: University of Nebraska Press, 1964.

Books (German and Yiddish)

Acher, Mathias. *Achad Ha-am: Ein Denker und Kämpfer der Jüdischen Renaissance.* Jüdischer Verlag. (German).
Birnbaum, Nathan. *Die Nationale Wiedergeburt des jüdischen Vokes in seinem Lande, als Mittel zur Losung der Judenfrage, Ein Appell an die Guten und Edlen aller Nationen.* (German). Vienna: 1893.
Breuer, Isaac. *Judenproblem.* (German). Halle Saale: O. Handel, 1918.
Cohn, Marcus. "Erinnerungen eines Baslers an den Ersten Zionistenkongress." In *Schweizericher Israelitischer Gemeindebund, 1904–1954.* (German). Basel: Festrschrift zum 50 Jahrigen Bestehen, 1954. 225–336.
Rumshinsky, Joseph. *Klangen fun mein leben.* (Yiddish). New York: Biederman, 1944.

Articles

Almog, Shmuel. "Khayav umoto shel Alfred Nossig" (The Life and Deth of Alfred Nossig). In *Studies in Zionism* 2 (1985): 73–98. (Hebrew).
Almog, Shmuel. "The Relation of Seculars to Religion in Early Zionism." In *The Religious Trend in Zionism.* Edited by Anita Shapira, 31–38. (Hebrew). Tel Aviv: Am Oved, 1983.
Bein, Alex. "Gilgulay Hara'ayon Shel Hacongress Hatzioni" (The History of the Zionist Congress). In *Report (World Congress of Jewish Studies)*, 1 (1942): 469–476. (Hebrew).
Carlebach, Ezriel. "Hamanheeg Ha'enoshi" (The Human Leader). In *Profiles.* (Hebrew). Tel Aviv: Ma'ariv Books, 1959.
Cohen, Moshe. "Medinat Hayehudim Be'ayara Hayehudit" (The Jewish State in the in the in the Shtetel). In *Die Welt* 23, (Febuary 1946): 221–222. (Hebrew).
David, Ohad. "The 'King of the Jews' (Herzl) as a Communications Wizard." *Kesher* 27 (May 2000): 49–58. (Hebrew).

Eliav, Mordechai. "Herzl and Zionism in the Eyes of Morutz Gudemann." In *Zionism* 7 (1981): 399–425. (Hebrew).
Friesel, Evyatar. "The Meaning of Zionism and Its Influence among the American Jewish Religious Movement." In *Zionism and Religion*. Edited by Shmuel Almog, Jehuda Reinharz and Anita Shapira, 207–221. (Hebrew). Jerusalem: The Zalman Shazar Center for Jewish History, 1994.
Grossman, Haim. "Et lekhol khefetz" (A Time for Every Matter). In *Et Mol*, 176 (2004): 11. (Hebrew).
Gutwein, Daniel. "The Reconstruction of Herzl's Image in Israeli Collective Memory: From Formative Radicalism to an Adapting Fringe." In *Iyunim*, vol. 12, (2002): 29–73. (Hebrew).
Heymann, Michael. "Herzl and the Russian Zionists – Dissension and Agreement." In *Zionism* 3 (1973): 56–99. (Hebrew).
Katchensky, Miriam. "Hadrasha beyidish besherut tnuat tzion" (The Yiddish Sermon in Service of the Zionist Movement). In *Talking Culture: The First Aliya, an Interperiod Discourse*. Edited by Yaffa Berlowit, 198–222. (Hebrew). Tel Aviv: Hakibbutz Hameuhad, 2010.
Klausner, Israel. "Hatnu'a Hatzionit Bebesarabia" (The Jewish movement in Baserabia). In *Yahadut Bessarabia*. Edited by Y. Koren and B. Michali, 493–620. (Hebrew). Jerusalem: Khevrat entziklopediya shel galuyot, 1971.
Klausner, Israel. "Joseph Zeff – 'Lover of Zion' and Emissary of Herzl to America." In *Zionism* 3 (1973): 7–41. (Hebrew).
Kotz, Gideon. "Economic and Organizational Aspects of the Early Hebrew Newspapers in Europe." In *Kesher* 29 (May 2001): 18–26. (Hebrew).
Kotz, Gideon. "Nahum Sokolov and the 'Official Function' of the Hebrew Press." In *Kesher* 2 (November 1987): 23–28. (Hebrew).
Kressel, Getzel. "Dramatizatsia Lehayav Upoalo Shel Herzl" (Dramatization to Herzl's Life and Work). In *Moznayim* 46, 2 (1978): 128–133. (Hebrew).
Laskov, Shulamit. " Altneuland." In *Zionism* 15 (1990): 35–53. (Hebrew).
Mann, Rafi. "Herzl and the Press: From 'Sword of Steel' to Cable Newspaper." In *Kesher* 21 (May 1997): 20–36. (Hebrew).
Naor, Mordechai. "Herzl as a Public Relations Practitioner." In *Kesher* 40 (2010): 4–10. (Hebrew).
Naor, Mordechai. "Herzl and the Media." In *Kesher* 3 (May 1988): 32–38. (Hebrew).
Rabbi Binyamin. "Herzl." In *Shivat Tzion: Sefer Shana Lekheker Hatzionut Vetkumat Yisrael*. vol. 1, 347–353. (Hebrew). Jerusalem: Hasifriya Hatzionit, 1949.
Rabbi Binyamin. "Truth from the Land of the Jews." In *Hakeshet* 3 (1903): 117. (Hebrew).
Raphael, Geula. "The Cultural Question in the First Congresses." In *Sugiot Betoldot Hatzionu Veyishuvt*. 39–54. (Hebrew). Tel Aviv: Am Oved and Tel Aviv University, 1983.
Reinharz, Jehuda. "Zionism and Orthodoxy: A Marriage of Convenience." In *Zionism and Religion*. 141–166. (Hebrew). Jerusalem: The Zalman Shazar Center for Jewish History, 1994.
Rosenfeld, Shalom. "Dr. Theodor Herzl, Journalist". In *Kesher* 21 (May 1997): 2–4. (Hebrew).
Sadan, Dov. "Bein Pitaron Lekhida (Herzl Be'igrotav)" (From Solving a Riddle to Creating One.) In *Shivat Tzion – Sefer Hashana Lekheker Hatzionut Utkumat Yisrael*. Edited by Ben-Zion Dinur, 354–359. (Hebrew). Jerusalem: Hasifria hatzionit, 1950.

Salmon, Yosef. "The Response of East European Orthodoxy to Political Zionism." In *Zionism and its Jewish Opponents*. 51–73. (Hebrew). Jerusalem: Hasifria Hatzionit, 1990.

Salmon, Yosef. "Zionism and Anti-Zionism in Traditional Judaism in Estern Europe." In *Zionism and Religion*. 33–53. (Hebrew). Jerusalem: The Zalman Shazar Center for Jewish History, 1994.

Sarna, Jonathan. "Converts to Zionism in the American Reform Movement." In *Zionism and Religion*. 223–243. (Hebrew). Jerusalem: The Zalman Shazar Center for Jewish History, 1994.

Schwartz, Dov. "Hatzionut hadatit veherzl: Dgamim shel tadmit". In *Herzl Then and Now: 'The Jewish State' in the State of the Jews*. Edited by Avi Saguy and Yedidya Stern, 291–332. (Hebrew). Ramat Gan-Jerusalem: Bar Ilan University and Hartman Institute, 2008.

Schweid, Eliezer. "Confronting 'The Question of Jewish Existence': An Inquiry into the Thought of Nathan Birnbaum." In *Zionism and its Jewish Opponents*. Edited by Haim Avni and Gideon Shimoni, 301–319. (Hebrew). Jerusalem: Hasifriya hatzionit, 1990.

Shamir, Boas. "Sod Hakesher Hakarismati" (The Secret of Charismatic Connection). In *Leadership and Leadership Development*. Edited by Itzik Gonen and Eliav Zakai. (Hebrew). Tel Aviv: Ministry of Defense, 1999.

Toury, Jacob. "The Creation of 'The World' (Die Welt); Herzl's Newspapers." In *Zmanim* 6 (1981): 52–67. (Hebrew).

Wistrich, Robert. "Zionism and Its Religious Critics in Fin-de-Siecle Vienna." In *Zionism and Religion*. 167–188. (Hebrew). Jerusalem: The Zalman Shazar Center for Jewish History, 1994.

Zur, Yaakov. "German Jewish Orthodoxy's Attitude toward Zionism." In *Zionism and Religion*. 127–140. (Hebrew). Jerusalem: The Zalman Shazar Center for Jewish History, 1994.

Zur, Yaakov. "Zionism and Orthodoxy in Germany." In *Zionism and its Jewish Opponents*. 75–85. (Hebrew). Jerusalem: Hasifriya hatzionit, 1990.

Index

Abdul Hamid II 37, 43, 49, 56, 67, 71, 79, 107, 127f., 132, 134–136, 138f., 147, 149, 224, 236, 240, 311, 319, 330
Abner, Mayer 59, 183f.
Abraham (Avinu) 337
Abraham Ibn Ezra 296
Abramowitz 208
Adler, Naftali Zvi 98, 100, 168
Agudat Yisrael 169, 197
Ahad Ha'am see Ginsberg Asher Zvi
Aaron ha'Cohen 22, 24, 59, 297
Ahlem (Ulm) 61
Ahva (society) 140
Aleksot 170, 172, 198, 222, 339
Alfes, Ben-Zion 67f.
Alfonso XIII, King of Spain 21
Algeria 16
Alkalai Yehuda Chai 9, 107
Allgemeine Zeitung des Judentums (newspaper) 112
Alliance (school) 143
Almog, Shmuel 187, 308
America, see United States of America
Appel, Judah 56f.
Argentina 92, 211, 239f.
Augusta Victoria, German Empress 57, 145, 150
Austria 14, 70, 91, 125, 167, 292, 330 see also Austro-Hungarian Empire; Edlach; Salzburg; Vienna
Austrian Israelite Union (association) 166
Austro-Hungarian Empire 8, 132, see also Austria; Franz Joseph; Galicia; Hungary; Kolomyia; Prague
Avinovitsky, Philip (Feibush) 209

Ba'al Shem Tov Israel 336
Bad Aussee 246
Badeni, Count Kasimir Felix 70
Bahr, Hermann 33
Balfour, Arthur James 338, 345
Bambus, Willy 75f., 111f.
Bank, see Jewish Colonial Trust

Bar Kokhba 26
Bar-Ilan, Meir 27, 318, 320, 336, 338
Barabash, Shmuel 51
Barzilai-Eisenstadt, Yehoshua 47, 272
Basel 31, 39, 78, 97, 101f., 115–117, 119–121, 123–126, 171, 184f., 190f., 199, 206–209, 212, 246–248, 250, 257f., 260, 264, 275332
– Burgvogtei 116f.
– City Hall, Municipal Casino 184, 295
– Hotel Les Trois Rois 1, 22, 38, 59, 119, 312
– Municipal Concert Hall (location for the first Zionist Congress) 1f., 102, 117, 287
Bautenberg, A.L. 260
Bedzin 63
Beer, Friedrich 59
Beethoven, Ludwig van 2
Bein, Alexander (Alex) 49, 53f., 108, 110, 114, 119, 131, 139, 178, 185f., 224, 234, 238, 249f., 253, 329–331, 333
Belarus 62, see also Brisk; Grodno; Minsk; Mogilev; Novogrudok
Belkovsky, Zvi 264f., 269f., 273
Ben-Avi, Itamar 33, 143f., 150, 309
Ben-Gurion, David 29
Ben Hillel Hacohen, Mordecai 33, 39, 51, 95, 299, 320f., 324
Ben-Tovim, Zalman 144, 151
Ben-Yehuda, Eliezer 99, 137, 152, 229, 233, 307
Benedikt, Moriz 73
Berdyczewski, Micha Josef 94
Berkowicz, Michael 86, 88, 91, 239
Berkowitz, Michael 30
Berlin 33, 59, 71, 75, 90, 109, 111f., 134f., 160, 200, 228, 269f., 277
– Hovevei Zion in- 112
– Potsdam 135
– Zionists, Zionist Federation and Zionist Students Association in- 75, 109, 111, 201

See also Kadimah (zionist society in Berlin)
Berlin, Naftali Zvi Yehuda (The Netziv of Volozhin) 197
Bernstein-Kogen, Jacob 51, 53, 191, 201, 208, 213, 215, 217, 223, 247f., 250, 254, 263–266, 271, 276, 279, 296, 307, 309, 317, 343
Bialik, Hayim Nahman 218, 261
Bialystok 113, 173, 317
Bierer, Ruben 49, 51
Bilu (Beit Ya'akov Lekhu Venelkha) (organization) 141, 170, 309
Birnbaum, Nathan 11, 26, 31, 51, 109, 175, 183–185, 187, 191, 206, 228, 231f.
Birzhevye Vedomosti (newspaper) 102
Bismarck, Otto von 41, 61
Bloch, Joseph Samuel 10, 163f.
Bnai Moshe 98, 171, 226, 260f.
Bodenheimer, Hannah 131
Bodenheimer, Max 11, 31, 38, 109, 118, 139f., 175, 248, 274
Bohm, Adolf 169
Bonaparte Napoleon 40
Bordeaux 338
Borochov Dov Ber 209,
Botosani 204
Brainin, Reuben 33, 64, 86, 105, 120, 125, 290, 302, 310
Braudes, Reuben Asher 93
Breitenstein, Max 166
Breuer, Isaac 169
Brisk (Brest) 200
Brno 51
Brock, Zvi 265
Buber, Martin 82, 180, 205, 207, 212, 214, 222, 231, 277, 320, 324, 327, 341f.
Buber-Winkler Paula 327
Buchmil, Joshua 38, 51, 113, 206, 208, 257, 333
Budapest 5–8, 24, 42, 70
– Gymnasium; Jewish Elementary School; Jewish Preparatory School; Realschule (grammar school) 5f., 298
Buducnost (newspaper) 228
Bulgaria 43, 49, see also Ferdinand, Crown Prince of Bulgaria

Bülow, Bernhard von 42, 133–136, 139, 293, 343
Bund (party) 105

Carlebach, Ezriel 45f.
Chabad, Hassidism 197
Chajes, Zvi Perez 37, 297, 310f.
Chamberlain, Joseph, British Colonial Secretary 12, 235, 237, 241–243, 247, 267, 296, 344
Chatam Sofer, see Moshe Sofer
Chazanovitch, Joseph 272, 317f.
Chelouche, Yosef Eliyahu 47, 148
Chlenov, Yehiel 181, 203, 219, 246, 248–250, 255–259, 262, 264f., 267, 271f., 275f., 279, 333, 342f.
Church State 115
Citron, S.L. 281
Clemenceau, Georges 40, 295
Cohen, Gustav 162
Cohen, Leopold 203
Cohen, Meir 54
Cohen, Moshe 101
Cohen, Shlomo 50
Cohen-Reiss, Ephraim 148f., 152
Cohn, Asher (Arthur) 31
Cohn, Marcus 31
Committee for the Defense of the Zionist Organization 268, 270, 333
Congress, see Zionist Congress
Constantinople, see Istanbul
Cowen, Joseph 180, 288, 304
Cromer Evelyn Baring, Lord 241
Cromwell, Oliver 40
Cyprus 185, 237, 240f.
Cyrus the Great 128

Daily Chronicle (newspaper) 72, 100, 131
Daily Mail (newspaper) 101
Damascus 147
Das Volk (newspaper) 103
David, Ohad 78
Dawidowicz, Yehuda Leib 51
De Haas, Yaacob 75, 111, 113, 331
Del Val Merry 331
Democratic Fraction 22, 52, 82, 98, 122, 178, 180f., 185f., 192, 201f., 206, 209,

212, 215–217, 219 f., 222 f., 230–233, 257, 263, 273, 276, 278 f., 311, 331, 339 f.
Der Fraynd (newspaper) 102, 229 f.
Der Jude (weekly newspaper) 80, 230, 232
Die Welt (newspaper) 14, 28, 72 f., 77–80, 82, 93, 97, 100, 114 f., 131, 137, 164–166, 208, 227, 229 f., 234, 269, 287 f.
Dinur, Ben-Zion 336–338
Diskin, Yehoshua Leib 171
Disraeli, Benjamin 22, 24, 181
Dobling 238
Dreyfus, Alfred (Dreyfus Affair) 8, 66 f., 90, 102 f.
Drumont, Edouard 8
Druskininkai, see Hibbat Zion, Druskininkai Conference
Dunant, John Henry 12

East Africa 235–237, 241 f., 247–249, 251, 253, 258, 266–269, 271, 274 f., 297, 330, 343, see also Nandi; Uganda
Edlach 266, 273
Edward VII, King of England 21
Egypt, 241, 245, 293–295,, see also Sinai
Ehrenpreis, Mordecai Ze'ev 22 f., 31, 33, 36, 40 f., 48, 95, 114, 120, 183, 191, 296
Ehrlich Asher 257
Einstein, Albert 2
El Arish, see Sinai
Eliasberg, Mordechai 197
Eliash, Yosef 247 f., 256, 258, 296 f.
Eliav, Mordechai 76, 162
Ellerin Bette 130
Ellerin, Hermann 130
Elon, Amos 31 f., 35, 256 f., 335
Elyashar, Yaakov Shaul 148 f.
England, see Great Britain
Eretz Israel (Palestine, Zion) 1, 3 f., 7, 9, 12, 15, 17, 33, 42, 44, 49, 56 f., 62, 67, 71, 76, 78, 83, 87, 91–93, 96, 98 f., 104, 108 f., 112 f., 121 f., 126, 127–130, 132, 134, 136–138, 140–142, 145–147, 149–153, 157, 164, 167 f., 179, 185, 189, 200, 202, 224, 226, 236–243, 248, 250–255, 258, 262, 264, 268 f., 272, 279, 281, 293, 297, 302, 306, 308–310, 315, 330–332, 334, 343, 345
– Old Yishuv 99, 150, 309
See also Gedera; Haifa; Hadera; Jaffa; Jerusalem; Jewish National Fund; Keren Hayesod; Mikveh Yisrael; Ness Ziona; Ottoman Empire; Rehovot; Rishon Lezion; Rosh Pina; Safed; State of Israel; Teachers Association of the Land of Israel; Tel Aviv; Tiberias; Tzionei Tzion; Wadi Khanin; Zikhron Ya'akov; Zionist Associations
Esra (Society for Jewish Settlement in Eretz Yisrael) 76
Eulenburg, Philipp von 132–135, 138, 330
Europe 1–4, 8, 12, 16 f., 61, 64, 79, 99, 101, 107, 109, 117, 126, 127, 130, 133, 137–139, 141, 145 f., 150, 157, 167, 174, 220, 224, 237, 263, 273, , 288 f., 291, 302 f., 332–334
– East- 3, 13, 15, 22, 29–31, 38, 72, 80–83, 96, 105 f., 108 f., 118, 157, 169–172, 174–176, 184, 189, 191, 197, 202, 205, 227, 229 f., 236, 239, 241, 247–250, 279, 295, 297, 313, 321, 343
– West- 3, 13, 15, 29–31, 80–84, 96, 105, 109, 118, 122, 157, 169, 171, 174–176, 189, 191, 229, 248, 278 f., 295, 300, 321, 343
Evans Mary Ann (George Eliot) 22
Ezra 296
Ezrahi Krishevsky, Mordechai 143, 149

Farbstein, David 94, 116
Farbstein, Yehoshua Heschel 191
Feiwel, Berthold 52, 82, 180, 212, 231 f., 277
Ferdinand, Crown Prince of Bulgaria 12, 244
France 5, 67, 90, 100, 133, 139, 164, 168 f,, 186, 292, see also Bordeaux; Dreyfus Alfred; Montpelier; Paris
Frankfurt 310
Frankfurter Zeitung (newspaper) 100
Franz Joseph I, Emperor 8, 21, 105, 163
Frederick I, the Grand Duke of Baden 58, 128–132, 135 f., 224, 243, 332
Freedman, Eliezer Eliahu 102
Freud, Sigmund 8

Friedman, Adolf 331
Friedman, Isaiah 239f., 250, 252, 254, 256, 261, 263, 275
Friedmann, Paul 87
Frishman, David 320, 324, 326, 329
Frumkin, Yisrael Dov 99
Fuchs, Jacob Samuel 91–93

Galicia, 93, 104, 176, 186, 196, 236, 247, see also Lvov
Galileo Galilei 2
Gaster, Moshe 100, 196, 203, 219, 221, 269
Gedera 170
Geijerstam, Gustaf af- 310
Gelber, Nathan 91
Gelbhaus, Isaiah 163
Geneva 276, 279
George Eliot, see Evans Mary Ann
Germany 22, 53, 75f., 100, 109, 128, 130–133, 138f., 164, 169, 175, 189, 228, 330, 343
    Zionist Associations in- 52f., 109
    See also Ahlem; Berlin; Frankfurt; Hamburg; Hanover; Heidelberg; Katowice; Karlsruhe; Memmel; Munich; Wilhelm II
Getzowa, Sonia 209
Geula (Settlement Society) 262
Ginsberg, Asher Zvi (Ahad Ha'am) 9, 22, 76, 83, 93–97, 121, 125, 171, 184, 190, 201, 206, 208, 217–219, 222, 225–231, 233f., 248, 260, 300, 307f., 315, 320, 323–326, 328f., 339–341
Ginsburg, Chanoch Henig 57
Gissin, Dov 256
Gladstone, William Ewart 181
Glicksman Avraham Zvi Hirsch 28, 30, 46, 72, 198, 294f.
Glicksman, Pinhas Selig 198
Glickson, Moshe 320, 323
Glogau, Heinrich 70
Goiten, Yaakov Leib 53
Goldberg, Yitzhak Leib 51, 262, 264–266, 272, 333
Goldbloom, Jacob Koppel 60
Goldsmid, Albert 168
Goldstein, Yossi 95–96, 224, 260, 340f.

Golinkin, David 293, 300
Goluchowski Agenor Maria Adam (Austrian foreign minister) 224, 268, 330
Gordon, Yehuda Leib 83, 190
Goren, Aryeh 173f.
Gottesman, Arie Moshe 53
Gottheil, Gustav 65, 174
Gra, Gershon 51f.
Grayevsky, Pinhas 144
Great Britain, England 7, 24, 71f., 75, 87, 92, 98f., 101, 113, 130, 133, 168, 181, 237, 241, 243, 249, 251, 254, 263, 267, 269, 271, 275, 279, 292, 330, 334, 345
– British Jews 33
    See also Chamberlain Joseph; London
Greenberg, Leopold 98, 241–243, 249, 254, 267–270
Grodno 173
Grodzinski, Chaim Ozer 56
Gronemann Sammy 30, 53, 59, 61, 118, 123, 175, 187, 255, 269, 295
Gross, Wilhelm 152
Grossman, Haim 58f.
Grunhut, Lazar 152
Gudemann, Moshe Moritz 54, 76, 162–164, 168, 294, 297, 300, 302, 341
Gutwein, Daniel 32, 334–336

Hacohen, Shlomo 28
Hadera 57
Hague (The Hague) 79, 244, 288
Haifa 134
Hakeshet (newspaper) 228
Halevi, Moshe 147, 149
Hamagid (weekly newspaper) 82, 91–93, 102
Hamburg 22, 312
Hamelitz (newspaper) 28, 82–86, 89–91, 93, 95, 102, 140, 194, 207, 228, 233
Hamodia (newspaper) 197
Hanover 53
Hantke, Arthur Menachem 270
Ha'olam (newspaper) 66, 91, 101, 108, 157, 163,
Hapeles (newspaper) 197
Hapisga (newspaper) 98, 173
Hartwig, Nicholas 245

Hashiloah (newspaper)   26, 37, 76, 93–97, 225–227, 230, 260, 315, 324
Hashkafah (newspaper)   229
Hatzfira (newspaper)   1, 39, 46, 82f., 86–91, 93, 97, 102f., 121, 228, 267, 270, 321
Hatzofeh (newspaper)   102, 228, 230, 275f.,
Hatzvi (newspaper)   99
Havatzelet (newspaper)   99, 150
Hayom (newspaper)   102
Hazan, Yosef Haim   142
Hazman (newspaper)   97, 224, 226, 231
Hechler, William   58, 129–132
Heidelberg   179
Heine, Heinrich   6, 24, 316
Hermoni (Ginzburg), Aharon Zvi   57, 146, 215,
Herzl, Family   6, 14f., 77, 137, 221, 345, see also Herzl Hans; Herzl Jacob; Herzl Jeannette; Herzl (Naschauer) Julie; Herzl Paulina, Herzl Simon Loeb; Neumann (Herzl) Trude; Norman Stephan (Neumann, Herzl)
Herzl Hans   304, 338
Herzl Jacob,   14, 77, 165, 238, 345
Herzl Jeannette (T. Herzl's mother)   6, 163, 165, 298
Herzl (Naschauer), Julie   14, 288, 338
Herzl Paulina (T. Herzl's daughter)   304, 338
Herzl Paulina (T. Herzl's sister)   6
Herzl Simon Loeb (T. Herzl's grandfather)   221
Hess, Moses   9f., 107
Heyman Michael   265, 271
Hibbat Zion, Hovevei Zion   3, 9–11, 17, 24, 31, 40, 51, 57, 62, 64, 83, 86, 88f., 92, 94, 98f., 108f., 112, 114–116, 140, 152, 157f., 165, 168, 170f., 173, 175f., 179, 184f., 189–191, 194, 196f., 217, 220, 232, 260f., 275, 307, 331
– Druskininkai Conference   108, 217
– Katowice Conference   108
– Odessa Committee   158
– See also Berlin, Hovevei Zion in-
Hickel, Max   52

Hildesheimer, Zvi Hirsch   76, 112
Hill, Clement   254
Hirsch, baron Maurice de-   15, 24, 53, 71, 87, 110–112, 127, 131, 291, 298, 301
Hitler, Adolf   8, 289
Hochberg, Zvi   45, 145
Hofmann Richard Beer   294
Hohenlohe, Prince Chlodwig   42, 135f.., 344
Holland (Netherlands)   133, see also Hague
Horowitz, H.D.   309
Horowitz, Mordechai Halevi   310
Hovevei Zion, see Hibbat Zion
Hungary   100. see also Budapest; Pressberg

Imber, Naftali Herz   66, 283
Irgun Hamorim, see Teachers Association of the Land of Israel
Ish-Kishor, Ephraim   48, 294
Istanbul (Constantinople)   33, 43, 49, 56, 88, 113, 132–139, 153, 186, 287, 319, 330f.
Isthmus of Panama   5
Italy   269, 330f., see also Rome; Venice; Vittorio Emanuele III
Izraelita (newspaper)   89
Izzet Bey   236, 330

Jabotinsky, Ze'ev   123f., 178, 258, 289
Jacobson, Avigdor   256, 265f., 271, 277
Jaffa   43f., 47, 140f., 143, 145, 148, 150–152, 262, 330
Jasinowski, Israel   248, 264, 266, 280
Jassy (Iasi)   171
JCA, see Jewish Colonisation Association
Jerusalem   42, 49., 78124, 134–136, 138–141, 143–151, 153, 200, 202, 237f., 259, 309, 319
– Beit HaKerem   324
– Mount Herzl, Herzl's Tomb   2, 306
– David's Citadel   148
– Evangelical Church of the Redeemer   132
  See also Khalidi Yussuf Zia al-
Jesus of Nazareth, see Redeemer
Jewish Agency, see Austria, Zionist Organization; Berlin, Zionists; Jewish Colonial

Trust; Jewish National Fund; Munich, Zionist Youth Conference; Russian Empire, Zionist associations, Members of the Zionist Organization; South Africa, Zionist Associations; Tzionei Tzion; United States of America, Zionist Organization of America; Vienna, Reconciliation Conference; (Ibid), Zionists of Vienna and Action Committee; Vilna, Zionist Societies Assembly; Zionist Congress; Zionist Movment; Zionist Organization;
Jewish Chronicle (newspaper)   5, 7, 18, 71, 75, 98, 100, 113f., 164, 241, 256, 291
Jewish Colonial Trust   14, 37f., 67, 79, 96, 106, 121, 133, 137, 149, 165, 185,187, 201f., 204, 212, 223, 233, 245, 254, 260, 273, 288, 316, 326, 330
Jewish Colonisation Association (JCA)   74
Jewish National Fund (JNF)   26, 38, 106, 179, 187, 254, 316, 326
Jewish Territorialist Organization, see Territorialists
Jewish World (newspaper)   75f., 113, 135, Josephus Flavius   305f.
Joshua ben Nun   22
Jüdische Presse (newspaper)   76, 112
Jüdische Rundschau (newspaper)   228
Jüdische Volksstimme (newspaper)   52
Jüdisches Volksblatt (newspaper)   77

Kadimah (Zionist association in Berlin)   201
Kadimah (Zionist student's organization)   26, 49f., 165f., 183,
Kahn, Zadoc   74, 127, 168
Kalischer, Zvi Hirsch   9, 107
Karaite Judaism   197
Karlsruhe   58, 130f.
Katchensky, Miriam   62
Katowice, see Hibbat Zion, Katowice Conference
Katznelson, Berl   18, 160, 335
Kellner, Leon   293
Keren Hayesod   52, 106
Keren Kayemeth Leisrael, see Jewish National Fund
Khalidi, Yussuf Zia al-   127

Kharkov (Kharkiv)   113, 188, 209, 270
– Zionists in-   63
    See also Russian Empire, Kharkov Conference
Kiev (Kyiv)   65, 71, 209
Kishinev   28, 51, 66, 71, 113, 209, 232, 234, 236f., 241f., 244f., 248, 251, 257, 294
Klausner, Albert   160
Klausner, Joseph   86, 97, 203, 212, 215, 218, 230, 326
Klausner, Yisrael   65f., 80, 192, 201, 209, 213, 274, 277,
Kleinman, Moshe   108f., 157
Koerber, Ernest von   237, 330
Kohn, Jacob   77
Kohn, Jacob   166, 292
Kol Yisrael Haverim (KIAH), Alliance Israelite Universelle   107, 315, see also Alliance
Kölnische Zeitung (newspaper)   100
Kolomyia   103
Komarov, Avraham   45
Komarov, Efraim Yehuda   145
Kook, Avraham Yitzhak   307
Koopay, Joseph Arpad, Archduke   59
Korvin Piatrowska, Pauline von-   244
Kotz, Gideon   90, 102,
Kovno (Kaunas)   197
Kozirovsky, Haim   60, 66f., 103
Kraus, Karl   167
Kremenezky, Johan   26, 51, 269
Kremer, Mendel   147
Kressel, Gershon (Getzel)   32, 74, 82, 85–87, 89f.

Laharanne, Ernest   11
Landau Mendel Leibush   204f.
Landau, Saul Raphael   74, 77, 129
Landau, Yehuda Leib   85, 183
Laskov, Shulamit   226, 328
L'Echo de Paris (newspaper)   100
Leonardo de Vinci   2
Lesseps, Ferdinand   5
Levin, Moshe   262
Levin, Shmaryahu   60, 97, 123, 173, 226, 231, 252, 255, 341
Levine-Epstein, Eliyahu Ze'ev   142, 151

Levy, Yitzhak   331
Lewinsky, Elhanan Leib   94, 225.
Lifschitz, Yaakov   197
Lifshitz, Eliezer Meir   27
Lilien, Ephraim Moses   22 f., 58, 180, 209, 212, 214, 311 f.
Lilienblum, Moshe Leib   26, 31, 51, 83, 95, 190
Lippay, Berthold Dominik   42, 331
Lippe, Karpel   118, 171
Lipsky, Louis   65, 178, 181, 261
Liszt, Franz   39
Lithuania   123, 270, See also Aleksot; Hibbat Zion, Druskininkai Conference; Kovno; Ponevezh; Švenčionys
Lloyd George   338, 345
Lodz   28
Loewe, Heinrich   109, 143 f., 152, 175
London   1, 5, 24, 29 f., 33, 48, 60, 74 f., 87, 90, 100, 107, 111, 113, 121–123, 127, 134 f., 159, 164, 186, 196, 202, 204, 220, 239, 254, 269, 294 f., 319, 337
– East End   48, 75, 294
– King's Hall   33
Louban, Chaim Zelig   269
Lowy, Rabbi   240, 292
Lubavitch Sholom Dovber known as the Rashab   63
Lubman, Dov Haviv   27, 45, 142, 146
Lucanus, Hermann von   132
Ludwipol, Avraham   26 f., 37, 81, 90, 118, 314 f.
Lueger, Karl   8, 105
Luria, G.   56
Luria, Joseph   52, 56, 109, 113, 120, 231
Luz, Ehud   61 f., 67, 172, 190, 205, 209, 216, 219, 222, 239, 309
Lvov (Lviv, Lemberg)   69, 183, 186

Maccoby, Chaim Zundel (Maggid of Kaminetz)   62
Mahler, Gustav   8, 105
Maimon, Yehuda Leib   28 f., 41, 216
Maltz, David   183
Mandelstamm, Max Emmanuel   71, 264 f., 267, 280
Mani, Avraham   152

Maor, Yitzhak   245
Marcus, Aaron   196
Margalit, Michael   139
Margolin, Y.   233
Marmorek, Alexander   248, 299
Marmorek, Oscar   53, 118, 249
Marschall von Bieberstein, Adolf   132, 139
Masie, Aharon Meir   147
Masliansky, Zvi Hirsch   44 f., 64 f.
Meir, Yaakov   149
Melville, Herman   174
Memmel (Klaipeda)   10
Mendelssohn, Moses   314, 337
Michelangelo Buonarroti   290
Michlin, Haim Michal   149
Mikveh Yisrael   56–59, 78, 141 f., 146, 151, 315
Minsk   200, 217 f., 248, 270, 277 f., see also Russian Empire, Minsk Conference
Mizrahi   28, 68, 123, 217–19, 272, 279 f.
Mizrahi society   217
Mogilev   256
Mohilever, Shmuel   62, 170 f., 173, 194, 197, 217, 332
Moltke, Helmuth Karl Bernhard von   61
Montefiore, Frances   33, 35, 59, 212, 268 f., 343
Montefiore, Moses   59, 268
Montpelier (Montpellier)   51
Moscow   62, 65
Moses (Moshe Rabbenu)   16 f., 22, 24, 48, 59, 61, 68, 100 f., 162, 211, 245, 287, 289, 290–306, 310–313, 322
Moshe ben Maimon (Maimonides)   314, 337
Moshe Sofer (Hatam Sofer)   310
Motzkin, Leo   61, 119, 121, 178, 181, 200, 202, 204, 206, 208, 213 f., 223, 274, 278
Mozambique   237, 240
Munchhausen Baron Borries von   61
Munich   78, 112, 162, 169, 294
– Zionist Youth Conference   206
Myers, Asher   98

Nandi (western Kenya)   270
Naor, Mordechai   79, 98,

Index

Napoleon III 11
Napoleon, see Bonaparte Napoleon
Naschauer Family 14
Natonek, Yosef 9
Nehemiah 296, 317
Neigo, Yosef 151
Ness Ziona 45, 145
Netanyahu, Benzion 4, 39., 289, 335
Neue Freie Presse 5f., 8, 14, 16, 23, 69f., 70, 73, 77–79, 83, 133, 137, 150, 163, 165–167, 221, 287f., 300
Neumann (Herzl), Trude 304, 338f.
Neumark, David 124, 180, 183, 323
New York 33, 90, 100f, 174, 185, 295
– Temple Emanu-El 174
New York Herald (newspaper) 100
New York Times (newspaper) 101, 295
Newlinsky, Philipp Michael 244, 287
Newton, Isaac 40
Nicholas II, Tsar 244f., 247, 243
Nissenbaum, Yitzhak 61, 63f.
Nordau Anna 161f.
Nordau, Max (Simon Meir Sudfeld) 24, 33, 39f., 97, 162, 219, 243, 246, 269, 299, 310, 320, 327
Nordau, Maxa 161f.
Norman, Stephen (Neumann, Herzl) 304, 338f.
North Africa 16
Nossig, Alfred 12, 186f., 253, 273, 333
Novogrudok 209

Odessa 26, 51, 93, 113, 140, 266, see also Hibbat Zion, The Odessa Committee
Ohavei Tzion in Vilna (society) 56
Oliphant, Laurence 12, 87
Oppenheimer, Franz 255
Ost und West (newspaper) 97, 227–229, 231251
Ottoman Empire and its regime in the land of Israel 9, 49, 56, 79, 87f., 93, 99–101, 107–109, 127f., 133, 136–141, 147–150, 152f., 157f., 179, 189, 236–238, 240, 243–246, 263, 268, 270, 302, 321, 329, 331–333, see also Abdul Hamid II; Damascus; Istanbul

Paganini, Niccolo 39
Palestine, see Eretz Israel
Pall Mall Gazette (newspaper) 73, 100, 131
Panama 5
Paraty, Miguel de 238
Paris 1, 5–8, 12, 14, 24, 32, 34, 45, 73–75, 90, 107, 113, 133, 142f., 160–162, 165, 186, 206, 269, 287Patrikowski 87
Pawel, Ernst 112, 131f., 247, 261f., 302f.
Pester Lloyd (newspaper) 70, 100
Pevzner, Shmuel 296
Philadelphia 108
Pineles, Shmuel 32, 40
Pines, Berl 200
Pines, Yechiel Michal 152, 254
Pinsk 56, 277
Pinsker, Leo (Yehuda Leib) 10f., 26, 31, 84, 107f., 173, 261
Pius X, Pope 7, 12, 37, 42, 115, 319, 331
Plehve, Vyacheslav von (russian interior minister) 12, 71, 235, 243–245, 247, 250, 264, 266, 294, 319, 330
Plonsk 29, 204
Podolia 103
Poland 62, 72, 80, 89, see also Bialystok; Bedzin; Hibbat Zion, Katowice Conference; Lodz; Pinsk; Plonsk; Sosnowiec; Warsaw
Poltava 64, 170, 194
Ponevezh 209
Pope, see Pius X; Church State
Portugal 237
Prague 90
Pressberg (Bratislava) 310
Prilotzky, Zvi 224
Priluki (Pryluky) 170, 194
Przyszluc 103

Rabbi Binyamin, see Redler-Feldman Joshua
Rabbinowicz, Saul Pinhas (Shefer) 81, 176
Rabinovich, Mordechai (Ben-Ami) 47, 78, 116, 119, 315
Rabinovich, Solomon (Scholem Aleichem) 65, 80, 102
Rabinowitz, Eliyahu Akiva 116, 170, 194–197

Rabinowitz, Leon   233
Rabinowitz, Shmuel Yaakov   170, 172, 198, 202, 209, 214, 216, 222, 267, 280, 339
Rambam, see Moshe ben Maimon (Maimonides)
Raphael, Geula   192
Rashi, see Shlomo Yitzchaki
Rav Tza'ir, see Tchernowitz Chaim
Ravnitzky, Hanna   217
Redeemer, Jesus of Nazareth   128
Redler-Feldman, Joshua (Rabbi Binyamin)   228, 288, 318–320, 322, 329, 333–334
Rehovot   45, 143, 150, 153, 308
Reich, A.H.   238
Reines Avraham Dov Ber   204
Reines Yitzchak Yaacov   123, 171, 202–205, 209, 212, 214, 216, 218, 280–282, 320
Reinharz, Jehuda   163, 171f., 274–276, 278
Reizen, Mordecai Zeev   85
Rishon Lezion   27, 45, 141f., 145f., 151–153, 315
Romania   62, 122, 204, 237, 247, see also Botosani; Jassy
Rome   10, 42, 319
Rosenbaum, Simon (Shimshon)   265, 269f., 273, 277
Rosenberger, Erwin   165f., 240, 292
Rosenfeld, Shalom   69
Rosenthal, Littman   317, 331
Rosenzweig, Franz   298
Rosh Pina   29
Rothschild, Edmond de-, and his clerks in the colonys   1, 9, 15, 45, 53, 71, 111, 127, 142, 147, 152f., 158, 160,
Rothschild, family   11, 162, 164, 168, 239
Rothschild Lionel Walter   345
Rothschild, Nathaniel   168
Rovno (Rivne)   65
Rulf, Isaac   10
Rumshinsky, Joseph   33
Russian Empire   8, 10f., 26, 28, 51f., 61–63, 71f., 80f., 83, 91, 93, 102, 105f., 113, 121f., 139, 157f., 170f., 179, 192, 195f., 199, 213f., 228, 235, 243–251, 253f., 257, 263, 268f., 279f., 295, 321, 330–332

– Zionist Associations, Members of the Zionist Organization and Regional Leaders in-   52f., 62–64, 118, 121, 202, 205, 209, 213f., 219, 222, 224f., 235, 244–251, 254, 266, 271, 274–279, 321
– Kharkov Conference   188, 235, 259, 263–266, 270, 276f., 281, 333
– Minsk Conference   217f., 222, 225, 230, 274, 278, 339
– Pale of Settlement   62
– Warsaw Conference   195, 266
   See also Belarus; Lithuania; Moscow; Nicholas II; Podolia; Poland; Saint Petersburg; Ukraine

Saadia Gaon   337
Sabbatai Zvi, Sabbateanism   197, 307f., 311
Sachs, Hans   291
Sadan, Dov   54f., 344
Safed   309
Saint Petersburg (Peterburg)   28, 49, 90, 246, 253, 277, 319
Salant, Shmuel   171
Salmon, Yosef   168, 170, 172, 197
Salzburg   6
Sankt Peterburg Vedomosti (newspaper)   46
Sapir, Y.   315f.
Schach, Myriam   181, 220, 318, 340, 343f.
Schalit, Isidor   26, 32, 51, 72, 79, 166
Schapira, Zvi Hermann   121, 179
Schatz, Boris   311f..
Schiff, Friedrich   160, 167, 301
Schiff, Jacob   174
Schiller, Shlomo   183
Schnirer, Moshe (Moritz)   51, 140
Schnitzler, Arthur   8, 300
Scholem Aleichem, see Rabinovich, Solomon

Schur, Wolf   95, 98, 173
Schwartz, Dov   27
Schwartz, S.   41f.
Schwarz, Karl   23
Scientific Society   109
Selbstemanzipation (newspaper)   84, 109
Serbia   43
Serubabel (newspaper)   75

Shakespeare, William 40
Shapira, Avraham Moshe 257
Shazar, Zalman 51f., 61
Sheinkin, Menachem Mendel 118
Shlomo Yitzchaki (Rashi) 305
Shub, Moshe David 29, 38, 43, 140–142, 144f., 151
Sil-Vara, G. 332
Silberbusch, David Yeshayahu 165, 183, 310
Silman, Kadish Yehuda-Leib 324
Simon, Alexander Moritz 61
Simon, Oswald John 99
Sinai, El Arish 185f., 235, 237f., 240–242, 247, 253–254, 268, 270, 296, 345
Slonimski, Chaim Selig 86
Slouschz, Nahum 100, 122, 193, 221
Slutzky, Avraham Yaakov 256
Smilansky, Moshe 45, 143, 150, 308
Smolenskin, Peretz 307Society for the Cultivation of Jewish Scholarship 53
Sofer, Oren 90
Sokolow, Nahum 1–3, 15, 24f., 30, 33, 39, 43, 46f., 66, 86–90, 121, 160, 180, 195, 202f., 220, 223, 228, 267, 272, 335
Soldewitz, Baruch 200
Soldewitz, Berel 200
Solomiak, Avraham 309
Soloveitchik Chaim Halevi (Rabbi Chaim of Brisk's) 200
Somme 67
Sosnowiec 63
South Africa 237
– Zionist Associations and Zionist Organization in- 53
Spain 6, see also Alfonso XIII
Spektor, Yitzhak Elchanan 197
Spinoza, Baruch 314, 337
Stand, Adolf 69
State of Israel, see also Eretz Israel 2, 4, 7, 106, 114, 279, 306, 319, 333, 338, 345
Sternbuch, Moshe 200
Stricker, Robert 52
Struck, Hermann 21–23, 28, 30, 59, 61, 311f.
Suttner, Bertha von- 79, 245, 288

Švenčionys 57
Switzerland 128, see also Basel; Geneva; Zurich
Syrkin, Nachman 257, 272

Tartakover, David 48, 58f.
Taubish, Leibel 103
Tawfiq, Bey pasha 147, 149
Tchernichovsky, Shaul 320, 324, 326f., 329
Tchernowitz, Chaim (Rav Tza'ir) 195
Teachers Association of the Land of Israel 262
Tel Aviv 47, 324
Territorialists, Jewish Territorialist Organization 272
The Netziv see Berlin Naftali Zvi Yehuda
The Order of Ancient Maccabeans (club) 92, 159, 239
Theresienstadt 304, 339
Thon, Yehoshua (Josias) 75, 111, 183, 307
Tiberias 309
Tiglath Pileser, Assyrian King 24
Times (newspaper) 99
Tiomkin, Vladimir (Ze'ev) 265f.
Toury, Jacob 70
Trachtman, Jacob Samuel 92
Trietsch, Davis 185–187, 253, 273, 333
Trotsky (Bronstein), Leon 256f.
Tsirelson, Yehuda Leib 170, 194, 196f.
Turkey, see Ottoman Empire
Tzionei Tzion (organization) 262, 268, 270, 272, 333

Uganda 16, 37, 82, 97, 99, 123, 179, 181f., 185, 189, 219, 223, 232, 234–238, 240–243, 246–256, 258–264, 267–276, 278–281, 288, 296, 311, 316, 324, 328–335, 339, 342–345
– Tanaland province 267
See also East Africa
Uman 65
Ungerfeld, Moshe 163
United Nations Organization 114, 279, 306, 338, 345
United States of America 16, 64f., 75, 98, 108, 173f., 185, 237, 243

– Administration, Zionist Federation, Zionist General Council and Zionist Organization of America   65, 174
– Conservative Congregation   173
– Reform Congregation   85, 99, 173 f.
– Zionist Associations   53
  See also New York; Philadelphia
Ussishkin, Menachem Mendel   11, 24–26, 31, 51, 62, 64 f., 82, 85, 115, 179, 182, 209, 238, 259–269, 271–273, 276–280, 316, 333

Vardi, Aharon   59, 135, 137 f., 140–148, 151–153,
Venice   331
Vienna   1, 4, 6–8, 11, 24, 26, 29, 37, 49, 51, 54 f., 72, 75, 78, 80, 84, 90, 99, 101, 105, 107, 109, 111 f., 114, 116, 119, 122, 129 f., 132 f., 135, 137, 142, 159–168, 175, 178, 183, 194, 198, 201, 213, 230–232, 238, 240, 262, 265 f., 269–271, 277, 279, 282, 287, 292, 294, 297, 299, 321, 330
– Anglican Church   129
– Reconciliation Conference   259, 262, 271, 273, 277 f.
– University   166
– Zionists of Vienna and Action Committee   165, 230, 259, 263, 270 f., 277, 287
  See also Kadimah (Students Association in Vienna)
Vienna Congress   4
Vilna   28, 33, 44, 49–51, 56 f., 62, 68, 175, 200, 217, 246–248, 266
  Zionist Societies Assembly in-   296
Vital, David   256, 265
Vittorio Emanuele III, King of Italy   12, 21, 37, 308, 331
Voskhod (newspaper)   97, 226

Wadi Khanin   153
Wagner, Richard   6, 291
Warsaw   102, 191, 203, 205, 209, 248, 264, 266, see also Russian Empire, Warsaw Conference
Weber, Max   36

Weisz, Yitshak   18, 32, 240, 291, 298, 302, 335
Weizmann, Chaim   122 f., 178, 182, 201, 205–209, 212 f., 218, 222 f., 232, 252, 258, 260 f., 265, 273–279
Werner, Siegmund   77, 137
Whitman, Sidney   100
Wilhelm II, Kaiser   12, 21, 37, 42, 55–59, 78, 113, 126–139, 145, 148–151, 153, 157, 202, 237 f., 243 f., 301 311, 315, 319, 332, 343
Wintz, Yehuda Leib   86, 227, 229, 231, 234
Wise, Stephen S.   65, 337
Wistrich, Robert   15, 29 f.
Witte, Sergei   245
Wochenschrift (newspaper)   71, 163 f.
Wolffsohn, David   10, 30 f., 33, 43 f., 51, 59, 111, 140, 151, 167, 287, 294, 296, 299, 304
World Zionist Organization   2, 11, 13, 18, 38, 65, 77, 79 f., 82, 89 f., 106, 109 f., 114, 158, 172, 174, 177, 183 f., 187 f., 193, 197, 202, 218 f., 223, 255, 258, 265 f., 268, 316, 323, 326, 368, 341

Yaffe, Hillel   140, 143, 152, 315
Yaffe, Leib   158, 165, 179
Yavetz, Ze'ev   50, 152
Yekatrinoslav (Yekaterinoslav)   263, 266
Yellin, David   152
Yermans, Yosef   152
Yevzerov, Yehuda Zvi   64
Young Israel (society)   75, 109, 111

Zangwill, Israel   24, 26, 30, 180, 272, 288, 304, 316
Zapf, Joseph   64 f.
Zederbaum, Alexander   83
Zeidner, Josef   59, 140
Ziffer, Gershon   103
Zikhron Ya'akov   43, 262
Zion (newspaper)   71, 75
Zion, see Eretz Israel
Zionist Administration   68
Zionist Associations (Zionist Societies, Zionist Committees, Unions) worldwide   52, 66 f., 109, 112, 122, 166 f., 191, 198,

207, 220, 247, 255, 296
See also Ahva; Bilu; B'nei B'rith; Bnai Moshe; Esra (Society for Jewish Settlement in Eretz Yisrael); Geula; Hibbat Zion; Young Israel (society); State of Israel; Jewish Colonisation Association (JCA); Zionist Organization

Zionist Congress
- The I   1, 10, 15f., 24, 26, 31, 33, 37f., 47, 49f., 52f., 65, 72, 75, 77, 81f., 85f., 89, 92f., 96, 98f., 101f., 104, 105f., 108–110, 112, 114f., 119–122, 124–126, 128, 131, 157f., 162, 168–172, 176, 178, 180, 183–185, 187, 189–191, 193, 203, 209, 214, 221, 223, 287, 295, 299, 303, 310, 314f., 321, 331, 336, 345
- The II   16, 52f., 65, 75, 96, 112, 117, 121f., 124f., 127, 132, 137, 193f., 196f., 200, 212, 221f., 282, 339
- The III   52, 64f., 78, 97, 121, 123, 180, 185, 200–202, 204, 219, 222, 281, 310
- The IV   52, 60, 100, 122f., 204–206, 209, 212, 216f., 220, 222, 295, 340
- The V   22, 59, 77, 123, 193, 206f., 209, 211, 216f., 238, 257, 278, 339f.
- The VI   16, 37, 49, 99, 116, 122f., 178, 187f., 217, 219, 232, 234f., 238, 246–248, 250, 253, 259f., 262, 265, 274, 279. 281, 296, 317, 324, 331, 341, 343
- The VII   69, 253, 271, 328
- The VIII   321
- The XVII   119
- Committees for the Defense of the Congress and the Organization   333
- Culture Committees   194–196, 204, 212, 214, 216–218, 221f.
- Preparatory Conference (Organizing Committee) for the I Zionist Congress   78, 112, 114
- Standing Committee   60, 182
- Uganda Advisory Committee   258, 275
- Zionist Congresses   16, 37, 42, 52, 65, 76, 100, 105, 110, 112, 116, 152, 158, 170, 178, 187f., 192, 271, 317f., 329, 332, 339, 343
   See also Basel; Democratic Fraction
Zionist General Council, Actions Committee   16, 51, 64, 65, 106, 158f., 183, 187, 193f., 201–203, 207, 213, 217, 220, 247, 250, 254–256, 258f., 263, 265f., 269f., 277, 324
Zionist General Council names of members in-   203, 248, 262, 266
Zionist Movement   4, 10f., 14, 17, 26, 30, 41, 49, 51, 53, 58, 62f., 69, 75f., 78–81, 90f., 97–99, 101, 110, 114, 119, 121, 130–132, 146, 149, 153, 157f., 166f., 169–171, 174f., 179–183, 185, 187–190, 192–196, 198–209, 214, 217, 219f., 222–224, 227, 229, 232, 236, 238f., 244f., 258f., 261–263, 265–268, 270, 272f., 278f., 281f., 287f., 308, 311, 316, 320, 322, 324, 328–330, 333, 339–340, 342, see also World Zionist Organization
Zitomir (Zhytomyr)   65
Zlatopolsky, Hillel   265
Zlotnick, Yeshayahu   320–322
Zur, Yaakov   169
Zurich   116f.
Zweig, Stefan   8, 23, 30, 47, 167, 175, 320f.

www.ingramcontent.com/pod-product-compliance
Lightning Source LLC
Chambersburg PA
CBHW031751220426
43662CB00007B/367